THE BEST OF
FOOD&WINE
THE ITALIAN COLLECTION

THE BEST OF
FOOD&WINE

THE ITALIAN COLLECTION

American Express
Publishing Corporation
New York

Cover: Tuscan Beans with Tuna, Pancetta and Lemon (page 89)

The Best of Food & Wine/THE ITALIAN COLLECTION
Designer: Loretta Sala
Assistant Editor: Martha Crow
Writer/Researcher: Melanie Falick
Illustrations: Steven J. Charney

American Express Publishing Corporation
Editor in Chief/Food & Wine: Carole Lalli
Art Director/Food & Wine: Elizabeth Woodson
Managing Editor/Books: Kate Slate
Marketing Director: Elizabeth Petrecca
Production Manager: Joanne Maio

Published by American Express Publishing Corporation
1120 Avenue of the Americas, New York, New York 10036

Manufactured in the United States of America

ISBN 0-916103-15-3

TABLE OF CONTENTS

ITALY'S WINES— AND GREAT FOOD MATCHES

A Regional Affair
by Tom Maresca

Food and wine are inseparable in Italy. The two have spent nearly three millennia now evolving in tandem, achieving a matchless interplay of flavors. Italian food and Italian wine are literally made for each other, and they are made uniquely in each and every corner of the country—which is why pairing Italian dishes and the wines they grew up with makes such exquisite dining.

The long Italian peninsula is divided and subdivided by mountains: Over the centuries this has produced an extreme regionalization, so that the country never developed a nationwide *alta cucina* like the French, nor anything like a standard pantheon of grapes and wines. Instead, each region and town went—and largely still goes—its own way, cultivating the grape varieties that grow best in its soil and taste best with its food. The result for contemporary wine drinkers is a plenitude of wonderful wines—a blessing—but most of them utterly unfamiliar and, more often than not, confusingly named—a curse. What follows should provide a trail through that jungle of Italian vines.

NAMES

Italian wines bear three different kinds of names:

Varietal names: These are wines made exclusively or predominantly from, and named for, a single variety of grape. They often have a region of origin attached to the varietal name: for example, Nebbiolo d'Alba (a wine from Alba made from Nebbiolo grapes) or Greco di Tufo (a wine from Tufo made from Greco grapes). Most Americans are familiar with this sort of nomenclature from U.S. wines such as Sonoma Chardonnay or Napa Cabernet.

Regional names: These are wines named for the towns or areas in which they have traditionally been made: for example, Chianti or Barolo. Most winedrinkers are familiar with this kind of name from the classifications of French wine by region—Bordeaux or Burgundy—and by township—Pauillac, Corton, etc. Varietal and regional wine names are usually covered by Italy's DOC or DOCG classifications. DOC means that the wine's place of origin, the grape varieties used in it, and its methods of vinification and aging have been controlled by law. DOCG means all that plus a guarantee of the wine's quality (theoretically insured by regular tastings and inspections).

Proprietary names: Italians often call these "fantasy" wines, because they embody experiments that are not covered by existing laws. Examples are wines like Antinori's Tignanello, or Granduca's Barilot, or Jermann's Vintage Tunina. The official classification of such wines is almost always *Vino da Tavola*, the lowest legal ranking, but they often command respect—and prices—well beyond those of wines bearing the officially more prestigious DOC and DOCG classifications.

LOCALES

Local custom governs winemaking in Italy: In some regions the rule is always to blend grape varieties, in others never to blend them. Roughly speaking, the

6

north of Italy is the stronghold of 100% varietal wines, the center is the bastion of blending, and the south and the islands some of both.

The northeastern regions of Trentino-Alto Adige, The Veneto, and Friuli-Venezia Giulia produce most— but by no means all—of Italy's really interesting white wines; though perfectly acceptable, pleasant drinking, ordinary white wine is made almost everywhere in the peninsula. Similarly, while everyday quaffing red wines abound, the really distinguished red wines come from a few specially favored zones:

• the Piedmont, especially around Alba
• the area around Verona
• the hills and valleys of Tuscany, especially the central zone from just south of Siena to just north of Florence and east to Arezzo
• parts of Umbria near Assisi
• the Avellino hills east of Naples.
• scattered spots in Sicily

WHITE WINES

Different grape varieties predominate in these different areas. In the white wine regions of the northeast, for instance, many of the bottles bear the Italian versions of well known varietal names—Pi-

not Bianco and Pinot Grigio, Sauvignon and Riesling Renano, for instance. The contents of the bottles are similarly Italianized: In most cases, the familiar varietal flavors and pleasing, fresh, clean fruit of these wines have been lightened and brightened by the high acidity that is typical of Italian white wines. This characteristic acid brightness and freshness make these white varietals instantly appealing as well as very versatile with a wide variety of foods, from antipasti and canapés through fish and shellfish to fowl and light, white meats. Such varietal wines serve too as excellent aperitifs or cocktails, leaving the palate clean and fresh and the appetite uncloyed for the dinner to follow.

The international favorite Chardonnay is grown in many spots around Italy, but almost all of it is made into a relatively light-bodied and fresh wine, very much in the pan-Italian style. A few producers (Gaja and Pio Cesare in Piedmont, Lungarotti in Umbria) make a bigger, Burgundian or California-style Chardonnay, and the distinction is almost always reflected in the wine's higher price. (In regions where blending grape varieties is the norm, Chardonnay often finds itself in interesting mixed company. In Tuscany, for instance, it joins Pinot Bianco and Trebbiano to make Pomino Bianco, perhaps Tuscany's most distinguished white wine. In Friuli, the iconoclastic Silvio Jermann blends Chardonnay with Pinot Bianco, Sauvignon and a small amount of Picolit to make Vintage Tunina, a big, full-bodied wine of intriguing unique flavor.)

In addition to the internationally cultivated grape varieties, Italy's white wine regions also grow important local grapes that make wines well worth getting acquainted with. Tocai, for instance, is a specialty of the Collio and Colli Orientali zones of eastern Friuli (near the Yugoslav border, north of Trieste). Its unique, nutty flavor makes it a splendid dinner wine with a wide variety of foods, including some of the less aggressive meat dishes.

The same region produces the prestigious—and very pricey—Picolit, a unique dessert wine of simultaneous sweetness and dryness. This is a kind of wine Italians informally classify as *vino da meditazione*, a wine to meditate with or to meditate over—a nice idea, and an accurate depiction of the wine's nature.

Arneis and Cortese (both grown in the Piedmont), Trebbiano (grown almost everywhere) and the three Vees—Verdicchio (The Marches), Verduzzo (Friuli) and Vernaccia (Tuscany)—complete the list of the most important native varieties yielding dry, white

continued on page 11

VARIETAL WHITE WINES

GRAPE	WINE NAME	REGION	CHARACTERISTICS	FOOD MATCHES
Arneis	Arneis	Piedmont	Made in sytles ranging from light and acidic (Ceretto's Blange) to full and fruity (Giacosa's Arneis)	The lighter style makes a fine aperitif and goes well with antipasti, fish and light luncheon dishes; the fuller style matches well with risotto, fish and fowl
Chardonnay	Chardonnay	Many regions	A few Chardonnays are made in the full-bodied, California style (Gaja, Lungarotti), but most are light, fresh, acid, aperitif and luncheon wines	According to style, antipasti and light pastas and risottos, or fowl and white meats
Cortese	Cortese, Gavi	Lombardy, Piedmont	Dry, medium-bodied, lightly acid, with slightly citric fruit flavors	Matches well with simply prepared fish and shellfish, as well as roasted or broiled chicken or pork, or simply sauced veal dishes
Fiano	Fiano di Avellino	Campania	Light to medium body; balanced, with a dry and gentle, nutty flavor	This complex, elegant wine may be used as an aperitif, but is better with dinners of complexly sauced fish and fowl or white meats
Greco	Greco di Tufo	Campania	Medium-bodied, dry and weighty, with a big, oily flavor and feel	Popular throughout southern Italy with antipasti and pastas of all sorts, and especially with seafood. Excellent also with chicken, pork and veal, but avoid cream sauces
Moscato	Asti Spumante (sparkling), Moscato (still)	Piedmont, many regions	Luscious, sweet, smooth, mouthfilling, with intense, exotic-fruit flavors	In the sparkling form, Italy's most popular festive dessert wine. In the still form (especially from Piedmont and the Sicilian islands—Pantelleria, etc.), some of the loveliest dessert wines available
Picolit	Picolit	Friuli-Venezia Giulia	Rare and endangered; golden, honey-scented, sweet and dry at the same time	An expensive and unique dessert wine, with characteristics of both dry sherry and botrytised Sauternes. Serve by itself, with dried fruit or a few nuts or some simple biscotti
Pinot Bianco	Pinot Bianco	Lombardy, Trentino-Alto Adige	Medium to full body; dry; more closely resembles the American idea of Chardonnay than do most Italian Chardonnays	Matches well with fish, fowl, white meats either grilled or simply sauced; will also handle modest cream sauces
Pinot Grigio	Pinot Grigio	Friuli-Venezia Giulia, The Veneto, Trentino-Alto Adige	Dry and brightly acidic, with a pleasing, slightly spicy aroma and flavor	A pleasing aperitif and an excellent companion to all sorts of canapés and antipasti. Fine as a light luncheon wine or with lighter, warm-weather entrées.

GRAPE	WINE NAME	REGION	CHARACTERISTICS	FOOD MATCHES
Riesling Renano	Riesling, Riesling Renano	Lombardy, Friuli-Venezia Giulia, Trentino-Alto Adige	Dry, medium-bodied, perfumed, about midway between the German and Alsace styles	Uses very similar to Pinot Grigio
Sauvignon	Sauvignon	Friuli-Venezia Giulia, Trentino-Alto Adige	Medium-bodied, dry and acid. Fragrant, with an herby, citrus flavor and, in some cases, a distinctive coppery edge	A pleasant aperitif, but best as a middleweight dinner wine for rich fish or shellfish, fowl or white meats. Matches well with either acid (wine-based, tomato-based) or cream sauces
Tocai	Tocai	Friuli-Venezia Giulia, The Veneto	Dry, spicy-smelling and -tasting; nutty flavors—almonds especially—in a medium to occasionally full body	A wine of all uses in Friuli, where the best of it comes from and where it is drunk with literally everything. Best with risottos, gnocchi and polenta, rich fish and shellfish (monkfish, lobster, tuna, swordfish) and all white meats
Traminer Aromatico	Gewürztraminer, Traminer, Traminer Aromatico	Trentino-Alto Adige, Friuli-Venezia Giulia	Light to medium body, spicy aroma, relatively modest, fruity flavor (modest compared to Gewürztraminer made outside Italy)	Much the same range of foods as Pinot Grigio and Riesling
Trebbiano	Lugana, Trebbiano d'Abruzzo, Trebbiano di Romagna	Lombardy, Abruzzi, Romagna	Many different clones, most yielding wines of light to medium body, with a slight fruity aroma and taste to match	Simple and useful all-purpose wine, inoffensive with almost everything
Verdicchio	Verdicchio, Verdicchio dei Castelli di Jesi (also di Matelica and di Montanello	The Marches	Light-bodied, acidic, with a bright, clean flavor	A fish and shellfish wine par excellence; the fresher the fish and the simpler the preparation, the better the Verdicchio will taste with it
Verduzzo	Verduzzo, Ramandolo	Friuli-Venezia Giulia	A pleasant, light, dry wine and, in its *amabile* version, an unforgettable sweet dessert wine	The dry version matches well with very light foods, especially canapés and antipasti. Serve the sweet as you would any fine dessert wine
Vernaccia	Vernaccia di San Gimignano, Vernaccia	Primarily Tuscany	Light, clean, with small fruit flavors. A few barrel-aged specimens exhibit oaky or vanilla overtones	A light wine of all uses, especially with "summer food." Match with lighter, less aggressive flavors or dishes with an acid character

9

BLENDED WHITE WINES

WINE NAME	GRAPES	REGION	CHARACTERISTICS	FOOD MATCHES
Bianca di Custozza	Trebbiano, Garganega, Tocai	The Veneto	Light, clean, soft, with gentle fragrance and flavor; resembles Soave	Pleasing as an aperitif or with light foods of all sorts: canapés; antipasti (especially fish or vegetable); seafood; fowl; and pastas with tomato, fish or shellfish
Bianco di Toscana	Mostly Trebbiano and Malvasia	Tuscany	Light, clean, simple, with small fruit flavors	In Tuscany, this and similar white wines fill the ecological niche of Soave in the Veneto
Breganze Bianco	Mostly Tocai	The Veneto	Light to medium body, clean-tasting and spicy-smelling: nuts and herbs	Excellent aperitif, fine with all sorts of antipasti, pastas and risottos. It has character enough to match well with fish, fowl and white meat entrées unless they are very aggressively sauced
Frascati	Trebbiano, Malvasia and other local grapes	Lazio (Rome)	The wine of everybody's Roman memories: light, fragrant and delicate	Drunk in Rome with anything one feels like. Best bets, however, are mild-flavored dishes: Red meats just won't work
Galestro	Mostly Trebbiano and Malvasia	Tuscany	Light, clean, simple, with small fruit flavors	Essentially this is another version of Bianco di Toscana: Uses are the same
Lacryma Christi	Primarily Coda di Volpe	Campania (Naples)	Dry, medium-bodied and smooth, with round, mouthfilling flavors	A bit full-bodied for an aperitif, but excellent with many foods, from the traditional white wine partners through to some red wine foods (grilled sausages or braised lamb shanks, for example)
Orvieto	Grechetto and other local grapes	Umbria	Light, fruity, fresh; usually fully dry but there are still some of the traditionally sweet *abboccato* bottlings	The dry Orvietos can be used exactly like Frascati; the sweet (really lightly sweet) makes a very pleasant sipping wine for aperitif or dessert
Pomino Bianco	Pinot Bianco, Chardonnay, Trebbiano	Tuscany	A polished, full-bodied white, capable of bottle-age and distinction	Serve Pomino Bianco with entrées of rich fish, roasted fowl, or pork and veal in richly flavored preparations
Soave	Garganega, Trebbiano di Soave, other local varieties	The Veneto (Verona)	A light, simple wine, with uncomplicated flavor. Some *cru* bottlings achieve distinction	Fine as an aperitif and with light, mildly flavored foods. Best with canapés, antipasti and pastas

continued from page 7
dinner wines. All are light to medium-bodied and fresh, with gentle, often slightly citric fruit and palate-cleansing acidity. Verduzzo also yields an important sweet dessert wine, but the unqualified Italian champion in that category has to be the peninsula's beloved and ubiquitous Moscato. Both its still and its sparkling versions (Asti Spumante) furnish luscious closings to an elaborate dinner.

A handful of other native and very traditional varieties produce some distinguished varietal white wines in very restricted locales: The most notable are Campania's Greco di Tufo and Fiano di Avellino, the former a round, mouthfilling, almondy wine that loves shellfish, and the latter an elegant, complex white that responds brilliantly to veal and chicken dishes.

In addition to varietal wines, native grapes are blended throughout the country to make some of Italy's most traditional white wines. Three of the most popular—with Italians, tourists, and the export market alike—are Soave from Verona, Orvieto from western Umbria and Frascati from the hills south of Rome. Made from three completely different mixes of very localized grapes, the three wines nevertheless resemble each other in general character: Each is pale in color, fragrant, light-bodied, dry and delicately fruity. Each of them is pleasing as a lightly chilled luncheon wine or aperitif. All of them also show very well with pastas, seafood, fowl and white meat dishes.

Torre di Giano, from Umbria, Breganze Bianco, from The Veneto, Lacryma Christi from the Naples area and Pomino Bianco from Tuscany fairly represent the middleweights of blended whites. Though they are once again made from utterly different, very local grapes, all are medium-bodied, round, and clean, with complex spicy to nutty flavors. They make excellent dinner companions to richer or more strongly flavored fish and shellfish preparations as well as all sorts of fowl and white meats.

RED WINES

The vast majority of Italy's great red wines, whether 100% varietals or blends, are made from grapes little known or cultivated outside of Italy. This means that they offer both flavors uniquely tailored to their native foods and exciting opportunities for a curious connoisseur to explore brand new territory.

The Big Three of red wine grapes are, unquestionably, Nebbiolo in the north, Sangiovese in the center of Italy, and Aglianico in the south. All three yield intense, full-bodied wines, frequently austere and tannic in youth, but capable of great bottle development, and evolving over time into complex aristocrats of the table.

Nebbiolo grows throughout Piedmont and Lombardy, but its quality epicenter is the small city of Alba, which also happens to be the white truffle capital of this galaxy. A mature Nebbiolo-based wine shares the deep, earthy redolence of Alba's truffles: The scent of a newly opened bottle can fill an entire room. Although the Nebbiolo grape almost always makes a 100% varietal wine, ironically only the least of its children bears its name: The others carry the names of their various towns of origin—Barolo and Barbaresco above all, but also Gattinara and Ghemme and Carema. Spanna is also a Nebbiolo wine: It is in fact another regional name for the grape.

Sangiovese grows widely in central Italy, but rises to greatness in Tuscany. At its best, Sangiovese combines an intense grapey character with durability and persistent freshness. This can be seen best in some of the 100% varietal Sangiovese wines, such as the long-lived Brunello di Montalcino or the complex Pergole Torte from Monte Vertine. But even where Sangiovese's intensity is ameliorated by mixtures of lighter varieties, as in simple Chiantis, its rich, fruity character still shines through. In the great Tuscan blends—the riserva wines from the Chianti Classico and the Chianti Rufina, from Montepulciano and Carmignano—and in Umbria's Rubesco, Sangiovese is both the spine that holds those wines together and the spirit that gives them long life.

Aglianico is the least known of these three greats, even within Italy. An ancient vine, introduced into southern Italy by Greek colonists before 500 BC, Aglianico continues to play a role as a blending grape in the occasionally exported Falerno. As a 100% varietal wine, Aglianico produces the princely Aglianico del Vulture and the regal Taurasi. Mature Taurasi is admirably harmonious, rich, and velvety on the palate, a wonderful companion for richly flavored or complexly sauced meat and game dishes.

continued on page 15

11

VARIETAL RED WINES

GRAPE	WINE NAME	REGION	CHARACTERISTICS	FOOD MATCHES
Aglianico	Aglianico del Vulture, Taurasi	Basilicata, Campania	One of Italy's noblest red grapes: rich, generous and elegant; capable of bottle age	A wine to match with your finest meats, most complex sauces and most elegant dinners. Excellent also with fine cheeses
Barbera	Barbera from various townships (Alba, Asti, Monferrato)	The Piedmont	Medium- to light-bodied and acidic, with a pleasing, black cherry tang	The lightest and least tannic of the fine Piedmont reds, Barbera is an important and versatile food wine, excellent with all but the most aggressively flavored dishes
Dolcetto	Dolcetto with different township designations (most commonly Alba, Acqui, Diano d'Alba)	The Piedmont	Medium-bodied, fruity, fresh. The so-called "Beaujolais of Piemonte"	An easy-drinking wine, fine with simple foods—grilled meats, cheeses, pasta and risotto. On its home territory, often the first-course wine, preparatory to a big Nebbiolo
Merlot	Merlot	Many regions	Italian Merlot tends to be a bit more tannic than French or California, but has the same, soft fruit	Good with roast birds or roast meats; grilled or stewed meats; cheeses
Monte-pulciano	Rosso Conero, Montepulciano d'Abruzzo	The Marches, Abruzzi	Used elsewhere primarily as a blending grape; in The Marches amd Abruzzi Montepulciano makes a pleasing, full-bodied, soft red wine quite useful for everyday meals, country dinners, and such	Fine with antipasti of meat and vegetables, pastas (especially those with tomato and meat sauces), risotto and simply prepared meats
Nebbiolo	Nebbiolo d'Alba, Barbaresco, Barolo, Roero, Carema, Spanna	The Piedmont	A truly noble grape, Nebbiolo produces the Piedmont's finest red wines: big, full-bodied wines, austere in youth but aging to great complexity and richness	This is a wine to serve with game and big roasts or with fine cheeses
Sangiovese	Brunello di Montalcino, Rosso di Montalcino, Morellino di Scansano and some Tuscan Vino da Tavola (see Chianti)	Primarily Tuscany	The backbone of Chianti, Sangiovese makes a big, richly flavored, tannic wine that ages with great grace: a noble grape not well enough respected outside its home territory	100% Sangiovese wines bear comparison to California's finest 100% Cabernets in their deep flavors, complexity and rich fruit. Serve with red meats, duck or game birds, fine cheeses
Teroldego	Teroldego Rotaliano	Trentino-Alto Adige	Generous and full, with a flavor that is often compared to Pomerol	A classic dinner wine: Serve with foods like those suggested for Merlot

BLENDED RED WINES

WINE NAME	GRAPES	REGION	CHARACTERISTICS	FOOD MATCHES
Amarone	Primarily Corvina, plus Rondinella and Molinara	The Veneto (Verona)	The biggest of Italian red wines, with alcohol levels approaching those of fortified wines: round, full-bodied, with intense fruit; great aging potential	The elegance and power of Amarone demand strong flavors in the foods you pair them with: big roasts (saddle and leg of lamb, prime rib), game (both feathered and furred), the strongest cheeses
Bardolino	Corvina, Rondinella, Molinara	The Veneto	A spindly younger brother to Amarone: light, fruity, somewhat acid quaffing wine	A perfect warm-weather red wine, Bardolino can take some chilling and matches well with all sorts of light foods (even strong-flavored fish and shellfish)
Breganze Rosso	Merlot, some Cabernet	The Veneto (Vicenza)	Dry, round, slightly tannic, with intense fruit	A good all-around dinner wine with the normal red-wine companions—grilled and roasted meats, savory stews and braises, cheeses of all sorts
Carmignano	Sangiovese, some Cabernet, other local grapes	Tuscany	Similar to Chianti Classico: medium to full body, round and smooth, with complex fruit and wood flavors	An ideal companion for important dinners and/or complexly flavored preparations. Use as you would Bordeaux châteaux
Castel del Monte	Uva di Troia, Montepulciano, Bombina Nero	Apulia	Simple but generous flavor, consistent quality	A very useful red wine for everyday meals, barbecues, outdoor dining, Castel del Monte works with just about everything from hamburgers to roasts, chili con carne to boeuf à la mode
Chianti, Chianti with regional name (Siena, Aretine Hills, etc.)	Sangiovese plus other local varieties	Tuscany	Combines the deep flavor of Sangiovese with fruit and acidity to make a fine, youthful wine of some complexity	Matches well with almost everything except cream sauces: an excellent wine for middle-range dinners or to use as a modulation from a white or simple red to a very complex red wine in an important dinner
Chianti Classico (Riserva), Chianti Rufina (Riserva)	Sangiovese, local varieties	Tuscany	More austere and complexly flavored than simple Chiantis, especially in the long-aged *riserva* versions	Serve these Chiantis with your finest dinners, with all the classic red-wine companions—the great roasts, game, fine cheeses
Etna Rosso	Nerello Mascalese, Nerello Mantellato, other local varieties	Sicily	Pleasing, full-bodied red wine for drinking young	Excellent wine for everyday drinking and informal occasions: compatible with the whole range of red-wine foods, from antipasti through pastas and meats

WINE NAME	GRAPES	REGION	CHARACTERISTICS	FOOD MATCHES
Franciacorta	Cabernet, Merlot, Nebbiolo and Barbera	Lombardy	Dry, round and pleasing, with complex fruit: should be drunk relatively young	A good all-around dinner wine with the normal red-wine companions—grilled and roasted meats, savory stews and braises, cheeses of all sorts
Gattinara	Primarily Nebbiolo	Piedmont	Often velvety and elegant, occasionally coarse and tannic; fine Nebbiolo flavors	Serve with red meats, stews and braises (especially those made with wine), game, cheese
Ghemme	Nebbiolo, other local varieties	Piedmont	Similar to Gattinara	Similar to Gattinara
Lacryma Christi	Piedirosso, with some Aglianico and other local grapes	Campania (Naples)	Perhaps the favorite red wine of southern Italy: deeply colored, aromatic, soft, with big, full, uncomplicated flavor	A readily enjoyable wine with greater scope than its apparent simplicity suggests; all the conventional red-wine matches, but especially good with veal dishes and dishes like lasagna, eggplant parmigiana, gnocchi
Salice Salentino	Negroamaro, other local varieties	Apulia	Assertively flavored, round mouthfilling: a big wine	Excellent with risottos, roast and grilled meats (especially good with lamb), cheeses
Torgiano Rosso	Sangiovese and several other local varieties	Umbria	Similar to Chianti Classico, but a touch softer, less tannic	Use as you would Chianti Classico
Valpolicella	Corvina, Rondinella, Molinara	The Veneto (Verona)	Similar to Bardolino, but somewhat fuller, rounder, more intense	Use as you would Bardolino or simple Chianti
Valtellina, Valtellina Superiore	Nebbiolo and other red grapes	Lombardy	Slightly tannic, with pleasing fruit when young and a good degree of complexity when older: an easy introduction to the Nebbiolo grape	A versatile wine, useful on almost all the standard red-wine occasions from the simplest to the most formal
Vino Nobile di Montepulciano	Sangiovese and other local varieties	Tuscany	Like Carmignano, a sort of super-Chianti	Use exactly as you would Carmignano

14

continued from page 11

Three near-greats—the Barbera, Dolcetto and Montepulciano grapes—qualify in quality, quantity, and importance as the next most significant tier of Italian red wines. Barbera and Dolcetto appear most often as pure varietal wines, especially in the Piedmont (though Barbera is elsewhere often blended, and even in Piedmont many blending experiments are now under way).

Barbera is the lighter of the two and the least tannic of all Piedmontese red wines, with the kind of pleasing fruit and acidity that make it a wine of all uses, even with some of the more assertively flavored of the traditional white wine foods. It seems to go well with almost every sort of food, which is not an observation you can make of many other red wines, or even many whites.

Dolcetto, a juicy, flavorful, medium-bodied wine, takes a more conventional red wine range of food companions. In the Piedmont, it almost always prepares the way for a great Barolo or Barbaresco at an important dinner.

The grape Montepulciano should not be confused with Vino Nobile di Montepulciano, which is made from Sangiovese (see above). The Montepulciano grape tends to be somewhat low in tannin, and thus yields soft, supple wines that are chiefly useful in blending. In The Marches and Abruzzi, however, it makes varietal wines that are robust and full-flavored—excellent with strong-flavored meats in simple preparations (for example, roasts and grills).

Some of the "international" varieties of red grapes—chiefly Cabernet Sauvignon and Merlot—are now grown in many parts of Italy and get a lot of publicity, but they are considerably less important than the native red wine grapes. In a few areas (Carmignano, Friuli-Venezia Giulia), Cabernet and especially Merlot have been cultivated for some time and are vinified according to prevailing local custom. In Carmignano they are blended into a Chianti-like mixture, and in Friuli and The Veneto made into separate varietal wines—the Merlot a little sturdier and the Cabernet softer and fruitier than is the norm outside of Italy.

Elsewhere, the arrival of Cabernet Sauvignon and Merlot has heralded upheavals in viticultural tradition. Throughout Tuscany, for instance, and especially in the Chianti Classico zone, growers are mixing Cabernet in their Chianti blend, or making a simple Sangiovese-Cabernet mix, or even vinifying 100% Cabernet wines on the California model. Many of these new-style wines, although quite excellent and of a superior level of craftsmanship, can bear only the *Vino da Tavola* designation, but you will be able to distinguish them from genuine, humble (and often barely drinkable) *Vino da Tavola* by their designer labels and their designer price tags. Some examples of these new-style wines are: Antinori's Tignanello, Avignonesi's Grifi, Caparzo's Ca del Pazzo, Castellare's I Sodi di San Niccolo, Castello di Volpaia's Coltassala, Fontodi's Flaccianello, Monte Vertine's Il Sodaccio and Le Pergole Torte.

In addition to the fine Chiantis and their kin, a good many other estimable Italian red wines result from blending native grape varieties. Of these, the best-known are probably the Veronese reds, the very light Bardolino, the slightly fuller Valpolicella, and their brawny brother Amarone. All three wines contain the same traditional grapes grown in the traditional areas—Bardolino right near Lake Garda and the other two in the hills around Verona.

Amarone achieves its great size and power by a process usually reserved for sweet wines (it does have a sweet sibling, called Recioto di Valpolicella): late picked, partially raisined grapes of intense sweetness and flavor are very slowly fermented at low temperatures—sometimes the fermentation takes all winter—to produce a wine that combines extraordinary berry-like fruitiness, enormous body, and a wonderfully elegant, velvet texture. Some people treat it like Port, serving it after a meal with walnuts or hazelnuts, but Amarone also matches well with selected entrées or *secondi*—chiefly either those of marked flavor themselves or composed dishes of great, balanced complexity. If you are able to obtain a chunk of top-quality eating Parmigiano, no wine in the world will do as much with it or for it as an Amarone.

Sicily produces some blended red wines of outstanding character. The Duca di Salaparuta firm, which makes the deservedly popular red and white Corvo wines, also produces the huge and elegant Duca Enrico, a stunning exemplar of the potential of Sicilian grapes. Regaleali's fine Rosso del Conte has for years embodied the same high quality.

15

Crostini with Tarragon Spread (page 45) and Crostini with Beef and Balsamic Vinegar (page 46).

At right, two possible antipasto plates chosen from among the antipasti displayed at left (from left to right and top to bottom): Shallots in Red Wine (page 23), White Beans with Squid (page 28), imported olives, anchovies, grilled zucchini, Roasted Peppers in Olive Oil (page 22), grilled eggplant, Ricotta Pecorino Cheese with Peppers and Lemon (page 27), Pickled Figs in Red Wine Vinegar (page 26), Marinated Chick-Peas (page 28), prosciutto-wrapped Sweet and Hot Melon (page 25) with pickled figs, Herbed Mozzarella (page 27), Frittata Wedges (page 41), Braised Celery with Olives (page 24) and poached fresh salmon, shrimp and ricotta pecorino, Tarragon Mushrooms (page 24), Artichokes with Garlic and Fresh Mint (page 25).

Crostini with Tomato (page 45).

ANTIPASTI & STARTERS

21

ROASTED PEPPERS IN OLIVE OIL

These roasted peppers are especially delicious when served on warm toasted or grilled Italian bread. They can also be slivered and served, with a little of their oil, over spaghetti or room-temperature pasta salads. The peppers can be stored in their oil in the refrigerator for several weeks.

Makes About 1 Quart

12 *red bell peppers*
2 *sprigs of rosemary or 2 bay leaves*
2 *garlic cloves, lightly crushed*
2 *strips of orange zest*
2 to 3 *cups olive oil*

1. Preheat the broiler. Arrange the peppers in a single layer in a large baking tray and broil, as close to the heat as possible, turning occasionally, until they are blackened all over, 15 to 20 minutes.

2. Transfer the peppers to a large brown paper bag; close the top and let stand for about 10 minutes, until the skins loosen.

3. One at a time, hold the peppers under cold running water, rinse and pull away the charred skin; drain on paper towels.

4. Quarter each pepper and, using a paring knife, remove the stem, seeds and ribs. Place the peppers in a clean, dry 1-quart jar. Add the rosemary, garlic and orange zest.

5. Pour in the olive oil, adding enough to cover the peppers and fill the jar. Slide a clean blunt knife blade between the peppers to release any trapped air bubbles. Secure the jar with a lid and store in the refrigerator.
—*Diana Sturgis*

MARINATED MUSHROOMS WITH ROASTED RED PEPPERS AND MARJORAM

You can use all white button mushrooms if you wish, but fresh shiitakes—or other fleshy wild mushrooms—add a more earthy flavor and varied texture.

4 to 6 First-Course Servings

⅓ *cup extra-virgin olive oil*
3 *large shallots, minced*
2 *large garlic cloves, minced*
1 *pound medium white button mushrooms, quartered*
1 *pound medium fresh shiitake mushrooms, stemmed and quartered*
¼ *cup balsamic vinegar*
2 *large red bell peppers*
1 *tablespoon chopped fresh marjoram*
1 *teaspoon freshly ground black pepper*
1 *teaspoon salt*
1 *large ripe avocado, preferably Hass, peeled and cut into 1-inch cubes*
1 *bunch of arugula*

1. In a large heavy skillet, heat the olive oil over moderate heat. Add the shallots and garlic and reduce the heat to low. Cook the mixture, stirring occasionally, until softened but not browned, about 5 minutes. Increase the heat to moderately high and add the button and the shiitake mushrooms, stirring well to combine. Cover the skillet and

THE ANTIPASTO COURSE

The versatility of the antipasto course makes a major contribution to the meal. Readily available ingredients such as melon, dried figs, shallots, mushrooms, cheese, celery, chick-peas and eggs can be easily transformed into dazzling antipasti (an antipasto is made up of several antipasti). With one or two homemade antipasti and the addition of some simply grilled vegetables or store-bought olives, roasted red peppers, anchovies and cured meats such as prosciutto, bresaola or pepperoni, you can put together a splendid assortment in a matter of minutes. Once you've decided on the main dish, you can take advantage of the myriad starting possibilities to complement and add dimension to the rest of the menu's flavors and textures.

22

cook, stirring once, until the mushrooms are slightly softened, about 4 minutes.

2. Uncover, increase the heat to high, add the balsamic vinegar and cook for 1 minute. Spoon the mushroom mixture into a large bowl and let it cool to room temperature, stirring occasionally.

3. Meanwhile, roast the red peppers directly over a gas flame or under the broiler as close to the heat as possible, turning until charred all over. Enclose the peppers in a paper bag and set aside for 10 minutes to steam. When cool enough to handle, peel the peppers and remove the cores, seeds and ribs. Slice the peppers lengthwise into ½-inch-wide strips.

4. Combine the roasted peppers with the mushrooms. Stir in the marjoram, pepper and salt. Refrigerate the mixture until ready to serve. (The recipe can be prepared 1 day ahead to this point and kept covered in the refrigerator.)

5. To serve, fold the avocado cubes into the mushroom mixture. Arrange the arugula leaves on a large serving place and place the mushroom salad on top. Serve chilled or at room temperature.
—Marcia Kiesel

SHALLOTS IN RED WINE

When peeling the shallots, barely trim the root end to keep the shallots intact during cooking. I like to leave the other end long, just for the look of it.

Makes About 30
Shallots

1 *pound large shallots, peeled*
2 *tablespoons sugar*

1 *small sprig of fresh rosemary or ¼
   teaspoon dried*
¼ *cup extra-virgin olive oil*
⅛ *teaspoon coarsely ground pepper*
1 *bottle (750 ml) dry red wine*

1. In a medium bowl, toss the shallots with the sugar and rosemary. In a medium nonreactive skillet, heat the olive oil. Add the shallots and cook over moderate heat, tossing frequently, until browned, 5 to 7 minutes. Add the pepper and wine and simmer until the shallots are tender, 20 to 25 minutes.

2. Using a slotted spoon, transfer the shallots and rosemary to a l-quart jar. Boil the liquid in the

ANTIPASTO GUIDELINES

• Don't serve too much. Antipasto can have equal status, but don't risk an anticlimactic first or main course.
• Select antipasti that will complement the first or main course. If the main course will be substantial, emphasize vegetables and fish; if light, take advantage of cheeses, meat and eggs.
• Try not to repeat flavors. Avoid using ingredients featured in the main course.
• Combine antipasti with texture, color, and flavor in mind.
• Antipasto can be served on a large platter or on individual plates. Platters have dramatic punch and express abundance and conviviality. They do, however, require at least six antipasti to make the statement properly.

Individual plating makes for a more graceful presentation and lends itself to using just a few items.
• For an idea of how much variety is appropriate, divide the number of diners by two. Eight guests divided by two equals four antipasti.
• For antipasti that come in slices or large pieces, allow two for each person plus a few extra. For small marinated vegetables, allow about ¼ cup.
• Last but not least, never make an antipasto at the last minute. Everything should be arranged, covered and left at room temperature about one hour before dinner.
—Anne Disrude

ANTIPASTI & STARTERS

skillet over high heat until reduced to 1¼ cups, 10 to 15 minutes. Pour this reduction over the shallots. Let cool completely, then cover and refrigerate. These shallots will keep in the refrigerator for several months.

—Anne Disrude

TARRAGON MUSHROOMS

These mushrooms will keep for several months in the refrigerator. Serve them tossed with additional chopped fresh tarragon and lemon juice.

Makes About 20 Pieces

1 ounce dried porcini mushrooms
2 tablespoons olive oil
½ small onion, minced
1 pound small fresh mushrooms, cleaned
¼ cup tarragon wine vinegar
1 teaspoon coarse (kosher) salt
6 sprigs of fresh tarragon or 2 teaspoons dried

1. Soak the porcini in 1½ cups of warm water until softened, about 30 minutes. Scoop the mushrooms out of the liquid and rinse thoroughly. Sort through and discard any sandy pieces or tough stems; coarsely chop the mushrooms. Strain the liquid into a saucepan through several layers of dampened cheesecloth; set aside.

2. In a large skillet, heat the olive oil. Add the onion and cook over moderate heat, stirring, until softened, 1 to 20 minutes. Add the fresh mushrooms and cook until warmed through, 1 to 2 minutes. Add the vinegar and cook for 1 minute. Add the chopped porcini and salt and cook for 1 minute. Using a slotted spoon, transfer the mushrooms to a 1-quart heatproof jar. Add the tarragon sprigs.

3. Bring the reserved porcini liquid to a boil and pour it into the jar. Add enough boiling water to fill the jar. Let the mixture cool, then cover and refrigerate.

—Anne Disrude

BRAISED CELERY WITH OLIVES

It's easy to forget about using celery as a cooked vegetable, but prepared in this manner, it makes a tasty and relatively inexpensive antipasto that will keep in the refrigerator for up to two weeks. Or, serve it with poached or grilled salmon flaked over the top or with strips of fresh Parmesan and an extra grinding of coarse black pepper.

Makes About 4 Dozen Pieces

1 large bunch of celery, ribs separated
2 tablespoons extra-virgin olive oil
3 garlic cloves, crushed
⅓ cup Niçoise olives (2 ounces)
4 imported bay leaves
Pinch of crushed red hot pepper
½ cup dry white wine
½ cup chicken stock or canned broth
¼ teaspoon salt
¼ teaspoon coarsely cracked black pepper

1. Trim the leaves and any bruised ends from the celery ribs.

24

ITALIAN OLIVE HARVEST

Italian olives are harvested between the months of November and March, either by workers perched on ladders, picking with their hands or wooden tools, or by wrapping large nets around the base of the olive trees and shaking them or hitting them with sticks so that the olives fall into the nets. Green olives are picked when they are underripe; purple olives when they are just ripe and black olives when they are overripe.

It is traditional to celebrate the olive harvest with *bruschette*, grilled slices of bread rubbed with garlic cloves and drizzled with freshly pressed olive oil.

Peel the ribs, then slice lengthwise into ½-inch strips. Cut the strips crosswise into 4- to 5-inch pieces.

2. In a large skillet or flameproof casserole, heat the olive oil. Add the garlic, olives, bay leaves and hot pepper. Cook over moderate heat, stirring frequently, until aromatic, 3 to 5 minutes. Do not let the garlic brown.

3. Increase the heat to high, add the wine and boil for 1 minute. Add the chicken stock and celery. When the liquid returns to a boil, reduce the heat to low. Cover and cook, tossing occasionally, until the celery is crisp-tender, about 20 minutes. Remove from the heat.

4. Let the celery cool in the liquid. Season with the salt and black pepper. Transfer the celery and its cooking liquid to a glass dish or jar, cover and refrigerate.
—Anne Disrude

ARTICHOKES WITH GARLIC AND FRESH MINT

An enameled cast-iron pot with a tight-fitting lid is ideal for cooking these artichokes. They should fit as snugly as possible in the pot.

Makes 16 Pieces

4 medium artichokes
12 sprigs of fresh mint
½ teaspoon salt
½ teaspoon freshly ground pepper
½ cup extra-virgin olive oil
8 garlic cloves, peeled

1. Trim the artichoke stems to the base and cut off any spiny leaf tips. Rinse the artichokes. Pry open the centers and stuff 3 mint sprigs into each one. Place the artichokes in a heavy pot just deep enough to accommodate them. Sprinkle with the salt and pepper and drizzle on the oil. Add the whole garlic cloves and ¼ cup of water.

2. Bring to a boil. reduce the heat to moderately low and cook, covered, adding water as necessary to keep a sizzle going, until a leaf pulls out easily, about 40 minutes. Let the artichokes cool in the pot. (The artichokes can be prepared to this point up to 10 days ahead. Cover and refrigerate.)

3. To serve, remove the mint sprigs and set aside. Using a pair of scissors and beginning at the tips, quarter each artichoke lengthwise. Or quarter the artichokes with a large sharp knife. Carefully remove the chokes with a spoon and discard them. Chop the mint sprigs and garlic cloves and mix with the pan juices. Pour over the quartered artichokes.
—Anne Disrude

SWEET AND HOT MELON

Makes 16 Pieces

1 small ripe cantaloupe, halved
    lengthwise and seeded
½ to ¾ teaspoon crushed hot red
    pepper
¼ cup dry Marsala
Pinch of salt

Cut each melon half into 4 lengthwise wedges. Using a paring knife, remove the rind. Cut each wedge in half crosswise and place in a medium bowl. Add the hot

pepper, Marsala and salt and toss well. Serve, or cover and refrigerate, tossing occasionally, for up to 2 hours.
—Anne Disrude

FRESH RICOTTA CHEESE WITH ROSEMARY AND OLIVES

The full yet delicate flavor of freshly made ricotta is a real treat, and it is easy and quick to prepare. For this delicious hors d'oeuvre, the fresh cheese is highlighted with sprinklings of salt and pepper, rosemary, green olives and a small amount of extra-virgin olive oil. Serve with crackers or thinly sliced Italian bread.

*Makes About
1 Cup*

1 quart milk
½ cup heavy cream
*1 tablespoon plus 1 teaspoon fresh
    lemon juice*
⅛ teaspoon salt
⅛ teaspoon freshly ground pepper
Pinch of finely crushed rosemary
*2 brine-cured green
    olives, minced*
*2 teaspoons extra-virgin
    olive oil*

1. In a large nonreactive saucepan, bring the milk and cream to a boil over high heat. When the liquid is boiling vigorously, stir in the lemon juice; the mixture will separate into curds and whey in 5 to 10 seconds. Immediately remove from the heat and pour through a fine sieve lined with a double thickness of dampened cheesecloth. What collects in the cheesecloth are the curds; discard the whey. Immediately place the ricotta on a small plate and let cool, uncovered, at room temperature. (*If making ahead, cover the cooled ricotta and refrigerate until ready to use.*)

2. With the back of a spoon, spread the ricotta in an even layer on the plate. Sprinkle with the salt, pepper, rosemary and minced olives. Drizzle the olive oil evenly over the cheese.
—Anne Disrude

PICKLED FIGS IN RED WINE VINEGAR

These figs make an excellent sweet/tart accompaniment to prosciutto and other cured meats. Since the figs become increasingly vinegary and their liquid increasingly sweet, I suggest using them within two weeks.

*Makes About 2
Dozen*

*1 pound dried figs, hard
    stems removed*
2 cups red wine vinegar
2 to 3 strips of orange zest

In a medium nonreactive saucepan, combine the figs with the vinegar and enough water to cover. Add the orange zest, cover and simmer over low heat until the figs are very soft, about 2 hours. Let cool in the liquid. Transfer the figs and their cooking liquid to a glass jar, cover and store at room temperature.
—Anne Disrude

HERBED MOZZARELLA

I like to grate or chop a cube or two of this flavored cheese and sprinkle it over room-temperature pan-grilled zucchini or eggplant.

This recipe always works well as long as you use good fresh mozzarella and extra-virgin olive oil. Fresh mozzarella is available at Italian markets, many fine cheese shops and some supermarket deli counters. I use fresh or dried herbs for this, or sometimes a combination—it all depends on what's on hand. The dried herbs below, for example, can be augmented with or replaced by 1 tablespoon each of chopped fresh basil, chives and parsley.

Makes 16 to 20
Pieces

1 *pound fresh whole-milk mozzarella,*
    cut into 1-inch cubes
½ *teaspoon coarsely ground black*
    pepper
1 *teaspoon coarse (kosher) salt*
½ *cup extra-virgin olive oil*
½ *teaspoon dried oregano*
¼ *teaspoon dried rosemary*
¼ *teaspoon crushed hot red pepper*
1 *teaspoon dried thyme*

In a medium bowl, combine all the ingredients. Toss to coat evenly. Cover and refrigerate, for up to 2 weeks, tossing occasionally. Let return to room temperature before using.
—*Anne Disrude*

RICOTTA PECORINO CHEESE WITH PEPPERS AND LEMON

Makes 16 to 20
Pieces

12 *fresh green or red hot peppers*
1 *pound Ricotta Pecorino or feta*
    cheese, sliced 1 inch thick
Zest from 2 lemons
½ *cup extra-virgin olive oil*

1. Roast the peppers directly over a gas flame or as close as possible to the broiler, turning, until blackened all over. Place in a bag to steam for 10 minutes to loosen the skins. Peel the peppers as best you can without tearing them open.

2. Place half the cheese slices in the bottom of a 2- to 3-quart shallow glass dish. Top with half the lemon zest and half the roasted peppers. Drizzle ¼ cup of the oil over the peppers. Repeat with the remaining cheese, lemon zest, peppers and oil. Cover with plastic wrap and let infuse at room temperature for at least 30 minutes, or refrigerate, covered, for up to 3 weeks.

3. To serve, break the cheese into 1-inch pieces or cut into thin triangles. Mince the peppers and lemon zest and sprinkle over the top.
—*Anne Disrude*

FRESH MOZZARELLA

In Italy, the coveted water-buffalo-milk mozzarella is rarely used for cooking. Instead, it is purchased at its prime—one day old, tender and dripping with whey—and tossed with tomatoes, olive oil and fresh basil leaves. Or, it is served, unadorned, as a dessert. Served this way, the subtle and rich flavors of the mozzarella are allowed to shine.

However, there are also practical reasons for not cooking with any type of fresh mozzarella—cow's milk or water-buffalo's milk. Because the fresh cheese is still so soft and full of whey, it cannot be easily sliced or grated and it contributes too much liquid and not enough flavor when it is cooked with other ingredients. An Italian cook planning to use fresh mozzarella in a cooked dish will "age" the cheese for several days to let it give up some of its moisture, making it firmer and its flavors more concentrated.

ANTIPASTI & STARTERS

CLASSIC COCKTAILS

Italians like their drinks simple and refreshing. They are devoted to vermouth and other aperitif wines, usually on the rocks with a splash of mineral water. But they've also invented classic cocktails: the Bellini, the Negroni and the Americano, smooth, sophisticated and delicious. The following recipes are for 1 serving each.

AMERICANO
In an old-fashioned glass, pour 1 ounce Campari and 1 ounce Italian sweet vermouth over cracked ice; stir well. Granish with a twist of lemon peel.

CAMPARI AND SODA
In a highball glass, pour 2 ounces of Campari and 4 ounces of club soda over ice cubes; stir well. Garnish with a twist of orange peel.

PUCCINI
This Italian variation of a Mimosa uses freshly squeezed tangerine juice and an Italian sparkling white wine to make a refreshing drink. If tangerines are not in season, frozen concentrate may be substituted. Pour
continued on next page

CHICK-PEAS WITH CURRANTS AND PEPPERONI

Makes About 1¾ Cups

3 tablespoons red wine vinegar
2 tablespoons currants
½ teaspoon salt
1½ cups Marinated Chick-Peas (below)
1 tablespoon olive oil
1 tablespoon chopped parsley
3 tablespoons minced pepperoni

1. In a small saucepan, bring the vinegar, currants and salt to a simmer over moderate heat. Remove from the heat and set aside until plumped.
2. In a medium bowl, combine the Marinated Chick-Peas, raisins and their liquid, olive oil, parsley and pepperoni.
—Anne Disrude

MARINATED CHICK-PEAS OR WHITE BEANS

I like to serve these beans tossed with additional olive oil, lemon juice, minced parsley and salt and pepper.

Makes About 8 Cups

1 pound dried chick-peas or white pea beans
2 celery ribs
2 onions halves
Bouquet garni: 1 bunch of parsley stems, 1 small sprig of rosemary or ½ teaspoon dried, 7 sprigs of fresh sage or ½ teaspoon dried leaf sage,

2 imported bay leaves and 1 small dried hot red pepper, all tied in cheesecloth
½ cup extra-virgin olive oil
1 teaspoon salt
½ teaspoon coarsely cracked black pepper

1. In a large saucepan or flameproof casserole, soak the chick-peas or beans overnight in water to cover by 6 inches. Drain and add fresh cold water to cover by 6 inches. Add the celery, onions and bouquet garni.
2. Bring to a simmer over high heat. Reduce the heat to low and simmer until the beans are soft but still hold their shape, about 2½ hours for chick-peas or 1½ hours for white beans. Drain well and spread on a large baking sheet to cool. Remove and discard the vegetables and bouquet garni.
3. Toss the chick-peas or beans with the oil, salt and black pepper. Let cool to room temperature. Transfer to a jar, cover and refrigerate. The chick-peas will keep for 2 to 3 weeks; beans will keep for 1.
—Anne Disrude

WHITE BEANS WITH SQUID

Makes About 4 Cups

1½ pounds fresh squid, cleaned
1½ cups Marinated White Beans (at left)
2 tablespoons fresh lemon juice

3 tablespoons olive oil
½ teaspoon salt
¼ teaspoon pepper
3 tablespoons chopped parsley

1. In a medium saucepan of lightly salted boiling water, blanch the squid for 1 minute. Drain and cut the squid into ¼-inch rings.

2. In a medium bowl, combine the squid, Marinated White Beans, lemon juice, olive oil, salt, pepper and parsley.
—Anne Disrude

BAGNA CAUDA SALAD

Bagna cauda is a classic traditional Italian hot anchovy dip, usually served with crudités. In this takeoff, the vegetables are cooked briefly to enhance color and texture, then arranged attractively on the plate and served with the tangy anchovy dipping sauce as a dressing.

4 Servings

½ pound red potatoes, cut into 1½-by-¼-inch sticks
1 medium zucchini
¼ pound sugar snap peas
¼ pound green beans
½ small head of cauliflower, broken into ½-inch florets
½ small bunch of broccoli, broken into ½-inch florets
3 large mushrooms, quartered
2 tablespoons fresh lemon juice
¾ cup olive oil, preferably extra-virgin

6 large garlic cloves, thinly sliced
8 flat anchovy fillets, minced
1 tablespoon capers
¼ teaspoon coarsely cracked pepper
½ teaspoon grated lemon zest

1. Cook the potatoes in a medium saucepan of boiling salted water until tender, 5 to 8 minutes. Drain and set aside.

2. Cut the zucchini crosswise into ¼-inch-thick rounds. Stack the rounds and slice again into ¼-inch sticks. Bring a large saucepan of salted water to a boil. Put the zucchini in a strainer and dip in the foiling water for about 2 seconds to bring out the green color. Rinse under cold running water until cool. Drain on paper towels.

3. Add the sugar snap peas to the strainer and again blanch for about 2 seconds. Rinse under cold running water until cool. Drain on paper towels. Repeat separately with the green beans, cauliflower and broccoli, blanching the beans for 1 minute and the cauliflower and broccoli for 30 seconds each.

4. In a small bowl, toss the mushrooms with the lemon juice.

5. To assemble the salad, arrange the vegetables decoratively on 4 plates.

6. Make the sauce by warming the olive oil in a medium skillet over moderate heat. Add the garlic and slowly cook until light brown, about 10 minutes. Remove and discard the garlic. Add the anchovies to the skillet. Cook, mashing with the back of a spoon, until dissolved. Add the capers, pepper and lemon zest. Pour the hot sauce over the vegetables. Serve warm.
—Anne Disrude

¼ cup fresh (or reconstitute-frozen) tangerine juice over cracked ice in a champagne tulip or saucer glass. Add ¾ cup dry sparkling white wine (preferably Prosecco) and stir well.

NEGRONI
The original recipe for a Negroni calls for sweet vermouth, but you may prefer to substitute dry to bring out further the taste of the Campari and gin. For a "Perfect" Negroni, divide the quantity of vermouth equally between sweet and dry. Yet another variation: pour the ingredients over ice cubes in an old-fashioned glass. Shake 1 ounce each gin, Campari and Italian sweet vermouth together with ice until chilled. Strain into a cocktail glass. Garnish with a twist of orange peel.

BELLINI
The classic Bellini uses the juice of white peaches, with a hint of lemon juice to accentuate their flavor, and is refrigerated before serving. This variation substitutes peach nectar and serves it over cracked ice. A lovely garnish is a peach half floating in the glass. Pour 1 tablespoon peach nectar over cracked ice in a stemmed cocktail glass. Add 3 or 4 drops of fresh lemon juice and ¼ cup dry sparkling white wine (preferably Prosecco) and stir.

MIXED GREENS WITH POLENTA CROUTONS AND GORGONZOLA

6 Servings

1½ teaspoons salt
1 cup instant polenta*
1 head of radicchio
1 small head of chicory (curly endive)
1 small head of romaine lettuce
1 large Belgian endive
1 tablespoon red wine vinegar
3 tablespoons plus ⅓ cup olive oil,
*   preferably extra-virgin*
1 tablespoon walnut oil
½ teaspoon Dijon mustard
⅛ teaspoon freshly ground pepper
4 ounces gorgonzola cheese, at room
*   temperature*
*Available at Italian markets and
*   specialty food shops*

1. In a medium saucepan, bring 2¼ cups of water to a boil over high heat. Add 1 teaspoon of the salt and stir in the polenta. Cook, stirring, constantly with a wooden spoon, until the polenta thickens. Reduce the heat to a simmer and cook, stirring occasionally, until the polenta pulls away from the sides of the pan when stirred, about 15 minutes. (Note: The cooking time, longer than specified on the box, is needed to produce a tight, relatively dry polenta that will hold together when fried.)

2. Scrape the thickened polenta out of the pan onto a nonreactive baking sheet. Using a lightly oiled wooden or plastic spatula, spread the polenta into an even rectangle about 12 by 6 by ¼ inch. Let cool to room temperature, then cover and refrigerate until well chilled.

3. Meanwhile, prepare the salad greens. Cut the core from the radicchio and separate the head into individual leaves. Separate the chicory and romaine into individual leaves, remove the tough ribs and tear the leaves into bite-size pieces. Separate the Belgian endive into separate spears. Combine the greens, rinse thoroughly and dry. Wrap the greens in paper towels in a plastic bag and refrigerate if not serving at once. (*The recipe can be made 1 day ahead to this point.*)

4. In a small bowl, whisk together the vinegar, 3 tablespoons of the olive oil, the walnut oil, mustard, remaining ½ teaspoon salt and the pepper. Set the dressing aside.

5. Preheat the broiler. Remove the polenta from the refrigerator. Cut the polenta into 6 rectangles 6 by 2 inches each. Heat the remaining ⅓ cup olive oil in a large skillet. Add the polenta and sauté over moderately high heat, turning once, until crisp and golden, about 4 minutes. Remove with a slotted spatula and drain on paper towels. (*The recipe can be prepared to this point up to 1 hour ahead.*)

6. Spread the gorgonzola over the fried polenta.

7. To assemble the salad, toss the greens with the vinaigrette until coated. Divide among six plates.

8. Run the polenta croutons under the broiler until the cheese melts, about 1 minute. Slice each rectangle crosswise into 6 smaller rectangles or cut into triangles and, while still warm, arrange on top of the salad.
—John Robert Massie

POLENTA

Polenta is a staple in the Veneto region and in some of the other far northern parts of Italy. It is traditionally made in a deep copper pan, called a *paiola*, that is suspended over an open fire, and is stirred with a special long-handled spoon made of chestnut or acacia wood. When it is finished cooking, the piping hot polenta is first poured onto a white cloth and then placed on a wooden board. Polenta is traditionally cut with a wooden spatula or a thick cotton thread.

TUSCAN-STYLE WHITE BEAN SALAD

While this dish makes a delicious antipasto or an accompaniment to almost any simple meat, it also can be offered as the centerpiece of a compose-your-own salad for a long, lazy summer lunch. Present the beans, surrounded by ripe red tomato wedges, with an assortment of tasty and colorful components for each guest to choose according to individual taste: Italian tuna packed in olive oil, good black olives, crisp greens, scallions, sliced cucumbers and the like. Set out a cruet of extra-virgin olive oil, lemon wedges and a pepper mill for seasoning. Serve with crusty loaves of Italian bread and a chilled, light-bodied wine.

6 to 8 Servings

2 *cups dried cannellini (about 12
    ounces), Great Northern white or
    cranberry beans (see Note)*
1 *small yellow onion*
2 *garlic cloves*
4 *sprigs of fresh sage or thyme or ¼
    teaspoon dried thyme*
4 *fresh plum tomatoes*
2½ *teaspoons salt*
1 *teaspoon freshly ground pepper*
1 *small red onion, chopped*
1 *small celery rib with leaves, cut into
    ¼-inch dice*
¼ *cup thinly sliced scallion greens*
2 *tablespoons shredded fresh basil*
1 *tablespoon chopped parsley*
⅓ *cup extra-virgin olive oil*
3 *tablespoons lemon juice*

1. Either soak the dried beans overnight in cold water to cover by 4 inches or place in a large saucepan with several inches of water to cover and bring to a boil. Boil, covered, for 2 minutes, then remove from the heat and let stand for 1 hour. Drain the beans.

2. Place in a large saucepan and cover with 4 inches of fresh cold water. Cover and bring to a boil over high heat. Tuck the yellow onion, garlic and 2 sprigs of the sage in with the beans. Simmer over low heat until the beans are tender but not mushy, about 1½ hours. Drain the beans; discard the onion, garlic and sage.

3. Core and seed one of the tomatoes and cut it into ½-inch dice. Cut the remaining 3 tomatoes lengthwise into 6 wedges each and set aside. Finely chop the remaining 2 sprigs of sage.

4. Place the beans in a large mixing bowl and season with the salt and pepper. Add the chopped tomato and sage, the red onion, celery, scallion greens, basil, parsley, olive oil and lemon juice. Toss gently with 2 rubber spatulas to combine the ingredients without crushing the beans. Cover and set aside for at least 1 hour at room temperature to blend the flavors. (*The recipe can be prepared 1 day in advance up to this point and refrigerated, covered.*) Transfer to a serving bowl or platter and surround with the tomato wedges. Serve at room temperature.

NOTE: If fresh cranberry beans are available, buy 3 pounds (in the pod) and shell them. Begin at Step 2, but cook the beans for only about 20 minutes, until tender. If you prefer to use canned beans, use 2 cans (19 ounces each) cannellini. Simply rinse them and drain well, then proceed to Step 3.
—*Richard Sax*

31

PASTA SALAD WITH BROCCOLI AND TUNA

This authentic Italian salad is one of the few pasta recipes that can be prepared ahead of time, up to three hours before serving. If doing so, do not add the tuna until just before serving.

♟ Crisp, simple white, such as a dry California Chenin Blanc

8 to 10 Servings

1 *bunch of fresh broccoli—tops cut into bite-size florets, stems peeled and cut into bite-size pieces (4 to 4½ cups)*
1 *pound rigatoni*
2 *cups sliced scallions (about 2 bunches)*
1½ *pounds fresh tomatoes (3 or 4 large), cut into wedges*
2 *cans (7 ounces each) tuna packed in olive oil, drained and coarsely flaked*
3 *garlic cloves, minced*
3 *tablespoons finely chopped flat-leaf parsley*
2 *tablespoons chopped fresh basil (optional)*
½ *cup extra-virgin olive oil*
1 *teaspoon salt*
½ *teaspoon freshly ground pepper*

1. In a large saucepan of rapidly boiling salted water, cook the broccoli until crisp-tender but still green, 2 to 3 minutes. Remove with a slotted spoon or skimmer and rinse under cold water.

2. Add the pasta to the same water and cook until tender but still firm, 12 to 15 minutes. Drain, rinse in cold water, drain again and pour into a large serving bowl

3. Add the scallions, tomatoes, tuna, garlic, parsley, basil, olive oil, salt and pepper to the pasta and toss lightly. Do not refrigerate this dish. Serve the salad at room temperature.
—*Edward Giobbi*

ANTIPASTO FISH SALAD

Make this antipasto with leftover firm-fleshed fish that has been grilled or broiled. Tuna, swordfish and mako shark all work beautifully, or use leftover poached shrimp and scallops, singly or together.

♟ This dish calls for a light, tart white. Try Principessa Gavi from Italy or Merlion Coeur de Melon Pinot Blanc from California.

6 Servings

½ *cup plus 3 tablespoons extra-virgin olive oil*
½ *cup homemade pickled red bell peppers, finely chopped, or 1 can (4 ounces) pimientos, drained and finely chopped*
½ *cup minced parsley*
¼ *cup fresh lemon juice*
2 *large scallions, thinly sliced*
2 *tablespoons chopped fresh oregano or 2 teaspoons dried*
1 *tablespoon drained capers, rinsed*
½ *teaspoon salt*
1½ *pounds cooked firm-fleshed fish, cut into 1-inch pieces, or cooked shrimp or scallops*
1 *medium garlic clove, minced*
2 *small zucchini, sliced crosswise ¼ inch thick*
3 *bunches of arugula, large leaves torn*
¼ *pound brine-cured black olives, such as Gaeta, for garnish*
Lemon slices, for garnish

1. In a small nonreactive skillet, combine the ½ cup olive oil with the pickled red peppers, parsley, lemon juice, scallions, oregano and capers.

Heat gently over moderately low heat until the flavors are blended, 5 to 7 minutes. (Do not let the ingredients fry.) Season with the salt.

2. In a large bowl, add the fish and three-quarters of the warm dressing and toss to coat. Season with salt to taste and set aside.

3. In a small skillet, heat the remaining 3 tablespoons oil with the garlic over moderate heat until the garlic is softened but not browned, about 2 minutes. Add the zucchini, increase the heat to moderately high and cook, stirring, until tender, about 5 minutes. Immediately add the remaining dressing and toss to coat.

4. Arrange the arugula on 6 small plates. Top with the fish, zucchini and any residual dressing. Garnish with the olives and lemon slices and serve at room temperature.
—Nancy Verde Barr

GRILLED SHRIMP AND SCALLOP SALAD WITH LINGUINE AND PARSLEY PESTO

This sunny dish combines several tastes and textures, from the sweet bell peppers and scallops to the bitter radicchio and endive. The shellfish and vegetables would be even better cooked on a grill.

❦ The zesty flavors and bitter-sharp accents of this dish call for a dry white with a bit of a bite, such as Gavi dei Gavi "La Scolca."

4 Servings

1½ pounds large shrimp, shelled and
 deveined
½ pound jumbo sea scallops
⅔ cup Oregano Vinaigrette (p. 259)
1 medium yellow bell pepper
1 medium red bell pepper

Italian Parsley Pesto (p. 258)
1½ tablespoons fresh lemon juice
¼ teaspoon crushed hot red pepper
2 medium heads of radicchio, trimmed
 and quartered lengthwise through
 the core
4 medium Belgian endives, trimmed
 and halved lengthwise
⅓ cup extra-virgin olive oil
Salt and freshly ground black pepper
½ pound fresh or imported dry
 linguine
1 medium bunch of arugula, large
 stems removed
Flat-leaf parsley leaves, for garnish

1. In a medium bowl, toss the shrimp and scallops with ½ cup of the Oregano Vinaigrette. Cover and marinate in the refrigerator for 2 to 3 hours.

2. Preheat the broiler. Place the bell peppers on a baking sheet and broil as close to the heat as possible, turning, until charred all over. Transfer the peppers to a brown paper bag, fold over the top and set aside to steam for 5 minutes. Peel the peppers. Discard the cores, seeds and ribs. Slice the peppers into thin strips and set aside.

3. Combine ½ cup of the Italian Parsley Pesto with the lemon juice and hot pepper. Set aside at room temperature.

4. Brush the radicchio and endives with the oil and place on a baking sheet. Sprinkle lightly with salt and black pepper. Broil the vegetables for about 2 minutes per side, until lightly charred. Core the radicchio and endives and place on a plate. Drizzle the remaining vinaigrette over them.

5. Arrange the shrimp and scallops on a baking sheet and broil, turning once, until lightly browned and just opaque throughout, about 2 minutes per side.

6. In a large pot of boiling salted water, cook the linguine until ten-

33

PESTO

Some food historians claim that pesto—the classic Genoese sauce, the basis of which is basil, olive oil, garlic, Parmesan and Pecorino cheese—gets its name from the wooden pestle with which the ingredients are traditionally pounded together. Similarly, the Bolognese sausage called mortadella is said to have derived its name from the mortar with which it (and all the other forcemeats that used to fall under this name) were originally prepared.

ANTIPASTI & STARTERS

der but still firm. Drain and toss with the reserved bell pepper strips and the pesto mixture. While the pasta is still hot, add the arugula and toss until wilted.

7. Arrange 2 pieces each of radicchio and endive on 4 large heated plates. Divide the linguine among the plates and arrange the seafood on top. Garnish with parsley leaves.
—David Holben and Lori Finkelman Holben, The Riviera, Dallas

MIXED SEAFOOD SALAD

♟ This light, delicate *insalata di mare* would be complemented by an equally light wine. Look for one with a crisp acidity to accent the briny flavors of the seafood, such as Columbia Crest Sémillon from Washington State or Lungarotti Pinot Grigio from Italy.

4 First-Course
Servings

3½ teaspoons salt
1 pound small waxy potatoes, peeled
    and cut into 1-inch chunks
½ cup dry white wine
1 medium shallot, thinly sliced
6 whole black peppercorns
4 sprigs of flat-leaf parsley
8 small clams, such as Manila or
    littleneck, scrubbed
4 large shrimp (about 4 ounces),
    shelled and deveined
4 medium sea scallops (about 3
    ounces)
4 cleaned medium squid (about 12
    ounces), bodies sliced into ¼-inch
    rings
¼ cup extra-virgin olive oil
1 cup minced red, yellow and green bell
    peppers, from 3 small peppers
1 teaspoon dried oregano
½ teaspoon freshly ground black
    pepper

6 fresh basil leaves, very thinly sliced
Lemon wedges, for serving

1. In a medium saucepan, bring 4 cups of water to a boil over high heat. Add 2 teaspoons of salt and the potatoes. Return to a boil, reduce the heat to moderately high; cook until the potatoes are tender, about 8 minutes. Drain and set aside.

2. In a medium nonreactive saucepan, combine 4 cups of water with the wine, shallot, peppercorns, parsley and ½ teaspoon of the salt. Bring the mixture to a boil over high heat, reduce the heat to moderate and simmer for 10 minutes.

3. Add the clams to the saucepan and cook them just until they open, 30 to 60 seconds. As they open, transfer the clams in their shells to a large bowl using a slotted spoon; set aside. Discard all clams that do not open.

4. Cook the remaining seafood in the simmering broth, one type at a time, removing it to the bowl of clams with the slotted spoon: about 1½ minutes for the shrimp, 2 minutes for the scallops, and 1 minute for the squid. All the seafood should be just tender and cooked throughout. Toss together the seafood and set aside.

5. Stir in the oil, mixed bell peppers, oregano and the reserved potatoes. Season with the black pepper and the remaining 1 teaspoon salt. Mix gently and season with additional salt and pepper to taste.

6. To serve, mound the salad on 4 plates and sprinkle the basil on top. Serve with the lemon wedges.
—Tony Mantuano, Mangia, Kenosha, Wisconsin

34

ANTIPASTO DI PESCE

There are three categories of Italian antipasto. An *antipasto misto* (mixed antipasto) can include all of the antipasto possibilities. An *affettato* is just sliced pork products, such as salami—a sort of Italian cold-cut platter. And an *antipasto di pesce* is seafood only. It might include a variety of seafood salads; stuffed mussels, clams or squid, and such simple preparations as fish marinated in olive oil and lemon juice or a sweet-and-sour sauce.

SQUID SALAD WITH CELERY ROOT

♟ Full-flavored Italian white, such as Gavi

8 Servings

1½ pounds squid, cleaned
3 garlic cloves, crushed through a press
½ cup plus 3 tablespoons olive oil, preferably extra-virgin
2 tablespoons fresh lemon juice
6 tablespoons minced parsley
¾ teaspoon salt
½ teaspoon freshly ground pepper
1 medium celery root (about ¾ pound), peeled and cut into 2-inch julienne strips
2 tablespoons sherry wine vinegar
2 small heads of chicory (curly endive), washed and torn into small pieces
2 cups cooked fresh peas or thawed frozen

1. Remove the tentacles of the squid and cut crosswise in half. Slit the bodies lengthwise and spread flat. Score with a sharp knife in a crisscross pattern, then cut into 2-inch squares. Place in a bowl.

2. Add the garlic, 3 tablespoons of the olive oil, the lemon juice, 2 tablespoons of the parsley and ¼ teaspoon each of the salt and pepper. Toss to mix. Cover and refrigerate for 4 hours or overnight. Let return to room temperature before proceeding.

3. In a medium bowl, combine the celery root, the remaining ½ cup olive oil, 3 tablespoons of the parsley, ½ teaspoon salt, ¼ teaspoon pepper and the sherry vinegar. Toss to coat well.

4. Divide the chicory among 8 plates. Arrange the celery root in the center. Drizzle any extra dressing from the bottom of the bowl over the chicory.

5. Scrape the squid and marinade into a large skillet. Sauté over moderate heat, stirring frequently, until the squid is opaque, about 3 minutes. Add the peas and toss to warm through. Mound the squid on top of the celery root. Sprinkle with the remaining 1 tablespoon parsley and serve warm.
—Enoteca Pinchiorri, Florence, Italy

INSALATA DI CARNE CRUDA (FILET MIGNON SALAD)

2 Servings

Boston or Bibb lettuce
2 tablespoons olive oil
2 tablespoons fresh lemon juice
Salt and freshly ground pepper
5 ounces filet mignon, sliced paper thin
Chinese black mushrooms, softened if dried
Black truffles (optional)

1. Line 2 small plates with lettuce leaves. Mix 1 tablespoon of the oil, 1 tablespoon of the lemon juice and salt and pepper to taste and drizzle the dressing over the lettuce.

2. In a small bowl, combine the remaining 1 tablespoon oil and lemon juice and salt and pepper to taste. Dip the slices of filet mignon in the mixture for 2 seconds on each side. Arrange on top of the lettuce. Garnish each plate with Chinese mushrooms and/or truffles.
—Vito Gnazzo, Rex, Il Ristorante, Los Angeles

PROSCIUTTO

In Italian, the word prosciutto simply means ham: *Prosciutto cotto* is a cooked ham while a *prosciutto crudo* is a raw, air-dried ham that is cured with salt and seasonings. In the United States, the word prosciutto refers to the latter.

Although prosciutto is produced in Parma, San Daniele and Veneto—all boast the highly-desired D.O.C (Denominazione di Origine Controllata), the official Italian stamp of authenticity—prosciutto from Parma is by far the most widely consumed. It has a sweet flavor and a tender texture thanks to a special air-drying process that takes place in the hills around the province, which are believed to have the perfect air for curing hams. In fact, hams from all over are brought to Parma to dry.

At the end of August, the people of San Daniele, a town in the Fruili region of Northern Italy, host a prosciutto celebration, complete with a prosciutto parade for which locals dress up like their celebrated ham.

CIBREO'S ITALIAN BEEF SALAD

4 to 6 Servings

1½ pounds all-purpose potatoes (about 6 medium)—peeled, quartered lengthwise and cut crosswise into ¼-inch slices
⅓ cup minced parsley
1 large red onion, coarsely chopped
¼ cup olive oil, preferably extra-virgin
2½ tablespoons red wine vinegar
2 tablespoons minced fresh basil or 2 teaspoons dried
1 teaspoon salt
½ teaspoon coarsely cracked pepper
1½ pounds cooked beef (such as shin or brisket), cut into ½-inch dice (about 4 cups)
Boston or romaine lettuce leaves, for garnish

1. Bring a medium pot of salted water to a boil over high heat. Add the potatoes and cook until tender, about 15 minutes. Drain and transfer to a serving bowl.

2. Meanwhile, in a small bowl combine the parsley, onion, olive oil, vinegar, basil, salt and pepper. Stir until blended.

3. Add the cooked beef to the bowl with the potatoes. Pour the dressing on top and toss to coat well. Let marinate at room temperature, tossing occasionally, for 30 minutes to 1 hour. Season with additional salt and pepper to taste.

4. To serve, arrange a bed of lettuce on a platter. Mound the beef salad in the center.

—*Cibrèo, Florence, Italy*

GOLDEN ASPARAGUS-AND-PROSCIUTTO BUNDLES

This dish, *asparagi fritti al prosciutto*, looks best with one fat asparagus spear in each package, but it works fine if you pair two thinner ones.

4 Servings

12 thick or 24 thin stalks of asparagus, trimmed
6 tablespoons unsalted butter
6 long thin slices of prosciutto (2 to 3 ounces total), halved crosswise
½ cup all-purpose flour, for dredging
2 eggs
1 tablespoon vegetable oil

1. Fill a large, high-sided skillet with salted water and bring to a boil. Add the asparagus and cook until barely tender, about 10 minutes. Drain in a colander, refresh under cold water and drain again. Pat dry and spread on a platter.

2. In a small saucepan, melt 3 tablespoons of the butter. Drizzle it over the asparagus. Wrap 1 piece of prosciutto around the middle of 1 thick or 2 thin asparagus stalks.

3. Place the flour on a plate. Beat the eggs in a wide shallow bowl. Roll one of the asparagus bundles in the flour, then dip in the egg. Repeat with the remaining bundles.

4. In a large skillet, heat the remaining 3 tablespoons butter and the oil over moderate heat. Working in batches, add the asparagus bundles and fry, turning once, until golden, about 4 minutes. Drain on paper towels; serve at once.

—*Diane Darrow and Tom Maresca*

Mixed Seafood Salad (page 34).

Left, Zucchini and Arborio Rice Soup
(*page* 51). Above, Tuscan Red
Cabbage Soup (*page* 52). Right,
Ligurian Vegetable Soup (*page* 52).

Crostini with Pea Puree (page 44).

EGGPLANT IN THE STYLE OF MODUGNO

These eggplant rolls are from Apulia, the region that forms the heel of the Italian boot. They make a wonderful antipasto or a delicious luncheon dish. Serve them at room temperature to enjoy their fullest flavor.

6 to 8 Servings

1 *large eggplant (about 2 pounds),
  sliced lengthwise ¼ inch thick*
1 *tablespoon salt*
2 *cups olive oil*
¼ *cup dry bread crumbs*
2 *teaspoons minced garlic (3 medium
  cloves)*
½ *cup chopped parsley*
1¾ *cups grated mozzarella cheese
  (about ½ pound)*
½ *cup freshly grated Parmesan cheese
  (about 2 ounces)*
1 *egg, beaten*
Freshly ground pepper
1 *cup Marinara Sauce (p. 261)*

1. Layer the eggplant slices in a colander, sprinkling each layer with the salt. Set aside to drain for at least 1½ hours. Gently squeeze out the excess liquid. Pat dry with paper towels.
2. In a large skillet, heat the olive oil over moderately high heat to 375°, or until a small bread cube browns in about 1 minute. Add the eggplant slices in small batches and fry, turning once, until golden and cooked through, about 2 minutes per side. Remove and drain on paper towels.
3. Preheat the oven to 375°. In a medium bowl, combine the bread crumbs, garlic, parsley, mozzarella and all but 2 tablespoons of the Parmesan. Stir in the egg and season with salt and pepper to taste.

4. Spoon ¾ cup of the Marinara Sauce into a nonreactive 8-by-12-inch baking pan. Spread about 1 tablespoon of the mozzarella mixture on each slice of eggplant, roll up and place seam-side down in the pan. Spoon the remaining ¼ cup Marinara Sauce over the eggplant rolls and sprinkle the reserved 2 tablespoons Parmesan on top. This dish can be prepared to this point several hours ahead and kept covered at room temperature. Bake until the mixture bubbles and the cheese is melted, about 20 minutes. Serve the eggplant hot or at room temperature.
—Nancy Verde Barr

FRITTATA WEDGES

This type of Italian omelet will take any number of flavoring variations. You can, for example, substitute 1 tablespoon minced fresh basil and parsley or 1 tablespoon minced roasted red pepper and 1 teaspoon parsley for the pepperoni used below.

Makes 6 to 8 Pieces

2 *eggs*
⅛ *teaspoon salt*
Pinch of freshly ground pepper
1 *tablespoon minced pepperoni*
1 *teaspoon minced parsley*
½ *tablespoon extra-virgin olive oil*

1. In a small bowl, beat together the eggs, salt, pepper, 2½ teaspoons of the pepperoni and ¾ teaspoon of the parsley.

2. Place a 7-inch skillet, preferably nonstick, over moderately high heat. Add the oil and swirl to coat the bottom of the skillet. Add the egg mixture and swirl to coat the bottom of the skillet. Reduce the heat to low and cook, without stirring, until the top is set but still soft, 3 to 4 minutes.

3. Carefully slide the eggs onto a dinner plate and then invert back into the skillet. Cook until set, about 30 seconds. Slide back onto the plate. Cut the frittata into 6 or 8 wedges and serve hot or at room temperature, garnished with the remaining ½ teaspoon pepperoni and ¼ teaspoon parsley. (*The frittata can be cooked 1 to 2 hours ahead, cooled, covered and left at room temperature.*)
—Anne Disrude

ITALIAN HERBED BREAD TOASTS

For a festive holiday hors d'oeuvre, serve these flavorful toasts with an array of cheeses—mild Cheddars and goat cheeses are particularly good matches. The herbed oil is also a fine addition to salad dressings or oil-brushed breads such as focaccia.

Makes 4 Dozen
Melba Toasts

1 teaspoon rosemary
½ teaspoon crushed hot red pepper
2 whole bay leaves, crushed
1 teaspoon thyme
½ cup olive oil
1 loaf (10 ounces) Italian bread
¼ cup freshly grated Parmesan cheese

1. In a small container, combine the rosemary, hot pepper, bay leaves, thyme and oil. Cover and let stand at room temperature for at least 12 hours.

2. Cut the bread into three 4-inch lengths. Wrap individually and freeze for at least 4 hours or overnight.

3. Defrost the bread for 10 to 15 minutes. Trim off the end pieces and cut the bread into even, ¼-inch-thick slices.

4. Preheat the oven to its lowest setting. Arrange the bread slices in a single layer on a wire rack set in a large baking sheet. Place the bread in the barely warm oven and bake until dry, but not browned, about ½ hour.

5. Preheat the oven to 250°. Lightly brush one side of the bread with the herbed oil. Sprinkle the Parmesan cheese over the oiled side of each toast and bake until golden brown and crisp, about 1 hour.
—Diana Sturgis

VINEGAR AND OIL CROUTONS

Make these large crunchy croutons to have with pickled vegetables or as an accompaniment to soups or stews.

Makes 10
Croutons

5 thick slices of coarse country bread, halved into pieces about 2 by 3 inches
⅓ cup extra-virgin olive oil
¾ teaspoon salt
¾ teaspoon freshly ground pepper
2 to 3 garlic cloves, cut in half
2½ tablespoons balsamic or sherry wine vinegar

1. Preheat the broiler. Brush both sides of the bread slices with the oil and sprinkle with the salt and pepper. Place the bread on a rack set over a baking sheet. Broil on the bottom shelf of the oven for about 5 minutes on each side, until crisped and browned.

2. Rub both sides of the croutons with the garlic cloves. Brush one side of each crouton with the vinegar and serve hot.
—Anne Disrude

MUSHROOM TOASTS

In Italy, this recipe is done with the succulent wild mushrooms called porcini (cèpes in France, Steinpilz in Germany). A good substitute for those expensive delicacies is Italian cremini or fresh shiitake, both of which are beginning to appear in specialty food shops and some supermarkets in the United States. The dish is still quite flavorful when made partially or entirely with ordinary white button mushrooms.

4 to 6 Servings

3 tablespoons unsalted butter
1½ tablespoons olive oil
¾ pound firm fresh mushrooms— porcini, cremini or shiitake— coarsely chopped
1 garlic clove, minced
2 tablespoons chopped parsley
½ teaspoon salt
Freshly ground pepper
2 tablespoons dry Marsala
1 tablespoon heavy cream
12 to 16 slices of Italian bread, toasted

1. In a large skillet, melt the butter in the oil over high heat. Add the mushrooms, garlic and parsley. Sauté, stirring, until the mushrooms absorb the fat, 1 to 2 minutes. Reduce the heat to low and season with the salt and several grindings of pepper. Cook, stirring, until the mushrooms begin to release their juices. Increase the heat to moderate and cook, stirring occasionally, until the juices evaporate, about 6 minutes.

2. Add the Marsala to the pan and cook until reduced to about 1 tablespoon, scraping up any browned bits from the bottom of the pan.

3. Transfer the mushrooms and any remaining liquid to a food processor and puree to a paste, about 1 minute. With the machine on, gradually add the cream. Taste for salt and pepper. (It should be slightly oversalted while still warm.) Transfer the mushroom puree to a bowl and let cool completely. (*The mushroom puree can be made up to 1 day in advance. Cover and refrigerate. Let the mixture return to room temperature before serving.*)

4. When ready to serve, generously spread the mushroom puree over the toasted Italian bread.
—Tom Maresca and Diane Darrow

FRESH PORCINI

During the season (April through July, and September through November), Italian markets overflow with the large-capped wild mushrooms known as porcini (or little pigs). In this country, these rich and earthy-tasting funghi are harder to come by in their fresh form. But if you are lucky enough to live near a shop that stocks them, look for porcini with full and stocky stems and uniformly golden caps; pass them by if the underside of the cap is soft or has a grayish or greenish tinge.

OLIVE-STUFFED PEPPER WEDGES WITH TOMATOES AND ANCHOVIES

This dish is based on a recipe from chef Sandra Gluck, who brought it back from Pierino Govene, chef-owner of Ristorante Gambero Rosso in Cesenatico, on Italy's Adriatic coast. Since they are prepared in advance and served at room temperature, these hors d'oeuvres couldn't be easier.

🍷 Robust Italian white wine, such as Greco di Tufo

6 to 8 Servings

10 to 12 Calamata or other brine-
   cured black olives, pitted and
   chopped
2 garlic cloves, minced
3 tablespoons chopped flat-leaf parsley
2½ tablespoons drained capers, rinsed
   and chopped
2 to 3 anchovy fillets, chopped
5 canned plum tomatoes—drained and
   chopped
½ teaspoon freshly ground black
   pepper
3½ tablespoons extra-virgin olive oil
2 large red bell peppers
2 large yellow bell peppers

1. Preheat the oven to 375°. In a medium bowl, combine the olives, garlic, parsley, capers, anchovies, tomatoes, black pepper and 1½ tablespoons of the olive oil. Set the stuffing aside.

2. Cut the peppers in half lengthwise and remove the stems, seeds and ribs. Make 2 diagonal crisscross cuts in each half to form 4 triangular wedges.

3. Lightly oil a large shallow baking dish and arrange the pepper pieces in a single layer, hollow-sides up. Spoon 1 heaping teaspoon of the olive stuffing into each piece of pepper. Cover the dish with foil.

4. Bake until the peppers begin to soften, about 15 minutes. Uncover and bake until they are tender but not limp, about 10 minutes. Let cool to room temperature. Transfer the stuffed pepper wedges to a serving platter and drizzle with the remaining 2 tablespoons olive oil.

—*Richard Sax*

PROSCIUTTO AND CHEESE APPETIZER TOASTS

🍷 Italian white, such as Gavi

8 Servings

4 not-too-thin slices of prosciutto
   (about 3 ounces)
8 slices of Italian or French bread,
   about 3 inches in diameter, cut
   ½ inch thick
¼ pound Italian Fontina or mozzarella
   cheese, shredded
4 fresh sage or basil leaves
About ¼ cup extra-virgin olive oil
1 large garlic clove, smashed
1 small fresh or dried hot pepper
1 lemon, quartered
Sprig of fresh sage or basil, for garnish

1. Fold a slice of prosciutto on each of 4 slices of the bread. Top each with 1 heaping tablespoon of the grated cheese and a sage or basil leaf. Sandwich each with a second slice of bread.

2. In a large heavy skillet, heat ¼ cup olive oil with the garlic and hot pepper over moderate heat. When the garlic sizzles, carefully lay the sandwiches in the oil. Fry until the bottom slice of the bread is golden, about 4 minutes. With a wide spatula, turn the sandwiches over, add a little more oil if needed and

reduce the heat slightly. Fry until the second side is golden and the cheese is melted but not runny, about 3 minutes.

3. Place the sandwiches on a serving plate and cut them in half. If desired, warm the remaining oil in the pan and drizzle a little of the seasoned oil over the sandwiches. Garnish with the lemon quarters and a small sprig of fresh sage or basil. Serve hot.

—*Richard Sax*

CROSTINI WITH TARRAGON SPREAD

Tarragon is common in Siena but is practically unknown in the rest of Italy. This spread can be prepared the day before and refrigerated, as the olive oil will prevent the tarragon from discoloring. Serve at room temperature on toast or in a bowl as a dip.

Makes 24 Toasts

¼ cup finely chopped fresh tarragon or
  flat-leaf parsley
2 tablespoons capers, finely chopped
2 hard-cooked eggs, finely chopped
¼ cup extra-virgin olive oil
Salt
12 slices country-style round Italian
  bread, halved crosswise, or 24 slices
  from a long loaf

1. Preheat the oven to 375°. In a medium bowl, combine the tarragon, capers and eggs with a fork. Gradually whisk in the olive oil until well blended. Stir in a pinch of salt.

2. Place the bread slices on a large baking sheet and toast in the oven for 10 minutes, until crisp and golden.

3. Spread each slice with the tarragon mixture and arrange on a platter. Alternatively, spoon the tarragon spread into a small bowl and surround with the toasts.

—*Lorenza de' Medici*

CROSTINI WITH TOMATO

When you begin to receive ripe, flavorful tomatoes and fresh basil from the garden, you know it is time to offer these crostini with tomatoes to your friends.

Makes 24 Toasts

1½ pounds plum tomatoes (8 to 9
  medium), quartered
1 teaspoon salt
1 garlic clove, minced
1 tablespoon minced fresh basil
2 tablespoons minced flat-leaf parsley
¼ cup extra-virgin olive oil
Freshly ground pepper
12 slices country-style round Italian
  bread, halved crosswise, or 24 slices
  from a long loaf

1. Place the tomatoes in a food processor and pulse for 1-second intervals until finely chopped; do not puree. Transfer the tomatoes to a colander or strainer and toss with the salt. Let drain for 1 hour, stirring once or twice.

2. Preheat the oven to 375°. In a medium bowl, combine the drained tomatoes with the garlic, basil and parsley. Gradually whisk in the olive oil until well blended. Season with pepper to taste and more salt if necessary. Set aside.

3. Place the bread on a baking sheet and toast in the oven for about 10 minutes, until crisp and golden.

BALSAMIC VINEGAR

Balsamic vinegear, made from the cooked and concentrated must of white grapes, has been produced in Modena and Reggio Emilia for hundreds of years, but it has only recently become a staple in the American kitchen. A dark brown, wine-based vinegar with a heady fragrance and sweet-sour flavor, *aceto balsamico tradizionale* must, by law, be aged for a minimum of 10 years and is sometimes aged for up to 50 years or longer. To develop its distinctive flavor, it is transferred through a series of 12 kegs made of different aromatic woods, including juniper, mulberry, chestnut and red oak.

This distinctive vinegar has long been cherished: In fact, it was once considered so valuable that it was included in the dowries of young ladies of nobility and was specifically mentioned in wills. And in 1944, when reports of approaching American bombers reached the Modena area, small kegs of balsamic vinegar were packed up along with money, jewelery and other valuables.

4. To serve, place the tomato mixture in a small bowl in the center of a platter and surround with toasted bread.
—*Lorenza de' Medici*

CROSTINI WITH BEEF AND BALSAMIC VINEGAR

The best way to begin this dish is to ask your butcher to slice the meat paper thin by machine. However, if you do it at home, freezing the meat for about an hour will help make it easier to shave off thin slices. With all the ingredients ready, you can finish preparing this dish in a few minutes, right before your guests arrive.

Makes 24 Toasts

12 *slices country-style round Italian bread, halved crosswise, or 24 slices from a long loaf*
¾ *pound lean top round, sliced into 24 paper-thin slices*
2 *tablespoons balsamic vinegar*
2 *tablespoons extra-virgin olive oil*
Salt and freshly ground pepper
¼ *pound fresh porcini or button mushrooms—stems trimmed, wiped clean and sliced paper thin*
¼ *pound Parmesan cheese, thinly sliced*
2 *tablespoons minced flat-leaf parsley*

1. Preheat the oven to 375°. On a large baking sheet, toast the bread in the oven for 10 minutes, until crisp and golden.
2. Top each piece of toast with a slice of beef, folding in the ends to fit as necessary. Sprinkle lightly with the vinegar and oil; season with salt and pepper to taste.
3. Top each toast with several mushroom slices, a few slices of Parmesan and a sprinkling of parsley. Arrange the toasts on a platter and serve.
—*Lorenza de' Medici*

CROSTINI WITH PEA PUREE

The combination of flavors in this appetizer is pure Florentine; here the traditional Easter dish of whole green peas is given an entirely new treatment.

6 Servings

5 *ounces pancetta, thinly sliced*
4 *garlic cloves*
6 *tablespoons olive oil*
¾ *pound fresh peas or 1 package (10 ounces) frozen peas*
¼ *cup chopped parsley*
¼ *teaspoon salt*
¼ *teaspoon freshly ground pepper*
18 *slices of Italian bread, cut ⅜ inch thick*

1. Finely chop enough of the pancetta to yield ½ cup. In a large skillet, cook the chopped pancetta over moderate heat until crisp, about 5 minutes. Drain on paper towels and set aside.
2. In a food processor, puree the remaining pancetta with 3 of the garlic cloves. Scrape the puree into a large skillet, add 2 tablespoons of the olive oil and cook over moder-

ately low heat until the garlic is just golden, about 4 minutes.

3. Add the fresh peas, 2 tablespoons of the parsley, the salt, pepper and ¼ cup of water. Cook until the peas are completely tender, 15 to 20 minutes. If using frozen peas, omit the water and cook for only 10 minutes.

4. In a food processor, puree the cooked peas until smooth. Strain to remove the skins. Add 1 tablespoon of the olive oil and the remaining 2 tablespoons parsley and mix to blend well.

5. Preheat the oven to 400°. Bake the bread slices directly on the oven rack until lightly toasted, about 4 minutes. Cut the remaining garlic clove in half and rub over one side of the toast slices. Brush the garlic-rubbed sides with the remaining 3 tablespoons olive oil. Spread 1 scant tablespoon of the pea puree over each toast slice and sprinkle with the reserved crisp pancetta.
—Nancy Verde Barr

CHICKEN LIVER CROSTINI

This makes a typical Italian first course. The livers must soak for 24 hours, so plan ahead.
♇ Fruity red, such as Dolcetto

4 Servings

1 pound chicken livers
2 cups milk
½ cup olive oil, preferably extra-virgin
3 garlic cloves, coarsely chopped
¾ cup beef stock or canned broth
¼ cup dry red wine
1 teaspoon tomato paste
2 anchovy fillets, finely chopped

¾ teaspoon minced fresh sage or
* ½ teaspoon crumbled dried*
1 tablespoon small capers
¼ teaspoon coarsely cracked pepper
8 slices (about 2 by 4 by ¼ inch)
* coarse peasant bread*
1 tablespoon minced parsley

1. Trim the livers of any connecting membranes and fat. Place in a small bowl, cover with the milk and refrigerate, covered, for 24 hours. Drain the livers and pat dry; finely chop. Discard the milk.

2. In a medium skillet, heat ¼ cup of the oil. Add the livers and garlic and cook over moderately high heat, stirring, until lightly browned, about 2 minutes. Add the stock, wine, tomato paste, anchovies and sage. Simmer, uncovered, stirring occasionally, until most of the liquid has evaporated and the mixture is a thick paste, about 30 minutes. Stir in the capers and pepper.

3. Brush both sides of the bread slices with the remaining ¼ cup oil. In a large skillet, fry 4 slices at a time over moderate heat, turning once, until golden brown, about 3 minutes on each side. Drain on paper towels.

4. To serve, mound about 2½ heaping tablespoons of the liver mixture onto each crostini. Place 2 crostini on each of 4 warmed plates. Sprinkle with parsley and serve warm.
—Cibrèo, Florence, Italy

DUCK CAKES WITH SUN-DRIED TOMATO BUTTER AND ARUGULA

Chefs David Holben and Lori Finkelman Holben serve these duck cakes as an appetizer.

🍷 The richness of the duck cakes points to a full-bodied red but one with enough solid, direct flavor to stand up to the bite of the arugula and the slightly piquant sauce. A young Chianti, such as Frescobaldi Riserva or Castello di Ama would be ideal.

*8 First-Course
Servings*

*3 pounds whole duck legs with thighs
    attached*
⅓ cup hazelnuts (1½ ounces)
5 tablespoons extra-virgin olive oil
*½ medium red bell pepper, cut into
    small dice*
*½ medium yellow bell pepper, cut into
    small dice*
1 medium shallot, finely chopped
2 eggs, lightly beaten
2½ tablespoons mayonnaise
½ teaspoon salt
*¼ teaspoon freshly ground black
    pepper*
⅛ teaspoon cayenne pepper
*1½ tablespoons chopped fresh thyme or
    1½ teaspoons dried*
1 cup dry bread crumbs
1½ teaspoons red wine vinegar
⅛ teaspoon Dijon mustard
2 tablespoons hazelnut oil
Olive oil, for frying
*¼ pound fresh porcini mushrooms, cut
    into ¼-inch pieces*
1 pound arugula, large stems removed
*Sun-Dried Tomato Butter (recipe
    follows)*

1. Preheat the oven to 425°. Roast the duck legs in a roasting pan for about 40 minutes, until the juices run clear when the meat is pierced in the thickest part. Let the legs cool to room temperature.

2. Pull the meat from the legs, discarding the skin, bones and fat. Coarsely chop the meat into ½-inch pieces and set aside in a large mixing bowl. (*The duck can be prepared to this point up to 1 day ahead. Cover and refrigerate.*)

3. Reduce the oven temperature to 350°. Place the hazelnuts on a baking sheet and toast in the oven for about 12 minutes, until lightly browned. While the nuts are still warm, rub them in a dish towel to remove most of the skins. Coarsely chop and set aside.

4. In a heavy medium skillet, heat 2 tablespoons of the extra-virgin olive oil over moderately high heat. Add the red and yellow peppers and the shallot and cook until soft, about 5 minutes. Let cool, then toss with the duck meat. Stir in the eggs, mayonnaise, salt, pepper, cayenne, thyme and ¾ cup of the bread crumbs.

5. Using a ¼-cup measure, scoop out the duck mixture and form into sixteen ½-inch-thick cakes. (*The duck cakes can be prepared to this point up to 1 day ahead and refrigerated, covered.*)

6. Reserve 2 tablespoons of the chopped hazelnuts. On a large plate, toss the rest of the nuts with the remaining ¼ cup bread crumbs.

Coat both sides of the duck cakes thoroughly with the bread crumb-nut mixture, pressing lightly to help it adhere. Set the cakes aside.

7. In a small bowl, combine the vinegar and mustard. Gradually whisk in the hazelnut oil and 1 tablespoon of the extra-virgin olive oil. Season the vinaigrette with salt and pepper to taste and set aside.

8. Pour ¼ inch of olive oil into a large heavy skillet and heat the oil over moderately high heat until it begins to shimmer, about 5 minutes. Add as many cakes to the pan as will fit without crowding and fry, turning once, until golden brown, about 2 minutes per side. Drain on paper towels. Fry the remaining cakes. Cover with foil to keep warm.

9. In a medium skillet, heat the remaining 2 tablespoons extra-virgin olive oil over moderately high heat until very hot, about 2 minutes. Add the porcini and cook, stirring, until lightly browned, about 4 minutes. Cover and keep warm.

10. In a large bowl, toss the arugula with the vinaigrette. Mound the salad on 8 plates, covering about two-thirds of each plate. Top with the porcini. Ladle about 1 ½ tablespoons of the Sun-Dried Tomato Butter onto the remaining third of each plate. Place 2 duck cakes on top of the sauce, sprinkle with the reserved hazelnuts and serve immediately.

—*David Holben and Lori Finkelman Holben, Riviera, Dallas*

SUN-DRIED TOMATO BUTTER

Makes About ¾ Cup

2 *whole oil-packed sun-dried tomatoes*
3 *small shallots, finely chopped*
1 *cup dry white wine*
12 *parsley sprigs*
2 *tablespoons heavy cream*
1½ *sticks (6 ounces) cold unsalted butter, cut into small cubes*
1½ *teaspoons tomato paste*
½ *teaspoon salt*
¼ *teaspoon freshly ground black pepper*
Pinch of cayenne pepper

1. In a food processor, process the tomatoes until smooth; set aside.

2. In a medium nonreactive saucepan, combine the shallots, wine and parsley and bring to a boil over high heat. Reduce the heat to moderate and boil until almost all the liquid is evaporated, about 20 minutes.

3. Add the cream and the sun-dried tomato puree and bring to a boil over moderate heat. Remove from the heat and gradually whisk in the butter and then the tomato paste. Season with the salt, black pepper and cayenne. Strain the sauce into a small bowl through a fine sieve and set aside, covered. Reheat gently in a water bath before serving.

—*David Holben and Lori Finkelman Holben, Riviera, Dallas*

49

SCALLOPS VENETIAN STYLE

In Italy this dish is matchless when prepared with the large sea scallops that are sold with their crimson roe attached—a seasonal treat. It is still fine prepared without the roe as long as the sea scallops are very fresh.

4 Servings

5 tablespoons unsalted butter
3 tablespoons minced shallots
1 pound sea scallops, with roe if available, sliced horizontally into thirds
¼ cup dry white wine
4 slices of firm-textured white bread, toasted and quartered on the diagonal into triangles

1. In a large nonreactive skillet, melt 3 tablespoons of the butter over low heat. Add the shallots and cook until softened but not browned, about 3 minutes. Increase the heat to moderately high, add the scallops and cook, stirring constantly (and gently if the roe is attached), for 1 minute. Add the wine and ¼ cup of water. Reduce the heat to low, cover and cook until the scallops are just barely opaque throughout, about 2 minutes.

2. Using a slotted spoon, transfer the scallops to a warm plate and cover with foil to keep warm. Over high heat, quickly boil down the liquid in the pan until it is reduced to a thick syrup, about 2 minutes. Remove from the heat and stir in the remaining 2 tablespoons butter to make a creamy sauce.

3. Divide the scallops among 4 plates, distribute the sauce over them, garnish with the toast points and serve at once.
—*Tom Maresca and Diane Darrow*

MUSSELS MARINARA

At Amerigo's in the Bronx, this Neapolitan classic is served with *friselle*, a hard hot pepper biscuit, for dipping into the sauce.
♟ The full flavor and character of the sauce call for a medium-bodied Italian red with good fruit, such as Nozzole Chianti Classico.

4 First-Course Servings

⅓ cup extra-virgin olive oil
4 large garlic cloves
3 dozen mussels, scrubbed and debearded
1 can (35 ounces) crushed Italian plum tomatoes
1 tablespoon minced parsley
1 tablespoon minced fresh oregano or 1 teaspoon dried
Salt and freshly ground pepper

1. In a large flameproof casserole, heat the oil. Add the garlic and cook over moderate heat until lightly browned, 3 to 5 minutes. Add the mussels, tomatoes, parsley and oregano. Bring to a boil. Reduce the heat to moderate, cover and simmer, stirring occasionally, until the mussels open, 5 to 7 minutes.

2. Using a slotted spoon, transfer the mussels to soup bowls. Discard any that do not open. Season the sauce with salt and pepper to taste. Ladle the sauce over the mussels and serve hot.
—*Amerigo's, New York City*

ITALIAN ZUCCHINI SOUP

8 to 10 Servings

2 medium onions, chopped
4 tablespoons unsalted butter
1½ teaspoons curry powder
2 quarts chicken stock or canned broth
1 pound boiling potatoes (about
    2 large), peeled and cut into 1-inch
    chunks
1 pound zucchini, coarsely chopped
½ cup heavy cream (optional)
⅓ cup chopped parsley
Salt and freshly ground pepper
Coarsely shredded zucchini, for garnish

1. In a large saucepan, sauté the onions in the butter over low heat until softened and translucent, about 5 minutes. Add the curry powder and cook, stirring, for 1 minute longer. Pour in the chicken stock and bring to a boil over moderate heat.

2. Add the potatoes to the pot, reduce the heat to low and cook until barely tender, about 10 minutes. Add the chopped zucchini and continue to cook until the zucchini and potatoes are tender, about 15 minutes longer. Remove from the heat and let cool for 15 minutes.

3. In a blender or food processor, coarsely puree the mixture in 4 or 5 batches. (*The soup may be prepared ahead to this point.*) Return the soup to the saucepan and rewarm until hot. Stir in the cream, if desired, and the parsley. Season to taste with salt and pepper and garnish with the shredded zucchini.
—*Helen Millman*

ZUCCHINI AND ARBORIO RICE SOUP

This thick, hearty soup is often served at room temperature in Italy. Its flavors will blend while it sits.

6 to 8 Servings

1 medium onion, minced
1 garlic clove, minced
¼ cup extra-virgin olive oil
3 medium zucchini (about
    1½ pounds), cut into ½-inch
    dice
2 teaspoons salt
¼ teaspoon freshly ground pepper
¼ teaspoon freshly grated nutmeg
1½ cups drained plum tomatoes from a
    35-ounce can, chopped
6 cups Vegetable Broth (p. 264) or
    canned low-sodium chicken broth
1 cup arborio rice
3 tablespoons finely chopped flat-leaf
    parsley
3 tablespoons chopped fresh basil, if
    available
Freshly grated Parmesan cheese

1. In a large saucepan, cook the onion and garlic in the olive oil over moderately low heat, stirring, until softened but not browned, about 8 minutes.

2. Add the zucchini and season with the salt, pepper and nutmeg. Increase the heat to moderate and cook, stirring, until the zucchini is barely tender, about 10 minutes.

3. Add the tomatoes, Vegetable Broth, rice, parsley and basil, if using. Increase the heat to moderately high and bring the soup to a boil. Reduce the heat to moderately low and simmer until the rice is tender, about 20 minutes. Serve hot or at room temperature with the grated Parmesan cheese.
—*Nancy Verde Barr*

51

LIGURIAN VEGETABLE SOUP

Don't cut the vegetables too small since the finished soup should have a chunky look. If you're lucky enough to find vine-ripened tomatoes, use the same volume of fresh—peeled, seeded and chopped—as canned.

8 to 10 Servings

1 large onion, coarsely chopped
2 celery ribs, coarsely chopped
2 medium carrots, coarsely chopped
¼ cup extra-virgin olive oil
1 pound savoy or green cabbage, coarsely shredded or chopped
2 teaspoons salt
½ teaspoon freshly ground pepper
2 cups coarsely shredded romaine lettuce or escarole
3 medium potatoes (about 1 pound), peeled and cut into ½-inch dice
1¼ cups drained plum tomatoes from a 35-ounce can, coarsely chopped
4 cups Vegetable Broth (p. 264) or canned low-sodium chicken broth
1 cup fresh shelled or frozen peas
⅓ cup minced flat-leaf parsley
2 garlic cloves, minced
8 to 10 slices Italian bread, toasted
Freshly grated Parmesan cheese

1. In a large saucepan, cook the onion, celery and carrots in the olive oil over moderate heat until they are softened, about 10 minutes. Add the cabbage, salt and pepper and cook, stirring, until the cabbage is wilted, about 3 minutes. Add the lettuce and cook until wilted, about 1 minute. Stir in the potatoes and tomatoes and cook for another 3 minutes. Increase the heat to moderately high, add the Vegetable Broth and bring to a boil. Reduce the heat to moderately low, cover and simmer for 30 minutes. Add the peas and cook for 5 minutes, cov-ered. Combine the parsley and garlic and stir into the soup; cook for 5 minutes.

2. Place a piece of toasted bread in each soup bowl. Ladle the hot soup on top and serve with a light sprinkling of the cheese. Serve immediately.
—Nancy Verde Barr

TUSCAN RED CABBAGE SOUP

Tuscans pour a little extra-virgin olive oil, often in the shape of the letter C, on the surface of each bowl of soup to enrich it. The hot soup releases the fragrance of the fruity oil and, in this case, the rosemary. For this recipe you can soak the beans overnight or use the quicker method of boiling them briefly and allowing them to soak for just one hour.

6 to 8 Servings

1 cup dried white beans
⅓ cup plus ¼ cup extra-virgin olive oil
1 tablespoon chopped fresh rosemary or 1 teaspoon dried
3 garlic cloves—2 crushed through a press, 1 minced
1 medium onion, finely chopped
1 large celery rib, finely chopped
1 small carrot, finely chopped
1 head (about 1½ pounds) of red cabbage, shredded or thinly sliced
2 teaspoons salt
½ teaspoon freshly ground pepper
⅓ cup drained plum tomatoes from a 12-ounce can, chopped
6 cups Vegetable Broth (p. 264) or canned low-sodium chicken broth

1. Rinse the beans. Place them in a large bowl and cover with cold water. Set aside to soak for 6 to 8 hours or overnight. Alternatively rinse the beans and place them in a large saucepan. Cover with 2 inches of cold water and bring to a boil over high heat. Boil for 2 minutes, remove from the heat and set aside, covered, to soak for 1 hour.

2. Drain and rinse the soaked beans. In a medium saucepan, cover the beans with twice their volume of water and bring them to a boil, covered, over moderately high heat. Reduce the heat to moderately low and simmer, covered, until tender, about 1½ hours. Drain and reserve.

3. In a small saucepan, combine the ⅓ cup olive oil, rosemary and the 2 crushed garlic cloves. Cook over moderate heat until the oil is hot, about 1 minute. Remove from the heat and set aside.

4. In a large saucepan, cook the onion, celery, carrot and the minced garlic in the remaining ¼ cup olive oil over moderate heat, stirring occasionally. until the vegetables are softened, about 8 minutes. Add the cabbage, salt and pepper and cook, stirring often, until wilted, about 4 minutes. Add the tomatoes and cook 5 more minutes. Add the Vegetable Broth and bring just to a boil. Reduce the heat to moderately low, cover and simmer for 30 minutes. Add the beans and cook, covered, for 20 minutes.

5. Ladle the soup into bowls and pour the reserved rosemary oil through a strainer into the soup. Serve immediately.
—Nancy Verde Barr

BREAD SOUP, LIVORNO STYLE

In making this dish, which is more like a porridge than a soup, the bread should be squeezed very dry after it is soaked. Olive oil, broth, tomatoes, sage and garlic are the typical Tuscan ingredients here. The soup can be served at room temperature in warm weather or hot in winter to warm the bones.

6 to 8 Servings

1 *pound Tuscan bread store-bought or homemade (p. 177), several days old, cut into 1-inch cubes (about 8 cups)*
¾ *cup olive oil, plus extra for serving*
3 *large garlic cloves, minced*
8 *large sage leaves, fresh or preserved in salt,* chopped*
3 *cans (14 ounces each) Italian peeled tomatoes, drained*
5½ *cups boiling beef, veal or chicken broth*
Salt and freshly ground pepper
**Available at Italian markets*

1. Sprinkle the bread with about 4 cups of cold water, making sure the bread is evenly moistened. Let soak until all of the water is absorbed, 10 minutes or so. With your hands, squeeze the bread as dry as possible. Separate the bread into pieces.

2. Heat the oil in a medium non-reactive casserole. Add the garlic and sage and cook over moderate heat, stirring occasionally, until the garlic begins to color, about 4 minutes. Add the bread and toss constantly with a wooden spoon until the cubes are well coated with oil, about 5 minutes.

3. Place the tomatoes in a food mill fitted with a fine disk and puree them directly into the casserole.

Alternatively, puree the tomatoes in a food processor and strain into the casserole through a sieve to remove the seeds. Mix very well until blended.

4. Stir in the boiling broth, season with salt and pepper and return to a boil. Remove from the heat and give the mixture a good stir. Cover the casserole and set aside for 1 hour.

5. Using a wooden spoon, stir the mixture to break up most of the remaining lumps of bread. Taste for seasoning. Reheat over low heat if necessary. Spoon into bowls and drizzle 1 teaspoon of olive oil over each serving.

—*Giuliano Bugialli*

ENTREES

VITELLO TONNATO

This unusual but felicitous pairing of veal and canned tuna is a classic that's enjoyed throughout Italy. The meat can be cooked and refrigerated well ahead. However, since it must be thinly sliced and has a tendency to dry out, the dish should be assembled shortly before serving. Traditionally, the sliced veal is arranged on a large platter, and the sauce is poured over the meat. A crisp mixed salad would be lovely alongside.

8 Servings

3-pound trimmed veal roast, such as
   leg, top round or shoulder, tied
2 medium carrots, halved lengthwise
1 medium onion, halved, each half
   stuck with 1 whole clove
1 celery rib, quartered
1 bay leaf
2 sprigs of parsley
1 cup dry white wine
1 cup chicken stock or canned low-
   sodium broth
1 can (2 ounces) flat anchovy fillets
1 can (6½ ounces) tuna in olive oil
2 tablespoons fresh lemon juice
1 cup mayonnaise
¼ cup sour cream
⅛ teaspoon white pepper
Black olives, drained capers and lemon
   and tomato wedges, for garnish

1. In a medium flameproof casserole, combine the veal roast, carrots, onion, celery, bay leaf, parsley, wine and chicken stock. Bring to a boil over high heat. Reduce the heat to low, cover and simmer, turning the veal occasionally, until it is tender and the internal temperature reaches 160° on an instant-read thermometer, about 1 hour and 40 minutes.

2. Remove from the heat, uncover and let cool. Remove and discard the vegetables. Cover the meat and refrigerate overnight or for up to 2 days.

3. Skim the fat from the surface of the jellied cooking liquid. In a food processor, combine 6 tablespoons of the cooking liquid with 3 of the anchovies, the tuna with its oil and the lemon juice. Puree until smooth. Scrape the sauce into a bowl, cover and refrigerate for at least 30 minutes and up to 1 day.

4. Remove the roast from the casserole and place on a cutting board. Using a sharp knife, thinly slice the meat. Arrange the meat on a large platter or on individual plates. (If not serving immediately, cover the platter or the individual plates well with plastic wrap to prevent the meat from drying out.)

5. Add the mayonnaise, sour cream and pepper to the tuna sauce and stir until well blended. Pour the sauce over the plattered veal or drizzle it lightly over the individual servings and pass the remainder separately. Garnish with the remaining anchovies and the olives, capers and lemon and tomato wedges.
—W. Peter Prestcott

ROASTED VEAL SHANKS

Serve this dish, *stinco di vitello arrosto*, with any green vegetable.

🍷 To match the richness of the veal shanks, choose a balanced, elegant red wine, such as Mastroberardino Taurasi or Carmignano from Villa di Capezzana.

4 Servings

Four 2- to 2½-inch-thick meaty veal
    shanks (about 3 pounds)
Salt and freshly ground pepper
¼ cup olive oil
1 medium carrot, finely chopped
1 small onion, finely chopped
1 large celery rib, finely chopped
1 garlic clove, finely chopped
1 tablespoon chopped parsley
1 tablespoon chopped fresh sage or
    1½ teaspoons dried
1 teaspoon chopped fresh thyme or
    marjoram or ½ teaspoon dried
½ cup dry white wine
Sprigs of parsley, sage and thyme

1. Preheat the oven to 350°. Rinse and dry the veal. Season lightly with salt and pepper. Brush the bottom of a baking dish just large enough to hold the veal in a single layer with 1 tablespoon of the olive oil. Add the veal shanks, arranging them with the wider part of the bone facing up. Drizzle the remaining 3 tablespoons olive oil over the meat and roast for 45 minutes. Transfer the meat to a plate and set aside.

2. Add the carrot, onion, celery, garlic, parsley, sage and thyme to the baking dish and stir to mix with the pan juices. Season lightly with salt and pepper. Return the veal to the baking dish with the wider part of the bone facing up. Pour ¼ cup of the wine over the meat and roast for 10 minutes. Pour the remaining ¼ cup wine on top and roast for 20 minutes longer, basting twice with the pan juices. Reduce the heat to 325°, cover loosely with aluminum foil and roast for 30 to 45 minutes longer, until the meat is quite tender.

3. Transfer the veal to a warmed serving platter and garnish with the herb sprigs. Pass the contents of the baking dish through a food mill. Alternatively, pour into a strainer and press through with the back of a spoon. Pass the sauce in a gravy boat.
—Diane Darrow and Tom Maresca

OSSO BUCO WITH GREMOLATA

The classic garnish for *osso buco* is *gremolata*, a mixture of grated lemon zest, chopped parsley and garlic. It adds a welcome piquancy to this rich, meaty dish.

8 Servings

2 tablespoons unsalted butter
2 tablespoons olive oil
5 pounds veal shanks, cut into 2-inch
    pieces and tied with string around
    their circumference
1 cup all-purpose flour
2 medium onions, coarsely chopped
1 large carrot, coarsely chopped
1 medium celery rib, coarsely chopped
3 garlic cloves, crushed
½ teaspoon marjoram
½ teaspoon basil
½ teaspoon thyme
1 can (28 ounces) Italian peeled
    tomatoes, drained and coarsely
    chopped
2½ tablespoons tomato paste
2 cups dry white wine or dry vermouth
1 cup chicken stock or canned broth

57

A FORMAL DINNER

Roasted Veal Shanks (p. 57)

Parmesan Mashed Potatoes
(p. 194)

Green Beans Sautéed with Garlic

🍷 Mastroberardino Taurasi

Fruit Tart

🍷 Vietti Moscato

3 strips of lemon zest, about 2 inches
   long
1 large bay leaf
4 sprigs of parsley

Gremolata:
½ cup minced parsley
3 medium garlic cloves, minced
1 tablespoon grated lemon zest

1. In a large flameproof casserole, melt the butter in the oil over moderate heat.

2. Dredge the veal in the flour and shake off any excess. Working in batches, sauté the veal on all sides until golden brown. Do not crowd the pan. Remove to a bowl.

3. Add the onions, carrot, celery and garlic. Cover and cook until the vegetables are tender, about 15 minutes.

4. Place the veal on top of the vegetables, making sure the bones are upright. Sprinkle the marjoram, basil and thyme on top. Add the tomatoes, tomato paste, white wine, chicken stock, strips of lemon zest, bay leaf and parsley sprigs. If necessary, add enough water to cover the shanks.

5. Bring to a boil, reduce the heat to low and simmer, covered, until the meat is tender, about 2 hours. (The recipe may be prepared to this point up to 3 days ahead. Let cool; cover and refrigerate. Warm through before proceeding.)

6. Transfer the veal shanks to a heated platter; remove the strings and cover with foil to keep warm. Increase the heat to high and boil, stirring frequently, until the sauce is reduced by half, about 20 minutes. Pour the sauce over the meat.

7. Just before serving, combine the parsley, garlic and lemon zest to make the gremolata. Sprinkle on top.
—W. Peter Prestcott

BRAISED VEAL SHANKS MILANESE

Whether it is called *ossibuchi*, *ossobuco*, or *osso buco*, braised veal shank is a traditional Italian dish, usually garnished with *gremolata*, an aromatic mixture of lemon zest, garlic and parsley.

♟ The assertive flavors here demand a robust red wine, such as a Rainoldi Sassella or an Inferno from Nino Negri.

4 Servings

4 tablespoons unsalted butter
1 medium onion, thinly sliced
⅓ cup all-purpose flour, for dredging
Six 2½- to 3-inch-thick meaty veal
   shanks (5½ to 6 pounds total)
Salt and freshly ground pepper
½ cup dry white wine
1 tablespoon tomato paste dissolved in
   ½ cup water
1 large garlic clove, minced
1 tablespoon minced parsley, plus
   parsley leaves for garnish
1½ teaspoons finely grated lemon zest,
   plus thin strips of lemon zest for
   garnish

1. In a large flameproof casserole, melt the butter over moderate heat. Add the onion and cook until softened and just beginning to color, about 10 minutes. Using a slotted spoon, transfer the cooked onion to a strainer set over the casserole and press with the back of the spoon to extract the juices. Discard the onion.

2. Place the flour on a plate. Pat

58

the veal pieces dry and dredge in the flour. Working in batches, add the veal to the casserole and cook over moderate heat, turning once until browned all over, about 10 minutes; transfer to a plate. Return the veal to the casserole. Season lightly with salt and pepper, increase the heat to moderately high and pour ¼ cup of the wine over the meat. Cook for 30 seconds, then turn the pieces of veal over, season again with salt and pepper and cook until the wine has evaporated, 2 to 3 minutes. Pour the remaining ¼ cup wine over the meat and cook until all the wine has evaporated, another 2 to 3 minutes.

3. Arrange the veal pieces in the casserole with the wider part of the bone facing up and pour the diluted tomato paste on top. Cover and cook over low heat until the meatiest piece of veal is tender, about 1¾ hours. During cooking, move the veal pieces from time to time to prevent sticking and baste with the pan juices; don't turn the shank pieces over or the marrow will run out. If the sauce seems to be reducing too much, add a tablespoon or two of warm water.

4. Meanwhile, finely chop together the garlic, parsley and grated lemon zest to make a gremolata. Five minutes before serving, sprinkle the gremolata into the casserole. Serve the veal shanks on 4 warmed plates and garnish with parsley leaves and lemon zest strips.
—Diane Darrow and Tom Maresca

BOILED VEAL SHANKS WITH GREEN SAUCE

In *vitello bollito con salsa verde*, the veal's gentle unctuousness contrasts nicely with the zingy flavors of the sauce. ♟ This dish needs a wine with moderate body and acidity, such as a young Frescobaldi Pomino Bianco or a La Crema Chardonnay from Sonoma.

4 Servings

1 *medium carrot, coarsely chopped*
1 *small onion, coarsely chopped*
1 *medium celery rib, coarsely chopped*
⅓ *cup chopped parsley plus 3 sprigs*
¾ *teaspoon salt*
3 *whole peppercorns*
Four 2- *to* 2½-*inch-thick meaty veal shanks (about 3½ pounds)*
2 *anchovy fillets*
2 *garlic cloves*
1½ *tablespoons drained capers, rinsed*
¼ *cup fresh bread crumbs*
2 *teaspoons red wine vinegar*
¼ *cup olive oil*

1. In a large casserole, combine 2 quarts of water with the carrot, onion, celery and parsley sprigs. Stir in ½ teaspoon of the salt and the peppercorns. Bring to a boil over high heat. Add the veal shanks, arranging them with the wider part of the bone facing up, and return to a boil. Reduce the heat to low, cover and simmer until the veal is very tender, about 1½ hours.

2. Meanwhile, mince together the anchovies, garlic cloves and capers. Add the remaining ¼ teaspoon salt and the chopped parsley and chop again. Put the bread crumbs in a small bowl, sprinkle the vinegar on top and toss well. Stir in

ENTREES

the anchovy mixture, then add the olive oil to make a thick, coarse sauce. Season to taste with additional salt and vinegar, if desired. Set the salsa verde aside.

3. Using a spatula, transfer the veal shanks from their cooking liquid to a warmed serving dish, handling them carefully to keep the marrow intact. Spoon a little of the broth over the shanks (reserve the remaining broth for another use). Pass the salsa verde separately.
—Diane Darrow and Tom Maresca

VEAL MARSALA

🍷 Chianti, such as Ruffino Riserva Ducale

4 Servings

1¼ pounds veal scallops, pounded ¼ inch thick
2 to 3 tablespoons vegetable oil
½ teaspoon salt
¼ teaspoon freshly ground pepper
1 cup dry Marsala
1 tablespoon unsalted butter
2 teaspoons chopped parsley, for garnish.

1. Pat the veal dry with paper towels
2. In a large heavy skillet, heat 1½ tablespoons of oil until almost smoking. Add as many veal scallops as will fit in a single layer without crowding and sauté over high heat until browned on the bottom, about 2 minutes. Turn and cook until browned on the second side, about 30 seconds. Transfer to a serving

platter and cover loosely to keep warm. Season the cooked veal with half the salt and pepper. Repeat with the remaining scallops, adding additional oil to coat the bottom of the skillet as needed.

3. Blot the skillet with paper towels to remove excess oil. Pour in the Marsala. Boil over high heat, scraping up any browned bits from the bottom of the pan, until the wine is reduced slightly. Pour in any accumulated meat juices from the platter and continue cooking until the sauce is reduced to a thin syrup, about 8 minutes.

4. Whisk in the butter just until incorporated. Return the meat to the skillet and turn to coat with the sauce. Arrange on the platter, spooning extra sauce on top. Garnish with the parsley.
—Anne Disrude

SCALOPPINE CAPANNINA

🍷 Taurasi

4 Servings

3 ounces dried porcini mushrooms
2 medium red bell peppers
4 tablespoons unsalted butter
1 pound veal scallops (about 8 slices), pounded ⅛ inch thick
½ teaspoon salt
¼ teaspoon freshly ground pepper
2 tablespoons olive oil
½ cup dry white wine
2 tablespoons dry Marsala

1. Preheat the oven to 400°. Soak the mushrooms in a small bowl of boiling water to cover for 20 minutes. Drain and squeeze to remove as much liquid as possible; pat dry.

60

CAMPANIAN-STYLE DINNER

Americanos (p. 28)

Spaghettini and Uncooked Tomato Sauce with Olives (p. 112)

Scaloppine Capannina (p. 60)

Herbed Carrots and Green Beans (p. 189)

🍷 Chianti, such as Capponi

Radicchio and Arugula Salad with Oil and Tarragon Vinegar

Molded Ricotta and Mascarpone with Strawberries (p. 224)

Trim off the hard stems and cut the caps into thin julienne strips.

2. Meanwhile, place the red peppers in a small baking dish and bake until the skin begins to split, about 12 minutes. When cool enough to handle, peel off the skin with a paring knife and cut the peppers into thin julienne strips.

3. In a medium skillet, melt 2 tablespoons of the butter over moderately high heat. Add the mushrooms and sauté, tossing occasionally, until tender, about 3 minutes. Add the red peppers and toss to mix. Remove from the heat.

4. Season the veal with the salt and pepper. In a large nonreactive skillet, melt the remaining 2 tablespoons butter in the oil over moderately high heat. Place half of the veal scallops in the skillet and sauté until lightly browned, about 1 minute. Turn and sauté for 1 minute longer. Remove from the heat and place on a warm platter. Sauté the remaining scallops.

5. Pour the white wine into the skillet and bring to a boil, stirring to scrape up any browned bits from the bottom of the pan. Add the mushroom-pepper mixture and the Marsala. Boil to reduce the liquid to a thin glaze, about 2 minutes. Pour the hot sauce over the veal.
—*La Capannina, Capri, Italy*

VEAL ROLLS WITH PEAS

When ripe, fresh tomatoes are not in season, use canned plum tomatoes rather than fresh ones without any flavor. If you use frozen peas, defrost them by passing them under cold water before adding them to the tomatoes.

12 Servings

24 *very thinly sliced veal scallops (about 1½ pounds), pounded to an even thickness*
12 *thin slices of pancetta, halved crosswise (about ½ pound)*
24 *small fresh sage leaves*
3 *tablespoons extra-virgin olive oil*
1 *tablespoon finely chopped sweet onion*
1 *pound plum tomatoes (about 6 medium), peeled and coarsely chopped, or 1 can (35 ounces) Italian peeled tomatoes, drained and coarsely chopped*
2 *tablespoons unsalted butter*
1 *cup dry white wine*
2 *pounds fresh peas, shelled, or 1 package (10 ounces) frozen peas, thawed*
Salt and freshly ground pepper
1 *tablespoon minced flat-leaf parsley*

1. Trim each scallop into a 2-by-3-inch rectangle. Lay 12 of the scallops on a work surface. Top each with a half slice of the pancetta and 1 sage leaf. Roll the scallops, starting at the short end. Fasten each roll with a wooden toothpick, threading it into the veal rolls lengthwise, so that they can turn easily in the pan. Alternatively, secure the rolls with thin cotton thread that you can remove before serving. Repeat with the remaining scallops, pancetta and sage. Set the rolls aside on a large platter.

2. In a medium nonreactive casserole, heat 1 tablespoon of the olive oil over low heat. Add the onion; cook until translucent, about 4 minutes. Add the tomatoes; simmer for 10 minutes.

3. Meanwhile, heat a large, heavy, nonreactive skillet over moderately high heat. Add 1 tablespoon of the olive oil and 1 tablespoon of the butter. Add 12 of the veal rolls and cook, turning until well browned all over, about 7 minutes. Using tongs, transfer the cooked veal to a platter. Repeat with the remaining 1 tablespoon each of oil and butter and the remaining veal rolls. Add the wine to the skillet and bring to a boil, scraping up any browned bits from the bottom of the pan. Boil until the wine is reduced by half, about 1 minute.

4. Add the reduced wine to the tomatoes along with the peas. Place all the veal rolls in the casserole and cook until the sauce is thick and the veal is tender and cooked through but not dry, 20 to 25 minutes.

5. Transfer the veal rolls to a deep platter and remove the toothpicks or string. Season the sauce with salt and pepper to taste, stir in the parsley, and ladle over the veal to serve. Serve hot.

—*Lorenza de'Medici*

VEAL CROQUETTES WITH LEMON

These light croquettes are tender and delicate. Before cooking, the meat mixture is quite soft, so don't be alarmed when you are forming the croquettes. As they bake in the oven, the lemon and butter form a light, piquant sauce.

♟ The delicacy of these light croquettes and the piquancy of the lemon point to a crisp and tart Tuscan white, notably a Fontodi Meriggio or Avignonesi Chardonnay "Il Marzocco."

4 to 6 Servings

12 *slices of white sandwich bread,*
   crusts removed
2 *cups milk*
¾ *pound ground lean veal shoulder*
4 *eggs*
1 *cup freshly grated Italian Parmesan*
   cheese (¼ pound)
¼ *cup fresh lemon juice*
¼ *teaspoon salt*
½ *teaspoon freshly ground pepper*
4 *cups vegetable oil, for deep-frying*
1½ *cups unbleached all-purpose flour,*
   for dredging
4 *tablespoons cold unsalted butter, cut*
   into bits

1. In a medium bowl, soak the bread in the milk for 30 minutes.

2. Squeeze the bread as dry as possible and place it in a large bowl; discard the milk. Add the ground veal, eggs, Parmesan, 2 tablespoons of the lemon juice and the salt and pepper to the bread. Mix very well with a wooden spoon until blended.

3. Preheat the oven to 300°. In a large, deep skillet or deep-fat fryer, heat the vegetable oil over moderate heat to 375°.

4. Meanwhile, form the veal mix-

ture into egg-shaped croquettes, using ¼ cup of the mixture for each; the mixture will be quite soft. Lightly dredge the croquettes in the flour and fry in batches, turning once, until golden, about 5 minutes per batch. Drain on paper towels.

5. Arrange the croquettes in a single layer in a shallow roasting pan. Dot the tops with the bits of butter and drizzle on the remaining 2 tablespoons lemon juice. Bake for 10 minutes, until heated through. Serve with the pan juices spooned on top.

—*Giuliano Bugialli*

FILLET OF BEEF MARCO POLO

This roasted, marinated fillet of beef makes a fabulous buffet dish.
♟ Northern Italian red, such as Barbera

10 Servings

1 *whole fillet of beef, trimmed of excess fat but with silvery outer membrane left on (4½ to 5 pounds)*
¼ *cup Cognac or other brandy*
½ *cup soy sauce*
10 *thin slices of fresh ginger*
6 *garlic cloves, smashed*
1 *bottle (750 ml) dry red wine*
¼ *cup olive oil*
1 *teaspoon salt*
1 *teaspoon freshly ground pepper*

1. Place the beef fillet in a non-reactive container just large enough to hold it comfortably (a stainless steel fish poacher works very well); cut the meat crosswise in half if necessary to fit. Add the Cognac, soy sauce, ginger, garlic and enough red wine to reach halfway up the sides of the meat. Cover and marinate at room temperature, turning occasionally, for at least 4 hours, or overnight in the refrigerator if you wish.

2. Preheat the oven to 500°. Remove the meat from the marinade and pat dry; reserve the marinade. Brush the fillet with the oil and season with the salt and pepper. Place a large skillet over moderately high heat. Add the beef and cook, turning, until well browned all over.

3. Transfer the fillet to a baking dish and roast, uncovered, for 20 minutes. Turn off the heat and leave the meat in the hot oven for 20 minutes longer.

4. Meanwhile, strain the marinade into a medium nonreactive skillet. Boil over high heat until reduced by half, about 10 minutes. Remove the tenderloin from the oven and transfer to a cutting board; let rest for 5 minutes before slicing. Add the cooking juices and any juices from the sliced meat to the marinade. Boil for 3 minutes longer and serve with the beef.

—*Margaret and G. Franco Romagnoli*

FESTA ROMANA

Campari and Sodas (p. 28)

Assorted Antipasti

Shrimp-Garlic Risotto (p. 209)

♟ *Soave*

Fillet of Beef Marco Polo (p. 63)

Sautéed Zucchini

♟ *Barbaresco*

Caprella, Gorgonzola and Bel Paese Cheeses

Italian Bread

Green Grapes and Pears

Chocolate-Almond Torte (p. 232)

Espresso

♟ *Sambuca con Mosca*

BEEF TENDERLOIN WITH JUNIPER

Juniper berries abound in the woods of the Alps and Apennines. You can also find them in the spice rack at your supermarket. For *filetto al gine-pro*, use a small tenderloin because it is compact and holds together better than a larger one. Nice accompaniments to this dish are potatoes and green beans or swiss chard.

♉ Nera Sfursat or Le Ragose Recioto della Valpolicella Amarone

6 Servings

1 *garlic clove*
2½ *pounds beef tenderloin, trimmed and cut into 12 medallions (1 inch thick)*
½ *cup gin*
36 *whole juniper berries*
1 *teaspoon fresh thyme or ¼ teaspoon dried, plus 6 sprigs of fresh thyme, for garnish*
1 *to 2 tablespoons unsalted butter*
¾ *cup mascarpone cheese*
Salt and freshly cracked pepper

1. Cut slits in the garlic clove and rub the clove over the meat. Then rub the inside of a large heavy skillet, preferably cast iron, with the garlic. Set the skillet aside and discard the garlic.

2. Place the beef in a nonreactive dish. Pour ¼ cup of the gin over the meat. Using the side of a large knife or a mortar and pestle, crush 12 of the juniper berries and sprinkle them over the meat. Sprinkle the 1 teaspoon thyme on top. Cover and refrigerate for 1 hour, turning once.

3. Pat the meat dry, discarding any bits of juniper. Place the prepared skillet on the stove and turn the heat to high. When hot, after about 5 minutes, add 1 tablespoon of the butter. When the foaming subsides, arrange half of the meat slices in the pan and cook, turning once, until browned, about 1½ minutes on each side for medium-rare. Transfer to a platter. Add the remaining 1 tablespoon butter to the skillet if necessary, and repeat with the remaining meat.

4. Reduce the heat to low and add the remaining 24 juniper berries and ¼ cup gin to the skillet. Cook for about 45 seconds to burn off the alcohol. Stir in the mascarpone and cook until thoroughly melted, about 2 minutes. Season the sauce with salt and pepper to taste. Return the meat to the skillet and cook, spooning the sauce over the meat, until heated through, about 2 minutes.

5. Arrange the meat on 6 warmed dinner plates and spoon the sauce on top, making sure to include a few juniper berries in each serving. Garnish with the thyme sprigs.
—*Constance and Rosario Del Nero*

GRILLED SIRLOIN STEAKS WITH HOT OLIVE OIL VINAIGRETTE AND WATERCRESS

This dish appears on the menu at Spiaggia as *tagliata con crescione*.
♉ Steak has an affinity with a wide variety of reds, but the highly seasoned sirloin and the tart vinaigrette call for one with sufficient richness for balance. A round, fleshy California Merlot, such as Franciscan or St. Francis would do the trick.

6 Servings

Six 6-ounce sirloin steaks, about
   1-inch thick, trimmed of all fat
6 tablespoons fresh lemon juice (2 to 3
   lemons)
¾ cup extra-virgin olive oil
1 tablespoon plus ½ teaspoon coarse
   (kosher) salt
1 tablespoon plus ½ teaspoon coarsely
   ground pepper
3 bunches of watercress (about ¾
   pound), large stems removed
6 large sprigs of fresh rosemary, for
   garnish

   1. Preheat the broiler. Place 6
heatproof serving plates on the bottom rack of the oven to warm. On a
broiling pan, broil the steaks 2 inches from the heat, turning once, until
just rare, about 4 minutes per side.
Let the steaks rest on a cutting
board for 5 minutes.
   2. Meanwhile, in a small nonreactive saucepan, whisk together the
lemon juice, olive oil and ½ teaspoon each of the salt and pepper;
keep warm over moderately low
heat.
   3. Arrange the watercress around
the rim of each warm plate. Slice
each steak across the grain into six
½-inch slices. Transfer each steak
to the center of a plate, overlapping
the slices. Bring the vinaigrette to
a full boil over high heat. Spoon 3
tablespoons of the vinaigrette over
each steak. Sprinkle the steaks with
the remaining 1 tablespoon each
of salt and pepper. Garnish with the
rosemary sprigs and serve hot.
—Spiaggia, Chicago

BOILED BEEF SALAD
WITH TARRAGON SAUCE

Most Italians do not eat leftovers
per se; we prefer to convert them
into an entirely new dish. And
so many popular dishes have
evolved this way that nowadays
these *rifatti* (recooked) dishes are
started from scratch. Until the 19th
century, it was quite common to
have a course of boiled meat or fowl
as part of an elaborate dinner. These
boiled dishes have retained a strong
place in Tuscan cooking.
♟ A full-flavored red best under-
scores this dish. Try an earthy Rosso
di Montalcino, such as Poggio Anti-
co or Banfi Centine.

6 Servings

2 teaspoons coarse (kosher) salt
1 large carrot
2 red onions—1 medium, halved;
   1 large, thinly sliced
1 large celery rib
5 sprigs of flat-leaf parsley plus ¼ cup
   coarsely chopped
3 cherry tomatoes
2½ pounds beef brisket
½ cup olive oil
2 large garlic cloves
3 ounces sweet Italian sausage without
   fennel seeds, casings removed, or
   3 ounces ground pork
½ teaspoon salt
½ teaspoon freshly ground black
   pepper
Large pinch of crushed hot red pepper
1 can (28 ounces) Italian peeled
   tomatoes—well drained, seeded and
   coarsely chopped
15 large fresh basil leaves, torn into
   large pieces
1 tablespoon chopped fresh tarragon

   1. In a medium flameproof
casserole, combine 8 cups of cold

**EASY FAMILY
LUNCH**

Assorted Antipasti

*Boiled Beef Salad with Tarragon
Sauce (p. 65)*

*Sautéed Broccoli Raab with
Garlic*

Olive Bread (p. 178)

♟ *Italian Red, such as Banfi
Centine*

Ricotta Gelato (p. 219)

Coffee

water with the coarse salt and bring to a boil over high heat. Add the carrot, halved onion, celery, parsley sprigs and cherry tomatoes. When the water returns to a boil, add the beef. Reduce the heat to moderately low and simmer gently until tender, about 2½ hours. Using tongs, transfer the meat to a platter and let cool to room temperature. (*The meat can be cooked up to 2 days ahead and refrigerated in its broth.*)

2. In a medium bowl, soak the sliced onion in cold water to cover for 30 minutes. Drain and pat dry.

3. In a medium nonreactive skillet, warm the oil over moderate heat. Add the garlic cloves and cook, stirring, until lightly golden, about 2 minutes. Discard the garlic. Add the onion slices and chopped parsley to the skillet and cook, stirring frequently, until softened, about 5 minutes.

4. Add the sausage meat, salt, black and hot peppers. Cook, stirring occasionally to break up the meat, until no trace of pink remains, about 15 minutes.

5. Add the chopped tomatoes and cook until they break down and the sauce is thick and chunky, about 15 minutes longer. Stir in the basil and tarragon and cook for 1 minute more.

6. Thinly slice the boiled beef and arrange on a platter with the slices overlapping. Pour the sauce over the meat and serve.
—Giuliano Bugialli

ROAST LEG OF LAMB WITH MUSTARD COATING

This lamb dish is perfect in its simplicity and fine flavor.
♟ Chianti Classico

8 to 10 Servings

½ cup Dijon mustard
2 tablespoons soy sauce
1 teaspoon crumbled thyme or rosemary
1 large or 2 medium garlic cloves, crushed to a paste
2 tablespoons olive oil
7-pound leg of lamb, boned and tied, to yield a 5-pound roast

1. In a small bowl, blend the mustard, soy sauce, thyme and garlic. Gradually whisk in the oil until well blended. Using a rubber spatula or pastry brush, evenly coat the surface of the lamb with the mustard mixture. Marinate at room temperature for 3 hours, or refrigerate overnight. (If marinated overnight, bring the lamb to room temperature before roasting; this takes about 2 hours.)

2. Preheat the oven to 350° about 15 minutes before you plan to roast the meat. Cook it on a rack in a roasting pan until the internal temperature reaches 130° for rare meat (about 2 hours) or 140° for medium (about 2¼ hours). Let rest for 15 to 20 minutes before carving.
—Helen Millman

SIT-DOWN DINNER

Italian Zucchini Soup (p. 51)

Roast Leg of Lamb with Mustard Coating (p. 66)

Mustard Ring (p. 196)

Braised Fennel

♟ Chianti Classico

Bitter Greens Tossed with Fruity Olive Oil, Coarse Salt and Garlic

Italian Cheeses

Torta Caprese (p. 231)

DONATELLO'S LAMB CHOPS MILANESE

At Donatello, these lamb chops are served with string beans, cherry tomatoes sautéed with garlic and baked potato cakes.
♟ Italian Merlot, such as Friulvini

4 Servings

12 rib lamb chops, cut no more than
    ¾ inch thick—trimmed, frenched
    and pounded ½ inch thick
⅓ cup finely chopped fresh basil
1 large sprig of fresh rosemary or
    2 teaspoons dried, crumbled
4 imported bay leaves
8 medium garlic cloves, bruised and
    peeled
2 cups olive oil, preferably extra-virgin
½ cup all-purpose flour
3 egg whites
½ teaspoon salt
¼ teaspoon freshly ground pepper
1½ cups fresh bread crumbs,
    preferably from egg bread
4 tablespoons unsalted butter
⅔ cup vegetable oil

1. Place the lamb chops close together in a single layer in a shallow container. Sprinkle with the basil, rosemary, bay leaves and garlic and pour the olive oil over all. Marinate, turning frequently, at room temperature for 3 hours or refrigerate, covered, for up to 3 days.

2. Place the flour in a shallow dish. Beat the egg whites in a wide bowl with the salt and pepper until foamy. Place the bread crumbs in a shallow dish.

3. Preheat the oven to 350°. One by one, remove the chops from the marinade, scrape off the herbs and blot any excess oil with paper towels. Bread each chop by first dredging in the flour and shaking off any excess. Then dip in the egg white, drawing each side over the side of the bowl to remove any excess. Then coat with the bread crumbs, pressing so that they adhere. Shake off excess crumbs, then place the chops on a rack.

4. In a large skillet, warm 2 tablespoons of the butter in ⅓ cup of the vegetable oil over high heat until shimmering. Working in 4 batches, add 3 chops at a time and sauté, turning once, until well browned, about 30 seconds on each side (they will finish cooking later). Transfer to a large baking sheet and cover loosely with foil. After 2 batches, discard the oil and wipe out the skillet with a paper towel. Heat the remaining 2 tablespoons butter and ⅓ cup oil and sauté the remaining 2 batches.

5. Uncover the chops and bake for 2 to 3 minutes for rare, 3 to 4 minutes for medium rare. Serve immediately.
—Donatello, San Francisco

SWEET AND SOUR LAMB

One of the nicest features of this unusual Apulian stew is the fact that it tastes even better a day or two after it is made.
♟ Match the sweet-sour flavors in this stew with a tart but fruity red, such as an Italian Dolcetto d'Alba—a Vietti or Marchesi di Gresy—or a fruity California Zinfandel, such as Caymus.

6 Servings

¼ cup plus 1½ tablespoons olive oil
2 medium onions, sliced
3½ pounds boneless lamb shoulder,
    trimmed and cut into 1-inch cubes

⅓ cup tomato paste
½ cup red wine vinegar
2 tablespoons sugar
⅓ cup pine nuts
⅓ cup raisins
½ teaspoon salt
½ teaspoon freshly ground pepper

1. In a large flameproof casserole, heat ¼ cup of the olive oil. Add the onions and cook over moderately low heat until softened but not browned, 10 to 15 minutes.

2. In a large skillet, heat the remaining 1½ tablespoons of the oil over high heat. Add one-third of the lamb cubes and sauté, tossing frequently, until well browned, about 5 minutes. Transfer the browned meat to the casserole. Repeat 2 more times with the remaining lamb.

3. Pour off any fat from the skillet and add ¾ cup of water. Bring to a boil, scraping up any browned bits from the bottom of the pan. Add the liquid to the casserole along with the tomato paste, vinegar, sugar and another ¾ cup water. Simmer the stew over low heat, stirring occasionally, for 1 hour. Add the pine nuts and raisins and cook until the meat is very tender, about 30 minutes longer. Increase the heat to moderate and boil until the liquid thickens enough to lightly coat the meat, about 20 minutes. Season the stew with the salt and pepper before serving.
—Nancy Verde Barr

TUSCAN ROAST LOIN OF PORK

A classic Tuscan meat dish is the herb-scented roast loin of pork called *arista*, most often done on the spit over an open wood fire. The fact that this handsome roast is just as good warm or cool as hot (some say it's even better the second day) makes it an ideal dinner-party choice.

6 to 8 Servings

15 *medium garlic cloves, peeled*
4 *tablespoons fresh rosemary or*
    3 *tablespoons dried*
2 *tablespoons salt*
1½ *tablespoons freshly ground pepper*
2 *tablespoons olive oil*
5-*pound pork loin, bone in*

1. In a food processor or blender, mince the garlic and rosemary with the salt and pepper. With the machine on, drizzle in the oil. Process to a thick paste, scraping down the sides of the bowl as necessary.

2. Place the meat, bone-side down, on a rack. Rub the paste all over the meat. Let stand for 2 to 3 hours at room temperature .

3. Preheat the oven to 325°. Place the meat, on the rack, in a roasting pan. Bake for 1½ hours or until the internal temperature reaches 150° on an instant-reading thermometer. Increase the heat to 400° and roast for 10 to 15 minutes longer, until lightly browned.

4. Remove the roast to a carving board. Loosely cover with aluminum foil and let rest for 20 to 30 minutes before serving.
—Tom Maresca and Diane Darrow

PORK BUNDLES WITH PANCETTA AND SAGE

This dish is known as *uccelini scappati*, or Birds That Got Away, because the little stuffed bundles of pork resemble tiny quail. They don't taste like quail, but no one seems to mind.
♟ Nino Negri or Rainoldi Grumello or Ceretto Barbaresco

4 Servings

½ cup beef or chicken stock or 1 can (10½ ounces) low-sodium chicken broth
1 pound trimmed, boneless center-cut pork loin, cut into 16 slices (about ¼ inch thick)
¼ cup all-purpose flour
Salt and freshly ground pepper
16 thin slices of pancetta or prosciutto
32 large fresh sage leaves or 3 tablespoons dried sage leaves or 2 tablespoons dried rubbed sage (see Note)
2 tablespoons unsalted butter
1 tablespoon mild olive oil
1 medium shallot, minced
2 tablespoons minced parsley
1 cup Valtellina red wine or other dry red wine
¼ cup tomato puree
Fresh sage leaves, for garnish

1. If using canned chicken broth, bring it to a boil in a small saucepan over high heat. Cook until reduced to ½ cup, about 8 minutes. Pour the broth into a measuring cup. If you have more than ½ cup, boil again to reduce the liquid.

2. Meanwhile, flatten each pork slice with the palm of your hand to a 4-by-3-inch rectangle. Place the flour on a plate and season it lightly with salt and pepper. Dredge the pork slices in the flour, shaking off any excess. Place 1 slice of pancetta and 2 fresh sage leaves (or a sprinkling of dried) in the middle of each pork slice. Starting at a short end, roll up the pork and secure with a toothpick.

3. In a large nonreactive skillet, heat the butter and oil over high heat. Add half of the meat to the pan and cook, turning once, until browned, 1 to 2 minutes on each side. Transfer to a large plate. Repeat with the remaining meat.

4. Reduce the heat to moderate. Add the shallot and parsley to the skillet and cook, stirring constantly, until softened, about 1 minute. Add the stock (or broth), wine and tomato puree and bring to a boil over high heat, scraping up the browned bits on the bottom of the pan. Cook until the liquid reduces by half, about 5 minutes.

5. Remove the toothpicks from the meat. Add the meat and any accumulated juices to the skillet. Cover and cook over moderate heat, turning once, until heated through, about 5 minutes.

6. Using tongs, transfer 4 of the pork bundles to each of 4 warmed dinner plates. Spoon the sauce over the meat and garnish with fresh sage leaves.

NOTE: If fresh sage is unavailable, be sure to use dried sage leaves or rubbed sage—available in the spice rack of most supermarkets—not powdered sage.
—Constance and Rosario Del Nero

69

TUSCAN FEAST

Chicken Liver Crostini (p. 47)

Bean and Vegetable Soup

♟ Chianti Classico

Tuscan Roast Loin of Pork (p. 68)

Sauté of Potatoes and Slivered Artichoke Hearts

♟ Vino Nobile di Montepulciano or Tignanello

Zabaglione (p. 221)

♟ Vin Santo

GIAMBOTTA OF MIXED GREENS WITH SPARERIBS

♟ Light red, such as Montepulciano d'Abruzzo

4 to 6 Servings

1 head of garlic, crushed (about 15 cloves)
1 tablespoon hot Hungarian paprika
½ teaspoon coarsely ground pepper
½ cup plus 1 tablespoon extra-virgin olive oil
1 teaspoon salt
2½ pounds pork spareribs in one piece, sawed lengthwise into thirds and trimmed of all excess fat
1 small rutabaga—peeled, cut into eighths, then sliced crosswise ½ inch thick
1 pint tiny white pearl onions, peeled
½ teaspoon (loosely packed) saffron threads, crushed (optional)
2 imported bay leaves
2 tablespoons white wine vinegar
16 cups (about 3 pounds) coarsely shredded mixed greens (kale, escarole, swiss chard, mustard greens and/or broccoli raab)
1 large sweet potato—peeled, halved lengthwise and cut crosswise into ¼-inch slices
2 pounds spinach, stemmed and coarsely shredded

1. In a small bowl, mash the garlic, paprika, pepper, 1 tablespoon of the olive oil and ½ teaspoon of the salt to make a paste. Rub the ribs with this paste. Cover and let marinate at room temperature for 1 to 2 hours, or refrigerate overnight for a more garlicky flavor. Cut the meat into 2- to 3-rib pieces and set aside.

2. In a large, heavy nonreactive pot, preferably enameled cast iron, combine the remaining ½ cup olive oil and ½ teaspoon salt with the rutabaga, pearl onions, saffron, bay leaves, vinegar and 1 cup of water. Add the garlic-paprika paste. Add half of the mixed greens, cover and cook over high heat until the greens wilt, 2 to 3 minutes. Stir in the remaining greens and cook until wilted. Add the ribs.

3. Cover and cook over moderately high heat, maintaining a slow boil and stirring occasionally, until the ribs and rutabaga are tender, 45 to 60 minutes. (The recipe can be prepared several days ahead to this point. Let cool completely, then cover and refrigerate. Reheat before proceeding.)

4. Scatter the sweet potato slices over the giambotta and cook over moderately high heat, stirring occasionally, until softened, 10 to 15 minutes.

5. Remove the bay leaves. Add the spinach and cook, stirring, until just wilted, about 1 minute.
—Anne Disrude

UMBRIAN PORK SAUSAGE WITH PINE NUTS AND RAISINS

This recipe from the central Italian province of Umbria is delicious with sautéed polenta and a dollop of tomato sauce. The sausage can be crumbled on pizza or put into sausage casings and grilled.

4 to 6 Servings

½ cup raisins
¼ cup pine nuts
2 pounds ground pork
1 tablespoon finely grated orange zest
4 to 5 small garlic cloves, minced

1½ teaspoons salt
½ teaspoon freshly ground pepper

1. In a small bowl, plump the raisins in ½ cup hot water, set aside for 30 minutes. Drain and reserve the liquid.

2. Meanwhile, preheat the oven to 350°. Spread the pine nuts on a baking sheet and bake for 5 minutes, or until lightly browned. Let cool completely.

3. In a medium mixing bowl, combine the pork, orange zest, garlic, toasted pine nuts, raisins and 2 tablespoons of their soaking liquid (discard the remaining liquid). Season with the salt and pepper. Mix the ingredients well, using your hands, but do not overwork. Form into 16 sausage patties ½ inch thick.

4. Heat a large heavy skillet over high heat. Working in 2 or 3 batches, cook the patties until browned on the outside, about 5 minutes on each side. Transfer to a warm oven, wiping out the skillet between each batch. Serve hot.

—Joyce Goldstein, Square One, San Francisco

TUSCAN SAUSAGE

If possible, use natural pork casings for these sausages; they add a flavor not provided by manufactured casings. They can be obtained inexpensively from a butcher and are sold by the yard, preserved in salt. The casings will keep indefinitely (unrinsed) in the refrigerator.

*Makes About 45
Sausages*

5 pounds pork butt, chilled
1 tablespoon plus 2 teaspoons salt
2 teaspoons freshly ground pepper

½ cup skinned, seeded and diced
 (¼ inch) tomato
½ cup diced (½ inch) mozzarella cheese
¼ cup minced fresh basil or
 1 tablespoon plus 1 teaspoon dried
3 tablespoons fresh oregano or
 1 tablespoon dried
8 yards prepared casings (about
 4 ounces)
1 tablespoon vegetable oil

1. Grind the meat coarsely. Place in a large bowl.

2. Add the salt, pepper, tomato, cheese, basil and oregano. Mix well with your hands.

3. Working with about one-quarter of the sausage filling at a time (cover and refrigerate the remainder), stuff the casings loosely with the sausage filling. Pinch and twist into 4-inch links and cut to separate. Refrigerate while stuffing the remaining sausages.

4. To cook, prick the sausages all over to prevent the skins from bursting. Place as many sausages in a skillet as will fit in a single layer without crowding. Pour in about ½ inch of water, cover and simmer over low heat for 20 minutes. Pour off any liquid. Add the oil to the pan and cook uncovered, turning, until the sausages are evenly browned, about 10 minutes. Drain on paper towels and serve hot.

—Sonny D'Angelo, D'Angelo Brothers, Philadelphia

TORTA RUSTICA

This hearty, satisfying torta is as old as the hills of Tuscany. Ideal for a small party, it can be made up to four hours ahead.

8 to 10 Servings

1 *envelope active dry yeast*
1 *tablespoon sugar*
¾ *cup lukewarm water (105° to 115°)*
3 *cups plus 6 tablespoons flour*
2½ *tablespoons extra-virgin olive oil*
2½ *teaspoons salt*
½ *pound hot Italian sausage*
½ *pound sweet Italian sausage*
4 *tablespoons unsalted butter*
1 *large onion, minced*
2 *large garlic cloves, minced*
1 *teaspoon freshly ground pepper*
2 *teaspoons basil*
2 *teaspoons oregano*
2 *teaspoons thyme*
1 *cup hot milk*
1 *egg, lightly beaten*
1 *cup dry rigatoni, cooked*
1 *can (16 ounces) Italian peeled
   tomatoes, drained and chopped*
2 *cups freshly grated Parmesan cheese*
¼ *cup chopped parsley*

1. In a small bowl, combine the yeast, sugar and ½ cup of the water. Let stand until the yeast foams, about 5 minutes.

2. In a food processor fitted with the dough blade, combine 3 cups of the flour with the olive oil, ½ teaspoon of the salt and the yeast mixture. With the machine on, pour in the remaining ¼ cup water and process until the dough forms a ball. (You may need an extra tablespoon of water depending on the humidity.) The dough will be soft and slightly sticky.

3. Turn the dough out onto a lightly floured surface and knead for 1 minute; knead in 2 more table-spoons of flour, if necessary, to form a smooth, shiny dough. Transfer the dough to a large oiled bowl and turn to coat. Cover with a towel and let stand in a warm place until doubled in bulk, about 1½ hours.

4. Place the sausages in a medium saucepan with water to cover. Cook over moderately low heat until firm, 12 to 15 minutes. Skin the sausages and slice ⅓ inch thick.

5. In a large skillet, melt the butter. Add the onion, garlic, pepper, basil, oregano, thyme and the remaining 2 teaspoons salt. Cook over low heat, stirring occasionally, until the onion is soft, about 10 minutes. Stir in the remaining ¼ cup flour until blended and cook for 30 seconds. Whisk in the hot milk and cook, stirring occasionally, until the mixture is thick and bubbling, about 5 minutes.

6. Scrape into a large bowl and beat in the egg. Fold in the cooked rigatoni, hot and sweet sausages, tomatoes, Parmesan cheese and parsley.

7. Preheat the oven to 375°. Lightly oil a 10-inch springform pan. On a floured surface, roll out the dough to form a circle 20 inches in diameter. Fold the dough in half and then into quarters, then unfold the dough into the pan, letting any excess drape over the edge. Spoon the filling onto the dough and spread it evenly. Gather together the overhanging dough in the center leaving a small hole in the middle for steam to escape during baking. Brush a little additional olive oil over the top and bake for 1½ hours, or until golden brown. Serve hot or at room temperature, cut into wedges.
—W. *Peter Prestcott*

Sautéed Calf's Liver and Onions (page 77) and Grilled Radicchio with Anchovy-Mustard Sauce (page 194).

At left, Scallops Venetian Style
(*page 50*). Above, Rice with Peas
(*page 196*) and Baked Chicken
Breasts with Scallions and Lime (*page
79*).

Top left, Artichoke, Chick-Pea and Fennel Giambotta with Chicken (page 83). Top right, Giambotta of Squash and Kohlrabi with Tilefish (page 88). At right, Giambotta of Mixed Greens with Spareribs (page 70).

SAUTEED CALF'S LIVER AND ONIONS

Venice produces many versions of this classic combination of calf's liver and onions, but the underlying principle of all of them is that the better the liver, the less you have to do with it.

4 Servings

1 *pound calf's liver—trimmed, thinly sliced and cut into ½-inch-wide strips*
1 *cup milk*
3 *tablespoons unsalted butter*
3 *tablespoons olive oil*
1 *pound sweet onions (such as Bermudas or Vidalias), thinly sliced*
½ *teaspoon salt*
¼ *teaspoon freshly ground pepper*
2 *tablespoons minced parsley*
Lemon wedges, for garnish

1. Place the liver in a large, shallow bowl or glass pie pan, pour on the milk and set aside for 1 to 3 hours.
2. In a large skillet, melt the butter in the oil over low heat. Add the onions and cook, stirring occasionally until very soft and light golden, about 30 minutes.
3. Drain the strips of liver, pat dry and add to the skillet. Increase the heat to moderately high and sauté, stirring constantly, until the liver is browned outside, but still supple and rosy inside, about 3 minutes. Add the salt, pepper and parsley and toss to combine. Serve at once, garnished with lemon wedges.
—*Tom Maresca and Diane Darrow*

LA FINANZIERA

An authentic *la finanziera* is made with cocks' combs and wattles, but we've developed a recipe with substitutes to spare us all embarassment, consumers and butchers alike. The instructions are lengthy but the techniques are very simple.

6 to 8 Servings

1 *pound boneless veal shoulder, cut into 1-inch cubes, chilled*
2 *ounces prosciutto, coarsely chopped (about ¼ cup)*
1 *large shallot, coarsely chopped*
⅓ *cup fresh bread crumbs, preferably from Italian or French bread*
2 *tablespoons minced parsley*
½ *teaspoon salt*
½ *teaspoon freshly ground pepper*
Pinch of freshly grated nutmeg
1 *egg, lightly beaten*
1 *tablespoon distilled white vinegar or fresh lemon juice*
1 *pound veal sweetbreads*
1 *veal kidney*
½ *pound chicken livers*
¾ *pound skinless, boneless chicken breast*
1 *cup chicken or beef stock or canned broth*
⅓ *cup all-purpose flour*
4 *tablespoons unsalted butter*
4 *tablespoons olive oil*
½ *cup red wine vinegar*
6 *ounces Italian prepared mushrooms in vinegar or mushrooms in oil (about 1 cup)**
3 *ounces cornichons (French gherkin pickles), sliced lengthwise (about ½ cup)**
⅓ *cup dry Marsala*
*Available at specialty food shops

1. Grind the veal, prosciutto and shallot in a meat grinder, or chop

AUTUMN DINNER

Mushroom Toasts (p. 43)

🍷 *Loredan Vennegazzù della Casa or Pio Cesare Barbera*

Risotto with Fennel (p. 201)

Sautéed Calf's Liver and Onions (p. 77)

Grilled Radicchio with Anchovy-Mustard Sauce (p. 195)

🍷 *Maculan Cabernet Fratta or Antinori Chianti Classico Riserva*

Sand Tart (p. 238)

🍷 *Anselmi Recioto di Soave or Livio Felluga Picolit or Malvasia di Lipari*

in a food processor, turning the machine on and off quickly, until the mixture is minced but not pureed. Scrape into a bowl. Add the bread crumbs, parsley, salt, pepper, nutmeg and egg. Mix well to combine. Shape into 1-inch balls.

2. Bring a medium nonreactive saucepan of water to a boil. Reduce to a simmer, add the white vinegar and sweetbreads and blanch the sweetbreads for 5 minutes, or until lightened in color. Rinse under cold running water until cool. Peel off the outer membrane covering the sweetbreads and trim away any connective tissue. Cut into 1-inch chunks.

3. Halve the kidney lengthwise and trim away any fat, connective tissue and tubules. Cut into 1-inch chunks. Trim the chicken livers and separate the lobes. Cut the chicken into 2-by-½-inch strips. Keep the meats separate.

4. In a large saucepan, bring the stock to a simmer. Keep partially covered to prevent evaporation.

5. Dredge the meatballs and each of the meats separately in the flour; shake off any excess and set aside. In a large skillet, melt 2 tablespoons of the butter in 2 tablespoons of the oil over high heat. Add the chicken breast strips and sauté 2 minutes. Remove with a slotted spoon and set aside.

6. Reduce the heat to moderate and add 1 tablespoon each of butter and oil to the skillet. When the foam subsides, add the meatballs and sauté until browned, 4 to 5 minutes. Remove with a slotted spoon and transfer to the simmering broth.

7. Heat the remaining 1 tablespoon each of butter and oil in the skillet. Add the sweetbread chunks and sauté, tossing, until lightly browned, about 4 minutes. Remove with a slotted spoon and transfer to the broth.

8. Add the kidney chunks to the skillet and sauté, tossing, until lightly browned, about 6 minutes. With a slotted spoon, transfer to the broth.

9. Add the chicken livers to the skillet and sauté, turning, until browned, about 4 minutes. Remove with a slotted spoon and transfer to the broth. Add the reserved chicken strips and any juices to the broth.

10. Pour off any fat from the skillet. Add ¼ cup of the red wine vinegar and deglaze the skillet over moderately high heat, scraping any browned bits from the sides and bottom of the pan. Scrape into the saucepan with the meats. Stir in the mushrooms and cornichons.

11. Cover the meats and simmer for 10 minutes longer.

12. Stir in the remaining ¼ cup vinegar and the Marsala. Simmer, uncovered, for 5 minutes to blend the flavors.

—*Tom Maresca and Diane Darrow*

BAKED CHICKEN BREASTS WITH SCALLIONS AND LIME

The three greens of the scallions, parsley and lime zest make for a pretty presentation as well as a lively flavor. In the Veneto, this combination is used on fish—mainly on triglia, a kind of mullet, though we've tried it successfully on bluefish, sardines and smelts. But the nicest discovery was how well this treatment works with chicken breasts.

4 Servings

4 skinless, boneless chicken breast
   halves (about 5 ounces each)
½ cup all-purpose flour
5 tablespoons unsalted butter
⅔ cup minced scallions (white and
   tender green)
1 large garlic clove, minced
½ cup dry white wine
¼ teaspoon salt
¼ teaspoon freshly ground pepper
1 tablespoon fresh lime juice
2 teaspoons minced lime zest
1 tablespoon chopped parsley
1 tablespoon fine, dry bread crumbs

1. Preheat the oven to 400°. Trim off any fat or membranes from the chicken breasts. Pound the thicker ends lightly to flatten to an even thickness.

2. Dredge the chicken breasts in the flour; shake off any excess. In a large nonreactive skillet, melt 4 tablespoons of the butter over moderately high heat. Add the chicken and sauté, turning once, until golden brown, about 3 minutes on each side. Remove to a plate.

3. Reduce the heat to low and add the scallions and garlic. Cook until soft, about 5 minutes. Increase the heat to moderately high, add the wine and boil, scraping up any browned bits. Cook until reduced by half, 2 to 3 minutes.

4. Spread half the scallion sauce in a buttered baking dish just large enough to hold the chicken in a single layer. Add the chicken and season with the salt and pepper; drizzle on the lime juice. Cover with the remaining sauce. Sprinkle on the lime zest, parsley and bread crumbs. Dot with the remaining 1 tablespoon butter.

5. Bake the chicken in the top third of the oven for 15 minutes, or until the chicken is opaque throughout but still juicy. Serve at once.
—Tom Maresca and Diane Darrow

POACHED CHICKEN BREASTS WITH GREEN SAUCE

A lovely picnic or light supper dish from the north.
🍷 Pinot Grigio

6 Servings

6 skinless, boneless chicken breast
   halves
2 medium leeks (white and tender
   green), cut into ½-inch slices
1 imported bay leaf
1 teaspoon salt
4 whole peppercorns
3 tablespoons fresh lemon juice
Green Sauce (p. 260)
Tomato slices, radishes or roasted red
   bell pepper strips, for garnish

1. Place the chicken in a large nonreactive saucepan. Cover with

SPRING DINNER

Scallops Venetian Style (p. 50)

🍷 *Gradnik Sauvignon Blanc or*
Bollini Pinot Grigio

Rice with Peas (p. 197)

Baked Chicken Breasts with
Scallions and Lime (p. 79)

Buttered Asparagus

🍷 *Jermann Vintage Tunina or*
La Scolca Gavi

Strawberries with Lemon and
Sugar (p. 214)

Biscotti

Espresso

ENTREES

80

A GRAND BUFFET

Crostini with Tarragon Spread (p. 45)

Crostini with Tomato (p. 45)

Crostini with Beef and Balsamic Vinegar (p. 46)

A Chilled Tuscan White, such as Badia a Coltibuono or Il Cipressino Vernaccia di San Gimignano

Veal Rolls with Peas (p. 61)

Chicken Breasts with Fennel Sauce (p. 80)

Risotto Mold with Prosciutto (p. 211)

Spinach with Raisins and Pine Nuts (p. 195)

Asparagus with Parmesan Cheese (p. 189)

Chianti Classico Riserva, such as Badia a Coltibuono or Castello di Querceto

Mascarpone Cream Dessert (p. 223)

Strawberry Sherbet with Cherry Caramel Sauce (p. 218)

Raisins in Grappa (p. 214)

the leeks, bay leaf, salt, peppercorns and lemon juice; add enough cold water to cover. Bring the water to a boil over high heat. Immediately reduce the heat to moderate and poach for 10 to 15 minutes, until the chicken has just lost its pink in the center. Remove from the heat and let cool in the poaching liquid.

2. With a slotted spoon, remove the chicken and leeks from the poaching liquid and arrange on a platter. (Save the liquid to use as a stock.) Pour the Green Sauce over the chicken or serve it on the side. Garnish with tomatoes, radishes or strips of roasted peppers if desired. Serve at room temperature.
—Anna Teresa Callen

CHICKEN BREASTS WITH FENNEL SAUCE

Arrange the slices of chicken in the center of a large platter, slightly overlapping, and surround them with Spinach with Raisins and Pine Nuts (p. 195). Pass any extra fennel sauce in a separate bowl and let guests serve themselves.

12 Servings

1 ounce dried porcini mushrooms
3 eggs
1 tablespoon coarsely chopped fresh sage leaves
¼ cup freshly grated Parmesan cheese
1 teaspoon finely grated lemon zest
Salt and freshly ground pepper

5 tablespoons unsalted butter
2 large, whole, skinless and boneless chicken breasts (12 ounces each), lightly pounded to an even thickness
8 ounces sweet Italian sausage, casings removed
1 cup dry white wine
2 medium fennel bulbs (1 pound total)—washed, trimmed and cut into 1-inch pieces

1. In a medium heatproof bowl, soak the porcini mushrooms in 1 cup hot water for 30 minutes. Drain, squeeze the mushrooms dry and set aside in a small bowl.

2. In a small bowl, using a fork, beat the eggs with the sage, Parmesan cheese, lemon zest and a pinch of salt and pepper.

3. In a 7-inch nonstick skillet, heat 1½ teaspoons of the butter over moderate heat. Pour in half of the egg mixture and cook as you would a pancake, until firm, 1 to 2 minutes per side. Transfer to a large plate and repeat with another 1½ teaspoons butter and the remaining egg mixture. Let the omelets cool slightly.

4. On a work surface, lay the flattened chicken breasts skinned-side down, open like a book in front of you. Spread half of the sausage meat over each breast and sprinkle the reserved porcini mushrooms on top; press the mushrooms into the sausage. Lay the omelets over the mushrooms and roll up the chicken breasts from one side to the other. Secure the rolled chicken with kitchen string.

5. In a heavy, medium casserole, melt 2 tablespoons of the butter over high heat. Add the chicken rolls and cook, turning, until golden brown on all sides, 6 to 8 minutes. Pour in the wine, add a pinch of salt and ¼ teaspoon of pepper. Cover, reduce the heat to low and simmer, turning occasionally, until the

chicken is cooked through, about 30 minutes.

6. Meanwhile, in a large heavy saucepan, melt the remaining 2 tablespoons butter over low heat. Add the fennel, 1 cup of water and a little salt and pepper. Cover and cook, stirring occasionally, until the fennel is tender, about 20 minutes. Remove from the heat. Transfer the fennel and its cooking liquid to a food processor or blender and puree until smooth.

7. Remove the chicken rolls and clip the strings. Stir the fennel puree into the juices in the casserole and bring to a simmer; if the sauce is too thick to pour, add a little water to thin it. Season with salt and pepper to taste.

8. Slice the chicken rolls into ½-inch rounds and arrange in an overlapping circle on a round platter. Strain the fennel sauce over the chicken and serve any extra sauce on the side.
—*Lorenza de' Medici*

CHICKEN POTENTINA

Ripe tomatoes, fresh basil and the piquancy of hot pepper mark this as a typically southern dish.
♟ Southern Italian red, such as Corvo Rosso

4 to 6 Servings

1 *tablespoon lard or bacon fat*
2 *tablespoons olive oil*
1 *medium onion, thinly sliced*
1 *chicken (3 pounds), cut into 8 serving pieces*
½ *cup dry white wine*
1 *pound tomatoes—peeled, seeded and cut into strips*
½ *cup shredded fresh basil*

¼ *cup chopped parsley*
Pinch of crushed hot red pepper
Chopped parsley and shredded basil, for garnish

1. In a large nonreactive skillet, melt the lard in the olive oil over moderately high heat. Add the onion, stirring to coat with the fat. When the fat sizzles, add the chicken and cook, turning, until golden on all sides, about 5 minutes. Add 2 tablespoons of the wine and continue to cook, uncovered, turning often and gradually adding the remaining wine, 2 tablespoons at a time, until it evaporates.

2. Add the tomatoes, basil, parsley and hot pepper. Cover and cook over moderate heat until the chicken is juicy and almost falling off the bone, about 1 hour. Garnish with parsley and basil.
—*Anna Teresa Callen*

CHICKEN ALLA CANZANESE

This recipe is from Abruzzo, in the central region of Italy. Traditionally the whole cloves are left in the dish; if you prefer, you can tie them in cheesecloth so that they can be easily removed before serving.
♟ Light white, such as Trebbiano d'Abruzzo or Torgiano

8 Servings

2 *chickens (3 pounds each), cut into 8 serving pieces each*
1 *tablespoon coarse (kosher) salt*
½ *teaspoon sage*

81

4 *imported bay leaves*
2 *garlic cloves, sliced crosswise*
12 *whole cloves*
3 *sprigs of fresh rosemary or 1
teaspoon dried*
24 *whole black peppercorns, crushed*
½ *small dried hot red pepper*
4 *slices of prosciutto, ¼ inch thick, cut
into ¼-inch dice*
½ *cup dry white wine, such as
Trebbiano d'Abruzzo*

1. Place the chicken pieces in a large bowl, sprinkle with the salt and cover with cold water. Let stand for 1 hour.

2. Drain the chicken pieces and arrange in a single layer in a large flameproof casserole. Add the sage, bay leaves, garlic, whole cloves, rosemary, black peppercorns, hot pepper, prosciutto and white wine. Cover the casserole and cook over low heat, turning the pieces occasionally, for 1 hour.

3. Remove the cover, increase the heat to moderately high and cook, turning frequently, until the sauce is reduced and the chicken starts to color. If necessary, add a little water to prevent sticking.
—Anna Teresa Callen

COUNTRY-STYLE FRIED CHICKEN

When I was growing up, it was considered beneficial for youngsters to have what was called a "change of air." Consequently, although we took vacations as a family as well, each year I was shipped to the country by myself to spend at least 10 days as the guest of a country priest. The house was attached to a beautiful 10th-century church and had a well of crystal clear, ice-cold water. All the cooking, including frying, was done in an enormous walk-in fireplace, under the supervision of the priest's huge, bossy sister. I'll never forget this simple, succulent dish they made with the chickens they raised. The meat becomes meltingly tender as a result of its marinating in eggs.

🍷 The dry, lean nature of a Chianti, such as Podere Il Palazzino or Cecchi would accent the chicken nicely.

4 *Servings*

1 *teaspoon coarse (kosher) salt*
1 *frying chicken (3½ pounds)*
1 *teaspoon salt*
½ *teaspoon freshly ground pepper*
1 *cup unbleached all-purpose flour*
3 *eggs*
4 *cups vegetable oil, for deep-frying*
½ *cup olive oil, for deep-frying*
1 *lemon, cut in wedges*

1. Bring a large pot of water with the coarse salt to a boil over high heat. Add the chicken to the pot and parboil for 1 minute. Drain well and let cool.

2. Using a sharp knife, cut the chicken into 8 pieces. Season with the salt and pepper, then dredge in the flour. In a large bowl, beat the eggs lightly with a pinch of salt. Add the chicken pieces and turn to coat evenly. Cover and refrigerate for at least 1 hour and up to 2 hours, turning occasionally.

3. In a large heavy skillet, preferably cast iron, heat the vegetable and olive oils over moderate heat until the temperature reaches 375°.

Add half of the chicken pieces and increase the heat to high for 20 seconds. Then reduce the heat to moderate and fry, turning occasionally, until the chicken is golden and crisp and the juices run clear when the meat is pierced with a fork, about 25 minutes.

4. Using tongs, transfer the fried chicken to paper towels to drain. (Keep warm in a low oven.) Fry the remaining chicken pieces. Serve hot, sprinkled with salt and garnished with the lemon wedges.
—Giuliano Bugialli

ARTICHOKE, CHICK-PEA AND FENNEL GIAMBOTTA WITH CHICKEN

The chicken for this hearty meal is browned first to enhance the flavor of the giambotta.
🍷 California Sauvignon Blanc, such as Clos du Bois

4 to 6 Servings

6 large artichokes
1 cup chopped fresh basil
½ cup plus 1 tablespoon extra-virgin olive oil
2 large whole chicken breasts, split and halved crosswise, or 8 thighs or legs
2 red bell peppers, cut into 1-inch pieces
1 can (19 ounces) chick-peas— drained, rinsed and patted dry
1 fennel bulb, cut into 1-inch pieces
1 large parsley root or parsnip, cut into ½-inch pieces
3 plum tomatoes, chopped
1 large zucchini, cut into 1-inch pieces
1 carrot, cut into 1-inch pieces
1 bunch of scallions, chopped
6 garlic cloves, chopped
½ cup chopped parsley
2 tablespoons white wine vinegar
½ teaspoon thyme
½ teaspoon oregano
½ teaspoon crushed fennel seed
1½ teaspoons salt
½ teaspoon freshly ground black pepper
⅛ teaspoon crushed hot red pepper
2 imported bay leaves

1. Trim the artichokes by first snapping off the tough outer leaves near the base. Using a stainless steel knife, cut off the stems; cut the crowns to within 1½ inches of the base. Quarter the artichoke bottoms and cut out the hairy chokes.

2. Set aside ½ cup of the basil, 1 tablespoon of the olive oil and the chicken. Combine all the remaining ingredients, including the artichokes, in a large heavy pot. Stir in 1 cup of water. Cover and cook over moderately high heat, maintaining a slow boil and stirring occasionally, until the artichokes are tender, about 30 minutes. (The recipe can be prepared to this point up to 3 days ahead. Let cool, then cover and refrigerate. Reheat before proceeding.)

3. Meanwhile, pat the chicken dry. Heat the reserved 1 tablespoon oil in a large skillet. Add the chicken and sauté over moderately high heat until browned all over, about 20 minutes. Add the chicken to the cooked vegetables.

4. Pour off any fat from the skillet. Add ⅓ cup of water and bring to a boil. Pour this liquid over the chicken.

5. Cover the giambotta and cook at a slow boil until the chicken is cooked, about 5 minutes for breasts and 15 for thighs or legs. Remove the bay leaves and sprinkle with the reserved basil.
—Anne Disrude

ENTREES

COD BAKED IN PANCETTA WITH POLENTA AND BITTER GREENS

In this recipe salt cod accents the fresh cod, which is roasted in bundles wrapped in thin slices of pancetta.

4 Servings

4-ounce piece skinless, boneless salt cod of even thickness
1 cup coarsely ground cornmeal
¼ cup freshly grated Pecorino Romano cheese (about 1 ounce)
Salt and freshly ground pepper
4 cod steaks (6 ounces each)
2 teaspoons fresh thyme or 1 teaspoon dried
12 very thin slices pancetta (6 ounces)
¼ cup extra-virgin olive oil
1 small red onion, halved and thinly sliced crosswise
2 medium garlic cloves, minced
8 cups mixed greens, such as watercress, radicchio, mustard greens and Belgian endive, torn into bite-size pieces
3 tablespoons fresh lemon juice
6 tablespoons cold unsalted butter, cut into large pieces
2 tablespoons drained capers
Lemon wedges, for serving

1. In a medium bowl, cover the salt cod with plenty of cold water and set aside, uncovered, in the refrigerator for at least 8 hours, or overnight. Change the water 6 to 8 times, or as frequently as possible while soaking.

2. Drain the salt cod, place it in a small saucepan, cover with cold water and bring just to a boil over moderate heat. Remove from the heat and set aside until the cod is barely cooked through, about 5 min-utes. Drain again thoroughly. Cover and refrigerate the salt cod.

3. In a heavy medium saucepan, bring 3 cups of water to a boil over high heat. Meanwhile, in a medium bowl, combine the cornmeal with 2 cups of water. Gradually whisk the cornmeal mixture into the boiling water. Reduce the heat to low and cook, stirring frequently, until very thick, about 30 minutes. Remove from the heat and stir in the cheese. Season the polenta with salt and pepper to taste.

4. Pour the polenta into a buttered 9-inch glass pie plate. Cover and refrigerate until very firm, about 2 hours. (*The recipe can be prepared to this point up to 1 day ahead and refrigerated, covered.*)

5. Preheat the oven to 450°. Season the fresh cod with salt and pepper; sprinkle with the thyme. Separate the salt cod into 4 pieces and place a piece of salt cod on top of each portion of fresh cod. Spread out 3 overlapping slices of the pancetta on a work surface and place a piece of cod in the center. Bring the pancetta up and over the cod, wrapping it snugly around to form a neat package. Repeat with the remaining cod and pancetta to form 4 packages. Set aside.

6. Cut the polenta in half; wrap and reserve one half for another use. Cut the remaining half into 4 wedges. In a 12-inch cast-iron skillet, heat the olive oil over high heat until smoking. Add the polenta wedges and cook until crusty and golden brown on the bottom, about 5 minutes. Turn the polenta over and place the cod bundles in the skillet, alternating the polenta and the cod. Place the skillet in the oven and roast the cod for about 14 minutes, until just cooked through.

PANCETTA

Pancetta, an Italian bacon, is made from the same cut of pork as American-style bacon (the belly of the pig), but instead of being simply salt-cured (and usually smoked), pancetta is cured with a mixture of salt, pepper and cloves. Then, instead of being left as a slab, pancetta is rolled into a tight cylinder, like a salami. When buying pancetta, look for a well-balanced layering of creamy, white fat and lean, pink meat. Although it is worth hunting for the real thing, if you are unable to find pancetta—try an Italian delicatessan—you can substitute American bacon (if it is smoked bacon, blanch for about 3 minutes to remove some of the smoked flavor) or, in a pinch, salt pork (although it should be used sparingly since it is all fat and no lean meat).

7. Using a metal spatula, transfer the cod and polenta to a large platter. Add the onion to the skillet and cook over moderately high heat, stirring, until wilted, about 2 minutes. Stir in the garlic and then add the greens. Cook, stirring, until just wilted, about 1 minute. Using a slotted spoon, transfer the greens to warmed plates.

8. Add the lemon juice to the skillet, increase the heat to high and boil for about 30 seconds to reduce slightly. Remove from the heat and whisk in the cold butter, 1 tablespoon at a time. Pour any juices that have accumulated on the platter into the sauce. Stir in the capers and season with salt and pepper to taste. Transfer the cod and polenta to the plates, spoon the sauce around and serve with lemon wedges.

—*Jody Adams, Michela's, Cambridge, Massachusetts*

HALIBUT IN CAPERED BASIL MARINARA

At Giovanni's, this dish is prepared with whole yellow pike. Any firmfleshed white fish such as striped bass or whiting can also be used. Serve the remaining sauce over spaghetti to accompany the fish.

4 Servings

1 *medium onion, chopped*
3 *tablespoons olive oil*
1 *can (28 ounces) crushed Italian tomatoes*
1 *tablespoon drained capers, rinsed*
½ *teaspoon salt*
½ *teaspoon freshly ground pepper*
1 *teaspoon sugar*
¼ *cup (packed) shredded fresh basil*
4 *halibut steaks (8 ounces each), cut about 1 inch thick*

1. Preheat the oven to 350°. In a medium nonreactive saucepan, sauté the onion in the olive oil over moderate heat until softened but not browned, about 5 minutes. Add the tomatoes, capers, salt, pepper and sugar. Bring to a boil. Stir in the shredded basil and simmer until the sauce is reduced by one-third, about 10 minutes.

2. Pour the sauce into a nonreactive baking dish just large enough to hold the fish in a single layer. Add the fish steaks and baste with the sauce. Cover and bake for 15 minutes, or until the fish is just opaque throughout.

3. Transfer the fish to plates or a platter and spoon some of the sauce over it.

—*Carl Quagliata, Giovanni's, Cleveland*

SALMON WITH LEMON-HERB SAUCE

The sauce can be prepared a day or two ahead; the salmon can be arranged on the platter, ready to cook and covered with plastic wrap, up to three hours before serving.
♆ The tartness of this salmon dish calls for a crisp but rich white, such as Antinori Cervaro della Sala or Ruffino Libaio, both from Tuscany.

6 Servings

4 *hard-cooked egg yolks*
2 *teaspoons anchovy paste*
3 *tablespoons chopped parsley*
2 *tablespoons chopped fresh basil*
2 *tablespoons fresh lemon juice*

½ cup extra-virgin olive oil
2 tablespoons drained capers, rinsed
¾ teaspoon freshly ground pepper
½ teaspoon salt
2 pounds skinless salmon
    fillet, cut into 12 slices,
    ¼ inch thick

1. Preheat the oven to 400°. Press the egg yolks through a sieve into a small bowl. Beat in the anchovy paste, parsley, basil, lemon juice, olive oil, capers, ½ teaspoon of the pepper and ¼ teaspoon of the salt.

2. Lightly oil the bottom of a large ovenproof platter. Arrange the salmon slices on the platter, overlapping slightly. Brush lightly with olive oil, season with the remaining ¼ teaspoon each salt and pepper and bake for 4 minutes, or until just opaque throughout. Drizzle a little of the sauce over the salmon and pass the rest separately.
—Nancy Verde Barr

GRILLED HERB-STUFFED SNAPPER WITH EGGPLANT-TOMATO COMPOTE

At Mark's Place, this dish is made with local yellowtail snapper cooked outdoors over a hardwood fire to crisp the skin. The Eggplant-Tomato Compote is a robust accompaniment for the simply cooked fish. ♥ The play of many herbs in the fish and compote recipes is best matched with a crisp, elegant white such as Mastroberardino Fiano di Avellino.

4 Servings

¼ cup extra-virgin olive oil
1 teaspoon fresh lime juice
⅛ teaspoon crushed hot red pepper
14 large fresh basil leaves

4 whole red snappers (1¼ to 1½
    pounds each)
4 sprigs of fresh thyme
4 sprigs of fresh oregano
4 sprigs of fresh tarragon
4 sprigs of flat-leaf parsley
1 teaspoon coarse (kosher) salt
Eggplant-Tomato Compote (p. 190)

1. In a small saucepan, warm the olive oil until barely hot to the touch. Add the lime juice, hot pepper and 6 of the basil leaves. Remove from the heat and let steep for 30 minutes. Strain and set the basil oil aside.

2. Preheat the oven to 500°. Brush a large, rimmed baking sheet or shallow roasting pan with some of the basil oil. Stuff each snapper with 1 sprig each of the thyme, oregano, tarragon and parsley and 2 of the basil leaves.

3. Arrange the fish on the baking sheet. Brush with the remaining basil oil and sprinkle with the salt. Roast for about 15 minutes, until nicely browned and just opaque throughout. Serve with the Eggplant-Tomato Compote.
—Mark Militello, Mark's Place, Miami

STRIPED BASS WITH POTATOES AND PORCINI MUSHROOMS

At once rustic and elegant, this recipe from Pazzia counterpoints the delicate fish with earthy porcini and oven-crisped potatoes.

4 Servings

2 ounces dried porcini mushrooms
1 cup boiling water
6 tablespoons unsalted butter

2 medium all-purpose potatoes, sliced
⅛ inch thick
2 tablespoons extra-virgin olive oil
1 large garlic clove, minced
1 tablespoon minced fresh oregano or
¾ teaspoon dried
2 teaspoons minced parsley
½ teaspoon salt
½ teaspoon freshly ground pepper
2 whole striped bass (2 pounds each)—
filleted, skinned and cut diagonally
into ½-inch-wide strips
2 tablespoons fresh lemon juice

1. Preheat the oven to 400°. In a small heatproof bowl, cover the dried mushrooms with the boiling water and let soak for 20 minutes.

2. In a small saucepan, melt the butter. Rinse the potato slices in cool water, drain in a colander and pat dry with paper towels. Place the potatoes in a medium bowl and toss with the melted butter. Arrange the potatoes on a large baking sheet, overlapping them only slightly. Bake on the lowest rack of the oven for 25 to 30 minutes, until browned and crisp.

3. Meanwhile, drain the mushrooms. Strain the soaking liquid through a sieve lined with a double thickness of cheesecloth and reserve it. Rinse the mushrooms well to remove any grit. Cut off and discard any tough bits.

4. In a medium skillet, heat 1 tablespoon of the oil. Add the garlic and cook over moderate heat until golden, 2 to 3 minutes. Add the mushrooms, ¼ cup of the reserved soaking liquid, 1 teaspoon of the fresh oregano (or ¼ teaspoon of the dried) and the parsley, salt and pepper. Cook until the liquid has evaporated, about 3 minutes.

5. Meanwhile, brush a baking sheet with the remaining 1 tablespoon oil. Arrange the fish strips on the sheet about 1 inch apart. Drizzle on the lemon juice and sea-son with the remaining 2 teaspoons fresh (or ½ teaspoon of the dried) oregano. Bake for 2 to 3 minutes, until the fish is just cooked through.

6. Mound the porcini on 4 warmed plates. Arrange the fish and overlapping potato slices attractively around the mushrooms and serve immediately.
—Umberto Bombana, Pazzia,
Los Angeles

HOTEL PALUMBO'S BAKED STRIPED BASS

🍷 Southern Italian white, such as Corvo Bianco or Fiano di Avellino

4 Servings

6 tablespoons olive oil
1 whole striped bass (about 3 pounds)
or other firm-fleshed white fish
½ teaspoon salt
¼ teaspoon freshly ground pepper
2 garlic cloves, crushed
2 sprigs of parsley
5 sprigs of fresh mint
2 sprigs of fresh oregano or ½ teaspoon
dried
¼ cup dry white wine

1. Preheat the oven to 425°. Pour the oil into a large, nonreactive, ovenproof skillet and place over high heat until hot, about 3 minutes.

2. Meanwhile, rub the inside of the fish with the salt and pepper. Stuff with the garlic, parsley, mint and oregano. Pat the fish dry on paper towels.

3. Place the fish in the hot oil and cook until the bottom is browned, about 1 minute. Turn the fish over and brown on the second side,

87

about 1 minute. Remove from the heat.

4. Add the white wine and tightly cover the skillet with aluminum foil. Bake for 15 minutes, or until the fish is opaque and firm to the touch. To serve, fillet the fish and spoon some of the cooking liquid over each portion.

—Hotel Palumbo, Ravello, Italy

FENNEL-SCENTED GRILLED TROUT

At Al Forno, the trout and fennel are grilled over a medium-hot charcoal fire.

4 Servings

2 medium fennel bulbs
    (about 1 pound each), trimmed,
    feathery tops reserved
About 3 tablespoons fruity extra-virgin
    olive oil
2 teaspoons coarse (kosher) salt
4 whole trout (10 to 12 ounces each)
2 teaspoons Ricard or other anise-
    flavored aperitif
Lemon wedges

1. Prepare a charcoal fire or preheat the broiler. Slice the fennel bulbs lengthwise ¼ inch thick. Brush lightly with oil and sprinkle with 1 teaspoon of the salt.

2. Brush the trout inside and out with oil and sprinkle all over with the remaining 1 teaspoon salt. Drizzle ½ teaspoon of the Ricard into each cavity, then stuff each fish with the reserved fennel tops.

3. Grill or broil the trout and fennel for about 4 minutes a side, until the fish is browned outside and just flakes and the fennel is tender. Drizzle each fish with ½ teaspoon of the oil and serve with the lemon wedges.

—George Germon and Johanne Killeen, Al Forno, Providence, Rhode Island

GIAMBOTTA OF SQUASH AND KOHLRABI WITH TILEFISH

Instead of tilefish, you can try cod, salmon or pompano, either fillets, whole small fish or bigger fish cut into large pieces.

❦ Flavorful white, such as Corvo

4 to 6 Servings

1 cup chopped parsley
1½ pounds tilefish fillets or steaks
½ pound red potatoes, cut into
    1-inch pieces
2 large strips of lemon zest
½ cup extra-virgin olive oil
1 large piece of smoky bacon rind
    (8 by 4 inches) or 2 small smoked
    ham hocks
2 large leeks (white and tender green),
    thinly sliced
1 small celery root (celeriac), cut into
    ½-inch pieces
3 celery ribs, cut on the diagonal into
    ½-inch slices
4 small kohlrabi, peeled and cut into
    small wedges
6 garlic cloves, chopped
3 to 4 sprigs of fresh thyme or
    1 teaspoon dried
Pinch of crushed hot red pepper
2 imported bay leaves
1½ teaspoons salt
1 pound yellow summer squash, cut
    into 1-inch pieces

88

½ small spaghetti squash—peeled, seeded and cut into ½-inch cubes (optional)
2 tablespoons white wine vinegar

1. Set aside ¼ cup of the parsley and the fish. Combine all of the remaining ingredients in a large, heavy nonreactive pot. Add 1 cup of water. Cover and cook over moderately high heat, stirring occasionally and maintaining a slow boil, until the potatoes are tender, about 30 minutes. Remove and discard the bay leaves and bacon rind. (*The recipe can be prepared several days ahead. Let cool completely, then cover and refrigerate. Reheat before proceeding.*)

2. Place the fish on top of the vegetables, cover and cook over moderately high heat for 5 minutes. Check the fish for doneness and recover and cook for a few more minutes if necessary. Sprinkle with the reserved ¼ cup parsley just before serving.

—*Anne Disrude*

TUSCAN BEANS WITH TUNA, PANCETTA AND LEMON

This is the most Tuscan of all dishes—it combines our love of beans with cooking in terra-cotta in a wood-fired brick oven. The beans can be eaten on their own as a vegetable or served over a slice of Tuscan bread that has been toasted and then rubbed with garlic.

🍷 The strong, salty flavors of this hearty dish would be set off by a simple refreshing Italian white, such as Antinori Galestro from Tuscany or Mastroberardino Plinius from Campania.

8 Servings

2 cups dried white beans (12 ounces), rinsed and picked over
¼ cup olive oil
*12 large sage leaves, fresh or preserved in salt**
4 large garlic cloves
¼ pound thinly sliced pancetta or prosciutto, cut into 1-inch pieces
½ teaspoon salt
2 tablespoons fresh lemon juice
1 can (6½ ounces) tuna packed in olive oil, drained
Freshly ground pepper
**Available at Italian markets*

1. In a large bowl, soak the beans overnight in cold water to cover. Alternatively, place the beans in a medium saucepan with cold water to cover and bring to a boil over high heat. Cover and set aside for 1 hour.

2. Preheat the oven to 400°. Drain the beans and rinse well. In a medium casserole, combine the beans with the oil, sage, garlic, pancetta and salt. Cover tightly and bake for about 1½ hours, stirring occasionally, until the beans are tender. Remove from the oven. (*The recipe can be prepared to this point up to 2 days ahead. Reheat before proceeding.*)

3. Stir the lemon juice and tuna into the beans and bake uncovered for 10 minutes longer. Season with pepper to taste and serve hot.

—*Giuliano Bugialli*

SIMPLE TUSCAN SUPPER

Crostini with Pea Puree (p. 46)

Tuscan Beans with Tuna, Pancetta and Lemon (p. 89)

Green Salad with Walnut Oil Vinaigrette

🍷 *Italian white, such as Antinori Galestro or Mastroberardino*

Assorted Cheeses and Fruits

Marinated Cucumbers (p. 190)

Grappa

BABY CLAMS, LIVORNO STYLE

Livorno (Leghorn) has been Tuscany's main seaport since the silting up of Pisa's harbor. As with many port towns, its cooking reflects outside influences and employs the widest range of spices and flavorings of any town in the region. Livorno is especially known for its spicy dishes made with an abundance of crushed red pepper, such as the native fish stew called *cacciucco*. The wonderful tiny Mediterranean clams are almost always cooked and served in the shell, even when combined with pasta or, as in this dish, with eggs.

6 Servings

2 *pounds small clams, such as littlenecks or razor clams*
1 *lemon, halved*
¼ *teaspoon coarse (kosher) salt*
½ *cup olive oil*
1 *small red onion, finely chopped*
1 *large garlic clove, minced*
1 *pound ripe plum tomatoes, peeled and seeded, or 1 can (28 ounces) Italian peeled tomatoes, drained and seeded*
Salt *and freshly ground black pepper*
About ¼ *teaspoon crushed hot red pepper*
2 *eggs*
¼ *cup coarsely chopped flat-leaf parsley*

1. Wash the clams very well and scrub if necessary. Place the clams in a bowl of cold water to cover. Add the lemon and coarse salt and let soak for 30 minutes.

2. In a large nonreactive skillet, warm the oil over moderate heat. Add the onion and garlic and cook, stirring occasionally, until slightly softened, 2 to 3 minutes.

3. Cut the tomatoes into large pieces and add them to the skillet. Reduce the heat to low and cook for 5 minutes, stirring occasionally. Season with salt, black pepper and hot pepper to taste.

4. Drain the clams and rinse well under cold running water. Add them to the skillet, cover and increase the heat to moderately high. Cook, stirring occasionally, until the clams open, 2 to 3 minutes depending on their size. Discard any clams that do not open. Meanwhile, in a medium bowl, lightly beat the eggs with a pinch of salt.

5. Remove the skillet from the heat. Sprinkle the parsley over the clams, pour in the eggs and mix well until thoroughly blended. Return the skillet to moderate heat and cook, stirring frequently, just until hot. Serve immediately.
—Giuliano Bugialli

SPICY CLAM ROAST WITH SAUSAGE AND FENNEL

George Germon and Johanne Killeen are known for their inventive, hearty dishes, such as this one from Al Forno.

6 Servings

½ *pound hot Italian sausage*
½ *pound chorizo sausage*
4 *tablespoons unsalted butter*
2 *medium onions, halved and thinly sliced lengthwise*

1 *large fennel bulb—halved, cored and
    thinly sliced lengthwise*
2 *large garlic cloves, minced*
1 *teaspoon ground fennel seeds*
½ *teaspoon crushed hot red pepper*
¾ *cup dry white wine*
1½ *cups drained plum tomatoes (from
    a 28-ounce can)*
48 *littleneck clams, cleaned and
    scrubbed*
Gremolata Mashed Potatoes (p. 193)
3 *scallions, thinly sliced lengthwise,
    for garnish*

1. In a large saucepan of boiling water, cook the sausages over moderate heat for 5 minutes. Drain and let cool. Slice the sausages crosswise ½ inch thick. Set aside.

2. In a nonreactive stockpot, melt the butter over moderately low heat. Add the onions, fennel, garlic, fennel seeds and hot pepper. Cover and cook, stirring occasionally, until the vegetables are soft and lightly browned, about 20 minutes.

3. Increase the heat to high, add the wine and bring just to a boil. Add the tomatoes, crushing them with your hands and bring to a boil. Reduce the heat to moderate and simmer, stirring occasionally, until the sauce thickens slightly, about 15 minutes.

4. Stir the sausages into the tomato mixture. Increase the heat to high, stir in the clams and cover. After 5 minutes, remove all clams that have opened, and transfer to a medium bowl. Continue to cook, covered, until all of the clams have opened. Check frequently for open clams; discard any clams that have not opened after 15 minutes. Increase the heat to high and boil the mixture until it thickens slightly, about 5 minutes.

5. To serve, place a generous scoop of the Gremolata Mashed Potatoes in the center of 6 large serving plates. Arrange the clams around the potatoes. Spoon the sausage and fennel mixture over the clams, garnish with the scallions and serve immediately.
—George Germon and Johanne Killeen, Al Forno, Providence, Rhode Island

---

SHRIMP CAPRI

🍷 Gavi dei Gavi, such as La Scolca

4 Servings

⅓ *cup olive oil*
3 *garlic cloves*
2 *small dried hot red peppers, split
    and seeded*
1 *pound large shrimp, shelled and
    deveined*
1 *tablespoon drained capers, rinsed*
12 *brine-cured black olives, halved
    and pitted*
12 *cherry tomatoes, halved*
½ *cup dry white wine*
1 *tablespoon fresh lemon juice*
1 *tablespoon chopped parsley*
½ *teaspoon salt*
⅛ *teaspoon freshly ground
    black pepper*
3 *tablespoons unsalted butter*

1. In a large skillet, heat the oil. Add the garlic and hot peppers and sauté over moderately high heat until the garlic is golden and the peppers are dark brown. Discard the garlic and peppers.

2. Add the shrimp to the hot oil and sauté for 1 minute. Add the capers, olives and tomatoes and

91

cook for 1 minute, or until the tomatoes are softened but still hold their shape.

3. Add the wine, lemon juice, parsley, salt and black pepper. Boil for 1 minute. Add the butter, 1 tablespoon at a time, stirring gently until blended.

—*Margaret and G. Franco Romagnoli*

LOBSTER FRICASSEE WITH ARTICHOKES

At San Domenico, this luscious lobster dish is made with quartered baby artichokes that are added to the pan with the carrots and onions right at the start.

❢ The lobster and mild butter sauce call for a rich, complex white such as Edoardo Valentini Trebbiano d'Abruzzo or, if you prefer, a white Burgundy or California Chardonnay.

4 Servings

4 *large artichokes*
2 *ounces pancetta, minced*
1 *stick (4 ounces) plus 2½ tablespoons cold unsalted butter, cut into tablespoons*
1 *large onion, halved lengthwise and thinly sliced*
2 *medium carrots, thinly sliced*
2 *sprigs of parsley plus 1 tablespoon minced parsley*
2 *tablespoons fresh lemon juice*
2 *boiled lobsters (1½ pounds each), meat removed and cut into 1-inch chunks (about 1½ cups of meat weighing approximately ½ pound)*
1 *tablespoon chopped fresh tarragon*
¼ *teaspoon salt*
½ *teaspoon freshly ground pepper*

1. Trim off the stems of the artichokes. In a large steamer basket, steam the artichokes until tender, about 20 minutes. Let cool.

2. In a large saucepan, sauté the pancetta in 2½ tablespoons of the butter over moderately high heat until the fat begins to render, about 2 minutes. Reduce the heat to moderately low and cook until the pancetta is browned, about 7 minutes longer. Add the onion, carrots and parsley sprigs and cook until the onion has softened, about 10 minutes.

3. Meanwhile, remove the leaves from the artichokes and reserve for another use. Scoop out the hairy chokes. Cut the bottoms into 1-inch chunks and add to the onion and carrot mixture with 1 cup of water. Bring to a simmer over moderate heat and cook until the carrots are tender, about 10 minutes longer.

4. Strain, reserving the vegetables and liquid. Discard the parsley sprigs. Set the liquid aside for 10 minutes, then skim off as much fat as possible. Pour the liquid into a medium nonreactive saucepan and add the lemon juice. Bring to a boil over moderately high heat and boil until reduced to ¼ cup, about 5 minutes. Reduce the heat to low and whisk in the remaining stick of butter, 1 tablespoon at a time, until it is thoroughly incorporated and the sauce is creamy.

5. Add the reserved onion and carrots and the lobster, artichokes, minced parsley, tarragon, salt and pepper. Warm just until heated through. Serve in heated soup plates.

—*San Domenico, New York City*

Veal Croquettes with Lemon (page 62) served with fresh artichokes.

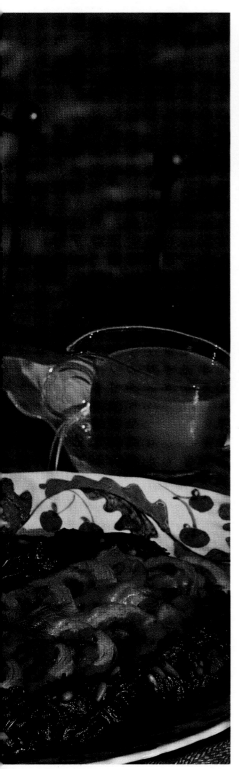

Far left (clockwise from lower left): Risotto Mold with Prosciutto (page 210) filled with Veal Rolls with Peas (page 61); Asparagus with Parmesan Cheese (page 189); Chicken Breasts with Fennel Sauce (page 80) on a bed of Spinach with Raisins and Pine Nuts (page 194).

Top, Braised Veal Shanks Milanese (page 58) with Saffron Risotto (page 198). Above, Boiled Veal Shanks with Green Sauce (page 59) and Tuscan Focaccia (page 174).

Above, Baby
Clams, Livorno
Style (*page* 90).
At left, Tuscan
Beans with Tuna,
Pancetta and
Lemon (*page* 89).

PEPPER, LEEK AND CELERY ROOT GIAMBOTTA WITH EGGS

Try to use a shallow casserole for this giambotta. Since removing the eggs intact can be a little tricky, use a large spoon.

6 Servings

3 Italian frying peppers, cut into
    1-inch pieces
1 red bell pepper, cut into 1-inch pieces
2 leeks (white and tender green), sliced
1 small celery root (celeriac), cut into
    1-inch pieces
1 large parsley root or parsnip, cut into
    ½-inch pieces
1 fennel bulb, cut into ¼-inch strips
2 carrots, cut on the diagonal into
    ½-inch pieces
1 small rutabaga, peeled and cut into
    ½-inch pieces
1 zucchini, cut into 1-inch pieces
2 celery ribs, cut on the diagonal into
    ½-inch pieces
½ small butternut squash, cut into
    1-inch chunks
6 garlic cloves, chopped
½ cup extra-virgin olive oil
2 tablespoons white wine vinegar
2 imported bay leaves
1 teaspoon thyme
1 teaspoon oregano
1 teaspoon fennel seed
¼ teaspoon crushed hot red pepper
1½ teaspoons salt
6 eggs
Freshly ground black pepper
¼ cup chopped fresh mint

1. In a large heavy flameproof casserole, combine all the ingredients except the eggs, black pepper and mint. Add 1 cup of water, cover and cook over moderately high heat, maintaining a slow boil and stirring occasionally, until the rutabaga is soft, about 30 minutes. Remove and discard the bay leaves. (*The recipe can be prepared several days ahead to this point. Let cool, then cover and refrigerate. Reheat before proceeding.*)

2. Use the back of a ladle to make 6 small indentations in the vegetables. Crack an egg into each, cover and cook over moderately high heat until set, about 5 minutes. Sprinkle with salt and pepper to taste and scatter the chopped mint over the top.
—Anne Disrude

GIANT FRITTATA

12 Servings

2 ounces dried mushrooms
2 cups boiling water
2 ounces sun-dried tomatoes
¼ cup plus 2 tablespoons olive oil
1 pound baking potatoes, peeled and
    cut into ½-inch cubes
½ cup dry white wine
2½ teaspoons salt
6 tablespoons unsalted butter
3 bunches of scallions (white and 2
    inches of the green), thinly sliced
2 medium garlic cloves, minced
½ cup pine nuts (pignoli)
½ pound boiled ham, cut into 1½-by-
    ⅛-inch julienne strips
½ pound sharp Cheddar cheese,
    shredded
24 eggs
½ teaspoon freshly ground pepper
1 tablespoon oregano
½ cup freshly grated Parmesan cheese
½ cup minced parsley
Pimientos and black olives, for garnish

1. Soak the dried mushrooms in the boiling water until softened,

about 1 hour. Drain the mushrooms, squeeze dry and chop coarsely.

2. Meanwhile, soak the sun-dried tomatoes in ¼ cup of the olive oil for 1 hour. Reserving the oil, drain the tomatoes and chop coarsely.

3. In a large saucepan of boiling salted water, cook the potatoes until just tender, 8 to 10 minutes; do not overcook. Drain well and transfer to a large bowl. While still hot, toss with the wine and ½ teaspoon of the salt.

4. In a 12-inch ovenproof skillet, melt 4 tablespoons of the butter in 1 tablespoon oil over moderate heat. Add the scallions and garlic and sauté until softened, about 7 minutes.

5. Add the pine nuts and sauté until lightly browned, about 5 minutes. Add the ham strips and cook for 5 minutes longer. Add this mixture to the bowl of potatoes; set the skillet aside.

6. Add the Cheddar cheese, chopped mushrooms and tomatoes with their reserved tomato oil to the potato mixture; toss well. Set this filling aside.

7. Preheat the oven to 450°. In a large bowl, beat 12 of the eggs with 1 teaspoon of the salt, ¼ teaspoon of the pepper and ½ tablespoon of the oregano. Using the reserved skillet, melt the remaining 2 tablespoons butter in the remaining 1 tablespoon oil over high heat. When the foam subsides, add the egg mixture. Cook until the omelet begins to set at the edges. Lift one side slightly and tilt the pan so that the uncooked egg runs underneath. Continue to cook, repeating this process, until most of the egg is set. Remove the skillet from the heat.

8. Spread the reserved filling evenly over the omelet. In a bowl, beat the remaining 12 eggs with the remaining 1 teaspoon salt, ¼ teaspoon pepper and ½ tablespoon oregano. Pour the egg mixture over the omelet filling. Place the skillet in the top third of the oven and bake for about 30 minutes, until the top layer of egg is set.

9. Invert the frittata onto a large heated platter. Sprinkle on the Parmesan cheese and parsley. Garnish with pimientos and olives.
—*W. Peter Prestcott*

PASTA FRITTATA

A well-seasoned ovenproof skillet, preferably cast iron, or nonstick skillet is best for this frittata. Any leftover pasta will work well in the recipe.

6 to 8 Servings

½ ounce dried porcini mushrooms (about ½ cup)
½ cup uncooked elbow macaroni or 1¼ cups cooked pasta
2 teaspoons olive oil
2½ tablespoons unsalted butter
1 large onion, chopped
10 eggs
4 large plum tomatoes—peeled, seeded and chopped
2 tablespoons heavy cream
1 teaspoon salt
1 teaspoon freshly ground pepper
1 tablespoon chopped fresh marjoram
4 ounces Gruyère cheese, grated (1¼ cups)
Marjoram leaves, for garnish

1. Preheat the oven to 400°. In a small bowl, soak the dried mushrooms in ½ cup of boiling water

until softened, about 20 minutes. Squeeze dry, discard any tough stems and chop coarsely. Set aside.

2. Meanwhile, cook the macaroni in a medium saucepan of boiling salted water until tender but firm, about 8 minutes. Drain, toss with the oil and set aside.

3. In a large ovenproof skillet, melt 1½ tablespoons of the butter over moderate heat. Add the onion, reduce the heat to low and cook, stirring occasionally, until golden and soft, about 12 minutes.

4. Meanwhile, in a large bowl, beat the eggs very lightly just to break the yolks. Stir in the tomatoes, mushrooms, heavy cream, salt, pepper and chopped marjoram. Beat the mixture briefly to blend the ingredients evenly. Stir in the reserved pasta.

5. When the onions are ready, increase the heat to high and add the remaining 1 tablespoon butter. Heat until the butter is almost smoking, then pour in the egg mixture, stirring just to combine the onion with the egg. Leave the mixture on the heat until it starts to bubble around the edges, about 30 seconds. Remove from the burner and place the skillet in the center of the oven.

6. Bake until the frittata is just set, about 30 minutes. Return the skillet to the stovetop and place over high heat for about 10 seconds, shaking the pan to loosen the frittata; run a spatula around the edges of necessary. Using a spatula, slide the frittata onto a large ovenproof serving dish.

7. Preheat the broiler. Sprinkle the grated cheese on top of the frittata and place it under the broiler 6 to 8 inches away from the heat. Broil until the cheese melts, about 10 seconds. Let the frittata stand at room temperature for at least 5 minutes before cutting into wedges. Serve warm or at room temperature. Garnish each serving with a sprinkling of marjoram leaves.
—*Marcia Kiesel*

CAPELLINI FRITTATA WITH PANCETTA AND PEAS

Anthony's features a panoply of fresh, regional specialties, like this golden brown frittata with smoky ham and peas. This can be prepared in advance and warmed later, or served at room temperature.
🍷 A good California Chardonnay, such as Clos du Bois, or the lively Pio Cesare Cortese di Gavi

2 to 4 Servings

6 *slices of pancetta or bacon (about 3 ounces), cut into ¼-inch squares*
¼ *pound capellini, broken into 2-inch pieces (about 1 cup)*
1 *cup fresh or frozen peas*
4 *eggs, lightly beaten*
1 *cup shredded whole-milk mozzarella cheese (about ¼ pound)*
¼ *teaspoon salt*
¼ *teaspoon freshly ground black pepper*
⅛ *teaspoon crushed hot red pepper*
⅓ *cup freshly grated Parmesan cheese*
2 to 4 *tablespoons extra-virgin olive oil*
3 *garlic cloves, crushed through a press*

1. In a small skillet, cook the pancetta over moderate heat, stirring occasionally, until browned and crisp, about 5 minutes. Remove

99

ITALIAN-STYLE BRUNCH
Bellinis (p. 29)
Assorted Olives
Rosemary Grissini (p. 176)
Capellini Frittata with Pancetta and Peas (p. 99)
Baked Tomato Halves with Brown Sugar, Mustard and Basil
Fresh Peach Slices with Marsala
Cappuccino

with a slotted spoon and drain on paper towels.

2. In a medium saucepan of boiling salted water, cook the pasta, stirring frequently, until al dente, about 2 minutes; drain well.

3. In a small saucepan over medium heat, cook fresh peas 3 to 5 minutes; thaw frozen under hot running water.

4. In a medium bowl. combine the cooked capellini, eggs, mozzarella, salt, black pepper and hot pepper. Mix well.

5. In a small bowl, toss together the pancetta, peas and Parmesan cheese.

6. In a large nonstick skillet, heat 2 tablespoons of the oil. Add the garlic and sauté over moderately high heat until fragrant but not browned, about 1 minute. Pour half the egg and capellini mixture into the skillet; top with the pancetta, peas and cheese. Cover with the remaining egg and capellini mixture. Cook over moderate heat, pressing down lightly with a spatula, until the bottom is golden brown, about 5 minutes.

7. Invert the frittata onto a large plate. If the pan is dry, add another 1 to 2 tablespoons oil. Slide the frittata back into the pan and cook until the second side is golden brown, 3 to 5 minutes. Serve warm or at room temperature.

—*Bruce McMillan, Anthony's, Houston*

PEPPER AND SPAGHETTI FRITTATA

6 to 8 Servings

6 tablespoons extra-virgin olive oil
2 medium onions, chopped
5 medium garlic cloves, minced
10 bell peppers, chopped (about 4 cups)
⅛ teaspoon sugar
½ teaspoon oregano
1 teaspoon salt
¼ teaspoon freshly ground black pepper
6 ounces spaghetti, cooked and drained
8 eggs
½ cup freshly grated Parmesan cheese
¼ cup minced parsley

1. In a large ovenproof skillet, heat the olive oil. Add the onions, garlic and bell peppers, and sauté over moderately high heat, stirring frequently, until the vegetables begin to brown, about 30 minutes. Season with the sugar, oregano, ½ teaspoon of the salt and ⅛ teaspoon of the black pepper.

2. Preheat the oven to 350°. Add the cooked spaghetti to the skillet and toss well. Cook, stirring occasionally, until the pasta is lightly browned, about 10 minutes.

3. In a medium bowl, beat the eggs with ¼ cup of water and the remaining ½ teaspoon salt and ⅛ teaspoon black pepper. Stir in ¼ cup of the cheese and 2 tablespoons of the parsley.

4. Pour the egg mixture over the pasta and stir with a fork to distribute evenly. Cook without stirring until the eggs are set around the edges. Place in the oven

and bake until the eggs are set, about 10 minutes.

5. Slide the frittata onto a platter and cut into wedges. Toss together the remaining ¼ cup cheese and 2 tablespoons parsley and pass separately.
—Anne Disrude

AVOCADO FRITTATA

1 Serving

½ avocado, cut into 1-inch chunks
½ teaspoon fresh lemon juice
¼ teaspoon salt
¼ cup crumbled goat cheese, such as
    Montrachet or Bucheron, crumbled
    (about 1 ounce)
¼ teaspoon rosemary, crushed
4 oil-cured black olives, pitted and cut
    into slivers
3 eggs
¼ teaspoon coarsely ground
    black pepper
1½ teaspoons olive oil

1. Preheat the broiler. In a small bowl, toss the avocado with the lemon juice and salt. Add the goat cheese, rosemary and olives; toss gently.

2. Beat the eggs with the pepper and a pinch of salt.

3. Set an ovenproof omelet pan or heavy medium skillet over moderately high heat and add the oil. When the oil is hot but not smoking, add the eggs. Cook for about 1½ minutes, stirring once or twice, until the bottom is set and the top is still slightly runny. Remove from the heat and sprinkle the avocado mixture evenly over the eggs.

4. Broil about 4 inches from the heat until the top of the frittata is set and the edges slightly browned, about 2 minutes.
—Anne Disrude

EGG WHITE FRITTATA WITH CARROTS

In Tuscany (in the pre-cholesterol-conscious days), aristocratic families would proudly insist on using only the yolks of eggs, which were considered fancier than the whites. Poor people ate the leftover egg whites, which they turned into remarkable dishes, thus managing to avoid the strokes and heart attacks that plagued the rich. A whole category of frittatas evolved based on egg whites, vegetables and herbs.

4 Servings

1 pound carrots, trimmed and
    scrubbed but not peeled
½ teaspoon coarse (kosher) salt
¼ cup olive oil
1 medium garlic clove, minced
¼ cup minced flat-leaf parsley
½ teaspoon salt
¼ teaspoon freshly ground
    black pepper
Pinch of crushed hot
    red pepper
6 egg whites

1. In a medium bowl, cover the carrots with cold water. Set aside for 30 minutes.

2. In a large saucepan, combine 4 cups of water and the coarse salt and bring to a boil over moderately high heat. Add the carrots and

cook for 8 minutes; drain and refresh under cold water. Cut the carrots into ½-inch dice.

3. In a medium skillet, heat 3 tablespoons of the oil over moderate heat. Add the garlic and parsley and cook for 30 seconds. Add the carrots, salt, black pepper and hot pepper. Cook for 10 minutes, stirring occasionally, to blend the flavors. Set aside to cool completely.

4. In an 8-inch nonstick skillet, heat ½ tablespoon of the remaining oil over moderately high heat. Meanwhile, in a medium bowl, lightly beat the egg whites. Stir in the carrot mixture.

5. When the oil is hot, add half of the frittata mixture to the skillet and cook until it just begins to set around the edges, about 2 minutes. Reduce the heat to low and cook until the underside is set and the frittata slides in the pan, about 2 minutes longer. Using a spatula, flip the frittata and cook on the second side for 2 minutes more. Transfer the frittata to a plate and cut into 4 wedges. Repeat with the remaining ½ tablespoon oil and frittata mixture. Serve 2 wedges per person.
—*Giuliano Bugialli*

PASTA

PASTA

CHRISTMAS EVE LASAGNA FROM PIEDMONT

This simple pasta dish has been made in Italian country kitchens for years. Fresh lasagna noodles are best, but if you use packaged noodles, be sure that they are sauced very quickly after they are cooked and drained.

6 Servings

1 stick (4 ounces) unsalted butter
8 anchovy fillets, preserved in oil,
   drained and finely chopped
2 large garlic cloves, crushed through a
   press
1 pound lasagna noodles
1 cup freshly grated Parmesan cheese
   (about ¼ pound)

1. In a large saucepan, melt the butter over moderate heat. Add the anchovies and garlic and cook, mashing the anchovies with a spoon, until the garlic is softened but not browned, 3 to 5 minutes.

2. In a large pot of boiling salted water, cook the pasta (fresh lasagna noodles will cook in about 1 minute, dried in about 10). Remove with a slotted spoon and drain very quickly. Toss immediately in a large bowl with ¼ cup of the Parmesan cheese to coat their surface. Quickly transfer the noodles to the anchovy butter sauce and toss to coat well. Serve everyone a few lasagna noodles on well-warmed plates. Pass the remaining Parmesan cheese on the side.

—Carol Field

COUNTRY-STYLE PASTA WITH RICOTTA

Adding some of the pasta cooking water to ricotta creates a sauce that is less rich than cream, yet clings nicely to the pasta. A bit of bacon and onion contribute extra flavor. ♥ This creamy pasta dish, with its mild, complementary flavors of cheese, bacon and onion, makes a perfect foil for fruity but refined Italian reds, such as Antinori Pèppoli Chianti Classico or Frescobaldi Tenuta di Pomino.

4 to 6 Servings

2 thick slices of bacon, coarsely chopped
¼ cup extra-virgin olive oil
1 medium onion, chopped
1 pound part-skim ricotta cheese
¼ cup coarsely chopped flat-leaf parsley
¼ cup coarsely chopped fresh basil
1 tablespoon finely chopped scallion
   green
1⅓ cups freshly grated Parmesan
   cheese
½ teaspoon salt
½ teaspoon freshly ground pepper
1 pound penne rigate

1. In a large heavy skillet, cook the bacon over moderate heat, stirring occasionally, until it is lightly browned and the fat is rendered, about 5 minutes. Add the oil and onion. Reduce the heat to low and cook until the onion is softened and translucent, about 8 minutes. Remove from the heat and set aside.

2. In a medium bowl, beat together the ricotta, parsley, basil, scallion green and ⅓ cup of the Parmesan cheese with a wooden spoon. Add to the cooked onion and bacon and season with the salt and pepper. Mix well.

3. Cook the pasta in a large pot

of boiling salted water until al dente, about 10 minutes. Meanwhile, add ¼ to ½ cup of the pasta cooking water to the ricotta sauce. Mix well.

4. Drain the cooked pasta and immediately transfer to a shallow pasta serving bowl. Quickly reheat the ricotta sauce if necessary, add to the pasta and toss to mix. Pass the remaining 1 cup Parmesan cheese on the side.
—Evan Kleiman and Viana LaPlace

SPAGHETTINI WITH ARUGULA

4 to 6 Servings

8 to 12 cups fresh arugula
  (see Note), large stem ends removed
  (4 to 6 bunches)
1 pound spaghettini
2 teaspoons minced garlic
¼ cup extra-virgin olive oil
¼ cup red wine vinegar
1 teaspoon salt
½ teaspoon freshly ground pepper

1. Rinse the arugula and drain off all moisture. Place in a large salad bowl.

2. Cook the pasta in a large pot of rapidly boiling salted water until al dente, 5 to 8 minutes. Drain well and add to the arugula.

3. Combine the garlic, oil and vinegar and toss with the pasta and arugula. Season with the salt and pepper.

NOTE: Other salad greens may be used such as Bibb, watercress or curly endive.
—Edward Giobbi

SPAGHETTI ALLA SAN PIETRO

🍷 Italian Sauvignon Blanc, such as Jermann

2 Servings

1 medium artichoke
½ lemon
4 tablespoons unsalted butter
3 tablespoons olive oil, preferably
  extra-virgin
2 medium garlic cloves, smashed
8 asparagus spears
½ pound spaghetti
2 tablespoons chopped flat-leaf
  parsley
1 teaspoon salt
½ teaspoon freshly ground pepper
Sprigs of flat-leaf parsley, for garnish
½ cup freshly grated Parmesan cheese

1. With a large stainless steel knife, cut the stem off the artichoke; rub the cut areas with the lemon half to prevent discoloration. Bend back and pull off the tough outer leaves. Cut off the top third of the artichoke. With scissors, snip off the sharp thorns from the tops of the remaining leaves.

2. Squeeze the lemon juice into a nonreactive saucepan filled with salted water. Bring to a boil, add the trimmed artichoke and cook, covered, until the tip of a knife easily pierces the bottom, 15 to 25 minutes; drain well. Set aside, loosely covered to keep warm.

3. Meanwhile, place the butter, oil and garlic in a small heavy saucepan over low heat. Cook until the garlic is softened and aromatic but not browned, about 10 minutes.

4. In a skillet of boiling salted water, cook the asparagus until just tender and bright green, about 3 minutes; drain well. Set aside loosely covered to keep warm.

5. While the vegetables and garlic sauce are cooking, bring a large pot of salted water to a boil. Add the spaghetti and cook until al dente, about 10 minutes; drain.

6. Place the drained cooked spaghetti in a large heated bowl. Reserving 1 tablespoon of the garlic sauce, strain the remainder over the pasta; toss until coated. Add the chopped parsley, salt and pepper and toss again.

7. Spread apart the inner leaves of the artichoke and scoop out the choke with a small spoon. Arrange the spaghetti on a large round platter. Place the artichoke in the center and arrange the spears of asparagus around it like the spokes of a wheel. Pour the reserved 1 tablespoon sauce into the center of the artichoke. Garnish the platter with sprigs of parsley. At the table, divide the artichoke in half. Pass the grated cheese and a pepper mill separately.

—Hotel San Pietro, Positano, Italy

TAGLIATELLE WITH ASPARAGUS

The asparagus can be blanched early in the day, but be sure not to overcook them so that they will maintain their bright green color. The noodles can be store-bought or your own freshly made.

6 Servings

1 *pound asparagus, peeled and cut into 1-inch pieces*
1 *stick (4 ounces) unsalted butter*
¼ *pound thinly sliced prosciutto, cut into thin strips*
⅔ *cup drained canned Italian peeled tomatoes, chopped*
½ *teaspoon salt*
1 *teaspoon freshly ground pepper*
1 *pound egg noodles*
½ *cup freshly grated Parmesan cheese*

1. Cook the asparagus in a large pot of boiling salted water until just tender, about 3 minutes. Rinse under cold running water to cool; drain well.

2. In a large skillet, melt 6 tablespoons of the butter over low heat. Add the prosciutto and cook for 2 minutes. Add the tomatoes, salt and pepper and simmer until the sauce is slightly thickened, about 5 minutes; remove from the heat.

3. In a large pot of boiling salted water, cook the noodles until al dente, about 8 minutes for dry and 2 minutes for fresh. Drain the noodles and return to the pot.

4. Add the asparagus to the tomato sauce and reheat. Pour the sauce over the noodles, add the remaining 2 tablespoons butter

and the Parmesan cheese and toss well. Transfer to a platter and serve at once.
—Nancy Verde Barr

TAGLIATELLE WITH CABBAGE AND SAGE

This *pasta alla valtellinese* calls for fresh pasta, but you can use dried. If you do, cook the pasta until almost tender to the bite before adding the greens to the water and proceeding.

♟ Nera Valgella or Dessilani Gattinara

4 Servings

Salt
¾ pound fresh tagliatelle or fettuccine
¼ medium head of red cabbage, thinly sliced crosswise (about 2 cups)
¼ medium head of Nappa cabbage, thinly sliced crosswise (about 2 cups)
¼ medium bunch of swiss chard, sliced crosswise ½ inch thick (about 2 cups)
1 stick (4 ounces) unsalted butter
4 garlic cloves, thinly sliced
8 fresh sage leaves, thinly sliced lengthwise or ¼ teaspoon rubbed sage (see Note), plus 4 sprigs of fresh sage, for garnish
Freshly cracked pepper
⅓ cup freshly grated Parmesan cheese

1. In a large pot, bring enough water for the pasta to a rolling boil, add salt and return to a boil again. Stir in the pasta and return to a boil. Stir in the red and Nappa cabbages and the swiss chard. Cook until the pasta is al dente, about 2 minutes. Do not overcook. Drain the pasta and vegetables thoroughly and place in a large serving bowl.
2. Meanwhile, in a medium skil-

let, melt the butter over moderate heat. Add the garlic and sage leaves and cook until the garlic is golden, about 4 minutes.
3. Pour the hot butter over the pasta and vegetables, season with salt and pepper and toss to mix well. Sprinkle the Parmesan cheese on top. Garnish with the sage sprigs and serve at once.
NOTE: If fresh sage is unavailable, be sure to use dried sage leaves or rubbed sage—available in the spice rack of most supermarkets—not powdered sage.
—Constance and Rosario Del Nero

PASTA SHELLS WITH CAULIFLOWER SAUCE

The combination of anchovies, raisins and pine nuts used in this sauce is a typical Moorish-inspired dish from Sicily. The use of only 2 tablespoons of tomato paste is the characteristically light way in which that ingredient is treated in southern Italy. Serve this sauce with pasta shells (conchiglie) or similar-shaped macaroni because they act as tiny catch basins for the flavorful sauce.

6 Servings

⅓ cup golden raisins
1 small head of cauliflower, broken into florets
6 tablespoons olive oil
1 large onion, coarsely chopped
2 tablespoons tomato paste dissolved in 1 cup water

107

TAGLIATELLE

Not surprisingly, the lexicon of Italian pasta names is enormous and complex. Even the subtlest change in size or shape or texture requires a new pasta term. Tagliatelle—the classic egg noodle from Bologna—on the other hand, have a straightforward, almost generic, name: Roughly translated tagliatelle means "cut noodles" (from the verb *tagliare*, to cut).

12 *anchovy fillets packed in olive oil,*
   drained, with oil reserved
⅓ *cup pine nuts (pignoli)*
1 *pound pasta shells*
1 *cup freshly grated Pecorino Romano*
   cheese (about ¼ pound)
¼ *cup chopped fresh basil and/or*
   parsley

1. Soak the raisins in lukewarm water for 15 minutes, or until softened, then drain.

2. Meanwhile, in a large pot of boiling salted water, blanch the cauliflower for 2 minutes. Drain and rinse under cold running water to stop the cooking.

3. In a large skillet, heat 3 tablespoons of the olive oil, add the onion and sauté over moderately low heat until softened and translucent but not browned, about 3 minutes. Add the dissolved tomato paste. Cover and simmer the sauce for 15 minutes.

4. In a small skillet, stir the anchovy fillets in the remaining 3 tablespoons oil over low heat until the anchovies dissolve.

5. Add the cauliflower to the onion-tomato sauce and simmer, covered, for 5 minutes. Add the anchovies, reserved anchovy oil, the pine nuts and raisins and cook until the cauliflower is tender but still holds its shape, about 10 minutes longer.

6. Cook the pasta in a large pot of boiling salted water until al dente, 8 to 10 minutes. Drain the pasta and serve topped with the sauce. Sprinkle with the cheese and basil.
—*Tom Maresca and Diane Darrow*

PENNE WITH SWEET PEPPER SAUCE

Red and yellow peppers make the most attractive presentation of this dish, but green will do.

6 Servings

2 *pounds red and/or yellow bell peppers*
¾ *cup olive oil*
⅓ *cup capers—rinsed, drained and*
   coarsely chopped
24 *oil-cured black olives, quartered*
   and pitted
3 *medium garlic cloves, minced*
½ *cup chopped flat-leaf Italian parsley*
⅔ *cup fine dry bread crumbs*
1 *teaspoon freshly ground black pepper*
1 *teaspoon oregano*
1 *pound penne, mezzani or other*
   tubular pasta

1. Preheat the oven to 425°. Roast the peppers over an open flame or broil 4 inches from the heat, turning with tongs as the skin blisters and blackens, until charred all over, about 5 minutes. Allow to cool for 1 minute; then seal in a plastic bag and let them "sweat" for 10 minutes. With your fingers, rub off the charred skin and rinse briefly under cold running water; pat dry. Remove the stems, seeds and ribs. Cut the peppers into ¼-inch strips and set aside.

2. In a large skillet, heat the oil over moderate heat. Add the bell peppers, capers, olives, garlic, parsley, bread crumbs and the black pepper. Mix well, cover, reduce the heat to low and cook for about 10 minutes, stirring occasionally. Add the oregano and set aside.

3. Cook the pasta in a large pot of boiling salted water until al dente, 8 to 10 minutes. Drain the pasta and toss with the sauce.
—*Tom Maresca and Diane Darrow*

PASTA WITH SWEET PEPPERS

This *pasta al peperone* makes an especially sweet sauce and is ideal for people who have problems with acidic foods.

🍷 Light, flavorful red, such as Montepulciano d'Abruzzo or Côtes du Rhône

4 to 6 Servings

¼ *cup olive oil*
1 *large onion, thinly sliced*
2½ *to 3 pounds red bell peppers, cut into ½-inch-wide strips*
2 *tablespoons chopped fresh basil or 1 teaspoon dried*
1 *teaspoon salt*
¼ *teaspoon freshly ground black pepper*
1 *to 1½ cups beef or chicken stock or canned broth*
1 *pound penne, ziti or farfalle (bow ties)*
¼ *cup freshly grated Parmesan cheese*
2 *to 3 tablespoons finely chopped flat-leaf parsley*

1. In a large skillet, heat the olive oil. Add the onion and peppers and cook over moderately high heat, stirring frequently, until the onion begins to brown, 10 to 15 minutes.

2. Reduce the heat to moderate and add the basil, salt and pepper. Cook for 15 minutes, or until the peppers are just tender. Remove 12 to 18 slices of pepper from the skillet and reserve. Add 1 cup of the stock to the skillet and cook for 3 minutes longer.

3. In the meantime, cook the pasta in a large saucepan of rapidly boiling salted water until al dente, 10 to 12 minutes. Drain well.

4. Pour the pepper sauce into a food processor and puree until it is the consistency of a thick tomato sauce. If the sauce is too thick, add as much of the remaining stock as necessary to thin to the desired consistency.

5. Toss the pasta with the hot sauce. Serve garnished with the reserved pepper slices, grated cheese and parsley.

NOTE: A teaspoon of fresh pesto on each portion will add to the beauty and the taste of this dish.
—*Edward Giobbi*

FUSILLI WITH GRILLED VEGETABLES

This recipe can be varied according to the vegetables in season and the amount of time you wish to spend cooking. Instead of cooking the vegetables on the grill, they can be brushed with oil, spread in a single layer on baking sheets and broiled about 4 inches from the heat.

6 to 8 Servings

4 *small zucchini, trimmed and cut lengthwise into thin slices*
4 *small, narrow Asian eggplants, stem end trimmed, cut in half lengthwise*
2 *medium red onions, cut crosswise into ½-inch slices*
3 *Belgian endives, trimmed and cut lengthwise in half*

FUSILLI

If you've ever been tempted to make the long, corkscrew-shaped pasta called fusilli at home, you should know that there is actually a piece of kitchen equipment designed for the task: A fusilli pin is a 12-inch-long steel rod, about ⅟₁₆ inch in diameter, with two pointed ends (its close resemblance to a double-ended knitting needle makes one suppose that this could be used as a substitute). To make fusilli, coil a strand of freshly made pasta around the pin, then slip it off and allow to dry.

¾ cup extra-virgin olive oil
2 tablespoons balsamic vinegar
1 tablespoon fresh lemon juice
4 garlic cloves, minced
3 tablespoons shredded fresh basil
½ cup coarsely chopped flat-leaf parsley
1 tablespoon minced fresh thyme or
    ½ teaspoon dried
12 oil-packed sun-dried tomato halves,
    cut into thin strips
¾ teaspoon salt
¼ teaspoon freshly ground pepper
1 pound fusilli or spaghetti
Freshly grated Parmesan cheese

1. Light a charcoal grill. Lightly brush the zucchini, eggplants, red onions and Belgian endives with some of the olive oil. When the coals are hot, grill the zucchini, turning once, for about 1 minute on each side, until lightly browned but still slightly firm. Transfer to a large shallow bowl.

2. Grill the eggplants, cut-side toward the heat, for about 2 minutes, until well browned. Turn and grill on the other side, just until the eggplants soften. Add the grilled eggplant to the zucchini.

3. Grill the onion slices, turning once, for about 5 minutes, until soft and translucent. Add to the other vegetables.

4. Grill the Belgian endives, turning, for about 4 minutes, until lightly browned all over and just wilted. Transfer to the bowl with the other vegetables.

5. When the grilled vegetables are cool enough to handle, cut the zucchini, eggplants and endives crosswise into thin strips. Cut the onion slices in half. Return the vegetables to the bowl and toss gently to mix.

6. In a small bowl, combine the remaining olive oil with the vinegar, lemon juice and garlic. Add the dressing to the grilled vegetables and toss gently to coat. Add the basil, parsley, thyme, sun-dried tomatoes, salt and pepper to the grilled vegetables and again toss gently. Set aside to marinate at room temperature for at least 1 hour.

7. When ready to serve, cook the fusilli in a large pot of boiling salted water until al dente, about 10 minutes. Drain well and add to the vegetables. Toss gently to mix. Pass a bowl of Parmesan cheese on the side.
—Evan Kleiman and Viana LaPlace

LINGUINE WITH NEAPOLITAN SAUCE

This is the simplest, quickest and most common way of dressing pasta in the region around Naples. The recipe may sound oily, but it makes a light and intensely flavorful sauce for spaghetti or linguine. The actual cooking time is less than 10 minutes. Try to time the preparation so the pasta and the sauce are ready at the same moment. No cheese is needed, but if you wish to use some, try Pecorino Romano rather than Parmesan.

There are many variations on this sauce, using shellfish, mushrooms, onions or any fresh vegetable cooked for the briefest possible time. We provide two, using shrimp or mushrooms.

6 Servings

¾ cup olive oil, preferably extra-virgin
2 small garlic cloves, halved

LUNCH IN THE GARDEN

Wine Spritzers

Olive-Stuffed Pepper Wedges
with Tomatoes and Anchovies
(p. 44)

Fusilli with Grilled Vegetables
(p. 109)

🍷 Fruity White, such as Robert
Mondavi Johannisberg Riesling
or Kesselstatt Piesporter
Goldtröpfchen Riesling Kabinett

Strawberry Granita (p. 217)

Cornmeal Crescent Biscotti
(p. 242)

Tea

1½ pounds ripe plum tomatoes—
    peeled, seeded and quartered—or
    1 can (35 ounces) Italian peeled
    tomatoes—drained, halved and
    drained again
1 pound linguine or spaghetti
2 tablespoons minced flat-leaf parsley
¾ teaspoon salt

1. Bring a large pot of water to a boil.

2. In a large skillet, heat the oil. Add the garlic and cook over moderate heat until browned, about 3 minutes, and then discard the garlic.

3. Add the tomatoes to the hot oil and simmer for 7 to 10 minutes, depending on the firmness of the tomatoes; the sauce should not be smooth.

4. Add the pasta to the boiling water and cook until al dente, 8 to 10 minutes. Drain the pasta. Stir the parsley and salt into the sauce and toss with the pasta.

SHRIMP SAUCE
Shell, rinse and pat dry ½ pound small shrimp (about 2 dozen). Add them to the finished sauce and cook, stirring, until they just lose their translucency, about 2 minutes.

MUSHROOM SAUCE
In a large skillet sauté 6 to 8 large mushrooms (5 ounces), thinly sliced, in 3 tablespoons of extra-virgin olive oil over high heat until browned, about 5 minutes. Add to the finished sauce.
—Tom Maresca and Diane Darrow

SPAGHETTI WITH TOMATO AND MILK

This recipe was one of our children's favorites. The starch from the pasta will make the sauce silky.

4 to 6 Servings

3 tablespoons olive oil
4 medium onions, thinly sliced
1 pound fresh tomatoes—peeled, seeded
    and chopped—or 1 can (28 ounces)
    Italian peeled tomatoes, drained and
    chopped
1 to 2 cups milk
1½ teaspoons salt
½ teaspoon freshly ground pepper
1 pound spaghetti
Freshly grated Parmesan cheese
    (optional)

1. In a large skillet, heat the oil. Add the onions, cover and cook over moderate heat, stirring occasionally, until they are softened and translucent, 10 to 15 minutes.

2. Add the tomatoes, 1 cup of the milk and the salt and pepper. Cover and simmer the sauce over moderate heat for 10 minutes.

3. Meanwhile, cook the pasta in a large pot of rapidly boiling salted water for 5 minutes. Drain well.

4. Bring the tomato sauce to a boil, add the pasta and cook over moderate heat, uncovered, for 1 minute. Add ½ cup more milk and cook, tossing the pasta frequently until al dente, 10 to 15 minutes. (Add the remaining ½ cup milk if necessary to thin the sauce.)

5. Serve the pasta immediately on heated plates. Sprinkle with Parmesan cheese if desired.
—Edward Giobbi

PASTA WITH UNCOOKED PUTTANESCA SAUCE

This is an uncooked version of one of the most loved of all Roman sauces. In our recipe the tomato turns dark red and develops a rich flavor after marinating with the olives and anchovies.

❦ The capers, garlic and anchovies in this rich red sauce contribute the sort of zesty flavors that only an assertive, spicy red can match. Look for a peppery California Zinfandel, such as Ravenswood Sonoma or Villa Mt. Eden.

4 to 6 Servings

2 pounds plum tomatoes—peeled, seeded and cut into ½-inch dice
4 anchovy fillets, chopped to a paste
½ cup oil-cured black olives, coarsely chopped
3 tablespoons drained small capers
½ cup chopped flat-leaf parsley
2 garlic cloves, minced
½ teaspoon crushed hot red pepper
¼ teaspoon salt
½ cup extra-virgin olive oil
1 pound cavatappi or fusilli
Freshly grated Parmesan cheese

1. In a medium bowl, combine the tomatoes, anchovies, olives, capers, parsley, garlic, hot pepper, salt and olive oil. Stir gently to combine. Cover with a towel and let the sauce marinate at room temperature for 30 to 60 minutes.

2. Cook the pasta in a large pot of boiling salted water until al dente, about 10 minutes. Quickly drain and toss with the sauce in a shallow pasta bowl. Serve at once, with a bowl of Parmesan cheese on the side.
—*Evan Kleiman and Viana LaPlace*

SPAGHETTINI AND UNCOOKED TOMATO SAUCE WITH OLIVES

Lively as a marinara sauce, this version of a very popular dressing has a distinctive southern accent. Fully ripe plum tomatoes and fresh basil are essential.

6 Servings

1½ pounds very ripe plum tomatoes (about 9 medium)—peeled, seeded and cut into 1½-inch strips
¼ pound Gaeta olives (about 40) or any small black oil-cured olives, halved and pitted
1 large garlic clove, minced
2 tablespoons chopped fresh basil
½ teaspoon salt
¼ teaspoon freshly ground pepper
½ cup olive oil
1 pound spaghettini

1. In a large serving bowl, combine the tomatoes, olives, garlic, basil, salt, pepper and oil.

2. Let stand at room temperature for 1 to 3 hours.

3. Cook the pasta in a large pot of boiling salted water until al dente, 8 to 10 minutes. Drain the pasta and toss with the sauce.
—*Tom Maresca and Diane Darrow*

Lasagna with Roasted Chicken and Porcini Mushrooms (page 138).

At left, *Tagliatelle with Cabbage and Sage* (page 107). Above, *Spaghetti alla San Pietro* (page 105).

Tagliatelle with Asparagus (page 106).

PASTA WITH TOMATO AND BLACK OLIVE SAUCE WITH ARUGULA

Imported canned tomatoes are the tomatoes of choice when good fresh ones are not available. Quick cooking keeps the flavor of this sauce lively.

4 to 6 Servings

¼ cup extra-virgin olive oil
3 garlic cloves, minced
½ teaspoon crushed hot red pepper
1 can (35 ounces) Italian peeled
    tomatoes, drained and chopped
½ cup Calamata olives, quartered
¼ teaspoon salt
¼ teaspoon freshly ground black
    pepper
2 bunches of arugula, trimmed and
    coarsely chopped (about 2 cups)
1 pound rigatoni or gnochetti rigati
Freshly grated Parmesan cheese

1. In a large nonreactive skillet, combine the oil, garlic and hot pepper. Cook over low heat until the garlic is softened and fragrant, about 3 minutes. Add the tomatoes, olives, salt and black pepper. Increase the heat to moderately high and simmer until the juices thicken to form a sauce, about 10 minutes.

2. Meanwhile, place the arugula in a pasta serving bowl. Cook the rigatoni in a large pot of boiling salted water until al dente, about 10 minutes. Drain well and toss with the arugula. Add the sauce and toss. Serve with a bowl of Parmesan cheese on the side.
—*Evan Kleiman and Viana LaPlace*

PASTA WITH FRESH TUNA

Here is our fast version of a Sicilian dish in which a chunk of fresh tuna is stuffed with mint and garlic before being braised in a tomato sauce. Here the tuna is diced and quickly sautéed, then added to the sauce to finish cooking.

4 to 6 Servings

¼ cup plus 2 tablespoons extra-virgin
    olive oil
1 large onion, cut into ½-inch dice
1 can (35 ounces) Italian peeled
    tomatoes, drained and
    coarsely chopped
¾ teaspoon salt
½ teaspoon freshly ground pepper
1 pound fresh tuna, cut into
    ½-inch dice
½ cup chopped fresh mint
3 garlic cloves, thinly sliced
1 pound spaghetti or linguine

1. Place ¼ cup of the oil and the onion in a large nonreactive skillet. Cook over low heat, stirring occasionally, until the onion is very soft, 10 to 12 minutes.

2. Add the tomatoes, ½ teaspoon of the salt and ¼ teaspoon of the pepper. Cook over moderate heat, partially covered, until the juices thicken to form a sauce, about 5 minutes. Remove from the heat and set aside.

3. Season the tuna with the remaining ¼ teaspoon each salt and pepper. In a medium skillet, heat the remaining 2 tablespoons oil. Add the tuna and cook over moderate heat, tossing occasionally, until the tuna is cooked on the surface but still raw in the center, about 4 minutes.

4. Add the tuna, mint and garlic to the tomato sauce and cook over

117

moderate heat, stirring, until the tuna is just barely opaque throughout, 2 to 3 minutes.

5. Meanwhile, cook the spaghetti in a large pot of boiling salted water until al dente, about 9 minutes. Drain well and transfer to a large shallow serving bowl.

6. Pour the hot sauce over the pasta and toss quickly to mix. Serve at once.
—Evan Kleiman and Viana LaPlace

FETTUCCINE WITH SMOKED SALMON

6 to 8 Servings

4 tablespoons unsalted butter
1 small onion, finely chopped
1 tablespoon Cognac
⅓ cup dry white wine
3 cups heavy cream
1 teaspoon freshly ground white pepper
½ teaspoon crushed hot red pepper
1 pound thinly sliced smoked salmon, cut into fine strips
1½ pounds fettuccine, preferably homemade
¾ cup chopped flat-leaf parsley

1. In a large nonreactive flameproof casserole, melt the butter over moderate heat. Add the onion and cook until soft and golden, about 3 minutes. Stir in the Cognac and wine and cook until about 1 tablespoon remains, about 4 minutes.

2. Add the cream, white pepper and hot pepper. Increase the heat to moderately high and boil, stirring, until the cream is slightly thickened, about 8 minutes. Remove from the heat; stir in the smoked salmon. Cover to keep warm.

3. In a large pot of boiling salted water, cook the fettuccine until al dente, about 1½ minutes for fresh, 8 minutes for dried. Drain and rinse;

drain well. Add the pasta and the parsley to the sauce. Cook, tossing, for 1 to 2 minutes to blend well. Add extra cream if the sauce seems too thick. Serve at once on warm plates.
—*Carol Field*

PASTA WITH SMOKED TROUT

6 Servings

2 whole smoked trout, about ½ pound each
1 pound penne, ziti or farfalle (bow ties)
3 tablespoons olive oil or other vegetable oil
2 tablespoons finely chopped shallot
½ pound fresh tomatoes—peeled, seeded and chopped—or 1 can (14 ounces) Italian peeled tomatoes—drained, pureed and strained, if desired, to remove the seeds
1 cup half-and-half or light cream
Dash of freshly grated nutmeg
¼ teaspoon salt
½ teaspoon coarsely ground black pepper
¼ cup brandy
Finely chopped flat-leaf parsley and/or freshly grated Parmesan cheese, for garnish

1. Skin and fillet the trout. (Use tweezers to pull out any small, hidden bones.) Cut the fish into 1-inch pieces.

2. In a large pot of rapidly boiling salted water, cook the pasta until barely tender, 8 to 10 minutes; drain.

LIGHT SUMMER LUNCH

Sweet Vermouth on the Rocks with Lemon Twist

Spiced Almonds

Pasta with Fresh Tuna (p. 117)

♟ Full-bodied Chardonnay, such as Charles Shaw or Navarro

Chicory, Romaine and Onion Salad

Cantaloupe Sorbet with Pepper and Port (p. 217)

Cappuccino

3. Meanwhile, heat the oil in a large skillet. Add the shallot and cook over low heat until soft and translucent, 3 to 5 minutes. Add the tomatoes, cover and simmer for 5 minutes. Add the half-and-half, nutmeg, salt and pepper. Cook for 3 minutes. (The sauce will still be a little thin at this point.)

4. Add the brandy and pasta. Increase the heat to high and cook, tossing frequently, until the pasta is al dente and the sauce thickens, 2 to 3 minutes. Add the trout and toss over heat until hot, about 30 seconds. Serve on warm plates, garnished with parsley and/or cheese.
—*Edward Giobbi*

LINGUINE WITH SARDINIAN CLAM SAUCE

This spicy clam sauce is from Alghero, Sardinia. The presence of green olives indicates a Spanish influence.

❦ Pair this salty dish and its accent of olives with a crisp Sauvignon Blanc, such as Beringer, or a weightier white with similar tartness, such as Buehler Napa Valley Pinot Blanc.

4 to 6 Servings

2 *pounds hard-shelled clams, such as cherrystones or littlenecks*
½ *cup extra-virgin olive oil*
4 *garlic cloves, minced*
½ *teaspoon crushed hot red pepper*
1 *can (28 ounces) Italian peeled tomatoes, drained and chopped*
¼ *cup pitted green olives, quartered lengthwise*
2 *tablespoons coarsely chopped fresh oregano or 1 teaspoon dried*
2 *tablespoons coarsely chopped flat-leaf parsley*
1 *cup dry white wine or pasta cooking water*
1 *pound linguine*

1. To clean the clams, soak them in a sink full of lightly salted cold water for ½ hour; scrub them, if necessary, to remove any sand from the shell. Rinse the clams under cold running water and place them in a bowl. Clean the sink thoroughly of all sand and fill again with cold salted water. Add the clams to the water and let soak for another 30 minutes. Lift the clams out of the water and rinse under cold water. Place the cleaned clams in a bowl, discarding any that are open and do not close to the touch, any with cracked shells and any that seem too heavy (they are probably filled with mud). Set the clams aside, refrigerated, for up to 3 hours, until needed.

2. In a large nonreactive skillet or flameproof casserole, heat the oil over moderate heat. Add the garlic and hot pepper and cook until the garlic is fragrant, about 1 minute.

3. Add the chopped tomatoes, olives, oregano and 1 tablespoon of the parsley. Cover and cook just until the tomatoes begin to break down, 3 to 5 minutes.

4. Add the clams and the wine to the tomato sauce. Cover, increase the heat to high and cook, shaking the pan occasionally to make sure each clam has contact with the heat, just until they open up, 3 to 5 minutes. (Discard any clams that refuse to open.) With a slotted spoon,

quickly transfer all the clams to a bowl and cover to keep warm.

5. Meanwhile, cook the pasta in a large pot of boiling salted water until barely tender and still quite firm, 8 to 9 minutes; drain. Add the pasta to the skillet with the tomato-clam sauce and toss over high heat to allow the pasta to absorb some of the sauce; cook until the pasta is al dente, about 1 minute.

6. With tongs, transfer the pasta to a large shallow serving bowl. Place the cooked clams in the shell all over the top of the pasta. Pour any juices left in the skillet over the clams. Sprinkle with the remaining 1 tablespoon chopped parsley.
—Evan Kleiman and Viana LaPlace

PASTA PRIMAVERA WITH CLAMS

This variation on the original Italian pasta primavera is made with fresh tomatoes, herbs and clams. Since the sauce is uncooked, and the clams are barely warmed through, the ingredients must be impeccably fresh and the tomatoes garden ripe. Make sure that everything but the clams are at room temperature before you begin preparing.
♟ Characterful white, such as Pinot Grigio or Muscadet

4 to 6 Servings

1 pound spaghettini
1½ pounds ripe tomatoes (3 or 4 large), seeded and chopped
2 garlic cloves, finely chopped
3 tablespoons coarsely chopped fresh basil

1½ tablespoons finely chopped flat-leaf parsley
¼ cup extra-virgin olive oil
½ teaspoon salt
¼ teaspoon freshly ground pepper
1½ dozen littleneck clams, shucked and coarsely chopped

1. Cook the pasta in a large pot of rapidly boiling salted water until al dente, 5 to 8 minutes.

2. While the pasta is cooking, put all of the remaining ingredients except the clams into a food processor and blend to a coarse puree.

3. Drain the pasta and toss it with the chopped clams. The heat from the pasta will warm the clams. Add the pureed sauce, toss well and serve at once.
—Edward Giobbi

SCALLOP AND PINE NUT SAUCE WITH SPAGHETTINI AND BASIL

♟ Italian white, such as Corvo

6 to 8 Servings

1 pound bay scallops
¼ cup olive oil, preferably extra-virgin
2 medium garlic cloves, minced
⅓ cup pine nuts (pignoli)
2 tablespoons plus ½ teaspoon salt
¼ teaspoon freshly ground pepper
1 pound spaghettini
1 stick (4 ounces) unsalted butter, melted
¾ cup (packed) fresh basil leaves, coarsely chopped

1. Wash the scallops. Remove the tough tendon on the side and dry well on paper towels.

2. In a large saucepan or flameproof casserole, heat the oil. Add the garlic and cook over moderate

ly low heat until softened but not browned, about 3 minutes. Add the pine nuts, increase the heat to moderate and cook, stirring frequently, until the nuts are lightly browned, about 2 minutes. Remove the sauce from the heat and season with ½ teaspoon of the salt and all of the pepper.

3. Bring a large pot of water to a boil. Add the remaining 2 tablespoons salt and the spaghettini. Cook the pasta until al dente, 8 to 10 minutes.

4. Meanwhile, add the scallops to the garlic and pine nut sauce. Cook over high heat, tossing frequently, until the scallops are just opaque throughout, 2 to 3 minutes. Remove from the heat and season with an additional pinch of salt and pepper.

5. Drain the spaghettini, add to the scallops and toss. Add the butter and basil and toss again. Serve hot.
—*Nancy Verde Barr*

NEAPOLITAN SPAGHETTI WITH SEAFOOD

4 to 6 Servings

1 tablespoon salt
1 pound spaghetti
⅔ cup olive oil, preferably extra-virgin
2 large garlic cloves, minced
¾ teaspoon crushed hot red pepper
1 pound bay scallops or quartered sea scallops
¼ cup minced parsley
Freshly ground black pepper

1. Bring a large pot of water to a boil. Add the salt and the spaghetti. Cook, boiling, until al dente, 9 to 10 minutes.

2. Meanwhile, in a large heavy skillet, warm the oil over moderate heat. Add the garlic and hot pepper and cook until the garlic is slightly golden, 1 to 2 minutes. Add the scallops and stir-fry until opaque, 1 to 2 minutes. Remove from the heat.

3. Drain the pasta and place in a warmed serving bowl. Scrape in the scallops and the flavored oil. Add the parsley and toss well. Season with black pepper to taste and serve hot.
—*Tom Maresca and Diane Darrow*

CAPELLINI WITH CALAMARI AND SHRIMP

Chopped walnuts and hot red pepper add a delightful dimension to this light pasta.
♟ The simple, pure flavors of the shrimp and squid marry very well with a light, uncomplicated red such as Bertani's Bardolino.

4 Servings

¼ cup chopped walnuts
¼ cup extra-virgin olive oil
2 large garlic cloves, minced
1½ cups chicken stock or canned broth
1 can (14 ounces) Italian peeled tomatoes, drained and chopped
¼ cup dry white wine
¼ cup chopped flat-leaf parsley
1½ teaspoons oregano
½ teaspoon salt
¼ teaspoon freshly ground black pepper
¾ pound capellini
10 ounces cleaned squid, sliced into thin rings
½ pound large shrimp—shelled, deveined and cut into thirds
¼ teaspoon crushed hot red pepper

121

DINNER AL FRESCO

Kirs

Fresh Ricotta Cheese with Rosemary and Olives (p. 26)

Pasta Primavera with Clams (p. 120)

Italian Herbed Bread Toasts (p. 42)

♟ *Italian White, such as Pinot Grigio*

Green Salad with Vinaigrette

Oranges with Sweet Basil Zabaglione (p. 220)

Espresso

1. Preheat the oven to 325°. Place the walnuts on a baking sheet and bake for 10 minutes, or until lightly toasted. Let cool.

2. In a large nonreactive skillet, heat the olive oil. Add the garlic and cook over moderate heat until beginning to brown, about 2 minutes. Stir in the chicken stock, tomatoes, wine, parsley, oregano, salt and black pepper. Bring to a boil. Reduce the heat to moderate and simmer until reduced by half, about 8 minutes.

3. In a large pot of boiling salted water, cook the capellini until al dente, about 3 minutes.

4. Meanwhile, add the squid and shrimp to the sauce and simmer until the seafood is just barely cooked through, about 2 minutes.

5. Drain the pasta and transfer to a large serving bowl. Add the seafood sauce and toss well. Sprinkle with the hot pepper flakes and toasted walnuts. Serve hot.
—*Mark Cox, Tony's, Houston*

ANGEL HAIR PASTA WITH SHRIMP AND RED PEPPER SAUCE

Chef Jimmy Schmidt's idea of combining a red and yellow pepper sauce with shrimp on angel's hair is a winning example of how American cooks have learned to use pasta in novel ways.
🍷 Fine beer or ale, such as Anchor Steam

4 to 6 Servings

3 medium red bell peppers
1 stick (4 ounces) plus 2 tablespoons unsalted butter
5 medium shallots, chopped
1 garlic clove, minced
½ cup dry white wine
3 cups Fish Stock (p. 265) or bottled clam juice
1 cup heavy cream
½ teaspoon salt
½ teaspoon freshly ground black pepper
1 yellow or red bell pepper
1 pound angel hair pasta or capellini
¼ cup olive oil, preferably extra-virgin
1 pound medium shrimp, peeled and deveined, shells reserved for the fish stock
¼ cup finely shredded fresh basil, for garnish

1. Chop 2 of the red peppers. In a medium saucepan, melt 2 tablespoons of the butter over moderately high heat. Add the shallots, garlic and chopped red peppers. Reduce the heat to low and cook, stirring occasionally, until the peppers are tender, about 10 minutes.

2. Increase the heat to high and add the white wine and Fish Stock. Boil until the mixture is reduced by half, about 20 minutes. Add the cream and boil until the sauce is thick enough to coat the back of a spoon, about 10 minutes. Season with the salt and black pepper.

3. In batches, if necessary, puree the sauce in a blender or food processor, about 1 minute. Strain through a sieve. Return the sauce to the saucepan. (*The recipe can be prepared to this point up to 1 day ahead. Refrigerate covered.*)

4. Bring a medium saucepan of water to a boil. Add the remaining red pepper and the yellow pepper and blanch for 2 minutes, or until the skin starts to wrinkle. Drain and rinse the peppers under cold run

ning water to cool. With a paring knife, remove the skin and cut out the cores and seeds. Cut the peppers into thin strips. Add to the sauce.

5. Preheat the broiler or a grill. Bring a large stockpot of salted water to a boil over high heat. Add the pasta and cook, stirring frequently, until al dente, 1½ to 2 minutes for dried, less if using fresh. Drain and return the pasta to the stockpot. Toss the pasta with 2 tablespoons of the olive oil.

6. Brush the shrimp with the remaining 2 tablespoons olive oil and broil or grill until medium-rare, about 1½ minutes without turning, or 30 seconds longer if you prefer them opaque throughout.

7. Bring the red pepper sauce to a boil and whisk in the remaining 1 stick butter, 1 tablespoon at a time. Adjust the seasoning if necessary. Pour the sauce over the pasta and toss to coat. Transfer the pasta to a large warm serving platter. Arrange the shrimp on top. Garnish with the basil and serve hot.
—Jimmy Schmidt

TAGLIARINI IN LOBSTER SAUCE

6 Servings

2 lobsters, 1¼ pounds each
1½ tablespoons extra-virgin olive oil
2 large garlic cloves, peeled and bruised
½ to 1 teaspoon crushed hot red pepper, to taste
½ cup dry white wine
¾ cup heavy cream
1 can (14 ounces) Italian peeled tomatoes, drained and chopped
1½ pounds fresh green or egg tagliarini or dried linguine

1. Bring a pot of water to a boil. Add the lobsters and cook for 10 minutes over high heat. Remove the lobsters and let cool; reserve the cooking water. Remove the lobster meat from the tail and claws. Chop the lobster meat into fine pieces.

2. In a large nonreactive flameproof casserole, heat the oil over moderate heat. Add the garlic and hot pepper and cook until the garlic cloves are golden all over, about 5 minutes. Remove from the heat and discard the garlic.

3. Add the wine to the pan; cook over moderately high heat until about 1 tablespoon remains, 1 to 2 minutes. Reduce the heat to low; stir in the cream and lobster meat. Cook until just hot, about 5 minutes. Add the tomatoes and cook for 5 minutes longer.

4. Salt the reserved lobster water and bring to a boil. Add the tagliarini and cook until al dente, about 2 minutes for fresh, 8 minutes for dried. Drain and rinse; drain well. Add to the sauce. Cook, tossing, for 1 to 2 minutes to heat through. Serve at once.
—Carol Field

GREEN PAPPARDELLE WITH LAMB, EGGPLANT, GOAT CHEESE AND TOMATOES

The innovative menu at Spiaggia avoids the obvious and marries Italian tradition to new American ideas, like this sunny dish in which fresh spinach pasta is cut into 1-inch-wide strips called pappardelle. This simplified version substitutes green fettuccine.

❦ Fine, flavorful red, such as Tignanello or Robert Mondavi Cabernet Sauvignon

4 to 6 Servings

½ cup olive oil
½ pound boneless lamb shoulder, trimmed of excess fat and cut into ¼- to ⅜-inch dice
4 garlic cloves, minced
2 cups lamb or beef stock or canned broth
1 can (35 ounces) Italian peeled tomatoes, drained and chopped
¾ pound small eggplant (about 4), thinly sliced
½ teaspoon salt
½ teaspoon freshly ground pepper
1 pound fresh spinach pappardelle or dried green fettuccine
¼ pound mild goat cheese, such as Montrachet, crumbled into bite-size pieces
¼ cup chopped flat-leaf parsley

1. In a large saucepan, heat ¼ cup of the olive oil over high heat. Add the lamb and sauté, tossing, until browned on all sides, about 2 minutes. Reduce the heat to moderate and add the garlic; cook, stirring, until it is fragrant but not browned, about 30 seconds. Add the stock and tomatoes. Reduce the heat to low and simmer, uncovered, for 1½ hours.

2. In a large skillet, heat the remaining ¼ cup olive oil over high heat. Add the eggplant slices and sauté, turning once, until browned, about 2 minutes on each side. Add to the lamb sauce. Season with the salt and pepper. (*The sauce can be made up to 2 days ahead. Refrigerate covered. Reheat before proceeding.*)

3. In a large pot of boiling salted water, cook the pasta until al dente,

2 to 4 minutes for fresh, 10 to 12 for dried; drain well.

4. Return the pasta to the pot. Toss with the hot lamb sauce. Add the goat cheese and toss again. Divide the mixture among serving plates or heap on a platter. Garnish with the parsley.
—*Spiaggia, Chicago*

PENNE WITH LAMB RAGU

This is a piquant sauce from the mountainous Abruzzo region. Only in sauces like this, where the object is to extract as much flavor as possible from a small amount of meat, do southern Italians cook tomatoes for a long time—and then always gently.

6 Servings

3 tablespoons olive oil
¾ pound lean boneless lamb shoulder, cut into ½-inch cubes
2 medium garlic cloves, coarsely chopped
½ teaspoon rosemary, crushed
1 tablespoon chopped flat-leaf parsley
1 small dried hot red pepper
½ teaspoon salt
½ cup dry white wine
1 can (35 ounces) Italian peeled tomatoes, well drained and pureed
1 pound penne

1. In a large skillet, heat the olive oil. Add the lamb and sauté over high heat, tossing frequently, until lightly browned, 1 to 2 minutes.

2. Add the garlic, rosemary, parsley, hot pepper and salt and sauté for 30 seconds.

3. Pour in the wine and boil, scraping up the browned bits clinging to the bottom of the pan, for 2 to 3 minutes, to reduce slightly. Add

the pureed tomatoes, cover and simmer over low heat until the lamb is very tender, about 1½ hours.

4. Cook the pasta in a large pot of boiling salted water until al dente, 8 to 10 minutes. Drain the pasta. Remove the hot pepper from the sauce and toss with the pasta.
—*Tom Maresca and Diane Darrow*

RIGATONI WITH HAM SAUCE

This quick, hearty sauce from Apulia gets a lot of mileage out of a quarter-pound of boiled ham. For those who like spicy food, add a small *peperoncino* (hot red pepper) with the garlic and remove it before serving.

6 Servings

¼ cup plus 2 tablespoons olive oil
2 large garlic cloves, minced
¼ pound lean boiled ham, sliced ¼ inch thick and cut into ¼-inch dice
1 can (35 ounces) Italian peeled tomatoes, with their juice
½ teaspoon freshly ground pepper
1 pound rigatoni
1 cup freshly grated Pecorino Romano cheese (about ¼ pound)
¼ cup minced fresh basil
Salt

1. In a large skillet, heat the olive oil. Add the garlic and ham and sauté over moderate heat until the garlic is lightly browned, 3 to 5 minutes.

2. Add the tomatoes with their juice and the pepper. Bring to a boil, reduce the heat to moderately low and simmer the sauce, uncovered, for 15 minutes.

3. Cook the pasta in a large pot of boiling salted water until al dente, 8 to 10 minutes. Drain the pasta and toss with the sauce, cheese, basil and salt to taste.
—*Tom Maresca and Diane Darrow*

CAPELLINI ALLA PROVINCIALE

Now half a century old, Amerigo's is a great Bronx restaurant that represents the robust and generous cooking of southern Italy. *Capellini alla provinciale* is full of the lusty flavors of the Neapolitan kitchen.
♟ A full-bodied red, such as Bolla Amarone or Vino Nobile di Montepulciano

6 to 8 Servings

1½ cups olive oil
6 large Spanish onions (about 3½ pounds), thinly sliced
4 anchovy fillets, chopped
2 tablespoons chopped parsley
1 tablespoon chopped fresh basil
1 small green bell pepper, thinly sliced
½ cup oil-cured black olives (about 4 ounces), pitted and coarsely chopped
¼ cup tiny capers, chopped
2 teaspoons freshly ground black pepper
10 ounces prosciutto, finely chopped (about 2 cups)
2 cups dry white wine
1 can (14 ounces) Italian peeled tomatoes, drained and chopped
1 pound capellini or angel hair pasta
Freshly grated Parmesan cheese

1. In a large flameproof casserole, heat the olive oil. Add the onions and cook over moderately low heat, stirring occasional-

PASTA-SAUCE MATCHES

Pasta lends itself to improvisation, which works best when supported by a knowledge of some basic techniques and authentic traditions. There are reliable formulas for matching pasta shapes with sauces. When selecting dried pasta to go with a soupy shellfish sauce, for example, choose the very thin, long strands; they absorb the juices without becoming soft. Tubular shapes are excellent for trapping bits of vegetables and meat. The more pronounced flavor of thick pasta suits the stronger-tasting, more assertive preparations. Dried eggless pasta, which is milder in flavor than a rich egg noodle, is the best choice when you are using sauces based on olive oil. By contrast, fresh or egg pasta—which is usually long and flat—has an extremely porous surface that is good for absorbing delicate butter or cream sauces.
—Viana LaPlace and Evan Kleiman

ly, until the onions are softened and well browned, about 50 minutes.

2. Add the anchovies, parsley, basil, green pepper, olives, capers and black pepper. Cook for 30 seconds. Then add the prosciutto and white wine. Boil over high heat until the liquid is almost evaporated, about 10 minutes. Add the tomatoes and return to a boil. Reduce the heat to low, cover and simmer for 30 minutes. (*The sauce can be made up to 3 hours ahead. Set aside at room temperature. Reheat before proceeding.*)

3. In a large pot of boiling salted water, cook the capellini until al dente, about 2 minutes. Drain and return the pasta to the pot.

4. Add half the sauce to the capellini and toss to coat. Arrange the pasta on a large serving platter, pour on the rest of the sauce and serve. Pass a bowl of Parmesan cheese if desired.
—*Amerigo's, New York City*

CHRISTMAS PASTA

Pastas made for Christmas Eve are always without meat (a tradition dating from church vigil days, when Catholics ate only fish on Fridays), but let Christmas Day come, and pastas stuffed with prosciutto and mortadella and cheeses and eggs pour forth. In the north of Italy, *il cenone*, the big dinner, is served on Christmas Eve, while Christmas Day lunch is a much bigger celebration in the south. In some places people manage to put away two major meals in less than 24 hours.
—Carol Field

PENNE WITH CHRISTMAS PASTA SAUCE

Here's a bold but rustic *ragù* from Emilia-Romagna, which many Italians serve with the traditional pasta course at Christmas. It's full of sausage, pancetta and beef, and it can be used with any type of pasta. On the other 364 days of the year, you can toss the sauce with fusilli, penne or fat rigatoni because the sauce slides right into their spirals and tubes and fills them with its flavor.

4 Servings

1 ounce dried porcini mushrooms
¼ cup extra-virgin olive oil
1 small carrot, finely chopped
1 small onion, finely chopped
1 small celery rib, finely chopped
1 small garlic clove, crushed through a press
1 pound sweet Italian sausages, casings removed
⅓ pound (about 5 ounces) lean ground beef
6½ ounces pancetta, diced
½ teaspoon salt
½ teaspoon freshly ground pepper
¼ teaspoon freshly grated nutmeg
½ cup dry red wine
½ cup tomato paste
1 cup drained canned Italian peeled tomatoes, chopped
¾ pound penne
2 tablespoons finely chopped parsley

1. Soak the porcini in warm water for at least ½ hour. Remove from the water, squeeze dry and chop.

2. Meanwhile, in a large saucepan or flameproof casserole, heat the olive oil over moderate heat. Add the carrot, onion and celery and sauté until the onion is golden, about 4 minutes. Add the garlic and cook until fragrant, about 1 minute.

3. Add the sausage, ground beef and pancetta to the pan. Cook over moderate heat, stirring to break up the meat, until the beef and sausage are no longer pink. Drain off any fat. Season the meat with the salt, pepper and nutmeg.

4. Pour in the red wine and cook, stirring occasionally, until it evaporates about 5 minutes. Add the tomato paste, tomatoes, porcini and ½ cup of warm water Simmer for 30 minutes. If the sauce gets too thick, add a little more water. (*The*

recipe can be made to this point up to 2 days ahead. Cover and refrigerate; reheat before serving.)

5. Cook the pasta in a large pot of boiling salted water until al dente, 8 to 10 minutes. Drain the pasta. Add the parsley to the sauce and toss with the pasta.

—*Carol Field*

FETTUCCINE BEN ARRIVATI

6 to 8 Servings

1½ pounds hot Italian sausage
1½ pounds sweet Italian sausage
2 cups dry white wine
2 tablespoons olive oil
2 medium onions, sliced into rings
2 garlic cloves, chopped
3 medium green bell peppers, sliced into rings
2 medium celery ribs, coarsely chopped
½ cup chopped parsley
4 tablespoons unsalted butter
3 tablespoons all-purpose flour
1½ cups hot beef stock or canned broth
⅓ cup sweet vermouth
⅓ cup dry vermouth
3 egg yolks
½ cup heavy cream
Salt and freshly ground pepper
1 pound fettuccine
1 cup freshly grated Parmesan cheese (about ¼ pound)

1. Prick the sausages and place them in a large nonreactive skillet; add the wine and cook rapidly over moderately high heat until the wine has evaporated and the sausages are glazed, 15 to 20 minutes. Cut the sausages into ½-inch rounds. Remove to a plate and keep warm.

Discard the fat in the skillet, but do not wash the pan.

2. In the same skillet, warm the oil over low heat. Add the onions, garlic, peppers and celery and cook until crisp-tender, about 7 minutes. Sprinkle on the parsley, remove to a plate and cover loosely to keep warm.

3. Using the same skillet, melt the butter over low heat. Add the flour and cook, stirring, for 2 to 3 minutes without coloring to make a roux. Off heat, whisk in the hot beef stock. Return to low heat and simmer, stirring occasionally, until thickened and smooth, about 5 minutes.

4. Add the sweet and dry vermouths and simmer for 5 minutes longer.

5. Remove from the heat and whisk in the egg yolks, one at a time, beating rapidly until incorporated. Slowly add the cream and return to low heat to warm through; do not allow the sauce to boil. Season with salt and pepper to taste.

6. In a large pot of boiling salted water, cook the fettuccine until al dente, 2 to 3 minutes for fresh or 8 to 10 minutes for dried. Drain well.

7. Toss the pasta with the sauce to coat. Add the Parmesan cheese and toss again.

8. To serve, place the fettuccine in the middle of a large, warmed platter. Surround with a ring of the reserved pepper and onion mixture and then with a ring of the sausages.

—*W. Peter Prestcott*

RIGATONI AND SHEPHERD'S SAUCE WITH SAUSAGE AND RICOTTA

This utterly simple peasant recipe from Basilicata produces a surprisingly sophisticated sauce. It takes no time at all to prepare and can be started after the pasta water is put on to boil. The sausage used should preferably be genuine *luganega*; a good-quality breakfast sausage or other mild pork sausage may be substituted if necessary. Also important is good-quality, freshly grated Romano cheese. Finally, don't stint on the black pepper.

6 Servings

1 *pound luganega sausage,* skinned and crumbled*
12 *ounces whole-milk ricotta cheese*
1 *teaspoon freshly ground pepper*
1 *pound rigatoni*
½ *cup freshly grated Pecorino Romano cheese*
*Available at Italian and specialty food shops

1. Bring a large pot of water to a boil.
2. Meanwhile, place the sausage in a medium saucepan. Add 1 cup of water, cover and cook over moderate heat until the sausage is cooked through and no longer pink, about 10 minutes. Drain the sausage, reserving the cooking liquid; there will be about 1 cup.
3. Place the ricotta in a large serving bowl and gradually stir in the reserved sausage liquid to make a smooth cream. Add the sausage meat and the pepper.
4. Add the pasta to the boiling water and cook until al dente, 8 to 10 minutes. Drain the pasta and toss with the sauce and the cheese.
—*Tom Maresca and Diane Darrow*

POTATO GNOCCHI WITH TOMATO SAUCE

8 Servings

3 *pounds baking potatoes*
2 *cups all-purpose flour*
4 *eggs, lightly beaten*
1 *teaspoon salt*
¼ *teaspoon freshly ground white pepper*
⅛ *teaspoon freshly grated nutmeg*
1 *cup freshly grated Parmesan cheese (about ¼ pound)*
Tomato Sauce with Garlic (p. 262)

1. In a large heavy saucepan of boiling salted water, cook the potatoes until tender when pierced with a fork, about 20 minutes. Drain and set aside to cool, then peel and mash with either a ricer or a food mill.
2. Stir in the flour, eggs, salt, white pepper, nutmeg and Parmesan until just mixed.
3. Lightly flour a work surface. To form the gnocchi, divide the dough into 8 sections. Using your hands, roll each into a cylinder ½ inch in circumference. Cut into 1-inch lengths. (*The recipe can be made several hours ahead of time to this point. Arrange the gnocchi on baking sheets in a single layer. Cover and refrigerate.*)
4. Bring a large pot of salted water to a simmer over moderately high heat. Add one-fourth of the gnocchi and cook until they all rise to the surface, 3 to 5 minutes. Remove with a slotted spoon and drain in a colander. Transfer to a large, warmed serving bowl and cover to keep warm. Cook the

remaining gnocchi in 3 more batches; transfer to the bowl.

5. To serve, ladle the hot Tomato Sauce with Garlic over the gnocchi and toss until well coated. Serve hot.

—Da Celestino, Florence, Italy

CORNMEAL GNOCCHI WITH PORCINI MUSHROOM SAUCE

8 Servings

2½ teaspoons salt
2 cups yellow cornmeal
1 ounce dried porcini mushrooms
5 tablespoons unsalted butter
1 tablespoon olive oil
1 small onion, finely chopped
½ cup finely chopped prosciutto or
    pancetta (2 ounces)
1 can (28 ounces) Italian peeled
    tomatoes, chopped, with their liquid
¼ teaspoon freshly ground pepper
½ cup freshly grated Parmesan cheese

1. In a large heavy saucepan, bring 6 cups of water to a boil over high heat. Add 2 teaspoons of the salt. Gradually stir in the cornmeal in a thin stream. Cook, stirring constantly, until the polenta mixture is very thick, about 45 minutes. Pour the hot polenta onto a large jelly-roll pan or tray. Immediately smooth to a ½-inch thickness. Let the polenta cool to room temperature.

2. In a small bowl, soak the mushrooms in 2 cups of hot water until softened, about 30 minutes. Remove the mushrooms from the water, reserving the liquid. Strain the soaking liquid through a paper coffee filter or a double thickness of dampened cheesecloth. Rinse the mushrooms in several changes of cold water. Finely chop.

3. In a medium saucepan, melt 3 tablespoons of the butter in the oil. Add the onion and cook over moderate heat until softened but not browned, about 5 minutes. Add the prosciutto and cook for 1 minute.

4. Add the chopped porcini, the soaking liquid, the tomatoes, the remaining ½ teaspoon salt and the pepper. Simmer uncovered, stirring occasionally, for 30 minutes.

5. Preheat the oven to 425°. Cut the cooled polenta into 1-inch squares to form gnocchi and arrange them in overlapping rows in a lightly buttered large baking dish. Spoon the porcini sauce over the gnocchi and sprinkle with the cheese. Dot with the remaining 2 tablespoons butter. Bake until the butter is melted and the gnocchi are heated through, about 20 minutes.

—Michele Scicolone

RICOTTA GNOCCHI WITH MEAT AND TOMATO SAUCE

8 Servings

2 cups ricotta cheese
1¼ cups freshly grated Parmesan
    cheese (about 5 ounces)
2¼ cups all-purpose flour
Meat and Tomato Sauce (p. 263)

1. In a large bowl, blend the ricotta and 1 cup of the Parmesan cheese. Gradually stir in as much of the flour as possible. When the dough becomes too stiff to stir,

GNOCCHI

Like pasta, gnocchi can be eaten as a first course or a side dish, but unlike pasta, they require no special equipment to prepare—not even a rolling pin. Indeed, they are really no more difficult to make than a batch of cookies.

The dough can be formed from a base of potatoes, flour, cornmeal or bread crumbs, and a variety abounds all over Italy. In the Val d'Aosta near Switzerland, for instance, gnocchi are made from buckwheat flour and are served with melted Fontina cheese. Saffron colors the tiny gnocchi of Sardinia, and pumpkin is favored in Lombardy. In the Alto Aldige region, bordering on Austria, gnocchi are made with rye bread crumbs. The people of Verona prefer potato gnocchi, which they traditionally eat on Good Friday. In the mountainous Abruzzi region, gnocchi are served like spaghetti carbonara, with an egg and pancetta sauce. North of Venice in Friuli, sweet gnocchi, flavored with raisins, cocoa and cinnamon are a traditional Christmas treat.
—Michele Scicolone

turn it out onto a lightly floured surface. Knead in the remaining flour and continue to knead until the dough is smooth and forms a ball, about 5 minutes.

2. Divide the dough into 8 pieces. On a lightly floured surface, roll one piece of dough into a cylinder about ¾ inch in diameter. Cut the cylinder into ¾-inch lengths.

3. Dip a table fork in flour. Holding the fork in one hand, roll each gnocchi over the back of the tines using enough pressure to leave ridges on the outside of the gnocchi and a concave indentation on the inside. Let the gnocchi drop ¼ inch apart onto baking sheets lined with waxed paper. Repeat with the remaining dough. Refrigerate the gnocchi for 30 minutes before cooking.

4. In a large pot of boiling salted water, cook the gnocchi in 2 batches, dropping them in a few at a time to prevent sticking. After the gnocchi rise to the surface, cook for 2 minutes longer. Remove with a slotted spoon or skimmer.

5. Pour half the Meat and Tomato Sauce into a serving bowl. Add the gnocchi and toss. Top with the remaining sauce and Parmesan cheese.

—*Michele Scicolone*

SPINACH, PROSCIUTTO AND RICOTTA GNOCCHI WITH SAGE BUTTER

These delicate gnocchi are popular in Florence, where they are called *ravioli nudi*, or nude ravioli, because their ingredients are similar to those used to stuff pasta. They would go well before a main course of veal or chicken.

♟ Crisp white, such as Vernaccia di San Gimignano or Orvieto

8 *Servings*

2 *pounds fresh spinach, rinsed and stemmed, or 2 packages (10 ounces each) frozen chopped spinach, thawed*
1½ *sticks (6 ounces) plus 2 tablespoons unsalted butter*
1 *small onion, finely chopped*
½ *cup finely chopped prosciutto (2 ounces)*
2 *cups ricotta cheese*
1½ *cups plus 2 tablespoons all-purpose flour*
1¼ *cups freshly grated Parmesan cheese (about 5 ounces)*
2 *eggs*
¼ *teaspoon salt*
¼ *teaspoon freshly grated nutmeg*
¼ *teaspoon freshly ground pepper*
6 *fresh sage leaves or ¾ teaspoon dried, crumbled*

1. If using fresh spinach, steam for 2 to 3 minutes, or until wilted and tender. Drain and cool. Squeeze out as much water as possible. Finely chop the spinach. If you are using thawed frozen spinach, simply squeeze it dry; do not cook.

2. In a medium skillet, melt 2 tablespoons of the butter over moderately low heat. Add the onion and cook until softened and translucent, 5 to 6 minutes. Add the prosciutto and cook for 30 seconds. Add the chopped spinach and blend. Transfer the mixture to a large bowl.

3. With a wooden spoon, beat in the ricotta cheese, 1½ cups of the flour, 1 cup of the Parmesan cheese, the eggs, salt, nutmeg and pepper. The mixture will be soft.

4. Spread the remaining 2 tablespoons flour on a dinner plate. Lightly flour your hands and shape the gnocchi mixture into balls about ¾ inch in diameter, rolling them

lightly in the flour. Put the gnocchi on baking sheets lined with waxed paper, cover and refrigerate for up to several hours until ready to cook.

5. In a small saucepan, melt the remaining 1½ sticks butter over moderately low heat. Add the sage leaves and a pinch of salt. Cook until the butter is lightly browned, 4 to 6 minutes. Keep warm over very low heat.

6. In a large pot of boiling salted water, cook the gnocchi in 2 batches, dropping them in a few at a time, to prevent sticking. After the gnocchi rise to the surface, cook for 2 minutes longer. Remove the gnocchi with a slotted spoon or skimmer and transfer to a warm platter. Drizzle with the sage butter and serve the remaining Parmesan cheese on the side.

—Michele Scicolone

SAUSAGE AND POTATO GNOCCHI WITH GARLIC BUTTER

Potato gnocchi are eaten all over Italy. In this version, sautéed sausages give them an added dimension. Fresh rosemary (which in Italy grows in bushes as tall as the houses) is, if you can find it, a fragrant addition to the garlic butter. These gnocchi would be a delicious side dish with roast pork or turkey.

❦ Big fruity red, such as d'Angelo Aglianico del Vulture

8 Servings

1½ pounds boiling potatoes
2 sweet Italian sausages without fennel (about 5 ounces)
2 eggs
1¾ teaspoons salt
¼ teaspoon freshly ground pepper

2 cups all-purpose flour
1½ sticks (6 ounces) unsalted butter
1 medium garlic clove, minced
1 teaspoon minced fresh rosemary (optional)
½ cup freshly grated Parmesan cheese

1. In a medium saucepan of boiling salted water, cook the potatoes until tender when pierced with a knife, 25 to 35 minutes; then drain. While still hot, peel them and pass them through a potato ricer or a food mill into a large bowl. Let cool completely.

2. Meanwhile, remove the sausage meat from the casings and sauté in a small skillet over moderately high heat, stirring, until browned, about 15 minutes. Using a slotted spoon, transfer to a cutting board and finely chop.

3. Using a wooden spoon, beat the eggs, 1½ teaspoons of the salt and ⅛ teaspoon of the pepper into the mashed potatoes. Gradually stir in the flour. When the mixture becomes too stiff to stir, turn out onto a lightly floured surface and knead in the remaining flour. Do not overwork the dough. Finally, knead in the chopped sausage.

4. Divide the dough into 8 pieces. On a lightly floured surface, roll each piece into a cylinder ½ inch in diameter. Using a knife dipped into flour, cut the cylinders into 1-inch lengths.

5. Dip a table fork in flour. Holding the fork in one hand, roll each gnocchi over the back of the tines with the thumb of the other hand, using enough pressure to leave

THE POPE OF GNOCCHI

On the last Friday of Carnivale, the town of Verona hosts a gnocchi festival at which the "Pope of Gnocchi" reigns. Dressed in red and white (representing the sauce and gnocchi, respectively) and proudly bearing a huge fork-shaped scepter with a gnocchi attached to the end, he leads a procession of bands, drum majorettes, revelers dressed up in 15th-century garb and floats celebrating foods indigenous to the area, including herring, strawberries and local wines. In front of the church at the Piazza San Zeno, gnocchi as well as sausages and plates of polenta with herring are served to the crowd.

131

ridges on the outside of the gnocchi and a concave indentation on the inside. Let the gnocchi drop (in a single layer without touching) onto baking sheets lined with waxed paper. Refrigerate the gnocchi for at least 30 minutes before proceeding.

6. In a medium saucepan, melt the butter over moderate heat. Add the garlic, rosemary and remaining ¼ teaspoon salt and ⅛ teaspoon pepper and cook for 1 minute. Keep the butter warm over low heat.

7. In a large pot of boiling salted water, cook the gnocchi in 3 or 4 batches, dropping them in a few at a time to prevent sticking. Simmer until all the gnocchi float to the surface, then cook for 30 seconds longer. Remove with a slotted spoon or skimmer and transfer to a colander; drain the gnocchi well.

8. In a large warm serving bowl, combine the gnocchi with the butter sauce; toss gently. Sprinkle with the cheese and serve hot.
—Michele Scicolone

ORECCHIETTE BAKED WITH OLIVES, VEGETABLES AND MOZZARELLA

Orecchiette, literally "little ears," is a disk-shaped pasta that is fun to eat, but hardly necessary to the success of this dish. Feel free to substitute ziti, rigatoni or fusilli. Quick and fresh and light, this pasta can serve as a simple main course or a side dish.

4 Main-Course or
6 First-Course
Servings

3 tablespoons olive oil
2 medium zucchini, cut into ½-inch cubes
¼ teaspoon salt
½ teaspoon freshly ground pepper
½ pound orecchiette or other shaped pasta, such as ziti or rigatoni
1 cup Calamata olives, pitted and coarsely chopped
3 firm-ripe tomatoes, peeled and diced
1 cup freshly grated Parmesan cheese (about ¼ pound)
½ pound whole-milk mozzarella, cut into ½-inch dice, at room temperature

1. In a large skillet, preferably nonstick, heat the olive oil. Add the zucchini and cook over moderately high heat, stirring occasionally, until lightly browned, about 5 minutes. Season with the salt and ¼ teaspoon of the pepper. Using a slotted spoon. transfer the zucchini to a large bowl.

2. In a large pot of boiling salted water, cook the orecchiette, stirring occasionally, until al dente, 10 to 12 minutes. Drain immediately, rinse under cold water and drain again. Toss the pasta with the zucchini. (The recipe can be made to this point several hours ahead. Cover with plastic wrap and set aside at room temperature.)

3. Preheat the oven to 375°. Add the olives, tomatoes, ½ cup of the Parmesan cheese and the remaining ¼ teaspoon pepper to the pasta and toss well. Spoon the mixture into a buttered, large shallow baking dish.

4. Scatter the mozzarella evenly over the pasta. Bake in the upper third of the oven until the cheese is melted and the pasta is heated through, about 10 minutes. Pass the remaining ½ cup Parmesan cheese at the table.
—Michael McLaughlin

BUCKWHEAT PASTA WITH POTATOES, SWISS CHARD AND ONIONS

Pizzoccheri—brown buckwheat noodles tossed with pink-skinned potatoes, green swiss chard, crisp red onions and a sauce of Fontina, Parmesan and garlicky butter—is a traditional dish from the Lombardy region of Italy.

Although it would never be served so in Italy, I like to present this wonderful dish as a meatless main course. It's just too sturdy to be a starter. Precede the *pizzoccheri* with pâté, prosciutto or other cold meat appetizers; follow with a green vegetable dressed with vinaigrette and then with fresh fruit.

❦ One of the region's accommodating reds (Grumello, Sassella, Inferno) would be an apt choice with this meal, but I prefer a white and suggest a Lugana. If you prefer a California wine, look for a good light Zinfandel or a Sauvignon Blanc.

6 Servings

1 *pound small red potatoes, cut into*
    ½-*inch chunks*
1 *large bunch of swiss chard, trimmed,*
    leaves and stalks separated
1½ *sticks (6 ounces) unsalted butter*
4 *garlic cloves, minced*
2 *tablespoons minced fresh sage or*
    oregano or 1 teaspoon dried oregano
1 *medium red onion, diced*
Fresh Buckwheat Pasta (p. 255)
Salt and freshly ground pepper
6 *ounces Fontina Val d'Aosta cheese,*
    grated (about 1½ cups)
½ *cup freshly grated Parmesan cheese*

1. Put the potatoes in a medium saucepan of cold salted water to cover. Bring to a boil over moderate heat. Reduce the heat slightly and cook until the potatoes are just tender but still hold their shape, about 6 minutes. Drain immediately, rinse under cold water and drain again.

2. Cut the stalks of the swiss chard crosswise into ½-inch pieces; rinse. Slice the leaves crosswise into thin strips. Place the leaves in a colander and rinse under cold running water. Set aside in the colander in the sink.

3. In a medium saucepan of boiling salted water, cook the chard stalks until tender but still crunchy, about 4 minutes. Pour the stalks and boiling water over the chard leaves in the colander. Transfer immediately to a bowl of ice water and let cool. Drain well and squeeze out as much water as possible. (*The recipe can be made to this point up to 3 hours ahead. Cover the potatoes and the swiss chard separately with plastic wrap and set aside at room temperature.*)

4. Preheat the oven to 375°. In a large skillet, melt the butter over low heat. Add the garlic and cook, stirring occasionally, until fragrant, about 2 minutes. Add the sage and red onion and cook, stirring, until the onion is softened but not browned, about 5 minutes. Add the potatoes and chard and toss to coat with butter. Cook, covered, until heated through, about 5 minutes.

5. In a large pot of boiling salted water, cook the Fresh Buckwheat Pasta until al dente, 10 to 20 seconds if freshly made and 1 to 1½ minutes if the noodles have been fully dried. Drain immediately and transfer to a large bowl. Add the chard/potato mixture and toss gently. Season with salt and pepper to taste. Add the Fontina and Parmesan cheeses and toss again.

6. Turn the pasta into a large, shallow buttered baking dish. (*The recipe can be made to this point up to 1 hour ahead. Cover and hold at room temperature.*) Cover with foil and set in the upper third of the oven. Bake for 10 minutes. Remove the foil and bake until the cheeses are melted and the dish is heated through, 5 to 7 minutes longer.

—Michael McLaughlin

BAKED RIGATONI WITH BRAISED BEEF, OLIVES AND MOZZARELLA

This dish is inspired by the Italian practice of saucing pasta with left-over pot roast juices as well as by a traditional French dish called *macaronade* (pasta sauced with braised beef juices, which precedes or accompanies the meat).

Most of the work for this dish is done days in advance, and if you're planning to feed a large crowd, double the recipe. To complete the menu, mix up a green salad, grill a batch of garlic bread and keep the red wine (Pinot Noir or Côtes du Rhône) flowing.

6 to 8 Servings

2 *pounds boneless chuck or other pot roast in one piece*
1 *large onion, sliced*
1 *large carrot, sliced*
4 *garlic cloves, minced*
1 *can (28 ounces) Italian peeled tomatoes, crushed, with their juice*
½ *cup dry red wine*
½ *cup beef stock or canned broth*
2½ *teaspoons thyme*
2½ *teaspoons marjoram*
2½ *teaspoons basil*
2 *imported bay leaves*
½ *teaspoon salt*
1 *pound rigatoni*

2 *tablespoons olive oil (optional)*
18 *Calamata olives, pitted*
½ *cup freshly grated Parmesan cheese*
½ *cup finely chopped flat-leaf parsley*
1 *pound whole-milk mozzarella, cut into ¼-inch dice, at room temperature*
1 *teaspoon freshly ground pepper*

1. Preheat the oven to 350°. Set the roast in a 2½- to 3-quart oven-proof casserole and surround it with the onion, carrot and garlic. Add the tomatoes with their juice, wine, beef stock, thyme, marjoram, basil, bay leaves and salt. Bake, covered, for 1½ hours. Turn the roast and bake until tender, about 1 hour longer. Leave the roast in the braising liquid and let cool to room temperature. Cover tightly and refrigerate overnight.

2. Remove the congealed fat from the surface of the braising liquid and discard the bay leaves. Transfer the roast to a cutting board. Trim away any strings or surface fat and cut the meat into ¼-inch dice. Stir the diced beef back into the braising liquid and cover. (*The recipe can be prepared up to 2 days ahead to this point. Cover and refrigerate.*)

3. In a large pot of boiling salted water, cook the rigatoni, stirring occasionally, until the pasta is just barely tender, 8 to 10 minutes (it will soften further during baking). Drain immediately, rinse with cold water and drain again. (*The recipe can be prepared to this point up to 3 hours ahead. To hold, toss the pasta with the oil, cover and keep at room temperature.*)

4. Preheat the oven to 375°. Reheat the beef sauce. Stir in

the olives, Parmesan cheese and chopped parsley.

5. In a large bowl, toss the beef sauce, mozzarella and pasta. Season generously with pepper and toss again. Spoon the pasta into a large heatproof casserole and set in the middle of the oven. Bake the casserole until the top is well browned and the cheese is melted throughout, 40 to 50 minutes.
—*Michael McLaughlin*

PORK CANNELLONI IN SHIITAKE, TOMATO AND CREAM SAUCE

This pasta dish, with its rich pork stuffing and wild mushroom sauce, is a worthy first or main course for any autumn dinner party. Bake each portion in an individual gratin dish for best results. Imported dried cannelloni or manicotti tubes, available in Italian specialty food shops, are somewhat thicker than freshly made pasta and are thus perfect for this hearty dish. Serve this as an impressive first course and follow with a simple main course, such as roast chicken.

6 First-Course or
3 Main-Course
Servings

7 tablespoons unsalted butter
½ cup minced onion
2 medium garlic gloves, minced
¼ cup minced boiled ham or prosciutto
   (2 ounces)
1 pound very lean, finely ground pork
Salt and freshly ground pepper
¼ teaspoon freshly grated nutmeg
½ cup dry white wine
1¾ cups heavy cream
⅓ cup minced flat-leaf parsley
2 tablespoons tomato paste
¾ cup freshly grated Parmesan cheese

3 egg whites
1 pound fresh shiitake mushrooms,
   stemmed and coarsely chopped
1 can (14 ounces) Italian peeled
   tomatoes, well drained and crushed
1½ cups chicken stock or canned broth
6 cannelloni or manicotti tubes

1. In a medium saucepan, melt 3 tablespoons of the butter over low heat. Add the onion, garlic and ham. Cook, covered, stirring occasionally, until the onion is soft and translucent, about 15 minutes.

2. Add the pork and increase the heat to moderately low. Cook, stirring, until the pork is crumbly and no longer pink, about 10 minutes.

3. Add a pinch of salt and season generously with pepper. Stir in the nutmeg, white wine and ¼ cup of the heavy cream. Increase the heat and bring the mixture to a boil. Reduce the heat slightly and cook, stirring, until all the liquid is evaporated, about 25 minutes.

4. Remove from heat and transfer to a bowl. Stir in the parsley, tomato paste and 3 tablespoons of the Parmesan cheese. Let cool to room temperature. Beat the egg whites until frothy; stir into the meat. (*The filling can be made 1 day ahead. Cover with plastic wrap and refrigerate. Let the mixture return to room temperature before proceeding.*)

5. In a medium skillet, melt the remaining 4 tablespoons butter over moderately high heat. Add the mushrooms and cook, stirring, until softened, about 5 minutes. Add the crushed tomatoes and cook, stirring, for 1 minute. Add the chicken

PASTA

stock and the remaining 1½ cups cream and bring to a boil. Reduce the heat slightly and cook, stirring occasionally, until reduced by about one-third, 15 to 20 minutes. Remove from the heat and stir in the remaining Parmesan cheese.

6. In a large pot of boiling salted water, cook the cannelloni, stirring gently, until al dente, 10 to 20 minutes. (Cooking time can vary greatly, depending on the brand of pasta.) Drain, rinse with cold water and drain again.

7. Divide half of the shiitake sauce among 6 individual gratin dishes. Divide the pork filling evenly among the 6 cannelloni tubes and place one in each gratin dish. (*The recipe can be prepared up to 3 hours ahead. Cover tightly with plastic wrap and refrigerate.*)

8. Preheat the oven to 375°. Divide the remaining shiitake sauce evenly over the cannelloni. Set the gratin dishes in the upper third of the oven and bake until the sauce is bubbling, the filling is heated through and the tops of the cannelloni are lightly browned, 15 to 20 minutes.
—Michael McLaughlin

LASAGNETTE WITH RADICCHIO

Palio features the light elegance of northern Italian cuisine, as exemplified by this delightful dish of grilled radicchio sandwiched between delicate sheets of pasta.
♆ A fruity white, such as Pinot Grigio or Gewürztraminer

12 First-Course
Servings

½ recipe Food & Wine's Fresh Pasta
    (p. 254)
2¼ pounds radicchio or escarole
1 cup olive oil
1 shallot, minced
1 garlic clove, minced
1 cup chicken stock or canned broth
½ teaspoon salt
½ teaspoon freshly ground pepper
Béchamel Sauce (p. 264)
1¼ cups freshly grated Parmesan
    cheese (4 to 5 ounces)
6 ounces whole-milk mozzarella cheese,
    thinly sliced
4 tablespoons unsalted butter, melted

1. Prepare the pasta through Step 4. Cut the dough into 3 sections and roll each flattened piece in a pasta machine down to the second-to-the-last setting; the pasta should be about ⅟₁₆ inch thick. Cut the sheets of pasta into 4-by-2-inch rectangles.

2. In a large saucepan of boiling salted water, cook half of the pasta rectangles, stirring constantly, until barely tender, about 30 seconds. With a slotted spoon, remove the pieces and place them in a large bowl of cold water. Repeat with the remaining pasta rectangles. Remove each piece of pasta separately from the bowl and drain on paper towels.

3. Preheat the broiler. Remove the tough outer leaves from the radicchio and cut out the cores. Separate the leaves. Working in batches, cover a large baking sheet or jelly-roll pan with radicchio leaves and drizzle 2 tablespoons of olive oil over the leaves. Toss to coat. Broil the leaves 6 inches from the heat until lightly browned, about 2 minutes (the radicchio will

HOMEMADE PASTA TIPS

Preparing fresh pasta at home is as easy as it is rewarding. Here are a few tips to ensure success:
• To prevent the dough from sticking to the machine, dust it lightly with flour as you roll it out. Don't use more flour than necessary, however, as it may toughen the dough.
• As you roll out one piece of dough, keep the others covered with a towel.
• For noodles, do all of your rolling out first, then do all the cutting.
• Cook 1 pound of fresh pasta in at least 5 quarts of boiling water.
• Fresh pasta can be ready in less than 1 minute, so stand by as it cooks.

shrink as it cooks). Repeat in 3 more batches with the remaining radicchio. Stack the leaves in piles and cut into ½-inch strips.

4. In a large skillet heat the remaining ½ cup olive oil. Add the shallot and garlic and cook over moderate heat until fragrant, about 30 seconds. Add the radicchio and chicken stock. Reduce the heat to low and simmer until the radicchio is tender and the stock has almost evaporated, about 10 minutes. Season with the salt and pepper.

5. Preheat the oven to 350°. Butter a large shallow rectangular baking dish that will hold half the pasta rectangles in a single layer. (If necessary use a large and a smaller baking dish.) Spread 1 cup of the Béchamel Sauce over the bottom. Place ¾ cup of the Parmesan cheese on a plate and dredge each pasta rectangle in the cheese to coat both sides. Arrange a single layer of cheese-coated pasta over the béchamel. Spread the radicchio on the pasta and arrange the mozzarella slices on top. Spoon 1 cup of the béchamel sauce over the mozzarella. Dip the remaining pasta rectangles in the Parmesan and cover the filling with the pasta. Spread the remaining béchamel sauce over the top. Sprinkle on the remaining ½ cup Parmesan cheese and drizzle the melted butter over all.

6. Bake in the middle of the oven for about 30 minutes, until the top is golden brown.
—*Palio, New York City*

LASAGNA WITH FOUR CHEESES

This very rich lasagna can be served as a separate pasta course or as a side dish with the meal.

8 to 10 Servings

½ pound lasagna noodles
4½ tablespoons unsalted butter
3 tablespoons all-purpose flour
4 cups hot milk
1 cup coarsely grated Swiss Gruyère cheese (about ¼ pound)
1¼ cups finely grated Parmesan cheese (4 to 5 ounces)
¾ cup diced mozzarella cheese (about ¼ pound)
1 cup grated Pecorino Romano or Italian Fontina cheese (about ¼ pound)
¾ teaspoon freshly ground white pepper

1. In a large pot of boiling salted water, cook the lasagna, stirring gently occasionally, until al dente, 10 to 12 minutes. Drain and lay the noodles in a single layer on kitchen towels.

2. Preheat the oven to 350°. Butter a 13-by-9-by-2-inch baking dish.

3. In a large heavy saucepan, melt 3 tablespoons of the butter over moderately low heat. Whisk in the flour and cook, stirring constantly, for 2 to 3 minutes without browning, to make a roux. Gradually whisk in the hot milk in a slow, steady stream, stirring until smooth. Bring to a boil, reduce the heat slightly and cook, stirring frequently, for 5 minutes. Add the Gruyère, 1 cup of the Parmesan, the mozzarella and Romano and cook until the cheeses melt, 5 to 7 minutes. Season with the pepper.

4. Line the bottom of the baking

dish with one-fourth of the lasagna noodles. Spoon on one-fourth of the cheese filling; spread to cover evenly. Repeat with the remaining ingredients to make 3 more layers of each. Sprinkle the remaining ¼ cup of Parmesan over the top layer of cheese filling and dot with the remaining 1½ tablespoons butter.

5. Bake for 30 to 40 minutes, until bubbly and golden brown. Serve immediately.
—Helen Millman

LASAGNA WITH ROASTED CHICKEN AND PORCINI MUSHROOMS

This lasagna, created by the corporate executive-chef Steven Singer, is layered in small molds that hold individual servings at the Sfuzzi restaurants.

🍷 A light, fruity red, such as an Italian Dolcetto d'Alba, would offer a welcome contrast to the richness of this dish. A Ceretto "Rossana" or Vietti "Sant'Anna" are excellent examples.

6 Large Servings

One 3-pound roasting chicken
1 tablespoon plus 1¼ teaspoons salt
¾ teaspoon freshly ground pepper
1 small lemon, cut in half
1 medium red onion, cut in half
1 fresh rosemary sprig or ½ teaspoon dried
⅓ cup plus 3 tablespoons extra-virgin olive oil
1½ ounces dried porcini mushrooms (about 1¼ cups)
¼ pound mixed fresh mushrooms (button, shiitake or oyster), sliced ¼ inch thick
2 large garlic cloves, chopped
¾ pound fresh spinach, stems removed
2 tablespoons chopped fresh oregano or ½ teaspoon dried
1 pound fresh mozzarella, cut into ¼-inch dice, plus ½ cup (¼ pound), shredded
1 pound ricotta cheese (2 cups)
1⅓ cups freshly grated Pecorino Romano cheese (4 to 5 ounces)
½ cup coarsely chopped fresh basil
Five 6-by-12-inch sheets of fresh pasta (see Note)
Tomato Butter Sauce (p. 263)
2 tablespoons chives, cut into 1-inch lengths, for garnish

1. Preheat the oven to 400°. Season the cavity of the chicken with ⅛ teaspoon each of the salt and pepper and stuff with the lemon halves, onion halves and rosemary sprig. Tie the legs together to close the cavity and rub the skin with 1 tablespoon of the olive oil and ⅛ teaspoon each salt and pepper. Set the chicken in a roasting pan and roast for 1 hour to 70 minutes, until the juices run clear when a thigh is pricked. Let cool slightly, then remove all of the meat, tearing it into 1-inch chunks. Discard the bones, skin and fat; set the meat aside. (*The chicken can be prepared up to 1 day ahead and refrigerated, covered.*)

2. In a small bowl, soak the dried porcini mushrooms in hot water to generously cover until softened, about 20 minutes. Drain and rinse carefully; pat dry and coarsely chop. Set aside.

3. In a large nonreactive skillet, heat ⅓ cup olive oil over moderately high heat until hot, about 2 minutes. Add the fresh mushrooms and the garlic and cook, stirring, until the mushrooms are softened, about

3 minutes. Add the reserved porcini and cook until heated through, about 2 minutes. Add the spinach, reduce the heat to moderate and cook, stirring, until almost all of the liquid has evaporated, about 10 minutes. Add the oregano, 1 teaspoon of the salt and the remaining ½ teaspoon pepper. Remove from the heat and stir in the reserved chicken. Season with additional salt and pepper, if necessary. Set aside.

4. In a large bowl, combine the diced mozzarella, ricotta, Romano and basil.

5. In a large saucepan, combine the remaining 1 tablespoon salt with 4 quarts of water and bring to a boil over high heat. Add the pasta sheets, one at a time, and boil until tender, about 1½ minutes. Using two slotted spoons or spatulas, carefully remove each sheet and transfer to a work surface. Using your fingers, coat each side with a little of the remaining olive oil to prevent sticking. Repeat with the 4 remaining sheets of pasta.

6. Preheat the oven to 350°. Lightly oil the bottom of a 13-by-9-by-2-inch glass baking dish. Line the bottom of the dish with one layer of pasta using one sheet and portions of another to cover. Spread evenly with half of the cheese mixture and then cover with another layer of pasta. Spread all of the spinach-mushroom-chicken mixture on the pasta and cover with another layer of pasta. Spread with the remaining cheese mixture and top with a final layer of pasta. Sprinkle the shredded mozzarella on top. (*The lasagna can be assembled 1 day ahead and refrigerated, covered.*)

7. Bake the lasagna for about 30 minutes, until heated through. Do not let it come to a boil or the cheese will become rubbery.

8. Preheat the broiler. Broil the lasagna 4 inches from the heat until the top is browned, about 1 minute. Cool for 10 minutes before cutting into 6 portions.

9. Spoon a heaping ¼ cup of the Tomato Butter Sauce onto 6 warmed dinner plates. Place the lasagna in the center and garnish with the chives. Serve immediately, with the remaining sauce passed separately.

NOTE: Fresh pasta sheets are usually available at specialty stores that sell freshly cut pasta.
—*Steven Singer, Sfuzzi*

CAPPELLETTI IN CAPON BROTH FROM GUBBIO

These filled hat-shaped pasta, similar to but smaller than *cappellacci*, are traditionally served in capon broth for Christmas lunch in Umbria. Ask your butcher to grind the meat for you, or you can grind it yourself in a food processor.

8 Servings

3 cups all-purpose flour
1¼ teaspoons salt
4 whole eggs plus 1 egg yolk
1 tablespoon unsalted butter
1¼ ounces ground lean veal
1¼ ounces ground lean pork
2½ ounces ground skinless, boneless chicken breast
⅓ cup freshly grated Parmesan cheese
Pinch of freshly grated nutmeg
Pinch of cinnamon
3 quarts Capon Broth (p. 265), chicken stock or unsalted canned chicken broth
Freshly grated Parmesan cheese, as accompaniment

FESTIVE PASTAS

Italians eat pasta all year long—stuffed pasta, dried pasta, fresh egg pasta. And then at Christmastime each town and village, each city and *paese* has its own special pasta dish. This may be the one time of year that these festive pastas appear on the table. If this is Mantua, it must be *agnolini*; and if it's Ferrara, it's pumpkin-filled tortelli. It's not Christmas in Gubbio, the quaint medieval city north of Perugia, unless there are hat-shaped cappelletti floating in rich broth.
—Carol Field

1. In a food processor, combine the flour and 1 teaspoon of the salt. Process briefly to mix. With the machine on, add the whole eggs one at a time to form a loose dough. (If the dough isn't quite moist enough, add a few drops of water.) Turn out onto a lightly floured surface and knead until it forms a smooth ball, about 1 minute. Cover with plastic wrap and let rest for at least 20 minutes. (*The recipe can be prepared to this point up to 1 day ahead. Cover and refrigerate.*)

2. In a small skillet, melt the butter over moderately low heat. Add the veal, pork and chicken and cook, stirring occasionally, until the pork is no longer pink, about 10 minutes.

3. Transfer the cooked meats to a medium bowl and let cool. Mix in the egg yolk, Parmesan, nutmeg, cinnamon and remaining ¼ teaspoon salt. (*This filling can be made up to 2 days ahead. Refrigerate, covered.*)

4. Divide the pasta dough into pieces the size of a lemon. Roll out each piece through a pasta machine to the thinnest setting. Using a 2-inch cookie cutter, cut the dough into rounds.

5. Spoon ½ teaspoon of the filling onto the center of each round. Moisten the edges with a bit of water and fold in half to form a half-moon shape. Using your fingertips, pinch the edges firmly together to seal well. Shape into little hats by bringing the two edges together, overlapping one pointed edge on top of the other and pressing them firmly together.

6. In a large saucepan, bring the Capon Broth to a boil over high heat. Add the cappelletti and cook until the pasta is tender, about 5 minutes. Ladle the broth and pasta into soup bowls at once. Pass a bowl of Parmesan cheese on the side.
—*Carol Field*

CAPPELLACI OF PUMPKIN

In Italy this hat-shaped pasta is filled with pumpkin. Here I frequently use butternut squash, available year-round.

8 Servings

4 cups unbleached all-purpose flour
2 teaspoons salt
5 extra-large whole eggs plus
  1 egg yolk
2½ pounds pumpkin or butternut
  squash, cut into large chunks,
  seeds removed
2 sticks (8 ounces) unsalted butter—1
  stick cut up and at room
  temperature, 1 stick melted
About 1⅓ cups freshly grated
  Parmesan cheese
¼ teaspoon freshly grated nutmeg
¼ teaspoon freshly ground pepper

1. In a food processor, combine the flour and 1 teaspoon of the salt. Process briefly to mix. With the machine on, add the whole eggs one at a time to form a soft dough. (If the dough isn't quite moist enough, add a few drops of water.) Turn out onto a lightly floured surface and knead until it forms a smooth ball, about 1 minute. Cover with plastic wrap and let rest for at least 20 minutes. (*The dough can*

be made 1 day ahead. Cover with plastic wrap and refrigerate; or freeze for up to 2 weeks.)

2. Preheat the oven to 350°. Put the pumpkin or squash chunks on an oiled baking sheet. Bake for 30 to 45 minutes, or until tender. Let cool, then remove the skin. Press through a ricer or a coarse sieve or puree briefly in a food processor.

3. Transfer the puree to a bowl. Add the stick of softened butter, the egg yolk, ⅓ cup of the Parmesan cheese, the nutmeg, pepper and the remaining 1 teaspoon salt. Mix well until the puree is firm and holds together well. If it is too soft, add a little more Parmesan cheese.

4. Divide the dough into pieces the size of a lemon. Roll out through a pasta machine to the next to the thinnest setting. Set the sheets of pasta on a well-floured work surface and cut with a 3-inch round cookie cutter. Keep the dough you are not working with under plastic wrap or a towel to keep it moist.

5. Spoon a heaping teaspoon of squash filling into the center of each circle. Moisten the edge of each pasta circle with a bit of water and fold in half to form a half-moon shape. Press with your fingertips to seal the edges firmly. Shape into little hats by bringing the two edges together, overlapping the pointed edges one on top of the other and pressing them firmly together. Repeat with the rest of the dough. (If you are not going to use the cappellacci immediately, arrange on a cookie sheet lined with parchment paper, cover with plastic wrap and set aside at room temperature for up to 1 hour. Or refrigerate to hold longer.)

6. In a large pot of boiling salted water, cook the cappellacci until they float to the surface, about 5 minutes. Be careful not to overcook, or the filling will ooze out. Drain and rinse. Transfer the cappellacci to a warm serving dish. Pour the melted butter over the top, sprinkle with some Parmesan and toss gently. Pass the remainder of the cheese separately.
—Carol Field

TORTELLI WITH TOMATO SAUCE

Tortelli such as my mother, Theresa Rossi-Ferretti, made entail some effort and were done on a leisurely Sunday.

6 Servings

4 cups all-purpose flour
¼ teaspoon plus a pinch of salt
2 eggs
1 pound ricotta cheese
½ cup freshly grated Parmesan cheese
1 tablespoon minced fresh basil
1 tablespoon minced parsley
1 garlic clove, minced
¼ teaspoon freshly ground pepper
Tomato Sauce (p. 261)

1. Place the flour and pinch of salt in a large bowl. Beat 1 of the eggs with ½ cup lukewarm water. Mix into the flour. If it is dry, add a bit more water by drops. Let the dough rest in the bowl, covered with plastic wrap, for at least 1 hour.

141

GRATING CHEESES

Grana, which, in Italian, means grain, is the generic term for the hard, granular Italian cheeses that were developed about AD 1200 in the Po Valley. The oldest and most well known of these cheeses is Parmigiano-Reggiano (known as *grana tipico* in Italy); others are Asiago, Romano, Lodigiano, Padano and Piacentino. These cheeses are usually made in thick wheels with a diameter of up to 18 inches.

Although these sharp, flavorful cheeses are often used for grating—over pasta or vegetables, into salads—or for adding to recipes, young *grana* (aged for less than a year) can be served as a table cheese.

2. In a medium bowl, beat the remaining egg. Add the ricotta, Parmesan, basil, parsley, garlic, remaining ¼ teaspoon salt and the pepper and beat well. Refrigerate, covered, until ready to use.

3. Divide the dough into 4 pieces. Wrap 3 of the pieces in plastic wrap and set aside. Cut the piece of dough into 2 smaller pieces and roll each piece with a hand-crank pasta machine through the third to last setting, ¹⁄₁₆ to ⅛ inch thick (or roll the dough by hand to ⅛ inch thick). Drop generous ½ teaspoonfuls of the cheese filling, 1 inch apart in straight rows, on 1 of the sheets of rolled dough. Place the second sheet on top of the filling. Using your finger, press lightly and indent between the filled mounds in both directions. With a fluted pastry wheel or a knife, cut across and down the sheets to create the 2-inch squares of tortelli. Repeat with the remaining dough and filling. (*The recipe can be made to this point up to 2 days ahead, wrapped and refrigerated, or frozen for up to 1 month.*)

4. In a large flameproof casserole, bring 2½ quarts of salted water to a boil over high heat. Add the tortelli and return to a boil. Cook until al dente, about 6 minutes. Drain; then toss in a large bowl with the Tomato Sauce.
—Fred Ferretti

TORTELLI WITH SWISS CHARD IN CREAMY TOMATO SAUCE

This pasta is stuffed with nutmeg-scented swiss chard and ricotta and is served in a creamy tomato sauce. The green filling and red sauce seem perfect for Christmas.

6 Servings

2 *bunches of swiss chard, white rib removed*
1¼ *cups whole-milk ricotta cheese*
1 *cup plus 2 tablespoons freshly grated Parmesan cheese (about ¼ pound)*
1 *stick (4 ounces) unsalted butter, at room temperature*
1 *egg*
¼ *teaspoon freshly grated nutmeg*
¾ *teaspoon salt*
¾ *teaspoon freshly ground pepper*
Egg Pasta *(p. 254)*
2 *tablespoons extra-virgin olive oil*
1 *large red onion, minced*
⅓ *cup dry white wine*
1 *can (28 ounces) Italian peeled tomatoes, drained and chopped*
2 *sprigs of fresh rosemary or sage*
⅓ *cup heavy cream*

1. Put the chard in a large saucepan, cover and cook over high heat with only the water that remains on the leaves, stirring once, until the chard is tender, 8 to 10 minutes. Drain, rinse with cold water and squeeze dry; finely chop.

2. In a medium bowl, combine the chard, ricotta, Parmesan, 4 tablespoons of the butter, the egg, nutmeg, ½ teaspoon each of the salt and pepper. (*The recipe can be prepared to this point up to 2 days ahead. Refrigerate, covered.*)

3. Divide the Egg Pasta into pieces the size of an egg. Roll out one piece of dough through the pasta machine to the next to the thinnest setting. Set the sheet of pasta on a well-floured work surface and trim to about 4 inches wide and 10 inches long.

4. Mound the filling onto the pasta by tablespoons, about 2½ inches apart (making 3 rows down and 3 across). Moisten all the edges and around the mounds with a pastry brush dipped in water. Roll out a second piece of pasta through the machine. Set on top of the pasta with the filling. Press down around the edges of each mound to enclose it tightly. Cut straight between the filling in both directions with a knife or pastry wheel to form square tortelli. Finish the process using all the pasta dough and filling. Sprinkle a little cornmeal on a tray or cookie sheet, arrange the tortelli on it and cover with a kitchen towel or plastic wrap. (*The recipe can be prepared to this point up to several hours ahead; refrigerate.*)

5. In a large nonreactive saucepan, melt the remaining 4 tablespoons butter in the oil over moderate heat. Add the onion and cook over moderately low heat until light golden and soft, 15 to 20 minutes. Add the wine, increase the heat to high and cook until it almost all evaporates, about 10 minutes.

6. Add the tomatoes and the rosemary. Cook, covered, over low heat for about 30 minutes. Stir in 2 tablespoons of hot water and the cream, cook for 2 to 3 minutes. Season with the remaining ¼ teaspoon each salt and pepper. (*The sauce can be made up to 1 day ahead. Refrigerate covered.*)

7. In a large pot of boiling salted

water, cook the tortelli until tender, 3 to 5 minutes; drain carefully. Immediately transfer to a large serving bowl. Pour the sauce over the tortelli, toss and serve.
—*Carol Field*

BASIC RAVIOLI

This is *Food & Wine*'s basic technique for forming and cooking ravioli. Use the following suggestions for flavored pasta doughs, ravioli fillings and sauces to create various combinations.

*Makes About 6
Dozen 2-Inch
Ravioli*

*Food & Wine's Fresh Pasta (p. 254),
    Spinach Pasta (p. 255) or Tomato
    Pasta (p. 256)
Chicken Liver Filling with Prosciutto
    and Lemon (p. 146), Spinach and
    Ricotta Filling (p. 145), Fennel
    Sausage and Chicken Filling with
    Garlic (p. 145) or Potato, Onion
    and Cheese Filling (p. 144)
Creamy Tomato Sauce (p. 262) or
    Béchamel Sauce with Cheese
    (p. 264)*

1. Divide the dough into sixths. Working with one piece at a time, pat the dough into a rectangle roughly 6 by 4 inches. Knead the dough by passing it through a pasta machine at the widest setting 2 or 3 times, until it is silky smooth and no longer sticky.

2. Continue to pass the dough through the pasta machine, reducing the space between the rollers

by one number each time, until the pasta has passed through the thinnest setting.

3. Cut the band of dough into two even lengths. Place one strip of dough on a flat work surface. Spoon or pipe mounds (about 1½ teaspoons) of filling onto the strip of dough, about ½ inch in from the edges and spaced about ½ inch apart.

4. Paint the exposed areas of dough lightly with water. Drape the second sheet of dough on top and shape the ravioli with your fingers, pressing on the air and sealing the edges. Cut the ravioli apart with a sharp knife, a jagged pastry wheel or a ravioli stamp.

5. Cook the ravioli, 12 at a time, in a large pot of boiling salted water until the pasta is al dente, 6 to 7 minutes; the filling will be hot and cooked. Do not overcrowd or the ravioli may stick.

6. Drain the ravioli well and serve with one of the sauces.
—F&W

POTATO, ONION AND CHEESE RAVIOLI FILLING

See the Basic Ravioli recipe (p. 143) for how to combine this filling with pasta and sauce to make delicious ravioli.

Makes Enough for
6 Dozen 2-Inch
Ravioli

2 medium baking potatoes (about 8 ounces each), peeled and quartered
1 tablespoon olive oil
2 medium onions, chopped
½ cup freshly grated Parmesan cheese
8 ounces farmer's cheese
1 egg
1¼ teaspoons salt
¼ teaspoon freshly ground white pepper
¼ teaspoon freshly grated nutmeg

1. In a medium saucepan of boiling salted water, cook the potatoes until tender, 15 to 20 minutes. Drain; then put through a ricer or the medium disk of a food mill.

2. Meanwhile, in a medium skillet, heat the oil. Add the onions and sauté over moderate heat until softened and translucent, about 5 minutes. Place the onions in a food processor and process to puree.

144

RAVIOLI MAKERS

There are a variety of ravioli-making devices, ranging from the simple to the not-so-simple. The easiest method of all, of course, it to press the dough together with your fingers and then use a knife or a pastry jagger (which leaves the ravioli with their typical zig-zag edging) to cut the stuffed squares of dough apart.

A more efficient method is to use a rolling cutter designed to press the edges of the dough squares together at the same time that it cuts them out. There are also cookie-cutterlike ravioli stamps that will do the same thing, although they cut out one ravioli at a time.

To make ravioli on an assembly line, there is a machine that looks like a hand-cranked pasta machine, but it has a conveyor belt. Sheets of dough with ravioli filling sandwiched between them is fed through the die-cut rollers, which stamp out the individual ravioli.

The compromise device, and the one that we favor, is a ravioli plaque, which consists of a metal tray with 12 round depressions (it looks like half of an egg carton) and a frame with 12 die-cut ravioli stamps. A sheet of dough is placed over the metal tray, the filling is placed over the depressions, the top sheet of dough is placed on top, and the stamping frame is pressed down to form the ravioli and cut them apart.

3. In a large bowl, combine the potatoes, onions, Parmesan cheese, farmer's cheese, egg, salt, pepper and nutmeg. Mix until well blended.

—John Robert Massie

SPINACH AND RICOTTA RAVIOLI FILLING

See the Basic Ravioli recipe (p. 143) for how to combine this filling with pasta and sauce to make delicious ravioli.

Makes Enough for
6 Dozen 2-Inch
Ravioli

1½ *pounds fresh spinach or 1½*
  packages (15 ounces) frozen
  spinach
1 *container (10 ounces) whole-milk*
  ricotta cheese
1 *cup freshly grated Parmesan cheese*
  (about ¼ pound)
2 *eggs*
1 *teaspoon salt*
⅛ *teaspoon freshly ground pepper*
¼ *teaspoon freshly grated nutmeg*

1. If using fresh spinach, steam for 2 to 3 minutes, until wilted and tender but still bright green. If using frozen, cook as directed on the package. Drain and rinse under cold running water until cooled. Squeeze the spinach by handfuls to remove as much water as possible.

2. Place the spinach in a food processor. Add the ricotta, Parmesan, eggs, salt, pepper and nutmeg. Puree for about 1 minute, until the spinach is finely chopped and thoroughly combined with the other ingredients.

—John Robert Massie

FENNEL SAUSAGE AND CHICKEN RAVIOLI FILLING WITH GARLIC

See the Basic Ravioli recipe (p. 143) for how to combine this filling with pasta and sauce to make delicious ravioli.

Makes Enough for
6 Dozen 2-Inch
Ravioli

2 *tablespoons olive oil*
1 *whole skinless, boneless chicken*
  breast (about 10 ounces)
6 *links (about 1¼ pounds) Italian*
  sweet sausages, casings removed
2 *garlic cloves, crushed through a press*
¼ *cup heavy cream*
Salt and freshly ground pepper

1. In a heavy medium skillet, heat the oil. Add the chicken breast and sauté over moderate heat, turning once, until lightly browned and resistant to the touch, about 10 minutes. Remove from the skillet and let cool.

2. Add the sausage to the same skillet. Sauté over moderate heat, stirring to break up the meat, for 4 minutes. Add the garlic and continue to cook until the meat begins to brown and there is no trace of pink, about 2 to 3 minutes longer. With a slotted spoon, remove the sausage from the skillet. Let cool to room temperature.

3. Cut the chicken into pieces; place in a food processor. Add the sausage, garlic and cream and chop for about 1 minute, until well blended. Season with salt and pepper to taste.

—John Robert Massie

CHICKEN LIVER RAVIOLI FILLING WITH PROSCIUTTO AND LEMON

See the Basic Ravioli recipe (p. 143) for how to combine this filling with pasta and sauce to make delicious ravioli.

Makes Enough for
6 Dozen 2-Inch
Ravioli

2 tablespoons olive oil
1 pound chicken livers, trimmed and cut in half
½ pound prosciutto, coarsely chopped
2 medium garlic cloves, crushed through a press
1 teaspoon grated lemon zest
1 teaspoon fresh lemon juice
½ cup freshly grated Parmesan cheese
3 tablespoons heavy cream

1. In a heavy, medium skillet, heat the oil. Add the livers and sauté over moderately high heat, tossing, until firmed but still rare and pink inside, 2 to 3 minutes. With a slotted spoon, remove the livers and let cool to room temperature.

2. In a food processor, combine the livers, prosciutto, garlic, lemon zest, lemon juice, Parmesan cheese and cream. Finely chop, turning the machine on and off quickly, until well blended.

—*John Robert Massie*

RAVIOLI WITH PORCINI SAUCE

At Rosa Ristorante, this sauce is served with ricotta and spinach ravioli. You can also serve it over plain pasta, as a first course, with freshly grated Parmesan cheese.

6 Servings

1 ounce dried porcini mushrooms
2 cups heavy cream
2 pounds cheese-and-spinach-filled ravioli
3 tablespoons unsalted butter
¼ teaspoon salt
⅛ teaspoon freshly ground pepper

1. In a medium bowl, cover the mushrooms with 1 cup of warm water and let soak for 30 minutes.

2. Strain the mushroom soaking liquid into a medium saucepan through several layers of dampened cheesecloth; set aside. Rinse the mushrooms well. Trim off any sandy stem ends. Coarsely chop the mushrooms and add to the saucepan.

3. Bring a large pot of water to a boil.

4. Meanwhile bring the mushroom liquid to a boil over high heat and cook until reduced to 3 tablespoons, about 7 minutes. Reduce the heat to moderate, add the cream and cook until reduced to 1½ cups, about 7 minutes longer.

5. Add the ravioli to the boiling water and cook until al dente, 6 to 7 minutes.

6. Remove from the sauce from the heat and whisk in the butter, 1 tablespoon at a time. Season with the salt and pepper.

7. Drain the ravioli and toss with the sauce.

—*Rosa Ristorante, Baldwin Park, California*

CRABMEAT RAVIOLI WITH CREAM SAUCE

Precut wonton skins are the same type of pasta normally used to make ravioli, but they do simplify the process considerably.

4 Main-Course or
9 First-Course
Servings

Ravioli:
1½ tablespoons unsalted butter
½ tablespoon all-purpose flour
¼ cup milk
1 egg, separated
2 scallions, chopped
½ pound lump crabmeat
1 tablespoon chopped parsley
2 tablespoons unsalted cracker crumbs
½ teaspoon salt
⅛ teaspoon freshly ground white
    pepper
Pinch of cayenne pepper
1½ packages (¾ pound each) wonton
    skins*

Cream Sauce:
2 cups heavy cream
1 stick (4 ounces) unsalted butter
½ teaspoon salt
⅛ teaspoon freshly ground white
    pepper
Pinch of cayenne pepper
4 scallions, thinly sliced
Freshly grated Parmesan cheese
*Available at Oriental groceries

1. *Make the ravioli:* In a small saucepan, melt ½ tablespoon of the butter over low heat. Add the flour and cook, whisking constantly, for 1 minute without letting the flour brown. Gradually add the milk, and bring to a boil, whisking constantly. Cook the sauce for 3 minutes, whisking from time to time. Remove from the heat and stir in the egg yolk. Set aside.

2. In a small skillet, melt the remaining 1 tablespoon butter. Add the scallions and cook over low heat until wilted, about 5 minutes. Scrape the scallions into a medium bowl and add the crabmeat, egg white, parsley, cracker crumbs, reserved sauce, salt, white pepper and cayenne.

3. Mound 2 teaspoons of the filling in the center of a wonton skin. Paint the edges with water, top with another wonton skin and press the edges together to seal. Repeat with the remaining wonton skins and filling. Cut the edges of each ravioli with a jagged-edged pastry wheel. Set the filled ravioli on a wire rack or lightly floured surface and let stand for 30 minutes, turning once.

4. Meanwhile, *make the cream sauce:* In a medium saucepan, bring the cream to a boil. Cook over moderate heat until reduced by one-third, 7 to 10 minutes. Remove from the heat and whisk in the butter, 1 tablespoon at a time. Season with the salt, pepper and cayenne and stir in the scallions.

5. Bring 2 large pots of salted water to a boil. Add half the ravioli to each and cook until al dente, about 8 minutes. Transfer the ravioli to a colander to drain.

6. Reheat the cream sauce and pour it into a large serving bowl. Add the ravioli and toss to coat. Pass the Parmesan separately.
—La Riviera, Metairie, Louisiana

UOVO AL TARTUFO

This simple but delicious tortello stuffed with spinach and egg is typical of Piero Selvaggio's respect for the traditions and pure tastes of Italian cuisine.

♀ Fruity red, such as California Gamay or Beaujolais

4 *Servings*

1 *stick (4 ounces) unsalted butter*
¾ *pound fresh spinach, stemmed*
2½ *tablespoons ricotta*
1 *cup freshly grated Parmesan cheese (about ¼ pound)*
5 *medium eggs*
⅛ *teaspoon salt*
¼ *teaspoon freshly ground pepper*
Pinch of freshly grated nutmeg
½ *recipe Food & Wine's Fresh Pasta (p. 254)*
1 *ounce truffles, shaved (optional)*

1. In a large skillet, melt 1 tablespoon of the butter over high heat. Add the spinach leaves and toss until just wilted. about 1 minute. Transfer the spinach to a sieve or colander and let cool. Squeeze out as much water as possible from the spinach and finely chop it.

2. In a small bowl, combine the chopped spinach, ricotta, ½ cup of the Parmesan, 1 of the eggs and the salt, pepper and nutmeg. Blend well.

3. Cut the Fresh Pasta dough into 4 equal pieces and roll out in a pasta machine to the thinnest setting. Using a pot lid as a guide, cut out 2 circles, 6 inches in diameter, from each pasta sheet.

4. Arrange 4 of the pasta rounds on a lightly floured baking sheet. Mound one-fourth of the spinach filling in the center of each of the 4 circles. Make a deep, wide well in the center of each spinach mound, leaving a ¾-inch border of pasta around the filling.

5. Break an egg into a saucer; if the egg white has a lot of watery liquid around it, gently blot with a paper towel. Slide the egg into the spinach well. Repeat with the remaining 3 eggs. Lightly moisten the rim of pasta around the spinach and place a top circle of pasta over each egg. Press the edges to seal. (*The recipe can be prepared to this point up to 2 hours ahead. Cover with plastic wrap and refrigerate.*)

6. Bring a wide saucepan or large flameproof casserole of salted water to a boil over high heat. Add the filled pasta rounds and cook, stirring occasionally, or until the pasta is al dente, about 2½ minutes. Remove with a slotted spoon onto 4 warm plates.

7. In a small skillet, melt the remaining 7 tablespoons butter over high heat and cook until just brown, about 1 minute. Immediately remove from the heat and drizzle over the pasta. Sprinkle on the remaining Parmesan cheese and garnish with truffles if desired. Serve at once.

—*Piero Selvaggio, Valentino, Los Angeles*

Cappelletti in Capon Broth from Gubbio (page 139).

At left, Tortelli with Tomato Sauce
(*page* 141). Above, Pasta Primavera
with Clams (*page* 120).

Christmas Eve Lasagna from Piedmont (page 104).

KRAFI WITH VEAL SGUAZET

Lidia Bastianich, co-owner with her husband, Felice, of Felidia Ristorante in Manhattan, hails from Istria, on the Italian-Yugoslav border, where *krafi* is a regional specialty. This delicate ravioli combines the heartiness of Italian pasta with the sweet-sour hints of Middle Eastern seasonings, like lemon, orange and raisins.

🍷 Fruity, rich red, such as red Burgundy or California Pinot Noir

4 to 6 Main-Course or 8 First-Course Servings

2 eggs
1½ teaspoons sugar
¾ pound Italian Fontina cheese shredded
¼ pound freshly grated Parmesan cheese (about 1 cup)
1 tablespoon dark rum
½ teaspoon grated lemon zest
½ teaspoon grated orange zest
½ cup golden raisins
¼ cup fresh bread crumbs
1 ounce dried porcini mushrooms
¼ cup olive oil
1 medium onion, chopped
2 slices of pancetta or bacon (about 2 ounces), chopped
¼ teaspoon salt
½ teaspoon freshly ground pepper
2 pounds boneless veal from the leg or shoulder cut into ½-inch cubes
2 bay leaves
1 small sprig of fresh rosemary or ½ teaspoon dried
2 whole cloves
½ cup dry white wine
2 tablespoons tomato paste
2 cups chicken stock or canned broth
Food & Wine's Fresh Pasta (p. 254)
Freshly grated Parmesan cheese

1. In a large bowl, beat the eggs and sugar until blended. Stir in the Fontina, Parmesan, rum, lemon zest, orange zest, raisins and bread crumbs. Mix well and set the filling aside.

2. Put the porcini in a small bowl. Add 1 cup of warm water and let soak until softened. about 30 minutes. Strain, reserving the soaking liquid. Rinse the mushrooms under running water to remove any grit; chop coarsely. Strain the liquid through several layers of dampened cheesecloth; reserve.

3. Meanwhile, in a large flame-proof casserole. heat the oil. Add the onion and pancetta, sprinkle on ⅛ teaspoon of the salt and ¼ teaspoon of the pepper and cook over moderate heat until the onion is golden, about 8 minutes.

4. Increase the heat to high, add half the veal cubes and sauté, tossing occasionally until browned, about 5 minutes. Push to the side, add the remaining veal and sauté until browned, about 5 minutes.

5. Add the chopped mushrooms to the casserole along with the bay leaves. rosemary and cloves. Add the wine and cook over high heat, stirring frequently, until the wine is almost evaporated, about 4 minutes. Reduce the heat to moderate, add the tomato paste and simmer,

stirring, for 2 minutes. Add the reserved mushroom soaking liquid and the chicken stock and bring to a boil over high heat. Reduce the heat to low and simmer, partially covered, until the veal is tender, about 45 minutes.

6. Remove the bay leaves and any rosemary stems. Skim off any fat from the surface and add the remaining ⅛ teaspoon salt and ¼ teaspoon pepper. (*The recipe can be prepared to this point up to 2 days ahead. Refrigerate, covered.*)

7. Divide the Fresh Pasta dough into 3 equal parts and roll in a pasta machine to the second-from-the-thinnest setting; trim the short ends to even, or roll out by hand on a lightly floured board to thickness of ¹⁄₁₆ inch. Cut lengthwise into 6-inch-wide strips and trim the short ends to even.

8. With a long side of the pasta facing you, dot the upper half of the rectangle with heaping tablespoons of the filling at 2½-inch intervals. Lightly moisten the dough all around the mounds. Fold the bottom half of the dough up and over to enclose the filling; press around the mounds with your fingers to seal. Stamp out the ravioli with a 3-inch round cutter. Press around the edges with the tines of a fork. (Lightly flour the work surface as necessary to prevent sticking.) Set on a lightly floured tray, cover with a slightly dampened kitchen towel and refrigerate, if desired, for up to 2 hours.

9. Reheat the veal sauce. Cook the krafi by dropping them one by one into a stockpot of boiling salted water. Stir gently with a wooden spoon to keep separate. Cook until the pasta is al dente, about 5 minutes. Drain gently into a colander. Return to the pot, add half of the sauce, toss to coat and divide among warm plates. Spoon the remaining sauce on top, and sprinkle with Parmesan cheese.
—*Lidia Bastianich, Felidia, New York City*

PIZZA & OTHER BREADS

FRESH ARTICHOKE PAN PIZZA

This method gives the artichokes an intense flavor that no other technique can supply. When you select artichokes, choose the biggest ones because they have the most flavorful hearts.

Here, there is far more garlic than most sane people would use, but this cooking method mellows and sweetens the garlic. If it seems too much for your taste, cut it back.

Makes 4 Individual
Pizzas

4 large artichokes
½ lemon
2 heads of garlic, cloves separated and
 peeled (about 24)
8 sprigs of flat-leaf parsley
¼ cup extra-virgin olive oil
1½ teaspoons fresh thyme leaves
¼ teaspoon salt
¼ teaspoon freshly ground pepper
1⅓ cups diced mozzarella cheese (about
 ½ pound)
Quick Semolina Pizza Dough (p. 257)

1. With a small sharp knife, cut the leaves from around each artichoke, using a circular motion, until you reach the tender, inner leaves. Cut the tops off the leaves and continue to trim the artichoke heart down to the base, removing all the tough, fibrous outer skin. Cut the heart in half and cut out the choke. Rub the heart all over with the cut lemon.

2. In a large bowl, combine the artichoke hearts, garlic, parsley, olive oil, thyme, salt and pepper; toss to mix.

3. In a large nonreactive saucepan, arrange the artichokes with the garlic-parsley mixture, bottom-side down, in the pan and sprinkle with 3 tablespoons water. Cover tightly and cook over low heat, turning occasionally, until the artichokes are light brown and very tender, about 30 minutes. Add a few tablespoons of water after 10 minutes to prevent burning.

4. Remove the pan from the heat. Remove the garlic and parsley from the pan and finely chop. In a small bowl, combine the mozzarella, garlic and parsley. Remove the artichokes from the pan and slice them ¼ inch thick. (*The recipe can be prepared to this point up to 1 day ahead; cover the artichokes and refrigerate.*)

5. Roll the Semolina Pizza Dough into a log 1½ inches in diameter. Cut into 4 equal pieces. Roll out each piece of dough into a 7-inch round about   inch thick. Cover the rounds with plastic wrap. Heat a 9- or 10-inch cast-iron skillet over moderately high heat until hot.

6. Place one of the dough rounds into the hot skillet, reduce the heat to low, cover and cook until the crust is dark brown on the bottom, about 3 minutes. (Check after 2 minutes and adjust the heat, if necessary, to avoid burning the dough.)

7. Remove the pizza crust from the skillet. Layer the crust with ⅓ cup of the mozzarella mixture and one-fourth of the artichoke slices; season with additional salt and pepper to taste. Brush the top with

any remaining oil from the pot. Return the pizza to the skillet and cook, covered, until the cheese melts, about 2 minutes. Repeat the process with the 3 other rounds.
—Anne Disrude

SCALLION AND OLIVE PAN PIZZA WITH ROSEMARY

This topping combines elements of several classic Italian vegetable recipes. Here, braised scallions with bay leaves and rosemary are offset by olives and a creamy goat cheese. Don't be afraid to experiment with other varieties of onions; red onions or Vidalia onions, when they are in season, are good alternatives.

Makes 4 Individual Pizzas

¼ *cup extra-virgin olive oil*
12 *bunches of scallions (white and light green), sliced ½ inch thick, plus ¼ cup minced scallion green*
3 *imported bay leaves*
2 *sprigs of fresh rosemary plus 1 teaspoon minced*
¾ *teaspoon salt*
¼ *teaspoon freshly ground pepper*
¼ *cup coarsely chopped olives, preferably Gaeta or Niçoise*
Quick Semolina Pizza Dough (p. 257)
½ *cup goat cheese (about ¼ pound)*

1. In a large heavy saucepan, heat the olive oil. Add the sliced scallions, bay leaves, rosemary sprigs and 3 tablespoons of water. Cover and cook over moderately low heat, stirring occasionally, until the scallions are very tender, about 20 minutes. Remove the pan from the heat. Discard the bay leaves and the rosemary sprigs. Stir in the minced rosemary, salt, pepper and olives. (*The recipe can be prepared to this point 1 day ahead; cover and refrigerate.*)

2. Roll the Semolina Pizza Dough into a log 1½ inches in diameter. Cut into 4 equal pieces. Roll out each piece of dough into a 7-inch round about ¹⁄₁₆ inch thick. Cover the rounds with plastic wrap. Heat a 9- or 10-inch cast-iron skillet over moderately high heat, until hot.

3. Place one of the dough rounds into the hot skillet, reduce the heat to low, cover and cook until the crust is dark brown on the bottom, about 3 minutes. (Check after 2 minutes and adjust the heat, if necessary, to avoid burning the dough.)

4. Remove the pizza crust from the skillet. Spread the crust with 2 tablespoons of goat cheese and top with about ½ cup of the cooked scallion mixture. Return the pizza to the skillet and cook, covered, until the cheese melts, about 2 minutes. Sprinkle with the minced scallion green and serve. Repeat the process with the 3 other rounds.
—Anne Disrude

PIZZA POINTERS

• Improvise your toppings, keeping in mind that the vegetables should not be too wet or heavy.
• Be generous with seasonings, but sparing with cheese.
• Keep on hand some store-bought toppings, such as pesto, artichoke puree or sun-dried tomatoes.
• Always try to use superior ingredients, such as top-quality mozzarella and extra-virgin olive oil. If you use packaged mozzarella, get only the whole-milk variety; the part-skim mozzarella is saltier and more rubbery.
• Try to pick toppings that can be made ahead. It will simplify the assembly process considerably.
• Make the pizza dough well ahead of time. If you are using the Quick Semolina Pizza Dough (p. 257), you can store it in the refrigerator or freezer. If you are using a yeast-risen dough, such as Basic Pizza Dough (p. 256), it can be stored for an hour or so in the refrigerator, but for longer storage it should be frozen.
• Let frozen pizza dough thaw, then roll it out, cover with plastic wrap and let it come to room temperature before topping and baking.

SPICY SPINACH AND
GARLIC PAN PIZZA

Any green—spring dandelion, baby mustard, beet greens, broccoli raab or even savoy cabbage—can be used instead of the spinach.

♟ The mildly spicy, savory toppings of this particular pizza would be best complemented by an equally flavorful medium-bodied red, such as Merlot. Look for Arbor Crest from Washington State or Louis M. Martini Russian River Valley from California.

*Makes 4 Individual
Pizzas*

3 pounds fresh spinach, stemmed and
    washed
¼ cup extra-virgin olive oil
8 garlic cloves, chopped
¼ teaspoon crushed hot red pepper
1 tablespoon plus 1 teaspoon anchovy
    paste
½ teaspoon salt
¼ teaspoon freshly ground black
    pepper
Quick Semolina Pizza Dough (p. 257)
1⅓ cups diced mozzarella cheese (about
    ½ pound)

1. In a large nonreactive saucepan, cook the spinach, covered, with only the water that clings to the leaves, over high heat, stirring occasionally, until tender, about 6 to 10 minutes. Drain, rinse under cold water and squeeze out as much moisture as possible.

2. In a large skillet, heat the olive oil over low heat. Add the garlic and hot pepper and cook until the garlic is lightly browned, about 8 minutes. Stir in the anchovy paste and cook for 1 minute longer.

3. Increase the heat to moderate and add the spinach. Toss the spinach to evenly coat with the oil. Reduce the heat to low and cook for 3 minutes. Season with the salt and pepper and remove the saucepan from the heat. (*The recipe can be prepared to this point up to 1 day ahead; cover and refrigerate.*)

4. Roll the Semolina Pizza Dough into a log 1½ inches in diameter. Cut into 4 equal pieces. Roll out each piece of dough into a 7-inch round about ¹⁄₁₆ inch thick. Cover the rounds with plastic wrap. Heat a 9- or 10-inch cast-iron skillet over moderately high heat until hot.

5. Place one of the dough rounds into the hot skillet, reduce the heat to low, cover and cook until the crust is dark brown on the bottom, about 3 minutes. (Check after 2 minutes and adjust the heat, if necessary, to avoid burning the dough.)

6. Remove the pizza crust from the skillet. Layer the crust with ⅓ cup mozzarella and top with ½ cup spinach. Return the pizza to the skillet and cook, covered, until the cheese melts, about 2 minutes. Repeat the process with the 3 other rounds.
—*Anne Disrude*

GARLICKY POTATO PAN PIZZA

The pan-roasted diced potatoes for this pizza are cooked in oil and butter with garlic and rosemary. Leave the potato skins on for extra flavor.

*Makes 4 Individual
Pizzas*

1 *tablespoon unsalted butter*
3 *tablespoons extra-virgin olive oil*
8 *large garlic cloves, thinly sliced*
1 *sprig of fresh rosemary*
1⅓ *cups diced mozzarella cheese (about
    ½ pound)*
1½ *pounds baking potatoes, cut into
    ⅜-inch dice*
¾ *teaspoon salt*
¼ *teaspoon freshly ground pepper*
3 *tablespoons chopped parsley*
Quick Semolina Pizza Dough (p. 257)

1. In a large heavy skillet, melt the butter in the oil over moderate heat. Add the garlic and rosemary and cook until the garlic is lightly browned, about 3 minutes. Remove the garlic and rosemary with a slotted spoon and chop. In a small bowl, combine the mozzarella, garlic and rosemary; toss to mix.

2. Add the potatoes to the skillet and toss to coat with the oil. Cook, tossing occasionally, until the potatoes are soft and well browned, about 25 minutes. Season with the salt and pepper and transfer to a large dish or bowl lined with paper towels to absorb the oil. Add the parsley and toss.

3. Roll the Semolina Pizza Dough into a log 1½ inches in diameter. Cut into 4 equal pieces. Roll out each piece of dough into a 7-inch round about 1/16 inch thick. Cover the rounds with plastic wrap. Heat a 9- or 10-inch cast-iron skillet over moderately high heat until hot.

4. Place one of the dough rounds into the hot skillet, reduce the heat to low, cover and cook until the crust is dark brown on the bottom, about 3 minutes. (Check after 2 minutes and adjust the heat, if necessary, to avoid burning the dough.)

5. Remove the pizza crust from the skillet. Layer the crust with ⅓ cup of the mozzarella mixture and top with about ½ to ¾ cup potatoes. Return the pizza to the skillet and cook, covered, until the cheese melts, about 2 minutes. Repeat the process with the 3 other rounds.
—Anne Disrude

CALABRIAN CAULIFLOWER PAN PIZZA

The versatile cauliflower topping on this pizza is a specialty of Calabria in southern Italy. It's delicious with almost anything, as a salad or tossed with spaghetti, Pecorino Romano cheese and lots of black pepper. In this variation, currants, salty capers and a splash of sharp vinegar give this pizza a salty, savory twist.

*Makes 4 Individual
Pizzas*

1 *small head of cauliflower (about 1
    pound), separated into florets and
    cut lengthwise into ⅛-inch slices*
¼ *cup extra-virgin olive oil*

4 garlic cloves, coarsely chopped
Pinch of crushed hot red pepper
½ teaspoon anchovy paste
2 tablespoons currants or raisins
1 tablespoon white wine vinegar
1½ tablespoons drained capers,
    coarsely chopped
3 tablespoons chopped parsley
½ teaspoon salt
¼ teaspoon freshly ground pepper
Quick Semolina Pizza Dough (p. 257)
1⅓ cups diced mozzarella cheese (about
    ½ pound)

1. In a large pot of boiling salted water, cook the cauliflower until just tender, about 5 minutes; drain well.

2. Meanwhile, in a large nonreactive skillet, heat the olive oil over moderate heat. Add the garlic and hot pepper and cook, stirring, until the garlic is golden brown, about 2 minutes. Add the anchovy paste and currants and cook for 1 minute. Add the vinegar and cook for 1 minute longer.

3. Add the cauliflower and toss to coat. Cook, tossing frequently, for 2 minutes. Remove from the heat and add the capers, parsley, salt and pepper. (The recipe can be prepared to this point up to 1 day ahead; cover and refrigerate.)

4. Roll the Semolina Pizza Dough into a log 1½ inches in diameter. Cut into 4 equal pieces. Roll out each piece of dough into a 7-inch round about 1/16 inch thick. Cover the rounds with plastic wrap. Heat a 9- or 10-inch cast-iron skillet over moderately high heat until hot.

5. Place one of the dough rounds into the hot skillet, reduce the heat to low, cover and cook until the crust is dark brown on the bottom, about 3 minutes. (Check after 2 minutes and adjust the heat, if necessary, to avoid burning the dough.)

6. Remove the pizza crust from the skillet. Layer the crust with ⅓ cup mozzarella and top with about ½ to ¾ cup cauliflower. Return the pizza to the skillet and cook, covered, until the cheese melts, about 2 minutes. Repeat the process with the 3 other rounds.
—Anne Disrude

ZUCCHINI AND SUN-DRIED TOMATO PAN PIZZA

In order to insure the optimum flavor of the zucchini, this recipe yields only two pizzas, but it's easy enough to make two batches. It is essential to cook the zucchini evenly in a large uncrowded pan. When tomatoes are in season, substitute one large fresh beefsteak tomato for the sun-dried tomatoes.

❦ The well-browned zucchini and the sweet piquancy of the sun-dried tomatoes in this mild vegetable pizza are best matched with a flavorful but not overpowering red, such as a young, medium-bodied Rioja. A Marqués de Cáceres or Marqués de Riscal would both be ideal choices.

Makes 2 Individual
Pizzas

3 small zucchini (about ¾ pound
    total), cut into ⅜-inch pieces
1 teaspoon salt
1 tablespoon oil from oil-packed sun-
    dried tomatoes

4 oil-packed sun-dried tomato
    halves, minced
3 garlic cloves, lightly smashed
Pinch of crushed hot red pepper
¼ teaspoon freshly ground
    black pepper
2 tablespoons minced fresh basil
½ recipe Quick Semolina Pizza Dough
    (p. 257)
⅔ cup diced mozzarella cheese (about
    ¼ pound)

1. Put the zucchini in a colander and sprinkle with ½ teaspoon of the salt; toss and let drain for 5 minutes. Gently blot the zucchini with a paper towel.

2. Meanwhile, in a large heavy skillet, heat the oil over moderate heat. Add the sun-dried tomatoes, garlic and hot pepper. Cook until the garlic begins to soften, about 2 minutes. Increase the heat to high, add the zucchini and toss to coat with the oil. Cook, tossing frequently, until the zucchini is evenly browned, about 3 minutes. Remove from the heat, season with the remaining ½ teaspoon salt and all the black pepper. Discard the garlic. (The recipe can be prepared to this point up to 1 day ahead; cover and refrigerate.) Add the basil and stir.

3. Roll the Semolina Pizza Dough into a log 1½ inches in diameter. Cut in half. Roll out each piece of dough into a 7-inch round about ⅛ inch thick. Cover the rounds with plastic wrap. Heat a 9- or 10-inch cast-iron skillet over moderately high heat until hot.

4. Place one of the dough rounds into the hot skillet, reduce the heat to low, cover and cook until the crust is dark brown on the bottom, about 3 minutes. (Check after 2 minutes and adjust the heat, if necessary, to avoid burning the dough.)

5. Remove the pizza crust from the skillet. Layer the crust with ⅓

cup mozzarella and top with about ½ cup of the zucchini. Return the pizza to the skillet and cook, covered, until the cheese melts, about 2 minutes. Repeat the process with the remaining round.
—Anne Disrude

ASPARAGUS AND PARMESAN CHEESE PAN PIZZA

This topping recipe is borrowed from Parma, where the great Parmigiano-Reggiano is made. Traditionally, the asparagus are served simply with a blanket of Parmesan cheese. Here the asparagus are cut in pieces and cooked until tender, flavored with onion and butter and covered with shavings of the cheese. ♟ Although the bittersweet flavor of asparagus can clash with wine, Parmesan complements it. A crisp, herbaceous California Sauvignon Blanc, such as Clos du Val or Kenwood, will bridge the two flavors perfectly.

Makes 4 Individual
Pizzas

1½ pounds asparagus, tough ends
    removed
3 tablespoons unsalted butter
½ cup diced red onion
¼ teaspoon salt
¼ teaspoon freshly ground pepper
Quick Semolina Pizza Dough (p. 257)
1⅓ cups diced mozzarella cheese (about
    ½ pound)

½ cup Parmesan cheese shavings, about 1 ounce (see Note)

1. Cut the asparagus stalks into 1-inch pieces if skinny, ½-inch pieces if fat. Reserve the tips. Cook the stalks in a large saucepan of boiling salted water until almost tender, about 2 minutes, then add the tips and cook until tender, 2 minutes longer. Drain and pat dry with paper towels.

2. In a large skillet, melt the butter over moderately low heat. Add the red onion and cook until softened, about 5 minutes. Add the asparagus, toss to coat with the butter and cook, tossing frequently, about 2 minutes. Remove from the heat and season with the salt and pepper.

3. Roll the Semolina Pizza Dough into a log 1½ inches in diameter. Cut into 4 equal pieces. Roll out each piece of dough into a 7-inch round about ⅛ inch thick. Cover the rounds with plastic wrap. Heat a 9- or 10-inch cast-iron skillet over moderately high heat until hot.

4. Place one of the dough rounds into the hot skillet, reduce the heat to low, cover and cook until the crust is dark brown on the bottom, about 3 minutes. (Check after 2 minutes and reduce the heat, if necessary, to avoid burning the dough.)

5. Remove the pizza crust from the skillet. Layer the crust with ⅓ cup of the mozzarella mixture and top with ¾ cup asparagus pieces. Return the pizza to the skillet and cook, covered, until the cheese melts, about 2 minutes. Top with one-fourth of the Parmesan shavings. Repeat the process with the 3 other rounds.

NOTE: Use a vegetable peeler to shave broad but thin pieces from a chunk of Parmesan. If using finely grated cheese, toss with the diced mozzarella instead of putting it on top.
—Anne Disrude

ZUCCHINI AND SAUSAGE DEEP-DISH PIZZA

Makes One 9-Inch Deep-Dish Pizza

½ pound sweet Italian sausage
6 tablespoons olive oil
2 medium zucchini, cut lengthwise into ¼-inch slices and trimmed to 4½ inches
14 ounces (½ recipe) Basic Pizza Dough (p. 256)
¼ cup freshly grated Parmesan cheese
6 ounces Monterey Jack cheese, shredded (1¼ cups)
½ cup Chunky Tomato Sauce (p. 260)
¼ teaspoon salt
⅛ teaspoon pepper

1. Preheat the oven to 450°. Remove the sausage from its casing and crumble into a medium skillet. Fry over moderate heat until browned. Drain on paper towels.

2. Lightly brush the bottom of a large, heavy, well-seasoned skillet with olive oil and warm over moderate heat until the oil is hot enough to evaporate a drop of water upon contact. Working in batches, lay as many zucchini strips into the skillet as will easily fit in a single layer. Lightly brush the tops of the

---

SHAPING A DEEP-DISH PIZZA

Roll out a 14-ounce ball of dough to a round that will comfortably line a 9-inch deep-dish pizza pan with an additional 1 inch for overlap.

Coat the interior of the pizza pan with a heavy film of olive oil to ensure a crisp crust. Drape the dough loosely over the pan and ease it in and against the bottom and sides of the pan.

After brushing the dough liberally with oil, top with the filling. Add the cheese first (if there is any) and any sauce last.

Using a pizza cutter or a small knife, trim off the dough about halfway up the sides of the pan to just above the top of the filling (the dough will rise as it bakes to comfortably contain all of the filling).

strips with oil and cook, turning once, until lightly browned, about 2 minutes on each side. Remove to a plate. Lightly oil the skillet and repeat with the remaining slices.

3. To assemble the pizza, oil a 9-inch deep-dish pizza pan. Roll the dough out and lay in the pan following the instructions in "Shaping a Deep-Dish Pizza," p. 164. Brush the dough with about 1 tablespoon of oil. Sprinkle with the Parmesan and 1 cup of the Monterey Jack. Dot with the sausage, then spoon the Chunky Tomato Sauce on top. Lay the zucchni slices on top in an overlapping pinwheel patter. Drizzle with the remaining oil and sprinkle with the salt and pepper.

4. Bake for 25 minutes, or until the crust is golden. Remove from the oven and sprinkle the remaining ¼ cup of Monterey Jack over the pizza. Bake for 5 minutes until melted.

5. Remove the pizza from the pan. Let stand on a rack for 10 minutes before slicing to allow the filling to set.
—Anne Disrude

EGGPLANT AND GOAT CHEESE DEEP-DISH PIZZA

Makes One 9-Inch
Deep-Dish Pizza

3 small eggplants (about 2½ pounds)
⅓ cup coarse (kosher) salt
½ cup olive oil
½ teaspoon minced fresh rosemary or
½ teaspoon dried
Salt and freshly ground pepper

14 ounces (½ recipe) Basic Pizza
Dough (p. 256)
5 to 6 ounces (about ½ large log)
Montrachet goat cheese

1. Cut 1 eggplant lengthwise into ¼-inch slices and trim to 4½ inches. Peel the 2 remaining eggplants and cut into ½-inch cubes.

2. Sprinkle both sides of the eggplant slices with half of the coarse salt and place on a rack to drain. Toss the cubed eggplant with the remaining coarse salt and place in a large colander to drain. Let stand for about 30 minutes.

3. Rinse the eggplant slices and cubes; drain well and press dry between towels. Wrap in kitchen towels, place in a colander or on a rack and weigh down to force out more liquid. Let stand for 1 hour.

4. Preheat the oven to 450°. Warm a large, heavy, well-seasoned skillet over high heat. In batches, lightly brush the eggplant slices with olive oil. Place in the skillet and cook until lightly browned, about 2 minutes on each side. Remove to a plate.

5. Add ¼ cup of oil to the skillet. When almost smoking, add the eggplant cubes and toss in the oil. Add the rosemary and cook, tossing occasionally, until the eggplant is translucent and browned around the edges, about 10 minutes. Season with salt and pepper to taste.

6. To assemble the pizza, oil a 9-inch deep-dish pizza pan. Roll the dough out and lay in the pan following the instructions in "Shaping a Deep-Dish Pizza," p. 164. Brush the dough with about 1 tablespoon of oil. Crumble the goat cheese over the dough. cover with the cubed eggplant. Arrange the eggplant slices in an overlapping pinwheel

pattern on top. Drizzle any remaining oil on top and sprinkle lightly with salt and pepper.

7. Bake for 20 minutes, or until the crust is golden, Remove from the pan and let stand on a rack for 10 minutes before slicing to allow the filling to set.
—Anne Disrude

OLIVE AND ROASTED RED PEPPER PIZZA

Makes 3 Individual
Pizzas (7 Inches)

3 flat anchovy fillets, rinsed and
*   patted dry*
1 large garlic clove, crushed
*   through a press*
¼ teaspoon freshly ground
*   black pepper*
¼ cup olive oil
1 can (6 ounces) pitted black olives,
*   rinsed and drained*
12 ounces (3 balls) Basic Pizza Dough
*   (p. 256)*
Cornmeal
¼ pound mozzarella cheese, cut into 9
*   thin slices*
1 red bell pepper—roasted, peeled,
*   seeded and finely chopped*

1. Preheat the oven and a pizza stone or tiles to 500° 1 hour before use. Place the anchovies, garlic, black pepper and 2 tablespoons of the olive oil in a food processor and puree until almost liquefied. Add the olives and process until chopped but not pureed.

2. Roll out one ball of the pizza dough to a round 7 inches in diameter and ¼ inch thick (if your oven is slow or has difficulty reaching 500°, make the dough a bit thicker). Sprinkle a baking sheet liberally with the cornmeal and transfer the round of dough to the sheet. Repeat with the other balls of dough.

3. Brush each pizza crust with about 1 teaspoon of olive oil. Spread ⅓ cup of the olive mixture evenly on each crust. Drizzling the remaining oil over all.

4. Slide the pizza onto the hot pizza stone. Bake for 6 to 8 minutes, or until the bottom of the crust is lightly browned. Remove from the oven and place 3 slices of the mozzarella on each crust. Sprinkle with the red pepper and return to the oven and bake for about 5 minutes, or until the cheese is melted.
—Anne Disrude

166

PERFECT PIZZA

Perfect dough is, quite literally, the foundation of a perfect pizza. Ideally, raw pizza dough should be supple, silky and not too stiff, to produce a baked crust that is light, crisp and a bit chewy—just substantial enough to stand up to a variety of savory toppings.

Making pizza dough, which is similar to bread dough, is a simple and deeply satisfying process. The Basic Pizza Dough recipe (p. 256) works equally well for hearty deep-dish pizzas as well as for the more usual flat pizzas.

The addition of olive oil to the dough helps keep the crust chewy and crisp. In the case of deep-dish pizza, a film of olive oil in the pan actually "fries" the crust as it's baking. Olive oil also acts as a seal between dough and topping to keep the crust from turning soggy.

Under ideal circumstances, pizza is baked in special ovens at extremely high temperature and emerges crisp and golden-crusted in 5 minutes. A home oven set to 500° will produce the desired combination of light and chewy textures in about twice that time. It is recommended, however, baking on a pizza stone or unglazed stone floor tiles and preheating both oven and stone or tiles for 1 hour before baking the pizza. Baking time should be as short and intensely hot as possible. If your oven cannot reach 500°, compensate by making the crust a little thicker than suggested.

FRESH TOMATO AND BASIL PIZZA

The quantities for the topping below make 1 small pizza, but the dough recipe will produce enough for seven of them. The topping ingredients are easily multiplied.

Makes 1 Individual
Pizza (7 Inches)

4 ounces (1 ball) Basic Pizza Dough
   (p. 256)
Cornmeal
3 tablespoons olive oil
1 small tomato, sliced ¼ inch thick
⅛ teaspoon salt
Pinch of freshly ground pepper
8 large basil leaves

1. Preheat the oven and pizza stone or tiles to 500° 1 hour before use. Roll the pizza dough to a round 7 inches in diameter and ¼ inch thick (if your oven is slow or has difficulty reaching 500°, make the dough a bit thicker). Sprinkle a baking sheet liberally with the cornmeal and transfer the round of dough to the sheet.

2. Generously brush the crust with about 1½ tablespoons of the olive oil. Arrange the tomato slices on top and sprinkle with the salt and pepper. Place the basil leaves on top. Drizzle the remaining olive oil over all. Slide the pizza onto the hot pizza stone or tiles. Bake for 8 to 10 minutes, or until the bottom of the crust is browned.
—Anne Disrude

CALZONE CON SALSICCIA

Better than a sausage and pepper hero, these savory calzone, individually wrapped, make great picnic fare.
♟ Montepulciano d'Abruzzo, such as Casal Thaulero

Makes 4 Calzone

Calzone Dough (p. 258)
4 links (about ¾ pound) Italian sweet
   or hot sausage
3 tablespoons olive oil, preferably extra-
   virgin
4 medium bell peppers (about 1
   pound), thinly sliced
3 medium onions, thinly sliced
½ to 1 teaspoon salt, depending on the
   saltiness of the sausage
⅛ teaspoon freshly ground black
   pepper

1. While the Calzone Dough is rising, make the filling: Prick the sausages all over with a fork. Place in a medium skillet with ½ inch of water. Cover and simmer over moderate heat until the water evaporates, about 20 minutes. Uncover and cook, turning occasionally, until the sausages are browned. Let cool; then cut into ¼-inch slices.

2. In a large skillet, heat the olive oil. Add the bell peppers and cook over moderate heat for 5 minutes. Add the onions, salt and black pepper. Cook until the peppers are soft and the onions are lightly browned, 15 to 20 minutes. Remove from the heat and let cool before assembling the calzone.

3. Punch the dough down and turn out onto a lightly floured surface. Divide into 4 equal pieces. One at a time, roll out into four 10-inch

circles. If you have time, wrap the dough in kitchen towels and plastic wrap and let it rest at this point for 30 minutes; it will yield a more tender dough. If time is of the essence, proceed to Step 4.

4. Preheat the oven to 450°. Arrange the dough circles on a large greased baking sheet with half of each circle off the edge of the sheet. Arrange the sausage slices over the half of each dough circle that is on the sheet, leaving a 1-inch border around the rim. Top with the peppers and onions. Fold the dough over to cover the filling and form a semicircle. Press the edges together to seal. Crimp decoratively by folding the lower edge up and over the top edge at about ¾-inch intervals.

5. Bake on the lowest rack of the oven for 20 to 25 minutes, or until brown and puffed. Transfer to a rack and let rest for 10 minutes before serving.

—*Michele Scicolone*

CALZONE SICILIANO

Oregano, anchovies and olives with onion are a favorite flavor combination in Palermo, Sicily.

♟ Sicilian white wine, such as Baronessa Anca Donnafugata

Makes 4 Calzone

Calzone Dough (p. 258)
3 tablespoons olive oil, preferably extra-virgin
2 medium onions, thinly sliced
1 can (35 ounces) Italian peeled tomatoes, drained and chopped
1½ teaspoons oregano
Pinch of salt
⅛ teaspoon freshly ground pepper
1 can (2 ounces) flat anchovy fillets

⅓ cup Calamata or oil-cured black olives, pitted and chopped

1. While the Calzone Dough is rising, make the filling: In a large skillet, heat the oil. Add the onions and sauté over moderate heat until tender and golden, 10 to 15 minutes. Add the tomatoes, oregano, salt and pepper. Simmer, stirring occasionally, until the sauce is thickened, about 20 minutes. Let cool to room temperature.

2. Punch the dough down and turn out onto a lightly floured surface. Divide into 4 equal pieces. One at a time, roll out into four 10-inch circles. If you have time, wrap the dough in kitchen towels and plastic wrap and let it rest at this point for 30 minutes; it will yield a more tender dough. If time is of the essence, proceed to Step 3.

3. Preheat the oven to 450°. Arrange the dough circles on a large greased baking sheet with half of each circle off the edge of the sheet. Spread the cooled onion-tomato mixture over the half of each dough circle that is on the sheet, leaving a 1-inch border around the rim. Arrange the anchovies on top and dot with the olives. Fold the dough over to cover the filling and form a semicircle. Press the edges together to seal. Crimp the dough decoratively by folding the lower edge up and over the top edge at about ¾-inch intervals.

4. Bake on the lowest rack of the oven for 20 to 25 minutes, or until brown and puffed. Transfer to a rack and let rest for 10 minutes before serving.

—*Michele Scicolone*

Herbed Italian Skillet Bread (page 174).

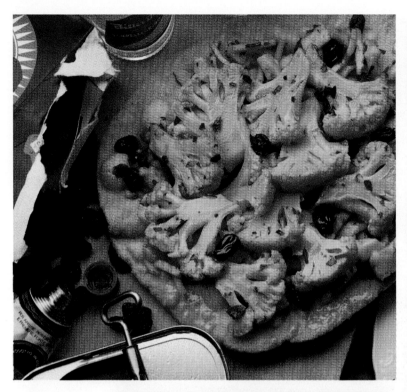

Above, Calabrian Cauliflower Pan Pizza (page 161). Near right, Garlicky Potato Pan Pizza (page 161). Far right, Fresh Artichoke Pan Pizza (page 158) and Scallion and Olive Pan Pizza with Rosemary (page 159).

Top left, Sage and Walnut Corn Cake (page 175). Top right, Focaccia (page 173). At right, Salt and Pepper Sea Biscuits (page 176).

CALZONE MARGHERITA

Use only red, ripe and meaty tomatoes for this filling. In winter, plum tomatoes are especially good. For a truly authentic Italian taste, look for freshly made mozzarella or imported water buffalo mozzarella.
❦ Chianti Classico, such as Ruffino

Makes 4 Calzone

Calzone Dough (p. 258)
1 pound tomatoes—peeled, seeded and finely diced
½ teaspoon salt
½ pound mozzarella cheese, finely diced
¼ cup freshly grated Parmesan cheese
2 tablespoons olive oil, preferably extra-virgin
2 medium garlic cloves, finely chopped
8 fresh basil leaves, minced, or ½ teaspoon dried
½ teaspoon oregano
⅛ teaspoon freshly ground pepper

1. While the Calzone Dough is rising, make the filling: Place the tomatoes in a colander, sprinkle with the salt and let drain for 30 minutes.
2. In a medium bowl, combine the mozzarella and Parmesan cheeses, the oil, garlic, basil, oregano and pepper. Add the tomatoes to the cheese mixture and toss to mix.
3. Punch the dough down and turn out onto a lightly floured surface. Divide into 4 equal pieces. One at a time, roll out into four 10-inch circles. If you have time, wrap the dough in kitchen towels and plastic wrap and let it rest at this point for 30 minutes; it will yield a more tender dough. If time is of the essence, proceed to Step 4.
4. Preheat the oven to 450°. Arrange the dough circles on a large greased baking sheet with half of each circle off the edge of the sheet. Place about ½ cup filling on the half of each circle that is on the sheet, leaving a 1-inch border around the rim. Fold the dough over to cover the filling and form a semicircle. Press the edges together to seal. Crimp decoratively by folding the lower edge up and over the top edge at about ¾-inch intervals.
5. Bake on the lowest rack of the oven for 20 to 25 minutes, or until brown and puffed. Transfer to a rack and let rest for 10 minutes before serving.
—Michele Scicolone

FOCACCIA

Many pizzerias will be very happy to sell you uncooked pizza dough. If there's no pizzeria around, defrosted supermarket bread or pizza dough works very nicely.

*Makes One
10-Inch Round*

½ cup sliced shallots (about 8 medium)
3 to 4 small sprigs of fresh rosemary or ½ teaspoon dried
½ teaspoon coarse (kosher) salt
½ teaspoon coarsely ground pepper
5 tablespoons extra-virgin olive oil
1 pound uncooked pizza dough

1. Preheat the oven to 425°. In a small bowl, toss the shallots, rosemary, salt and pepper with 3½ tablespoons of the olive oil; set aside.
2. On a lightly floured surface, roll out the dough to form a 10-inch circle about ½ inch thick.
3. Place a heavy ovenproof, 12-inch skillet over high heat for 1 minute. Add the remaining 1½ tablespoons oil. When the oil is

shimmering, remove from the heat and carefully lay the rolled-out dough in the pan.

4. Using your fingertips, make indentations all over the dough. Spread the shallot mixture on top. Bake the focaccia in the upper third of the oven for about 25 minutes, until browned on top. Let cool on a rack for 15 minutes before cutting into wedges.
—Anne Disrude

TUSCAN FOCACCIA

This flatbread with cheese, *schiacciata con formaggio*, is baked in a pizza pan to an amber-golden color.

4 to 6 Servings

½ envelope active dry yeast
2 tablespoons lukewarm water (105° to 115°)
2 cups all-purpose flour
⅛ teaspoon salt
2 ounces Pecorino Romano cheese— 1 ounce grated (¼ cup) and 1 ounce cut into ¼-inch dice
1 egg, beaten
About ½ cup milk, at room temperature
1 tablespoon olive oil

1. In a small bowl, dissolve the yeast in the water and stir in 1 tablespoon of the flour. Cover and set aside to proof in a warm place for 1 hour. (*This sponge can be made up to 1 day ahead and refrigerated, covered. Let return to room temperature before using.*)

2. In a bowl, combine 1¾ cups of the flour with the salt and grated cheese.

3. In a measuring cup, mix the egg with enough milk to equal ⅔ cup. Add the egg mixture and the reserved sponge to the flour and beat until combined. The dough should be soft but not sticky; beat in the remaining flour if necessary. Stir in the diced cheese.

4. Brush the bottom and sides of a 10-inch round pizza pan with the olive oil. With wet hands, press the dough to evenly cover the pan. Cover with a towel and set aside in a warm place to rise until doubled in bulk, 30 to 45 minutes. Meanwhile, preheat an oven to 425°.

5. Bake the focaccia for about 25 minutes or until golden brown on top. Transfer to a rack to cool.
—Diane Darrow and Tom Maresca

HERBED ITALIAN SKILLET BREAD

*Makes 2 Round
Flat Loaves*

1 tablespoon sugar
1½ cups lukewarm water (105° to 115°)
1 envelope active dry yeast
3¼ to 3¾ cups bread flour
1 tablespoon coarse (kosher) salt
1 teaspoon coarsely cracked pepper
1 teaspoon finely chopped fresh or dried rosemary
½ cup olive oil, preferably extra-virgin
4 garlic cloves, thinly sliced
4 sprigs of rosemary, for garnish

1. In a medium bowl, dissolve the sugar in ½ cup of the water. Sprinkle the yeast on top; set aside until it starts to foam, about 5 minutes.

2. In a large bowl, combine 3¼ cups of the flour with 2 teaspoons

174

FOCACCIA

Focaccia is sort of a scaled-down version of a pizza. It is a flat bread that is baked with a topping. However, focaccia toppings, unlike pizza toppings, are used merely as flavorings; the focus here is on the bread itself. (Coincidentally, the word focaccia derives from *focus*, the Latin word for hearth—which is where *focaccie* were traditionally baked.)

Focaccia toppings can be as simple as coarse salt, but range to various herbs, vegetables, cheeses and meats, and combinations thereof.

These flavored flatbreads are usually eaten as snacks, although they can also be served along with a meal.

of the salt, ½ teaspoon of the pepper and the chopped rosemary.

3. Stir ¼ cup of the olive oil and the remaining 1 cup water into the yeast mixture. Make a well in the flour and add the liquid ingredients. Stir until well mixed.

4. Turn the dough out onto a floured surface and knead until smooth and elastic, about 15 minutes. Use as much additional flour as necessary to prevent sticking and to form a slightly soft dough.

5. Form the dough into a ball and place in a large oiled bowl. Turn to coat with oil. Cover the bowl with plastic wrap and a towel. Place in a warm spot and let the dough rise until doubled in bulk, about 1 hour. Punch the dough down and let rise until doubled in bulk again, about 1 hour.

6. Preheat the oven to 400°. Place a 12- to 14-inch cast-iron skillet in the oven to heat.

7. Divide the dough in half. Return half the dough to the bowl, cover and refrigerate while you make the first loaf. (If you'd prefer to make only one loaf, the other half of the dough can be frozen and baked at a later time.) Roll the dough out to a ½-inch-thick round. With a sharp knife, score lightly in a crisscross pattern.

8. Remove the skillet from the oven and coat the bottom and sides with 1 tablespoon of the oil. Place the dough in the skillet. Press down around the edges to even the thickness. Distribute 2 of the sliced garlic cloves over the bread and top with 2 broken sprigs of rosemary if desired. Drizzle the bread with 1 tablespoon of the oil. Sprinkle with ½ teaspoon of the salt and ¼ teaspoon of the pepper.

9. Bake for 25 to 30 minutes, until browned. Repeat with the remaining dough and ingredients for the second loaf. Serve the bread warm or at room temperature.

—Anne Disrude

SAGE AND WALNUT CORN CAKES

Makes Two
10-Inch Cakes

1 cup milk
1 egg
5 tablespoons extra-virgin olive oil
1 cup all-purpose flour
1 cup finely ground cornmeal
2½ teaspoons baking powder
1½ tablespoons sugar
1 teaspoon salt
20 fresh sage leaves
⅔ cup chopped walnuts

1. In a bowl, combine the milk, egg and 3 tablespoons of the oil; beat well.

2. In a medium bowl, whisk together the flour, cornmeal, baking powder, sugar and salt. Make a well in the center and add the milk mixture. Stir to mix.

3. Heat a griddle, preferably cast iron, over moderate heat. Add 1 tablespoon of the oil and swirl to coat. When the oil shimmers, scatter 10 of the sage leaves over the griddle and sprinkle on ⅓ cup of the walnuts. Pour half the batter onto the griddle to just cover the nuts

and sage leaves. (The batter should be no more than ½ inch thick.)

4. Cook until bubbles appear on the surface, 5 to 7 minutes; the top should be barely wet. Slide the cake onto a plate and carefully invert onto the griddle. Cook the second side for about 4 minutes, until browned. Transfer to a rack and repeat with the remaining oil, sage, walnuts and batter. Serve warm.
—Anne Disrude

SALT AND PEPPER SEA BISCUITS

These delicate crackers make a wonderful accompaniment to soup or stew, especially those made with fish. Because the crackers are very tender, if you plan to store them, stack them carefully in an airtight cookie tin.

*Makes 12 Large
Biscuits*

2 cups cake flour, plus more for rolling
2½ teaspoons baking powder
1 teaspoon sugar
1 teaspoon salt
6 tablespoons cold lard, cut into small pieces
½ cup ice water
1 tablespoon coarse (kosher) salt
1 tablespoon coarsely ground pepper

1. Preheat the oven to 425°. Grease 2 large cookie sheets and set aside.

2. In a large bowl, whisk the flour, baking powder, sugar and salt to combine. Cut in the lard until only a few pea-size pieces remain. Make a well in the center and add the ice water. Gently stir to moisten. If the mixture is crumbly, add a little more water; if wet, add more flour. Scrape the dough onto a well-floured surface and knead briefly to form a cohesive ball.

3. Divide the dough in half. Roll out each piece of dough ⅛ inch thick, flouring as necessary to prevent sticking. Flour a 4- to 5-inch round cutter or a coffee can rim and stamp out circles of dough. Transfer the biscuits to the prepared cookie sheets and pierce with a fork at 1-inch intervals.

4. Brush the biscuits lightly with cold water and sprinkle with the salt and pepper. Bake for about 10 minutes, until the biscuits are barely beginning to brown on the bottom. Let cool on racks for 15 minutes before serving.
—Anne Disrude

ROSEMARY GRISSINI

Grissini (breadsticks), as well as bread, are usually served with an Italian meal. But they also make delicious appetizers, especially when served with a slice of prosciutto wrapped around one end. If kept in an airtight container, the breadsticks will remain fresh for several days.

*Makes 36
Breadsticks*

3 envelopes active dry yeast
1 cup lukewarm water (105° to 115°)
1 cup bread flour
1½ cups whole wheat flour
¾ cup coarse Italian semolina*
1 teaspoon salt
2 tablespoons plus 1 teaspoon extra-virgin olive oil
2 tablespoons fresh rosemary, finely chopped or 2 teaspoons dried
*Available at Italian markets

1. In a small bowl, dissolve the yeast in the water for about 10 minutes.

2. On a work surface, combine the bread flour, whole wheat flour, ½ cup of the semolina and the salt. Shape the dry ingredients into a mound, make a well in the center and pour in 2 tablespoons of the olive oil. Pour the dissolved yeast into the well, a little at a time, mixing with a fork in a circular motion and drawing in the flours until all the ingredients are combined and a dough forms.

3. Coat the inside of a large bowl with the remaining 1 teaspoon oil. Add the rosemary to the dough and knead with the heels of your hands until the dough is smooth and elastic, about 10 minutes. Form the dough into a ball and put it in the oiled bowl, turning to coat all sides of the dough with oil. Cover with a cloth and let rise in a warm place until more than doubled in bulk, about 2 hours.

4. Preheat the oven to 350°. On a work surface sprinkled with 2 to 3 tablespoons of the semolina, punch the dough down. Roll the dough out to form a rectangle approximately 8 by 9 inches and ½ inch thick. Cut into ¼-inch strips and roll gently into sticks about 10 inches long.

5. Sprinkle a heavy baking sheet with the remaining semolina and arrange the breadsticks on the baking sheet about 1 inch apart. Cover with a towel and let rise in a warm place for 10 minutes.

6. Bake in the middle of the oven for about 30 minutes, until lightly golden and crisp. Transfer to a rack to cool slightly, arrange in a basket and serve.
—*Lorenza de' Medici*

TUSCAN BREAD

This crusty, large-crumbed bread is traditionally baked in a wood-fired brick oven. If you like, you can replicate the effect by covering an oven shelf with the unglazed Italian or French terra-cotta tiles that are available at gardening shops.

*Makes One
2-Pound Loaf*

*2 envelopes active dry yeast
About 6 cups unbleached all-purpose
    flour
¾ teaspoon salt*

1. In a small bowl, combine the yeast and ½ cup very warm tap water. Stir well until the yeast dissolves.

2. To make the sponge, put ½ cup of the flour in a large bowl and add the dissolved yeast. Mix with a wooden spoon until a very loose dough forms. Sprinkle 1 tablespoon of the flour over the dough. Cover with a cotton dish towel and let rise in a warm, draft-free place until doubled in bulk, about 1 hour.

3. Mound 5 cups of the flour on a work surface and make a large well in the center. Add the sponge to the well, along with the salt and ½ cup very warm tap water; mix to blend with a wooden spoon. Add another 1¼ cups very warm water and begin mixing the dough with your

GRISSINI

Although not the only account, it is widely believed that *grissini* were created in Turin in 1688. Apparently, the doctor who was caring for duke Vittorio Amadeo asked a local baker to give him something to soothe the young duke's ailing digestion. The baker, in turn, stretched out the dough that he used to make the local bread and created a long and very thin "bread stick." Although it is not known whether or not the baker's creation helped the duke, *grissini* were popular throughout Italy by the 18th century, when Napoleon first tasted what he called "les petits batons de Turin" and set up a fast postal service so that he could enjoy them at his court on a daily basis.

ITALIAN BREAD SALAD

Over the years, thrifty Italian cooks have developed an entire subcuisine based on leftovers, from leftover roast meat and poultry, to pasta and bread. Bread in particular has inspired a number of famous solutions, including bread soups (see a Livorno-style soup, p. 53) and bread salad, or *panzanella*.

Panzanella is traditionally made of Tuscan bread, a salt-free, chewy Italian loaf, which dries rock hard. Buy the bread at least three days before you make the salad, so it will be completely stale. This recipe (from Helen Millman) makes 8 first-course servings:

1 *loaf (1 pound) crusty Italian*
    bread, preferably Tuscan
4 *medium tomatoes, cut roughly*
    into ½-inch cubes
1 *large cucumber, peeled and*
    thinly sliced
5 *scallions, chopped (about*
    1 cup)
¼ *cup chopped fresh basil*
6 *tablespoons olive oil, preferably*
    extra-virgin Tuscan
3 *tablespoons red wine vinegar*
1 *teaspoon salt*
1 *teaspoon freshly ground pepper*

1. Three days before assembling the salad, cut the bread roughly into 1-inch cubes and leave out, uncovered, turning several times, so that it becomes stale and hard.

2. The day you make the salad, spread the stale bread cubes, crust-side down, in a large shallow baking dish; the bread should be no more than 2 cubes deep. Drizzle 4 cups of cold water over the bread; moistening all the cubes. Let soak for 10 minutes, no longer.

3. Squeeze as much water as possible from the bread. Place the bread on one half of a large kitchen towel and pat out to about ¼ inch. Repeat until you have squeezed all the bread and spread it out in a thin layer over half the towel. Fold the towel over to cover the bread, slide onto a baking sheet and chill, about 2 hours.

4. Meanwhile, place the tomatoes, cucumber, scallions and basil in a large salad bowl. Cover and chill.

5. Transfer the cold bread to a dry towel. Form into a long, narrow cylinder; roll it up in the towel and twist to squeeze out as much water as possible.

6. Remove the vegetables from the refrigerator. Tear off small pieces of the bread and crumble it into the salad bowl; the bread will be sticky.

7. In a small bowl, whisk the oil, vinegar, salt and pepper until blended. Pour the dressing over the salad. With a fork, rake through the salad to mix the bread with the vegetables. Serve chilled.

hands, gradually drawing in the flour from the inside rim of the well.

4. After about 15 minutes, when all but about ½ cup of the flour has been incorporated, knead the dough with your palms, pushing it away from you and folding it over itself, until smooth and elastic, about 20 minutes longer. Incorporate any remaining flour as necessary to keep the dough from sticking to the work surface.

5. Shape the dough into a long or round loaf and wrap it loosely in a floured cotton dish towel. Set aside to rise in a warm, draft-free place until doubled in bulk, about 1 hour.

6. Preheat the oven to 400°. Set the loaf on a large, heavy, lightly floured baking sheet (or directly on heated unglazed oven tiles) and bake for about 55 minutes, until the bread sounds hollow when tapped. (Don't open the oven during the first 30 minutes of baking.)

7. Transfer the bread to a rack. Stand it on its side and let cool for at least 3 hours before slicing.
—*Giuliano Bugialli*

OLIVE BREAD

This bread is finer in texture than the traditional olive bread because it is made with a lighter dough. Use small brine-cured Tuscan olives, if possible, but Sicilian and Greek olives do nicely as well.

Makes 1 Large
Oval Loaf

2 *envelopes active dry yeast*
1 *cup lukewarm milk (105° to 115°)*
3 *cups bread flour*
¼ *cup plus 2 teaspoons extra-virgin*
    olive oil
1 *teaspoon salt*

½ cup pitted brine-cured black olives,
coarsely chopped

1. In a small bowl, dissolve the yeast in the milk and set aside until it begins to foam on the surface, about 10 minutes.

2. Sift the flour onto a work surface and make a well in the center. Pour in ¼ cup of the olive oil and add the salt. Pour the milk into the well, a little at a time, mixing with a fork in a circular motion and drawing in the flour until all the ingredients are combined and a dough forms.

3. Coat the inside of a large bowl with 1 teaspoon of the olive oil. Add the olives to the dough and knead with the heels of your hands until it is smooth and elastic, about 10 minutes. Form the dough into a ball and place in the bowl. Turn to coat all sides with oil, cover with a cloth and let it rise in a warm place until it is more than doubled in bulk, about 2 hours.

4. Preheat the oven to 375°. Punch the dough down and roll it out into an oval loaf approximately 10 inches long. Oil the baking sheet with the remaining 1 teaspoon olive oil. Place the loaf on the sheet, cover with a cloth and let rise for another 20 minutes.

5. Bake for about 30 minutes, or until the loaf sounds hollow when tapped. Let cool completely before slicing.
—Lorenza de' Medici

EASTER BREAD

My grandmother, Lucille Rossi, made this as an Easter treat, but it kept so well that we would eat it for many days after.

Makes 1 Loaf

2 envelopes active dry yeast
¼ cup lukewarm water (105° to 115°)
⅛ teaspoon salt
*¾ cup plus 1 teaspoon granulated
    sugar*
*4½ cups all-purpose flour plus
    additional for kneading*
*8 eggs at room temperature—3 lightly
    beaten, 5 in the shell, colored if
    desired*
¼ cup warm milk
*1 stick (4 ounces) unsalted butter,
    melted*
1 egg yolk

1. In a small bowl, combine the yeast, water, salt and 1 teaspoon of the sugar. Set aside until foamy, about 5 minutes.

2. In a large bowl, stir 4½ cups of the flour and the remaining ¾ cup sugar with a whisk to combine. Make a well in the center of the dry ingredients.

3. In a small bowl, mix the 3 beaten eggs with the warm milk and pour into the well with the yeast mixture and melted butter. With a wooden spoon, incorporate the liquids into the flour and sugar until the dough comes together. Turn out onto a lightly floured work surface. Knead the dough until smooth, about 5 minutes.

4. Rinse the large bowl with warm water. Return the dough to the bowl and turn to coat. Cover the bowl with plastic wrap and let rise in a warm place until doubled in bulk, 1½ to 2 hours. Punch down the dough and turn it out onto a work

surface, dusted with additional flour if necessary. Roll it into an 18-inch log. Transfer the dough to a large, ungreased baking sheet and curve the ends around to form a wreath. Set aside, lightly cover with a towel and let rise until doubled in bulk, 45 to 60 minutes. Preheat the oven to 350°.

5. Press the whole eggs into the top of the wreath. In a small bowl, mix the egg yolk with 1 teaspoon of water and glaze the bread around the eggs. Bake for 45 to 50 minutes, or until well browned and a tester comes out clean.
—Fred Ferretti

FAMILY FAVORITE
BRAIDED EGG BREAD

The recipe given here produces two generous braided loaves. The dough can also be baked in one dramatic large loaf or small rolls.

Makes 2 Loaves

2 *envelopes active dry yeast*
1⅓ *cups lukewarm water*
    (105° to 115°)
3 *tablespoons sugar*
6 *to 7 cups unbleached all-purpose*
    flour
4 *eggs*
1 *tablespoon salt*
¼ *cup vegetable oil*
About 2 tablespoons sesame or poppy
    seeds (optional)

1. In a small bowl, dissolve the yeast in ⅔ cup of the warm water. Add 1 tablespoon of the sugar and stir to mix.
2. Put 5 cups of flour in a large bowl. Make a deep well in the ceter and pour in the yeast mixture.
3. Lightly beat 3 of the eggs. In a medium saucepan, combine the beaten eggs with the remaining 2 tablespoons sugar, the salt, oil and the remaining ⅔ cup warm water. Place over low heat and stir until well blended and just warm to the touch, 1 to 2 minutes.
4. Using a wooden spoon, stir this mixture into the flour and yeast, blending well. Add 1 cup of the remaining flour and blend well until the dough forms a ball; it will be slightly sticky.
5. Turn the dough out onto a floured work surface and knead vigorously, adding small amounts of the remaining flour as needed to prevent sticking, until it is smooth and elastic, about 10 minutes.
6. Shape the dough into a ball. Place seam-side up in a large, oiled bowl. Turn the dough over, cover the bowl with a towel and set aside to rise in a warm, draft-free place until doubled in bulk, about 1 hour.
7. Punch down the dough and turn it out onto a lightly floured surface. Cut the dough in half. Cut each half into 3 equal pieces and, with your hands, roll each piece into a 12-inch-long rope. For each loaf, loosely braid 3 ropes together, starting in the center and braiding to one end, then turning the dough around and braiding to the other end. Tuck the loose ends under the loaf.
8. Place the loaves on separate lightly oiled baking sheets. Cover with kitchen towels and set in a warm, draft-free place to rise for 1 hour. Preheat the oven to 350°.
9. Lightly beat the remaining egg with 1 teaspoon of water to make an egg wash. Brush the loaves with some of the egg wash and, if you wish, generously sprinkle the sesame (or poppy) seeds over the loaves. Brush again with the egg

wash to "paste" the seeds onto the dough.

10. Bake the loaves for 40 to 45 minutes, until the bread is golden brown and sounds hollow when tapped on the bottom.

11. Transfer the loaves carefully from the baking sheets to wire racks and let cool.

—Helen Millman

ITALIAN FILLED BREAD

Served with a soup or salad, this hearty bread makes a filling meal.

Makes 1 Large
Loaf

2 tablespoons olive oil
1 small onion, minced
1 medium garlic clove, minced
1 can (35 ounces) Italian peeled tomatoes, with their juice, or 6 large fresh tomatoes, seeded and diced
2 tablespoons heavy cream
1 pound Italian sweet sausage, casings removed
½ teaspoon freshly ground pepper
½ teaspoon oregano
½ teaspoon basil
½ teaspoon salt
½ recipe Quick Loaf Bread dough (recipe follows)
¾ cup finely diced mozzarella cheese (about ¼ pound)
¼ cup freshly grated Parmesan cheese
1 egg, beaten

1. In a medium nonreactive saucepan, heat the oil. Add the onion and garlic and sauté over moderate heat until just translucent, about 3 minutes. Add the tomatoes and cream and cook for 15 minutes.

2. Meanwhile, in a medium skillet, fry the sausage over moderate heat, breaking up the meat as it cooks, until browned, about 15 minutes; drain well. Add the sausage, pepper, oregano, basil and salt to the tomato sauce and cook, stirring occasionally, for 15 minutes longer. The sauce should be very thick and reduced to about 2½ cups. Let cool to room temperature. (*The recipe can be made ahead to this point. Cover and refrigerate for up to 3 days. Let the sauce return to room temperature before proceeding.*)

3. Prepare the Quick Loaf Bread dough through Step 3. On a lightly floured surface, punch down the dough and let relax for 10 minutes. Preheat the oven to 425°.

4. Roll out the dough into a 16-by-12-inch rectangle about ⅜ inch thick. Leaving a 1½-inch border on the two short sides, spread the sauce in a 4-inch band down the center of the dough. Cover with the mozzarella and Parmesan cheeses.

5. Fold the two short ends of the dough up and over the filling. Dampen the long edges of the dough with cold water and pull up to completely enclose the filling, overlapping by about 1 inch on top; press gently to seal.

6. Flip the loaf over, seam-side down, onto a greased baking sheet. Slash the top in several places to allow the steam to escape. Brush with the beaten egg and bake at once until the outside is browned and the dough is cooked through, about 35 minutes. (Check the bread

after 20 minutes. If it is browning too quickly, reduce the oven temperature to 400°.)

7. Transfer to a rack and let cool for 20 minutes before cutting into thick slices.
—*Dolores Casella*

QUICK LOAF BREAD

So good and so simple that I start all bread-making students with this bread. It takes just 2 hours from start to finish unless you are using it to make a stuffed bread, in which case it will take a little less time. This bread also looks nice as a braid: Braid it after the first rising and let it rise again before baking.

Makes 2 Loaves

*2⅔ cups lukewarm water
   (105° to 115°)
2 envelopes active dry yeast
2 teaspoons honey or sugar
6½ to 7½ cups unbleached bread or
   all-purpose flour
2 teaspoons salt*

1. In a large bowl, combine the water, yeast and honey. Stir briefly and let stand until the yeast dissolves and begins to foam, 5 to 10 minutes.

2. Stir 3 cups of the flour and the salt into the yeast mixture and beat well until smooth and bubbly. Gradually add enough of the remaining flour, 1 cup at a time, to make a fairly soft dough; do not add more flour than the dough can absorb.

3. Turn out onto a lightly floured surface and knead lightly until the dough is just barely nonsticky, about 2 minutes. Place in an oiled bowl and turn to coat with a light film of oil. Cover and let rise in a warm, draft-free place until doubled in bulk, about 30 minutes.

4. Punch down the dough and divide in half, place each half in a well-greased 9-by-5-by-3-inch loaf pan. Cover and let rise in a warm, draft-free place until doubled in bulk, about 30 minutes. Meanwhile, preheat the oven to 400°.

5. Bake the loaves for 30 minutes, or until the tops are browned and the bottoms sound hollow when tapped. Turn out onto racks and let cool before storing.
—*Dolores Casella*

ZUCCHINI FRITTATA SANDWICHES

A tasty zucchini frittata is wedged between slices of garlic toast to make a comforting sandwich for lunch or brunch.

*Makes 4
Sandwiches*

*3 tablespoons olive oil
1 medium onion, coarsely chopped
2 garlic cloves
2 small zucchini (about 6 inches long),
   cut into ¼-inch slices
½ teaspoon basil
¼ teaspoon oregano
¼ teaspoon salt
¼ teaspoon freshly ground pepper
3 eggs
½ cup freshly grated Parmesan cheese
4 hero rolls, 5 to 6 inches long, or a
   loaf of Italian bread, cut into 5-inch
   lengths and split
4 tablespoons unsalted butter, at room
   temperature*

1. In a medium ovenproof skillet, warm the oil over moderate heat. Add the onion and sauté until soft and lightly colored, 5 to 7 min-

utes. Finely mince one of the garlic cloves and add it to the skillet along with the zucchini, basil, oregano, salt and pepper. Sauté until the zucchini is just tender, about 5 minutes; if the onions begin to brown too much, reduce the heat to low as the zucchini cooks.

2. Preheat the oven to 350°. In a medium bowl, whisk the eggs until evenly blended. Whisk in the Parmesan cheese. Add the egg mixture to the skillet and reduce the heat to very low. Without stirring, cook until the omelet is set but the top is still runny, about 15 minutes. Place in the oven and bake until completely set, 8 to 10 minutes.

3. Meanwhile, spread each roll with 1 tablespoon of the butter using half for each cut side of bread. Place the halves on a baking sheet and lightly toast in the upper portion of the oven, about 5 minutes. Cut the remaining garlic clove in half and rub the cut side of each toasted roll with the pieces.

4. Slide the frittata onto a plate. Slicing from the top to the bottom of the round, cut about one-third of the left side of the omelet away. Turn the plate so that the straight edge is at the top, and slice the remaining portion into 3 equal pieces. Place the 4 frittata pieces on the rolls (trim to evenly distribute as needed) and top with the corresponding tops. Cut in half lengthwise on the diagonal to make 2 long wedges and serve hot.
—Jim Fobel

CHICKEN SALAD SANDWICHES WITH ANCHOVIES AND EGGS

Sandwiches similar to these are served at Harry's Bar in Venice. For those who sit at the bar, the kitchen offers an assortment of inviting sandwiches, enough to last until the big meal of the day.

Makes 10 Small Sandwiches

1 *cup finely chopped cooked chicken (about ½ pound)*
4 *hard-cooked eggs, finely chopped*
1 *can (2 ounces) flat anchovy fillets in olive oil, drained and chopped*
1 *small onion, grated*
¼ *teaspoon freshly ground pepper*

THE ART OF ITALIAN SANDWICHES

A tempting display of colorful sandwiches greets hungry diners in cities throughout Italy. It doesn't matter whether you try a stand-up espresso bar, a cozy cafe, a lush hotel or a time-honored restaurant in Florence, Venice or Rome, you will inevitably be offered stacks of cool, stratified triangular sandwiches wrapped in linen napkins, or trays of toasted rolls packed full of fresh, local ingredients.

Throughout Italy, bread varies as greatly from region to region as the flour used to make it. In Florence, the local dense loaves are ideal for hearty sandwiches, while in nearby Siena, the soft and sometimes slightly sweet breads are made into delicate little sandwiches suitable for an afternoon picnic or overnight train ride. Pizza-like flatbread is a noticeable favorite in Genoa. Often topped with rosemary or sliced onions, these flatbreads are split horizontally and stuffed with meat and cheese.

Sometimes sandwiches are warmed on decorative grills that melt the cheese and toast beautiful designs onto the bread. To do this at home, you can use a lightweight metal skewer to make "grill" marks on the sandwiches: Place the skewer directly over a burner until red hot. Using potholders, pick up the skewer and use it as a branding iron to lightly burn lines in a geometric pattern over the top of each sandwich. If the skewer can be easily bent with pliers, do so in a zigzag line.
—Jim Fobel

⅓ cup mayonnaise
Salt
20 thin slices of firm white or whole
    wheat sandwich bread, crusts
    removed
7 tablespoons unsalted butter, at room
    temperature
¼ cup minced parsley

1. In a medium bowl, combine the chicken, eggs, anchovies, onion and pepper. Mix in the mayonnaise. Taste for salt and add if necessary, though the saltiness of the anchovies should be enough.

2. Spread each slice of the bread with about 1 teaspoon of the butter. Then spread 3 tablespoons of the chicken filling evenly over 10 slices of the bread. Mound about 1 teaspoon of the parsley over the center of the chicken filling. Place the remaining 10 bread slices, buttered-side down, over the filling and cut the sandwiches diagonally in half

3. Dip a clean kitchen towel or several layers of paper towels in cold water and wring out. Stack the sandwiches and wrap them tightly in the damp cloth. Refrigerate until serving time and serve cold. (*These can be made up to 6 hours ahead of time and kept this way. If making further ahead, wrap the sandwiches in plastic wrap.*)
—*Jim Fobel*

MUSHROOM AND MOZZARELLA SANDWICHES

These meltingly tender sandwiches can be served open-face, if you wish, by eliminating the top portion of each roll. To simulate the creamy texture of the southern Italian buffalo-milk mozzarella, domestic mozzarella is marinated in olive oil before cooking.

Makes 4
Sandwiches

1 cup coarsely shredded whole-milk
    mozzarella cheese (about ¼ pound)
1 tablespoon olive oil
4 round sandwich rolls (4- to 4½-inch
    diameter), split
3 tablespoons unsalted butter
8 large mushrooms, cut into ¼-inch
    slices
½ teaspoon salt
¼ teaspoon freshly ground pepper

1. Toss the cheese and olive oil together in a small bowl and let marinate for 15 minutes.

2. Preheat the oven to 400°. Place the rolls, cut-side up, on a baking sheet. Set aside.

3. In a medium skillet, melt the butter over moderate heat. Add the mushroom slices, increase the heat to moderately high and sauté until just cooked through, about 2 minutes.

4. Arrange one-fourth of the mushrooms over each of the four bottom portions of the rolls. Top each with one-fourth of the cheese. Season with the salt and pepper. Bake in the upper third of the oven until the sandwiches are hot and the cheese has melted, about 7 minutes. Add the toasted tops, if you are using them, and serve hot.
—*Jim Fobel*

GRILLED FONTINA AND GREEN OLIVE SANDWICHES

Although these are best when made with Italian Fontina cheese, any good melting cheese such as Port Salut, Muenster or Monterey Jack will work very well. In Italy these sandwiches are grilled with a decorative iron, which leaves a geometric design on the bread.

Makes 4
Sandwiches

8 *thin slices firm white or whole wheat sandwich bread, crusts removed*
8 *teaspoons mayonnaise*
1 *cup coarsely shredded Fontina or other melting cheese (about ¼ pound)*
8 *to 10 Italian brine-cured green olives, pitted and chopped*
8 *teaspoons unsalted butter*

1. Spread each slice of bread with 1 teaspoon of the mayonnaise.
2. Top each of 4 slices of the bread with one-fourth of the cheese. Mound one-fourth of the chopped olives onto the center over the cheese and top with the remaining bread, mayonnaise-side down.
3. In a heavy medium skillet, melt 2 teaspoons of the butter over moderately low heat. Place two sandwiches in the pan and cook until light golden brown, 2 to 3 minutes. Add 2 more teaspoons of butter to the pan, turn the sandwiches with a spatula and cook until golden brown, 2 to 3 minutes. Transfer to a platter. Repeat with the 2 remaining sandwiches. Serve hot.
—Jim Fobel

TUNA SALAD AND BLACK OLIVE SANDWICHES

For a truly Italian flavor, include these tasty morsels as part of any sandwich assortment. They can be prepared up to six hours ahead of time.

Makes 10 Small
Sandwiches

1 *can (7 ounces) light tuna packed in oil, drained and flaked*
4 *hard-cooked eggs, finely chopped*
1 *small red onion, finely chopped*
3 *tablespoons small capers, drained*
1 *tablespoon fresh lemon juice*
⅓ *cup mayonnaise*
¼ *teaspoon freshly ground pepper*
Salt
20 *thin slices firm white or whole wheat sandwich bread, crusts removed*
7 *tablespoons unsalted butter, at room temperature*
20 *to 25 Italian brine-cured black olives, pitted and chopped*

1. In a medium bowl, combine the tuna, eggs, onion, capers, lemon juice, mayonnaise and pepper. Stir to bind the ingredients with the mayonnaise. Season with salt to taste.
2. Spread each slice of bread with about 1 teaspoon of butter. Working with half of the slices, spread 3

185

FONTINA

Although Italian law specifies that Fontina cheese (more properly called Fontina d'Aosta) can only be made in the Val d'Aosta region of northern Italy, this buttery cheese with a nutty flavor is widely copied outside of Italy. The French version, known as Fontal, is softer, sweeter and more buttery, while Danish Fontina is tart and Swedish Fontina has a fuller yet less complex flavor. One easy way to spot the Italian original, considered by many to be the best of the bunch, is by the rind, which ranges in color from light to dark brown; the others sport red rinds. Fontina d'Aosta is traditionally used to make *fonduta*, a fondue topped with white truffles.

tablespoons of the tuna filling evenly over each slice of buttered bread. Top the center of each with about 1 teaspoon of the chopped olives. Place the remaining 10 slices, buttered-side down, over the filling. Cut the sandwiches diagonally in half and arrange in stacks.

3. Dip a clean kitchen towel or several layers of paper towels in cold water and wring out. Tightly wrap the stacks of sandwiches with the damp cloth and refrigerate until serving time. Serve cold. (*These can be made up to 6 hours ahead of time and kept this way. If making further ahead, wrap the sandwiches in plastic wrap.*)
—Jim Fobel

SAUSAGE AND RED PEPPER SANDWICHES

*Makes 4
Sandwiches*

*2 tablespoons olive oil
1 large onion, halved lengthwise and
    cut into thin slivers
1 large red or green bell pepper, cut
    into ¼-inch strips
4 Italian sweet sausages with fennel
    (about 1 pound)
½ teaspoon oregano, crumbled
½ teaspoon salt
4 hero rolls (5 to 6 inches long) or a
    loaf of Italian bread, cut into 5-inch
    lengths and spilt*

1. In a large heavy skillet, warm the olive oil over moderate heat. Add the onion and pepper and sauté until softened and lightly browned, about 10 minutes. Remove with a slotted spoon and set aside; reduce the heat to low.

2. Prick the sausages all over with a fork. Place the sausages in the skillet and cook, turning frequently, until they are well browned, about 10 minutes. Tilt the pan and pour off the fat.

3. Return the onion and pepper to the skillet and add the oregano, salt and 1 tablespoon of water. Cover and simmer over low heat until the sausages are cooked through, about 10 minutes.

4. Meanwhile, preheat the oven to 350°. Place the rolls on a baking sheet and warm until hot throughout, 3 to 5 minutes.

5. Remove the sausages with tongs and cut each one lengthwise into 6 long thin slices. Arrange over the bottom of each roll and top with one-fourth of the pepper and onion mixture. Add the tops, cut in half on the diagonal and serve hot.
—Jim Fobel

VEGETABLES & RICE

187

ARTICHOKE HEARTS WITH MUSHROOMS AND FENNEL

Although the artichokes require a little extra work, this recipe can be prepared ahead and reheated. Prepare through Step 4; cool, but do not refrigerate. Before serving, heat and add the cheese.

6 Servings

4 *medium artichokes*
½ *lemon*
1 *tablespoon fresh lemon juice*
2 *medium fennel bulbs, stalks removed*
¼ *cup olive oil*
1 *pound small mushrooms, halved*
½ *teaspoon salt*
¼ *teaspoon freshly ground pepper*
¼ *cup dry white wine*
¼ *cup freshly grated Parmesan cheese*

1. Using a large stainless steel knife, cut off the artichoke stems at the base; rub the cut area with the lemon half to prevent discoloration. Bend back and pull off all the outer green leaves until only the light, pale green leaves remain. Cut off and discard the top third of the artichoke. One at a time, with a small stainless steel knife, pare around the base to remove any tough green patches; rub with the lemon. Cut lengthwise into eighths, remove the chokes and drop into a bowl of water acidulated with the lemon juice.

2. Slice each fennel bulb crosswise into 1-inch strips. Discard the tough inner core.

3. In a large skillet, heat the oil. Add the mushrooms and sauté over moderately high heat, tossing frequently, until lightly colored, 3 to 4 minutes. Season with the salt and pepper, and cook 2 minutes longer. Drain the artichokes and add them to the mushrooms. Add the fennel and toss to mix.

4. Add the white wine and boil until the liquid is reduced to 2 tablespoons. Lay a sheet of waxed paper on top of the vegetables. Cover the pan, reduce the heat to low and cook until the vegetables are tender, 35 to 40 minutes. (*The recipe may be prepared several hours ahead to this point.*)

5. Remove the lid and waxed paper. The vegetables should be moist, but there should be no excess liquid. If there is, increase the heat to high and boil until the liquid has evaporated. Add the cheese and toss. Serve hot.
—*Nancy Verde Barr*

ROAST ASPARAGUS

Roasting fresh asparagus spears brings out their flavor in a whole new way and maintains a pleasingly firm texture. Treating asparagus in this fashion was first suggested to me by Johanne Killeen and George Germon, chef/owners of Al Forno in Providence, Rhode Island.

3 to 4 Servings

1 *pound fresh asparagus, trimmed and*
peeled halfway up from the bottom
1 *tablespoon extra-virgin olive oil*
1 *lemon, cut into wedges*
Freshly ground black pepper

Preheat the oven to 500°. Place the asparagus in a single layer on a baking sheet or shallow pan. Drizzle with the olive oil. Roast the asparagus in the middle of the oven, turning the spears occasionally for even cooking and to avoid browning, for 8 to 10 minutes, depending on the thickness of the stalks. Serve hot with lemon wedges and pass a pepper mill at the table.
—*Richard Sax*

ASPARAGUS WITH PARMESAN CHEESE

Cook fresh asparagus immersed upright in boiling water, leaving the tender tips standing clear.

12 Servings

4 pounds medium asparagus, trimmed
Salt
6 tablespoons lightly salted butter
¾ cup freshly grated Parmesan cheese
Pinch of freshly grated nutmeg

1. Divide the trimmed asparagus into 3 bunches and tie each bunch in the center with cotton string. Add enough water to a tall stockpot to almost cover the asparagus when standing vertically (the tips should not be immersed). Lightly salt the water and bring to a boil over moderately high heat. Stand the asparagus bundles in the pot, cover and simmer until just tender, about 10 minutes. The tips should be barely tender.

2. In a small saucepan, cook the butter over moderate heat until it bubbles and just begins to turn brown, 5 to 8 minutes. Remove from the heat.

3. Drain the asparagus well. Untie the bundles and heap the asparagus on a deep platter. Pour on 1 tablespoon of the brown butter and turn the asparagus with tongs or 2 spoons to coat. Sprinkle ¼ cup of the Parmesan cheese and the nutmeg over the asparagus and turn again to distribute the cheese. Pour the remaining browned butter over the asparagus and sprinkle the remaining ½ cup Parmesan cheese on top. Serve warm.
—*Lorenza de'Medici*

HERBED CARROTS AND GREEN BEANS

The subtle lemon and anchovy flavors of this dish marry well with most baked, grilled or broiled fish or chicken dishes.

6 Servings

4 tablespoons unsalted butter
1 medium garlic clove, crushed
¾ pound green beans, cut into 2-inch lengths
6 medium carrots, cut into 2-by-¼-inch julienne strips
¼ teaspoon salt
¼ teaspoon freshly ground pepper
3 tablespoons chopped parsley
2 teaspoons chopped fresh marjoram or ½ teaspoon dried
1 teaspoon finely chopped fresh rosemary or ¼ teaspoon dried, crushed
3 anchovy fillets, mashed
Grated zest of 1 lemon
2 teaspoons fresh lemon juice

VEGETABLES & RICE

1. In a large skillet, melt the butter over moderately low heat. Add the garlic and cook until lightly colored, about 2 minutes.

2. Add the beans, carrots, salt, pepper, parsley, marjoram and rosemary. Toss to combine. Cover tightly and cook, tossing occasionally, until just tender, 10 to 12 minutes. If the vegetables begin to stick, add 1 or 2 tablespoons of water.

3. Add the anchovies, lemon zest and lemon juice. Cook, tossing, for 2 minutes.

—Nancy Verde Barr

MARINATED CUCUMBERS

This simple, unusual and particularly Tuscan dish was traditionally associated with the gathering of the grain at harvest time. The sweetened cucumbers were probably served as a palate refresher before the dessert course at the big, festive dinner for all the neighbors who helped out. The dish was so well liked that it became a popular snack to have during a small rest break from hard work.

6 Servings

2 European cucumbers, peeled and
    sliced ⅛ inch thick
2 tablespoons fresh lemon juice
½ cup sugar

Place the cucumbers in a medium bowl. Drizzle the lemon juice on top and sprinkle evenly with the sugar. Do not mix. Cover and refrigerate for at least 2 and up to 24 hours. Just before serving, toss well. Spoon the cucumbers and their juices into dessert bowls and serve cold.

—Giuliano Bugialli

EGGPLANT-TOMATO COMPOTE

4 Servings

1 small onion, minced
½ cup extra-virgin olive oil
2 large garlic cloves, thinly sliced
1 large eggplant, cut into ¼-inch dice
6 medium tomatoes—peeled, seeded
    and chopped—or 1 can (28 ounces)
    Italian peeled tomatoes, drained and
    chopped
1 small zucchini—halved lengthwise,
    seeded and cut into ¼-inch dice
¼ of a medium red bell pepper, cut into
    ¼-inch dice
¼ cup Niçoise olives, pitted and
    chopped
2 tablespoons minced fresh herbs—
    thyme, basil, oregano and/or flat-
    leaf parsley
Salt and freshly ground pepper

1. In a large saucepan, cook the onion in the oil over moderately low heat until softened, about 5 minutes. Add the garlic and cook until tender, about 2 minutes.

2. Stir in the eggplant, tomatoes, zucchini and red pepper. Bring to a simmer over moderate heat. Cook uncovered until most of the liquid has evaporated and the vegetables are soft, about 15 minutes.

3. Add the olives and herbs. Season with salt and pepper to taste. Cook for 3 minutes to blend the flavors. Serve warm or at room temperature.

—Mark Militello, Mark's Place,
Miami

BAKED FENNEL WITH PARMESAN CHEESE

6 Servings

5 *small fennel bulbs (about 3 pounds),*
   trimmed and cut into quarters
4 *tablespoons unsalted butter*
¼ *teaspoon salt*
½ *teaspoon freshly ground pepper*
⅓ *cup chicken stock or canned broth*
¼ *cup freshly grated Parmesan cheese*

1. Soak the fennel in cold water for 20 minutes; drain.

2. Preheat the oven to 350°. In a large pot of boiling salted water, cook the fennel for 5 minutes. Drain, rinse under cold water and dry well.

3. Grease a large shallow baking dish with 1 tablespoon of the butter. Cut the remaining 3 tablespoons butter into small pieces. Layer half of the fennel in the dish, scatter the butter over the fennel and season with ⅛ teaspoon of the salt and ¼ teaspoon of the pepper. Top with the remaining fennel, pack down and season with the remaining ⅛ teaspoon salt and ¼ teaspoon pepper. (*The recipe can be prepared to this point up to 1 day ahead. Cover the baking dish and refrigerate.*)

4. Pour the stock over the fennel, cover with foil and bake for 45 minutes. Increase the temperature to 400° and cook until the liquid has evaporated, about 20 minutes. Sprinkle the Parmesan cheese over the fennel and bake uncovered until golden, about 10 minutes.
—*Nancy Verde Barr*

BRAISED MUSHROOMS WITH PANCETTA AND PINE NUTS

Pancetta can be very salty, so season this dish with discretion. If you cannot find pancetta, prosciutto is a good substitute.

6 Servings

1 *ounce dried porcini or cèpes*
¼ *pound pancetta, cut into ⅛-inch*
   dice
2 *to 4 tablespoons olive oil*
¼ *cup pine nuts (pignoli)*
1 *large garlic clove, minced*
1 *small onion, minced*
1 *pound mushrooms, thinly sliced*
¼ *cup dry Madeira or tawny port*
2 *tablespoons heavy cream*
¼ *cup minced parsley*
Salt and freshly ground pepper

1. In a small bowl, cover the porcini with warm water and let soak for 1 hour. Remove the mushrooms. Strain the soaking liquid through several layers of dampened cheesecloth; reserve ½ cup.

2. Rinse the mushrooms well to remove any sand; squeeze to remove as much liquid as possible. Coarsely chop the mushrooms and set aside.

3. In a large skillet, cook the pancetta in 2 tablespoons of olive oil over low heat until golden brown, 10 to 12 minutes. Remove the pancetta with a slotted spoon to a small bowl. Add enough oil, if necessary, to the fat in the skillet to measure 3 tablespoons.

4. Add the pine nuts to the fat and sauté, stirring frequently, over moderate heat until golden, about 3 minutes. Remove with a slotted spoon and add to the pancetta.

PINE NUTS

Pignoli, or pine nuts, are the small, ovoid seeds of pine cones. Rich and creamy, they used to be served in Liguria during Lent, when most foods of substance, including meat and cheese, were forbidden. Pine nuts are often used to flavor sweet breads and dessert fillings, in meat dishes, particularly game, and in sweet-and-sour sauces of Asian origin, such as caponata. Because they must be individually shelled and extracted, they are considerably more expensive than most other nuts.

5. Reduce the heat to low, add the garlic and onion and cook until softened, 2 to 3 minutes.

6. Increase the heat to high, add the reserved porcini and fresh mushrooms and cook, tossing, until the mushrooms begin to release liquid, 5 to 7 minutes.

7. Add the Madeira and the reserved soaking liquid and boil until the liquid is reduced to 2 tablespoons, about 5 minutes. Add the cream, reduce the heat to low and cook until the sauce thickens slightly, about 2 minutes.

8. Stir in the parsley, pancetta and pine nuts. Season with salt and pepper to taste.
—*Nancy Verde Barr*

PEAS BRAISED IN TOMATO

In this recipe, *piselli alla Napoletana*, peas simmer in a tomato sauce until they become very soft.

4 Servings

1½ teaspoons tomato paste
2½ tablespoons olive oil
¼ cup coarsely chopped onion
1½ packages (15 ounces total) *frozen green peas (about 2½ cups)*
¼ teaspoon salt

1. In a small bowl, combine the tomato paste with ⅓ cup of water. Stir to dissolve.

2. In a heavy, medium, nonreactive saucepan, heat the olive oil over moderate heat. Add the onion and cook until wilted, about 2 minutes. Add the peas, salt and the diluted tomato paste and bring to a boil. Reduce the heat to very low, cover and cook until the peas are very tender, about 15 minutes. Uncover, increase the heat to high and boil

vigorously until almost all the liquid has evaporated, 3 to 5 minutes. Serve at once.
—*Diane Darrow and Tom Maresca*

NEAPOLITAN STUFFED PEPPERS

Jenny Iannone, a favorite aunt of an Italian friend, taught me to prepare this dish. She said to cook the peppers until they sat down—mine kind of laid down, but they tasted terrific.

4 Servings

8 bell peppers
¼ cup plus 2 tablespoons extra-virgin olive oil
½ large onion, chopped
3 garlic cloves, chopped
3 tablespoons chopped parsley
4 plum tomatoes—peeled, seeded and chopped
1 teaspoon tomato paste
3 tablespoons chopped brine-cured black olives
3 tablespoons dry bread crumbs
1½ tablespoons chopped capers
16 anchovy fillets

1. Using a small sharp knife, cut around the pepper stems, leaving as small an opening as possible. Pull out the cores. Use a teaspoon to remove the seeds and ribs.

2. Preheat the oven to 350°. In a medium skillet, heat ¼ cup of the oil. Add the onion, garlic and parsley, and sauté over moderate heat until the onion is soft and translucent, 2 to 3 minutes.

3. Add the tomatoes, tomato paste and olives. Cook until the liquid from the tomatoes evaporates, about 5 minutes. Add the bread crumbs and capers. Cook, stirring, for 1 minute.

4. Spoon the filling into the peppers. Place 2 anchovy fillets in each. Spread the remaining 2 tablespoons of oil in a baking dish just large enough to hold the peppers in a single layer. Add the peppers and bake, uncovered, until they collapse, about 1½ hours.

5. Serve hot or cold as a first course, or place the peppers on top of pasta and dress with the juices. (*These peppers can be prepared up to 1 week ahead.*)
—Anne Disrude

PEPPERS WITH BALSAMIC VINEGAR AND FRESH HERBS

Alive with color and flavor, this dish is a natural accompaniment to grilled steak, hamburger or sausage.

8 Servings

¼ cup olive oil
1 large onion, halved and thinly sliced
4 medium red bell peppers, cut into ¼-inch strips
4 medium green bell peppers, cut into ¼-inch strips
⅓ cup minced parsley
⅓ cup shredded fresh basil or 1½ teaspoons dried
1 tablespoon fresh thyme or 1 teaspoon dried
¼ cup balsamic vinegar or good red wine vinegar
Salt and freshly ground black pepper

1. In a large skillet, warm the oil over moderate heat. Add the onion and cook until it is softened but not browned, about 3 minutes.

2. Add the red and green peppers and toss to coat with the oil. Cover and cook until the peppers are tender, 10 to 12 minutes.

3. Add the parsley, basil and thyme and cook, uncovered, for another 5 minutes.

4. Stir in the vinegar and continue cooking for 5 minutes. Season with salt and black pepper to taste.
—Nancy Verde Barr

GREMOLATA MASHED POTATOES

6 Servings

2 pounds small red potatoes, unpeeled and quartered
1 small lemon
1 cup (loosely packed) flat-leaf parsley leaves
1 garlic clove
½ cup heavy cream
1 stick (4 ounces) unsalted butter, at room temperature
1 teaspoon coarse (kosher) salt

1. Place the potatoes in a medium saucepan and add enough water to cover them by 1 inch. Bring to a boil over high heat. Reduce the heat to moderately high and cook the potatoes until tender, about 15 minutes.

2. Using a sharp vegetable peeler, cut away the zest of the lemon in strips, taking care not to include any of the bitter white pith. On a cutting board, finely chop the zest with the parsley and garlic. Set the gremolata aside.

3. Drain the potatoes in a colander and return them to the saucepan. Using a potato masher, coarsely mash the potatoes over very low heat, gradually incorporating the heavy cream and the butter. Stir in the salt and the gremolata and serve immediately.
—George Germon and Johanne Killeen, Al Forno, Providence, Rhode Island

PARMESAN MASHED POTATOES

Puree con parmigiano has more body than the usual mashed potatoes.

4 Servings

*6 medium boiling potatoes (about
1½ pounds), peeled and quartered
3 tablespoons freshly grated
Parmigiano-Reggiano cheese
½ teaspoon salt
⅛ teaspoon freshly ground pepper
½ cup warm milk*

1. In a saucepan, combine the potatoes and salted water to cover generously. Bring to a boil over moderate heat. Cover, reduce the heat to low and simmer until tender, about 20 minutes.

2. Drain the potatoes. Return them to the pan and mash with a potato masher. Using a wooden spoon, beat in the cheese, salt and pepper. Add the milk and beat until smooth. Serve at once.
—Diane Darrow and Tom Maresca

POTATOES WITH SWEET RED PEPPERS

A wonderful accompaniment to roasted or grilled meats, such as an herbed leg of lamb, steak or Italian sausage.

6 Servings

*3 medium all-purpose potatoes, peeled
and cut into ½-inch slices
2 medium onions, cut into eighths
4 medium red bell peppers, cut
lengthwise into thick slices
¼ pound thinly sliced prosciutto,
shredded
1 teaspoon finely chopped
fresh rosemary or ½ teaspoon
dried, crushed
½ teaspoon salt
¼ teaspoon freshly ground black
pepper
¼ cup extra-virgin olive oil*

1. Preheat the oven to 400°. Place the potatoes, onions and red peppers in a large roasting pan. Add the prosciutto, rosemary, salt and black pepper; drizzle on the oil and toss to coat the vegetables.

2. Bake, stirring 2 or 3 times, for about 35 minutes, or until the potatoes are tender.
—Nancy Verde Barr

194

PARMIGIANO-REGGIANO

Parmigiano-Reggiano is the highest quality Parmesan cheese available, and to many, it is the only Parmesan. Like French *appellation contrôlée* wines and Italian D.O.C. wines, its production is strictly limited, in this case to the provinces of Parma, Reggio Emilia, Modena, Mantova and Bologna.

On April 1, production begins with the the milk of cows that have fed in fresh pastures, and it ends promptly on November 11. Parmigiano-Reggiano is made completely by hand in an artisan's tradition that is hundreds of years old, and is aged for at least two years, and usually longer.

To distinguish Parmigiano-Reggiano from other, ersatz Parmesans, small dots spelling out its name are etched around the entire circumference of the 60- to 70-pound wheels.

When buying Parmigiano-Reggiano for grating, look for a faintly moist, straw-yellow chunk that crumbles softly in your hand. It should taste mellow but rich and minimally salty and should leave a slightly sweet aftertaste. If you want to serve Parmesan as an eating cheese, look for a younger, less yellow, moister wedge.

Whereas Americans have grown fond of sprinkling Parmesan on all sorts of dishes, in Italy, cheese is generally not grated on fish, game or mushroom dishes or dishes with hot red pepper. Parmesan should be grated just before using, since once grated, it loses its flavor quickly.

GRILLED RADICCHIO WITH ANCHOVY-MUSTARD SAUCE

Vivid garnet heads of radicchio are a comparatively new arrival at American vegetable stands. They reveal an intriguingly bitter savor when grilled. The tastiest radicchio is the Treviso variety, with long, narrow heads shaped like loose-leafed Belgian endive. Round-headed Verona radicchio, which resembles baby red cabbage, is less interesting in flavor, but this recipe works well with either variety. It is good as a warm salad after the main course, though it can also be served as an antipasto or as a vegetable.

4 to 6 Servings

2 *anchovy fillets*
1 *tablespoon Dijon mustard*
¼ *cup fresh lemon juice*
1 *garlic clove, lightly crushed*
½ *teaspoon rosemary, crumbled*
1 *tablespoon minced parsley*
½ *cup extra-virgin olive oil*
4 *small heads of radicchio (1 to 1¼*
    pounds), outer leaves removed,
    quartered lengthwise, with ends
    intact
Salt and freshly ground pepper

1. In a small bowl, mash the anchovies to a paste. Whisk in the mustard and lemon juice. Add the garlic, rosemary and parsley. Gradually whisk in 6 tablespoons of the olive oil in a thin stream. Set the anchovy-mustard sauce aside.

2. Heat a very large cast-iron skillet or griddle over moderate heat. Brush the radicchio with the remaining 2 tablespoons olive oil and lay them in the pan or on the griddle. Season with salt and pepper to taste. Cook, turning, until the radicchio is lightly browned and fork tender, about 8 minutes.

3. Arrange the grilled radicchio on a serving plate, cut-sides up. Give the sauce a final stir, discard the garlic and spoon the sauce over the radicchio. Serve warm or at room temperature.
—*Tom Maresca and Diane Darrow*

SPINACH WITH RAISINS AND PINE NUTS

In the springtime, fresh, tender spinach can be eaten either uncooked in a salad with just extra-virgin olive oil and a little lemon juice or sautéed with raisins and pine nuts. Don't toast the pine nuts because they will lose their delicate flavor.

12 Servings

1 *cup raisins*
4 *pounds fresh spinach leaves with*
    stems
¼ *cup extra-virgin olive oil*
Salt
½ *cup pine nuts (pignoli)*

1. In a small bowl, pour 1 cup of warm water over the raisins and set aside for 30 minutes. Drain the raisins thoroughly.

2. In a stockpot, bring 1 cup of salted water to a boil over high heat. Stir in the spinach and cook, stirring, until it is just wilted, about 2 minutes.

3. Drain the spinach in a colander and refresh under cold running water to keep the bright green color. Once the spinach has cooled, squeeze out the excess liquid.

4. In a large skillet, heat the oil over moderate heat. Add the drained spinach and the raisins and

cook, stirring, until heated through, about 5 minutes. Season to taste with salt and arrange the spinach on a platter. Sprinkle on the nuts.
—*Lorenza de' Medici*

FRIED ZUCCHINI

A garden without lots of zucchini could hardly be called Italian. This is one of the many Italian ways to prepare this popular vegetable.

6 to 8 Servings

1 egg
½ cup all-purpose flour
¼ teaspoon salt
3 cups olive oil or safflower oil
3 medium zucchini (about
 1¼ pounds), sliced crosswise
 ⅛ inch thick

1. In a small bowl, lightly whisk the egg. Gradually sift in the flour and salt, whisking until smooth. Slowly whisk in about ⅓ cup water. (The batter should be the consistency of thin pancake batter.) Set aside to rest for at least 20 minutes.
2. In a large deep skillet, heat the oil over moderately high heat to 375°, or until a small cube of bread browns in about 1 minute. One by one, dip the zucchini slices into the batter, shaking gently to release any excess. Slide into the hot oil and fry in small batches, turning, until golden, 1 to 3 minutes. Remove with a slotted spoon and drain on paper towels. Sprinkle with salt to taste and serve the zucchini immediately.
—*Nancy Verde Barr*

MUSTARD RING

This rich mustard ring is best described as a cross between an aspic and a condiment. Depending on the season, the center can be filled with coleslaw, tomatoes, black olives or watercress, as you wish.

*Makes About 4
Cups*

1½ envelopes unflavored gelatin
1 tablespoon dry mustard
½ cup dry white wine
4 eggs
½ cup apple cider vinegar
3 tablespoons Dijon mustard
1 teaspoon sugar
½ teaspoon salt
¼ teaspoon freshly ground white pepper
2 teaspoons drained, prepared white
 horseradish
1 cup heavy cream

1. Lightly oil a 4-cup ring mold.
2. In a double boiler, combine the gelatin and dry mustard with ¼ cup of cold water and stir until blended. Stir in the wine. Place over simmering water and stir until the gelatin dissolves, about 3 minutes.
3. In a small bowl, whisk the eggs until blended. Whisk in the vinegar, Dijon mustard, sugar, salt and pepper. Slowly stir the egg mixture into the gelatin mixture in the double boiler. Cook over simmering water, stirring constantly, until the mixture is the thickness of heavy cream, 8 to 10 minutes. Remove the pan

from the water and stir in the horseradish.

4. Cool by placing the pan in a bowl of ice and water or in the refrigerator, stirring frequently, until thickened but not set.

5. In a medium bowl, beat the cream until moderately stiff. Do not overbeat or it will be difficult to combine with the gelatin mixture.

6. Fold the cooled gelatin mixture into the whipped cream with a rubber spatula. Turn into the prepared mold, cover with plastic wrap and refrigerate for at least 6 hours, or until firm.

7. Before unmolding the ring, moisten the plate onto which it will be unmolded with a little cold water. (In case you unmold off center, the water makes it easy to slide the ring into the center.) To unmold the ring, dip the mold briefly, for about 15 seconds, into a large bowl of hot water and invert onto the serving plate, tapping sharply if necessary. Cut into small wedges to serve.

—Helen Millman

RICE WITH PEAS

This is a classic Venetian dish that is always served in early spring. This ambrosial combination absolutely requires sweet peas—the younger, the better. If your peas aren't fresh off the vine, you might want to add a pinch of sugar to the pot, or use the best-quality tiny frozen peas. The finished product should be slightly soupy, not as thick as a risotto.

4 Servings

6 cups light chicken stock or
 3 cups canned broth diluted with
 3 cups water
4 tablespoons unsalted butter
2 tablespoons olive oil
¼ cup chopped onion
½ cup chopped parsley
2 ounces pancetta, cut into ¼-inch dice
2 pounds fresh peas—shelled, rinsed
 and drained—or 1 package (10
 ounces) tiny frozen peas
1 cup arborio rice
3 tablespoons freshly grated Parmesan
 cheese
1 teaspoon salt
¼ teaspoon freshly ground pepper

1. In a medium saucepan, bring the stock to a simmer over moderate heat. Reduce the heat to low to keep it hot.

2. In a large flameproof casserole, melt 2 tablespoons of the butter in the olive oil over moderate heat. Add the onion, parsley and pancetta. Sauté until the fat is rendered from the pancetta and the onion is softened but not browned, about 3 minutes.

3. If you are using fresh peas, add them to the casserole at this point and cook for 1 minute, stirring to coat them with the fat in the pan. Gradually add 1½ cups of the hot stock. Reduce the heat to low and simmer, stirring frequently, until the peas are just tender, 15 to 20 minutes.

4. If using frozen peas, add them at this point. Add the remaining 4½ cups stock and bring to a boil. Stir in the rice. Reduce the heat to moderate to maintain a steady simmer and cook, uncovered, stirring occasionally, until the rice is tender but still firm, about 20 minutes.

5. Stir in the remaining 2 tablespoons butter, the Parmesan cheese, salt and pepper. Simmer for 2 minutes longer, then serve hot.
—Tom Maresca and Diane Darrow

3. Add the rice and stir for 1 to 2 minutes, until well coated with oil and slightly translucent.

4. Add ½ cup of the simmering stock and cook, stirring constantly, until the rice has absorbed most of the liquid. Adjust the heat if necessary to maintain a simmer. Gradually adding stock, ½ cup at a time, cook, stirring constantly, until the rice is almost tender but still slightly crunchy in the center, 20 to 25 minutes.

5. Add the cheese and season with the pepper and salt to taste. Continue to cook, stirring and adding stock as necessary, ¼ cup at a time, until the rice is tender but still firm and is bound with a creamy sauce, 3 to 6 minutes longer.

6. Stir in butter and serve hot.

VEGETABLE-CHEESE RISOTTO
Reduce the cheese to ¼ cup. Add 1 to 1½ cups sautéed vegetables (such as artichoke hearts, peas, mushrooms or green beans) in Step 5.
—F&W

198

GORGONZOLA

Gorgonzola, named after a village near Milan, has been produced in the Po Valley since the ninth century. Along with English Stilton and French Roquefort, it is considered one of the top three blue cheeses in the world; it is certainly one of the most pungent. Sweet, young gorgonzola (aged only four to six months) is rich and creamy; the aged version, which can be up to one year old, is even more robust. The characteristic veining of this celebrated blue cheese is actually more green than blue. The London Stock Exchange, whose marble interior has a greenish tone, is nicknamed "Gorgonzola Hall."

CHEESE RISOTTO

4 to 6 Servings

About 5 cups chicken stock or
  2½ cups canned broth diluted with
  2½ cups water
3 tablespoons olive oil
⅓ cup minced onion
1½ cups arborio rice
½ cup freshly grated Parmesan and/or
  a melting cheese, such as
  mozzarella, Fontina or Gorgonzola
½ teaspoon freshly ground pepper
Salt
2 tablespoons unsalted butter

1. In a medium saucepan, bring the stock to a simmer; maintain at a simmer over moderately low heat.

2. In a large nonreactive saucepan or flameproof casserole, heat the oil over moderate heat. Add the onion and cook until it is softened and translucent, about 2 minutes.

RISOTTO AL BAROLO

🍷 Dolcetto, such as Renato Ratti or Pio Cesare

6 Servings

3½ cups beef stock or canned chicken broth
1¼ cups Barolo wine
3 tablespoons unsalted butter
1 small onion, finely chopped
1½ cups arborio rice
½ cup freshly grated Parmesan cheese
¾ teaspoon salt
¼ teaspoon coarsely cracked pepper
2 tablespoons chopped parsley

1. In a medium nonreactive

saucepan, bring the broth and 1 cup of wine to a simmer.

2. Meanwhile, in a large nonreactive saucepan or flameproof casserole, melt 2 tablespoons of the butter over moderate heat. Add the onion and sauté, stirring occasionally, until softened but not browned, about 2 minutes.

3. Stir in the rice and cook, stirring, until the grains are well coated with butter and slightly translucent 1 to 2 minutes.

4. Stir in ½ cup of the simmering broth and cook, stirring constantly, until the rice has absorbed most of the liquid. Gradually adding broth, ½ cup at a time, cook, stirring constantly, until the rice is almost tender but still crunchy in the center, 20 to 25 minutes.

5. Stir in the cheese, salt and pepper. Continue to cook, stirring and adding the remaining broth as necessary, ¼ cup at a time, until the rice is tender but still firm and is bound with a creamy sauce, 3 to 6 minutes longer.

6. Stir in the remaining ¼ cup wine, the parsley and the remaining 1 tablespoon butter. Serve hot.
—F&W

SAFFRON RISOTTO

This is a variation of the classic dish *risotto alla milanese.*

4 Servings

*⅓ ounce dried porcini mushrooms
    (about ¾ cup)*
1 cup boiling water
6 cups chicken stock or canned broth
⅛ teaspoon saffron threads
4 tablespoons unsalted butter
½ small onion, minced
¼ cup dry white wine
1½ cups arborio rice
*¾ cup freshly grated Parmigiano-
    Reggiano cheese*
Salt and freshly ground pepper

1. Put the dried mushrooms in a small bowl. Pour the boiling water on top and let soak for 30 minutes. Drain the mushrooms, reserving the liquid. Rinse the mushrooms well and cut off any tough bits. Chop coarsely, rinse again and set aside. Strain the soaking liquid through a fine-mesh sieve lined with cheesecloth to remove any grit and set aside.

2. In a medium saucepan, bring the chicken stock to a simmer over low heat. Maintain at a simmer until ready to use. In a small bowl, combine ½ cup of the hot stock and the saffron and set aside.

3. In a medium casserole, melt 2 tablespoons of the butter over moderate heat. Add the onion and cook, stirring occasionally, until softened, about 5 minutes. Add the chopped porcini and cook for 1 minute. Increase the heat to moderately high, add the wine and cook until it evaporates, about 3 minutes.

4. Add the rice, stirring for 1 to 2 minutes to coat all the grains with the butter. Reduce the heat to moderately low and add ½ cup of the

RISOTTO ALLA MILANESE

According to one legend, the tradition of coloring risotto with saffron goes back to the 16th century when, in Milan and other large European cities, it was fashionable to gild food before serving it. In addition to providing the opportunity to show off one's wealth, gold was thought to be a cure-all for many of the health problems of the day.

In either case, this habit was out of the reach of all but the well-off. In 1574, as the story goes, the daughter of one of the craftsmen working on the stained-glass windows at the Duomo was getting married. In a moment of genius, one of the craftsman's apprentices came up with the idea of "gilding" the risotto planned for her wedding with the saffron that he used to enrich his yellow paints. The dish that was created, *risotto alla milanese*, has since been called "the national dish of Lombardy."

simmering stock. Stir frequently until it is absorbed. Continue adding more stock, ½ cup at a time, and stirring frequently until it is completely absorbed, for 20 minutes.

5. Pour in the saffron and its soaking liquid. Continue cooking and stirring until the rice is tender but still firm to the bite and has absorbed almost all the stock, 10 to 15 minutes longer. If you run out of stock before the rice is tender, use the reserved mushroom soaking liquid.

6. Remove the risotto from the heat and stir in the remaining 2 tablespoons butter and the cheese. Season to taste with salt and pepper. Serve at once.
—*Diane Darrow and Tom Maresca*

RISOTTO ALLA MILANESE

This classic saffron-tinged risotto, traditionally served with osso buco, is a delightful accompaniment to roast meats as well.

4 to 6 Servings

About 5 cups chicken stock or 2½ cups canned broth diluted with 2½ cups water
Pinch of saffron threads
3 tablespoons olive oil
⅓ cup minced onion
2 tablespoons finely diced prosciutto or beef marrow
1½ cups arborio rice
¼ cup dry Marsala or dry white wine
¼ cup freshly grated Parmesan cheese
½ teaspoon freshly ground pepper
Salt
2 tablespoons unsalted butter

1. In a medium saucepan, bring the stock to a simmer and crumble in the saffron. Maintain at a simmer over moderately low heat.

2. In a large nonreactive saucepan or flameproof casserole, heat the oil over moderate heat. Add the onion and prosciutto and cook until the onion is softened and translucent, about 2 minutes.

3. Add the rice and stir for 1 to 2 minutes until well coated with oil and slightly translucent. Add the Marsala and cook, stirring, until it evaporates.

4. Add ½ cup of the simmering stock and cook, stirring constantly, until the rice has absorbed most of the liquid. Adjust the heat if necessary to maintain a simmer. Gradually adding stock, ½ cup at a time, cook, stirring constantly, until the rice is almost tender but still slightly crunchy in the center, 20 to 25 minutes.

5. Add the cheese and season with the pepper and salt to taste. Continue to cook, stirring and adding stock as necessary, ¼ cup at a time, until the rice is tender but still firm and is bound with a creamy sauce, 3 to 6 minutes longer.

6. Stir in butter and serve hot.
—F&W

RISOTTO WITH PORCINI MUSHROOMS

Dried porcini and arborio rice can be found in Italian food markets and some supermarkets.
🍷 Rainoldi Inferno or Ceretto Nebbiolo d'Alba.

4 to 6 Servings

1¾ ounces dried porcini mushrooms
6 cups beef stock or 2 cans
    (13¾ ounces each) beef broth plus
    2½ cups water
1 stick (4 ounces) unsalted butter
1 medium white onion, chopped
4 fresh sage leaves, coarsely chopped, or
    a pinch of rubbed sage (see Note)
2 cups arborio rice
¾ cup dry red wine
3 tablespoons minced parsley
¾ cup freshly grated Parmesan cheese

1. In a small bowl, soak the mushrooms in 2 cups of lukewarm water for 30 minutes. Remove the mushrooms with a slotted spoon, rinse and set aside. Strain the mushroom liquid through a triple layer of cheesecloth and set aside.

2. In a saucepan, bring the stock to a boil over high heat; then lower the heat to maintain a simmer until ready to use.

3. Meanwhile, in a large nonreactive saucepan, melt 6 tablespoons of the butter over moderate heat. Add the onion and sage and cook, stirring occasionally, until the onion is translucent, about 5 minutes. Add the rice and cook, stirring constantly, until it is lightly toasted, about 5 minutes.

4. Add the wine and cook, stirring constantly, until the wine is absorbed, about 3 minutes. Stir in the reserved mushrooms and their liquid. Cook, stirring constantly, until the liquid is absorbed, 3 to 5 minutes.

5. Add 1 cup of the simmering beef stock and stir constantly until it is absorbed. Continue adding the stock, 1 cup at a time when the rice seems dry, stirring constantly, until tender but still firm to the bite and the mixture is creamy but not soupy, about 20 minutes.

6. Remove the saucepan from the heat and stir in the parsley, Parmesan and the remaining 2 tablespoons butter. Mix well and serve at once.

NOTE: If fresh sage is unavailable, be sure to use dried sage leaves or rubbed sage—available in the spice rack of most supermarkets—not powdered sage.
—*Constance and Rosario Del Nero*

RISOTTO WITH FENNEL

This pale, creamy and ethereal dish is soothing to the spirit as well as to the palate. Cooking fresh fennel in this manner transmutes its powerful licorice character into a mild, delicate fragrance.

4 Servings

6 tablespoons unsalted butter
½ cup chopped sweet onion
1 fennel bulb (1 pound)—trimmed,
    quartered, cored and cut into
    ¼-inch slices
¼ teaspoon salt
Pinch of freshly grated nutmeg
5 cups light chicken stock or 2½ cups
    canned broth diluted with 2½ cups
    water
1½ cups arborio rice
¼ teaspoon freshly ground pepper
¼ cup freshly grated Parmesan cheese

1. In a large heavy saucepan or flameproof casserole, melt 3 tablespoons of the butter over low heat. Add the onion and cook until softened but not browned, about 3 minutes. Stir in the sliced fennel. Season with the salt and nutmeg; mix well. Cover and simmer, stirring occasionally, for 10 minutes.

2. Meanwhile, bring the stock to a simmer in another saucepan.

3. After 10 minutes, add the rice to the fennel, stirring to coat each grain with butter. Add 2 cups of the hot stock. Bring to a simmer and cook, uncovered, stirring constantly, until the rice is just tender, adding more stock ½ cup at a time as the rice absorbs the liquid, about 20 minutes. (If you run out of stock before the rice is done, use hot water.) The finished dish should be moist but not soupy.

4. When the rice is tender but still firm, remove from the heat and stir in the pepper, the remaining 3 tablespoons butter and the grated Parmesan cheese. Season with additional salt to taste and serve immediately in warm bowls.

—Tom Maresca and Diane Darrow

TOMATO-BASIL RISOTTO

4 to 6 Servings

About 5 cups chicken stock or 2½ cups canned broth diluted with 2½ cups water
5 tablespoons unsalted butter
1 medium onion, finely chopped
⅓ cup minced prosciutto (about 3 ounces)
2 tablespoons tomato puree
1½ cups arborio rice
¼ cup freshly grated Parmesan cheese
½ teaspoon freshly ground pepper
Salt

1½ pounds plum tomatoes—peeled, seeded and coarsely chopped
¼ cup shredded basil leaves

1. In a medium saucepan, bring the stock to a simmer; maintain at a simmer over moderately low heat.

2. In a large nonreactive saucepan, melt 3 tablespoons of the butter. Add the onion and prosciutto and sauté over moderate heat until the onion is softened and translucent, about 3 minutes.

3. Stir in the tomato puree and cook for 1 minute.

4. Add the rice and stir for 1 to 2 minutes, until well coated with butter and tomato puree and slightly translucent.

5. Add ½ cup of the simmering stock and cook, stirring constantly, until the rice has absorbed most of the liquid. Adjust the heat if necessary to maintain a simmer. Gradually adding stock, ½ cup at a time, cook, stirring constantly, until the rice is almost tender but still slightly crunchy in the center, 20 to 25 minutes.

6. Add the cheese and season with the pepper and salt to taste. Continue to cook, stirring and adding stock as necessary, ¼ cup at a time, until the rice is tender but still firm and is bound with a creamy sauce, 3 to 6 minutes longer.

7. Stir in the tomatoes, basil and the remaining 2 tablespoons butter; serve hot.

—F&W

RISOTTO WITH SHRIMP AND CELERY

6 Servings

¼ cup olive oil, preferably extra-virgin
4⅓ cups finely chopped celery (9 to 10 ribs)
2 medium carrots, coarsely chopped
2 medium leeks (white and tender green), finely chopped
12 to 16 parsley stems
3 pounds fish heads and bones
8 cups beef stock or 4 cups canned broth diluted with 4 cups water
1 small onion, finely chopped
1 garlic clove, minced
1½ cups arborio rice
¾ pound small shrimp, shelled
⅛ teaspoon freshly ground pepper
Salt
1 tablespoon unsalted butter (optional)

1. In a large saucepan or stockpot, heat 2 tablespoons of the oil. Add 4 cups of the celery, the carrots, leeks and parsley stems. Cover and cook over moderate heat until softened, about 15 minutes.

2. Meanwhile, remove the gills and all traces of blood from the fish heads and bones. Cut into large pieces and rinse thoroughly under cold running water. Add to the vegetables in the saucepan, cover and cook, stirring occasionally, for 15 minutes.

3. Add the broth and simmer over moderately low heat for 45 minutes. Line a sieve with a double thickness of dampened cheesecloth and strain the stock into a large saucepan; discard the solids. If the stock measures less than 6 cups, add water to make up the difference; if there is more than 6 cups, boil to reduce. Adjust the heat so that the stock continues to simmer.

MAKING A PERFECT RISOTTO

There's no mystery to making a perfect risotto, but there are no shortcuts either. This sublime northern Italian rice dish can be adapted for almost any course of a meal with the addition of various seasonings and ingredients compatible with rice.

Risotto often takes the place of pasta in its area of origin, the regions of Lombardy and Piedmont, where—especially in Milan—it is popular after the theater as a late-night supper dish. It is marvelously versatile, serving as an elegant, rich first course, a sophisticated accompaniment to any number of meat or fish entrées, or even as a dessert. Or, with the addition of some cheese, sausage or shellfish, for example, or leftovers like poached fish or sautéed vegetables, it makes a satisfying main course.

The basic technique remains the same for virtually every risotto recipe. The rice (which must be one of the starchy, short-grain varieties, such as arborio; see "Rice for Risotto," p. 210) is first stirred in hot fat over heat for a couple of minutes until well coated and slightly translucent. It is then cooked, while being stirred constantly, as a hot liquid—stock, water, wine, or some combination thereof—is gradually added. This is the tricky part because the total amount of liquid that needs to be added can only be approximated.

The liquid is added about ½ cup at a time and ¼ cup near the end, until the rice is al dente and is loosely bound with a thick, creamy sauce. Each addition of liquid is made when the last has almost evaporated. Too much liquid, and the sauce will be too loose or the rice will become mushy. Too little, and the rice will remain crunchy and may not develop the creamy sauce that is the hallmark of a true risotto.

Other variables include the intensity of heat—the liquid should be maintained at a bare simmer—and the rate of evaporation, which is influenced by the surface area and the material of the pan. Consequently, timing may vary, but a properly cooked risotto will usually take at least 30 minutes.

Don't hesitate to keep tasting near the end of the cooking time, to gauge how much longer liquid should be added. Then, when the risotto is almost done, cheese and other garnishes are added and cooked just long enough to let them warm through. At that moment, act fast. Risotto waits for no one. Pour it into a warm dish and serve immediately, because as it cools, the risotto will tighten and lose its wonderful semifluid consistency.

4. In a large nonreactive saucepan or flameproof casserole, heat the remaining 2 tablespoons oil. Add the onion and the remaining ⅓ cup celery and cook over moderate heat until the onion is softened and translucent, about 2 minutes. Add the garlic and cook for 30 seconds. Add the rice and stir until coated with oil and slightly translucent, 1 to 2 minutes.

5. Add ½ cup of the simmering stock to the rice and cook, adjusting the heat to maintain a simmer and stirring constantly, until the rice has absorbed most of the liquid. Continue to cook, adding ½ cup of stock at a time and stirring, until the rice is almost tender but still slightly crunchy in the center, 20 to 25 minutes.

6. Add the shrimp; season with the pepper and salt to taste. Continue to cook, stirring and adding ¼ cup of stock at a time, until the rice is tender but firm and the shrimp are pink and just barely translucent in the center, 3 to 4 minutes; reserve any extra stock for another use. Stir in the butter, if desired, and serve immediately.
—*Sambuco, Porto Garibaldi, Italy*

TILEFISH AND SCALLOP RISOTTO

4 to 6 Servings

About 5 cups fish stock or 2½ cups bottled clam juice diluted with 2½ cups water
½ pound tilefish, cut into large chunks
¼ pound sea scallops, quartered
3 tablespoons olive oil
⅓ cup minced onion
1½ cups arborio rice
½ cup dry white wine
½ teaspoon freshly ground pepper
Salt
2 tablespoons unsalted butter

1. In a medium saucepan, bring the stock to a simmer; maintain at a simmer over moderately low heat.

2. Add the tilefish and scallops to the stock and cook until opaque almost to the center, but still not quite cooked through, about 1 minute. Remove from the stock with a slotted spoon and set aside, loosely covered to keep warm.

3. In a large nonreactive saucepan or flameproof casserole, heat the oil over moderate heat. Add the onion and cook until it is softened and translucent, about 2 minutes.

4. Add the rice and stir for 1 to 2 minutes, until well coated with oil and slightly translucent. Add the wine and cook, stirring, until it almost evaporates.

5. Add ½ cup of the simmering stock and cook, stirring constantly, until the rice has absorbed most of the liquid. Adjust the heat if necessary to maintain a simmer. Gradually adding stock, ½ cup at a time, cook, stirring constantly, until the rice is almost tender but still slightly crunchy in the center, 20 to 25 minutes.

6. Add the tilefish and scallops, breaking the tilefish up a bit with a spoon. Season with the pepper and salt to taste. Continue to cook, stirring and adding stock as necessary, ¼ cup at a time, until the rice is tender but still firm and is bound with a creamy sauce, 3 to 6 minutes longer.

7. Stir in butter and serve hot.
—F&W

Asparagus and Parmesan Cheese Pan Pizza (page 163).

Above, Easter Bread (page 179). At right, Risotto with Fennel (page 201).

Marinated Cucumbers (page 190) and Chestnut Flour Fritters (page 251).

SHRIMP-GARLIC RISOTTO

🍷 Vernaccia di San Gimignano

4 to 6 Servings

5 *tablespoons unsalted butter*
2 *garlic cloves, finely chopped*
1 *pound medium shrimp—shelled, deveined and sliced lengthwise*
2 *tablespoons minced parsley*
About 5 cups fish stock or 2½ cups bottled clam juice diluted with 2½ cups water
1 *large leek (white and tender green), thinly sliced*
1½ *cups arborio rice*
½ *cup dry white wine*
¼ *teaspoon freshly ground pepper*
Salt

1. In a large skillet, melt 2 tablespoons of the butter. Add the garlic and cook over low heat until softened, about 2 minutes.

2. Increase the heat to moderate, add the shrimp and cook, stirring occasionally, until just opaque, 1 to 2 minutes. Add the parsley and set aside.

3. In a medium saucepan, bring the stock to a simmer; maintain at a simmer over moderately low heat.

4. In a large nonreactive saucepan or flameproof casserole, melt the remaining 3 tablespoons butter over moderate heat. Add the leek and cook until softened, 3 to 4 minutes.

5. Add the rice and stir for 1 to 2 minutes until well coated with butter and slightly translucent. Add the wine and cook until it evaporates.

6. Add ½ cup of the simmering stock and cook, stirring constantly, until the rice has absorbed most of the liquid. Adjust the heat, if necessary, to maintain a simmer. Gradually adding stock, ½ cup at a time cook, stirring constantly, until the rice is almost tender but still slightly crunchy in the center, 20 to 25 minutes.

7. Add the pepper and salt to taste and continue to cook, stirring and adding stock as necessary, ¼ cup at a time, until the rice is tender but still firm and is bound with a creamy sauce, 3 to 6 minutes longer.

8. Stir in the shrimp mixture, along with any accumulated juices, and serve immediately.
—F&W

BACON-APPLE RISOTTO

4 to 6 Servings

About 5 cups chicken stock or water or 2½ cups canned broth diluted with 2½ cups water
8 *slices of bacon, fried until crisp and drained, with the drippings reserved*
2 *medium onions, coarsely chopped*
1 *tart green apple—peeled, cored and cut into ½-inch dice*
1½ *cups arborio rice*
2 *tablespoons Calvados or applejack*
⅓ *cup freshly grated Parmesan cheese*
½ *teaspoon freshly ground pepper*
Salt
2 *tablespoons unsalted butter*
1 *egg (optional)*

1. In a medium saucepan, bring the broth to a simmer; maintain at a simmer over moderately low heat.

2. In a large nonreactive saucepan or flameproof casserole, heat 3 tablespoons of the bacon drippings until sizzling. Add the onions and cook until softened and translucent, about 3 minutes. Add the apple and cook for 2 minutes longer.

3. Add the rice and stir for 1 to 2 minutes until well coated with the drippings and slightly translucent. Add the Calvados and cook until it evaporates.

4. Add ½ cup of the simmering stock and cook, stirring constantly, until the rice has absorbed most of the liquid. Adjust the heat, if necessary, to maintain a simmer. Gradually adding stock, ½ cup at a time, cook, stirring constantly, until the rice is almost tender but still slightly crunchy in the center, 20 to 25 minutes.

5. Add the cheese and season with the pepper and salt to taste. Continue to cook, stirring and adding stock as necessary, ¼ cup at a time, until the rice is tender but still firm and is bound with a creamy sauce, 3 to 6 minutes longer.

6. Crumble the bacon into the rice mixture. Stir in the butter. When the butter has melted, remove the pan from the stove and quickly stir in the egg for added richness and to further bind the sauce; serve immediately.
—F&W

RICE FOR RISOTTO

Italian short-grain rice is essential to a genuine risotto. It has the ability to absorb copious amounts of liquid while retaining a discernible firmness in texture, which allows the rice to be cooked al dente, like pasta. At the same time, it is high in amylopectin, a starch that dissolves into a thick, creamy sauce when the rice is cooked in liquid. We have tried several types and found Superfino Arborio (which is a variety of rice, not a brand name) superior because the individual grains seem best able to maintain their integrity.

Domestic short-grain rice can be used to produce a reasonable, pleasant-tasting dish, but the sauce formed by the amalgamation of the starch with the cooking liquid and the appealing interplay of textures will be missing. Converted rice should not be used for risotto.

SAUSAGE AND EGG RISOTTO

🍷 Valpolicella

4 to 6 Servings

½ pound breakfast sausage, cooked and drained, with the drippings reserved
6 hard-cooked eggs, quartered
¼ cup thinly sliced scallion greens
About 5 cups chicken stock or 2½ cups canned broth diluted with 2½ cups water
1 small onion, minced
1½ cups arborio rice
¼ cup freshly grated Parmesan cheese
½ teaspoon freshly ground pepper
Salt
2 tablespoons unsalted butter

1. Crumble the sausage into a small bowl. Add the eggs and scallion and toss briefly to mix.

2. In a medium saucepan, bring the stock to a simmer; maintain at a simmer over moderately low heat.

3. In a large saucepan or flameproof casserole, heat 3 tablespoons of the sausage drippings over moderate heat until sizzling. Add the onion and cook until softened and translucent, about 2 minutes.

4. Add the rice and stir for 1 to 2 minutes, until well coated with the drippings and slightly translucent.

5. Add ½ cup of the simmering stock and cook, stirring constantly, until the rice has absorbed most of the liquid. Adjust the heat, if necessary, to maintain a simmer. Gradually adding stock, ½ cup at a time, cook, stirring constantly, until the rice is almost tender but still slightly crunchy in the center, 20 to 25 minutes.

6. Add the cheese and the reserved sausage-egg mixture. Season with the pepper and salt to taste. Continue to cook, stirring and adding stock as necessary, ¼ cup at a time, until the rice is tender but still firm and is bound with a creamy sauce, 3 to 6 minutes longer.

7. Stir in butter and serve hot.
—F&W

RISOTTO MOLD WITH PROSCIUTTO

Instead of a ring mold, a cake pan can be used, but in that case leave it in the oven for a few more minutes to cook through to the center. Test by inserting the tip of a knife into the risotto: when the tip is thoroughly hot, it is ready to be served.

12 *Servings*

1 *stick (4 ounces) unsalted butter, at room temperature*
12 *slices prosciutto, preferably from Parma, thinly sliced*
11 *cups homemade chicken stock or canned low-sodium chicken broth*
2 *tablespoons minced onion*
6 *cups arborio rice*
1 *cup freshly grated Parmesan cheese*
Salt and freshly ground pepper

1. Butter two 6-cup ring molds or two 9-inch cake pans with 1 tablespoon or so of the butter. Evenly line the pans with the slices of prosciutto, patching with small-pieces as necessary.

2. In a medium saucepan, heat the stock over moderate heat, covered, until hot. Reduce the heat to low and keep covered.

3. In a large flameproof casserole or small, heavy stockpot, melt 3 tablespoons of the butter over low heat. Add the onion and cook, stirring frequently, until translucent, about 5 minutes. Increase the heat to moderate, add the rice and stir to coat evenly with the butter.

4. Increase the heat to high and stir in 3 cups of the hot stock. Cook, stirring constantly, until most of the liquid has been absorbed, about 3 minutes. Continue adding stock, 1 cup at a time about every minute, stirring constantly. The rice should always be covered with a thin veil of stock. After 12 minutes, the rice should be quite dry and al dente.

5. Remove from the heat and add the Parmesan cheese and the remaining 4 tablespoons butter. Stir until the butter is incorporated and season with salt and pepper to taste.

6. Pour the warm risotto into a large flat dish or roasting pan to cool completely and to prevent the rice from overcooking. Spoon the cooled rice into the prepared molds. (*The recipe can be prepared to this point several hours ahead; cover and refrigerate the molds.*)

7. Preheat the oven to 400°. Bake the risotto on the lowest rack in the oven, uncovered, for 20 minutes. Cover and bake 10 minutes longer, until heated through. Carefully unmold onto platters.
—*Lorenza de' Medici*

BAKED RISOTTO

This recipe is not a true risotto: It uses the typical risotto seasonings but shortcuts the process by adding all the stock at once and substituting long-grain for the arborio rice.

8 Servings

4 *tablespoons unsalted butter*
1 *tablespoon olive oil*
2 *medium onions, coarsely chopped*
2 *generous pinches of saffron threads*
2 *tablespoons white wine or dry vermouth*
3 *cups chicken stock or canned broth*
2 *cups long-grain rice*
1 *package (10 ounces) frozen green peas, thawed*
2 *cups freshly grated Parmesan cheese (about ½ pound)*

1. In a heavy medium saucepan, melt the butter in the oil over moderate heat. Add the onions, cover and cook until softened and translucent, about 10 minutes.

2. Meanwhile, sprinkle the saffron over the white wine in a small bowl and set aside. In a saucepan, heat the broth and 1 cup of water until just barely simmering.

3. Stir the rice into the onions and cook, stirring, until the rice becomes translucent, about 5 minutes. Increase the heat to moderately high and add the broth all at once. Add the saffron and wine and stir well. Reduce the heat to low, cover and cook until the rice has absorbed all the liquid, 20 to 30 minutes. (*The recipe may be prepared to this point a day ahead. Tightly cover the rice and refrigerate. Return to room temperature before continuing.*)

4. Preheat the oven to 425°. Stir the peas and 1½ cups of the Parmesan into the rice. Turn into a large, shallow ovenproof casserole. Sprinkle the remaining ½ cup cheese on top and bake for 20 minutes, or until the cheese is melted and the rice is heated through.

—W. Peter Prestcott

DESSERTS

DESSERTS

RAISINS IN GRAPPA

These raisins last for at least six months, so prepare several jars at a time. The raisins absorb almost all the grappa as they sit until they are barely covered. Dried apricots and prunes can also be conserved in this manner and are delicious served either separately or mixed together. Of course, one should use the best-quality grappa.

12 Servings

¾ cup golden raisins
1 cup good-quality grappa
1 whole clove

1. Place the raisins in a glass jar and pour in the grappa. Add the clove and seal with a lid. Store at room temperature for at least 2 weeks before serving.

2. To serve, discard the clove, put the raisins in individual tumblers and serve with a demitasse spoon.
—Lorenza de' Medici

STRAWBERRIES WITH LEMON AND SUGAR

Dressing strawberries with lemon juice is an old Italian trick. The acidity brightens the fruit's own flavor without adding a lemony taste to the dish.

4 Servings

1 teaspoon grated lemon zest
¼ cup fresh lemon juice
2 tablespoons sugar
1 quart strawberries

In a medium bowl, combine the lemon zest, lemon juice and sugar. Halve or quarter the strawberries, if they are large, and add to the bowl. Toss well. Serve at once or let stand for up to 2 hours.
—Tom Maresca and Diane Darrow

214

GRAPPA

Grappa is brandy—technically, pomace brandy, brandy distilled from the solids left after the fermentation of wine. Every wine-making region and town in Italy is therefore capable of making a distinctive grappa, and right now it appears as if they are all doing so. An Italian embarrassment a decade ago — rustic firewater beloved only by transalpine truckers and backward *contadini*—grappa has now become an internationally popular *digestivo*. Grappas now appear in sleek designer bottles from more and more sophisticated origins—single grape varietals, single vineyards, prized parcels of land.

Grappa was and is a matchless after-dinner drink, now easily available and in wide variety. After a big meal, grappa provides one of the great, soothing palatal pleasures. Unaged grappa—readily identifiable by its crystal clarity—should be served ice cold in a pony glass; the chill tames its fire and releases its aroma. Don't, however, ever serve grappa over ice. Instead, chill the whole bottle for about an hour in the freezer.

A wood-aged grappa—it will show coloration ranging from pale gold to deep amber—should be served at room temperature in a brandy snifter, the better to savor its perfume. In either case, treat grappa just as you would any fine brandy: sip it slowly, roll it all over your tongue, savor, and enjoy.
—Tom Maresca

COFFEE GRANITA

If you are sensitive to caffeine, use decaffeinated espresso coffee.

*Makes About 1½
Quarts*

¾ cup finely ground Italian espresso
    coffee
⅓ cup sugar
1 cup heavy cream

1. In an espresso maker or drip coffeepot, brew the coffee with 4 cups of water according to the manufacturer's directions. Add the sugar and stir until dissolved. Let cool slightly, then cover and refrigerate until cold.

2. Pour the coffee into a 9-by-13-inch metal pan. Freeze until ice crystals begin to form around the edges, about 30 minutes. Stir well and return the pan to the freezer. Continue freezing, stirring every 30 minutes, until the granita is frozen through, about 2 to 2½ hours. (*The recipe can be made to this point up to 1 hour before serving; transfer to a covered container to store.*)

3. To serve, whip the cream in a chilled bowl with chilled beaters until soft peaks form. Scoop the granita into serving bowls and top with the whipped cream.
—*Michele Scicolone*

MOLDED GRANITA DI ESPRESSO

8 Servings

1½ cups finely ground espresso
    coffee
¾ cup plus 2 teaspoons superfine
    sugar
¼ cup coffee liqueur, such as Tía
    Maria or Kahlúa
¾ cup heavy cream
1 tablespoon Cognac or
    other brandy
Strips of lemon zest, for
    garnish

1. Brew the coffee with 4½ cups boiling water.

2. Combine the hot coffee with ¾ cup of the sugar and the coffee liqueur. Stir until the sugar is dissolved. Let cool.

3. Pour into a shallow nonreactive pan and freeze for about 5 hours, stirring every hour to break up any large ice crystals that have formed. Pack into a decorative 6-cup mold and freeze again.

4. Before serving, whip the cream until it forms soft peaks. Add the remaining 2 teaspoons sugar and the Cognac; whip for 30 seconds more. Unmold the granita onto a large platter. Mound or pipe the whipped cream around it and garnish with strips of lemon zest.
—*W. Peter Prestcott*

215

GRANITA

Granita is a cool and refreshing water-based ice frozen into grainy crystals, hence its name. Some historians say that granita was enjoyed by the ancient Romans, who sent runners to the nearby mountains for snow, which they flavored with honey, wine, fruit syrups or herbs.

Coffee is probably the most popular granita flavor. In fact, *granita di caffè* is often served on sultry summer nights when a cup of steaming espresso is not so appealing. Sicilians even like to order *granita di caffè* for breakfast.

Granita, of course, is not limited to coffee. In the summer, every *gelateria* is well stocked with glass tubs of multicolored granitas, which are kept constantly swirling to maintain just the right consistency. The flavors are changed as different fruits come into season.
—Michele Scicolone

MINT GRANITA

This granita is especially refreshing after a fish dinner. Either spearmint or peppermint can be used.

*Makes About 1½
Quarts*

¾ cup sugar
Leaves from 2 bunches of fresh peppermint or spearmint, coarsely chopped (about 2 cups packed)
¼ cup fresh lemon juice

1. In a medium saucepan, bring 4 cups of water and the sugar to a simmer over moderate heat. Cook until the sugar is completely dissolved, about 2 minutes. Stir in the chopped mint and let cool. Refrigerate until chilled.
2. Strain the mint syrup through a fine sieve and discard the mint. Stir in the lemon juice. Pour into a 9-by-13-inch metal pan. Freeze until ice crystals begin to form around the edges, about 30 minutes. Stir well and return to the freezer. Continue freezing, stirring every 30 minutes, until the granita is frozen through, about 2 to 2½ hours. (*The recipe can be made up to 1 hour before serving; transfer to a covered container to store.*)
—Michele Scicolone

LEMON GRANITA

*Makes About 1½
Quarts*

1 cup sugar
Finely grated zest of 1 lemon
¾ cup fresh lemon juice

1. In a medium saucepan, bring 4 cups of water and the sugar to a simmer over moderate heat. Cook, uncovered, until the sugar is completely dissolved, about 3 minutes. Let cool slightly, then refrigerate until cold.
2. In a bowl, combine the sugar syrup, lemon zest and lemon juice. Pour into a 9-by-13-inch metal pan. Freeze until ice crystals begin to form around the edges, about 30 minutes. Stir well and return to the freezer. Continue freezing, stirring every 30 minutes, until frozen through, about 2 to 2½ hours. (*The recipe can be made up to 1 hour before serving; transfer to a covered container to store.*)
—Michele Scicolone

LIME AND GRAPEFRUIT GRANITA

This ice, *granita di limone verde e pompelmo*, is a refreshing end to any meal.
❦ With it or after it, serve a Tuscan grappa from Castellare or Barbi.

4 Servings

1 cup fresh grapefruit juice
⅓ cup fresh lime juice
½ cup sugar

1. In a medium bowl, combine the grapefruit and lime juices with ½ cup of water. Add the sugar and stir until completely dissolved.

Transfer the syrup to a nonreactive metal cake pan and freeze until partially frozen, about 30 minutes.

2. Using a fork, mash the mixture well to break up the ice crystals; refreeze. Repeat the mashing and freezing process every 30 minutes for 2 hours until the ice reaches a uniform texture like grainy snow. (*The ice will keep for up to 5 hours; cover and freeze. If it has solidified again when ready to serve, pulse briefly in a food processor or blender to loosen the texture; do not liquefy.*)

—Diane Darrow and Tom Maresca

STRAWBERRY GRANITA

Raspberries (*lamponi*) or blackberries (*more*) can be substituted for the strawberries. Adjust the amount of sugar to the sweetness of the fruit.

Makes About 1½ Quarts

1 cup sugar
1 pint strawberries
½ cup fresh orange juice
¼ cup fresh lemon juice

1. In a small saucepan, combine 3 cups of water with the sugar. Bring to a simmer over moderate heat. Cook until the sugar is completely dissolved, about 5 minutes. Let cool slightly, then cover and refrigerate until cold.

2. In a food processor, puree the strawberries until smooth. Add the chilled sugar syrup, the orange juice and the lemon juice. Puree until thoroughly blended.

3. Pour the mixture into a 9-by-13-inch metal pan. Freeze until ice crystals form around the edges, about 30 minutes. Stir well and return to the freezer. Continue freezing, stirring every 30 minutes, until the granita is frozen through, about 2 to 2½ hours. (*The recipe can be made up to 1 hour before serving; transfer to a covered container to store.*)

—Michele Scicolone

CANTALOUPE SORBET WITH PEPPER AND PORT

In Italy this type of dish is called an intermezzo, a palate-refresher served between courses, but it works just as well as a light dessert.

Makes About 3½ Cups

2 small cantaloupes
¼ cup sugar
1 tablespoon fresh lemon juice
½ teaspoon freshly ground pepper
Pinch of salt
Ruby port, chilled

1. Working on a large platter to catch the juices, split and seed the cantaloupes, cut into chunks and remove the rind. Strain the reserved juices to remove the seeds.

2. Combine the cantaloupe juice with enough water to equal ¼ cup. Pour into a small heavy saucepan and add the sugar. Bring slowly to a boil, stirring to dissolve the sugar. Boil for 1 minute, remove from the heat and let cool.

3. Place the sugar syrup, melon, lemon juice, pepper and salt in a

food processor. Puree until smooth. Strain through a sieve; to avoid any graininess, do not press on the solids.

4. Pour the puree into an ice cream maker and freeze according to the manufacturer's instructions. To serve, scoop into individual glasses and pour about 1 tablespoon of port on top of the sorbet.
—*Enoteca Pinchiorri, Florence, Italy*

STRAWBERRY SHERBET WITH CHERRY CARAMEL SAUCE

It is important to caramelize the sugar in a casserole with sides high enough so that when you add the rest of the ingredients, the foam that is created will not spill over. The caramel syrup is ready when the sugar is completely dissolved and turns a dark golden color.

12 Servings

1 *pound ripe black cherries, pitted, or 1 can (17 ounces) pitted black cherries in syrup*
2 *cups sugar*
3 *pounds strawberries, hulled*
2 *tablespoons fresh lemon juice*
½ *cup orange liqueur, such as Grand Marnier*

1. In a medium nonreactive casserole, combine the fresh cherries with 2 tablespoons of water and cook over low heat, covered, until softened, about 20 minutes. Puree the cherries in a food processor. (If using canned cherries, puree them in the processor with their syrup without cooking them first.) Set the puree aside.

2. In a medium saucepan, combine 1 cup of the sugar with ⅔ cup water. Bring to a boil over high heat, swirling the pan, until the sugar is dissolved, 2 to 3 minutes. Set the sugar syrup aside to cool slightly.

3. Reserve a few of the smallest strawberries for garnish. Put the remaining strawberries in a food processor and pour in the cooled sugar syrup. Add the lemon juice and puree until smooth. Transfer the puree to an ice cream maker and freeze according to the manufacturer's instructions. When the sherbet is ready, transfer it to a serving bowl and keep, covered, in the freezer until serving.

4. Meanwhile, pour the remaining 1 cup sugar into a heavy medium saucepan. Bring to a boil over moderate heat, swirling the pan to dissolve the sugar. Boil the syrup, without stirring, until the sugar becomes dark gold in color and reaches 240° on a candy thermometer, 15 to 16 minutes.

5. Standing back as the mixture may splatter, add the orange liqueur a little at a time, stirring constantly with a long-handled spoon until any lumps of caramel dissolve, about 1 minute. Stir in the reserved cherry puree and remove from the heat. Let cool to room temperature.

6. Pour the cherry caramel sauce over the sherbet and decorate with the reserved strawberries. Serve immediately.
—*Lorenza de' Medici*

ALLEGRO'S RICOTTA GELATO

🍷 *Picolit from Volpe Pasini*

Makes About 2 Quarts

1 *cup golden raisins*
¾ *cup grappa or other brandy*
2½ *cups light cream or half-and-half*
1 *vanilla bean, spilt lengthwise, or 1½ teaspoons vanilla extract*
1 *tablespoon grated lemon zest*
9 *egg yolks*
1½ *cups sugar*
2 *cups whole-milk ricotta*
1 *cup heavy cream*
1 *tablespoon chopped candied orange peel*
1 *tablespoon chopped candied lemon peel*

1. In a nonreactive saucepan, combine the raisins and grappa. Bring to a simmer over moderate heat. Remove from the heat, cover and set aside for 1 to 2 hours; then drain.

2. In a large heavy saucepan, combine the light cream, vanilla bean and lemon zest. Bring to a simmer over moderately high heat; immediately remove from the heat, cover and set aside.

3. In a large mixing bowl, beat the egg yolks until light and fluffy. Gradually beat in the sugar. Continue beating until the mixture is thick enough to hold a ribbon when the beaters are lifted.

4. Remove the vanilla bean and gradually whisk the hot cream into the egg yolk mixture.

5. Pour the custard into a large heavy saucepan. Cook over low heat, stirring constantly, until the mixture thickens enough to coat the back of a spoon, about 15 minutes. (The temperature should measure about 165°; do not allow the mixture to boil.) Remove from the heat.

6. Strain the custard through a fine sieve into a metal bowl set in a larger bowl of ice. Stir constantly until the mixture cools to room temperature.

7. In a large mixing bowl, beat together the ricotta and the heavy cream until blended and smooth. Fold into the cooled custard. Pour the mixture into the canister of an ice cream maker and freeze according to the manufacturer's instructions until almost frozen. Add the chopped orange and lemon peel and the drained raisins, and complete the processing. Pack the ice cream in a lidded container and freeze for at least several hours. Let soften slightly before serving.
—*Allegro, Waltham, Massachusetts*

ZABAGLIONE

Light and airy, made in only minutes, zabaglione is a perfect spur-of-the-moment dessert. The velvety, frothy custard is prepared from only three ingredients—eggs, sugar and Marsala—beaten for 10 to 15 minutes over heat until thick and quadrupled in volume. Traditionally served in large glass coupes, the gossamer texture of the whipped custard and the heady perfume of the hot wine make it a favorite Italian dessert. (When Sauternes is substituted for the Marsala, zabaglione is transformed into the French sabayon.)

While this dessert is most often enjoyed hot by itself, it can also be cooled quickly and spooned as a sauce over fruit. It is not stable enough to keep, however, and should be served immediately.

To make zabaglione, a 12- or 14-inch whisk is recommended, as is a specialized piece of equipment called a zabaglione pan. Made of copper, a zabaglione pan distributes heat evenly, and its rounded bottom makes whisking easy and efficient.

FROZEN COFFEE CREAM

Semifreddo al caffè, as this smooth, rich dessert is called, is a snap to prepare, and the distinctive flavor combination of coffee and chocolate makes it especially suitable for entertaining.

8 Servings

4 egg yolks
½ cup sugar
2 cups heavy cream, chilled
2 tablespoons instant espresso powder
Whipped cream and grated sweet chocolate, for garnish

1. In a medium mixer bowl, beat the egg yolks on high speed until smooth. Slowly add the sugar and beat until thick and lemon-colored, 2 to 3 minutes.

2. In a large mixer bowl, beat the cream until soft peaks form.

3. Sprinkle the coffee over the cream and fold in gently just until mixed.

4. Stir one-fourth of the cream mixture into the egg mixture to lighten it. Fold in the remaining cream until incorporated. Spoon the coffee cream into individual ½-cup ramekins. Cover lightly with plastic wrap and place in the freezer until firm but not hard, 1 to 1½ hours.

5. Serve garnished with whipped cream and grated chocolate.
—*Bette Duke*

ORANGES WITH SWEET BASIL ZABAGLIONE

If you'd rather not fuss with zabaglione, it can be omitted and the oranges served simply as a salad with red onions and a splash of vinegar.

4 Servings

8 large navel oranges
5 basil sprigs
½ cup (packed) fresh basil leaves
2 egg yolks
2 tablespoons sugar
¼ cup dry white wine

1. Remove a strip of zest from 1 of the oranges. Chop enough zest to measure ¼ teaspoon; reserve. Using a knife, peel all the oranges; cut in between the membranes to remove the sections.

2. Using your hands, lightly crush the basil sprigs and toss in a large bowl with the orange sections. Cover with plastic wrap and refrigerate for at least 2 hours, but no longer than 6.

3. Mince the ½ cup basil. In a medium bowl, combine the egg yolks, sugar, wine and reserved orange zest. Place over a saucepan of simmering water and whisk until the zabaglione is frothy, thick and doubled in volume, about 5 minutes. Stir in the minced basil.

4. Drain the orange sections and remove and discard the basil. Divide the fruit among 4 bowls and spoon a heaping tablespoon of zabaglione over each.
—*Marcia Kiesel*

ZABAGLIONE

Zabaglione can be served hot or cold. To chill, at the end of Step 1, place the zabaglione pan in a bowl of ice and water and stir until the mixture is cold. Spoon immediately into chilled glasses or over fruit and serve at once.

6 to 8 Servings

6 egg yolks
½ cup sugar
⅔ cup dry Marsala
1½ to 2 teaspoons finely grated lemon zest (optional)

1. In an 8½-inch copper zabaglione pan or a 3- to 3½-quart metal bowl, combine the egg yolks, sugar and Marsala. Place over a pan of simmering water and whisk until light and frothy. Continue beating over the water until quadrupled in volume, very thick and hot to the touch, about 10 minutes.

2. Immediately spoon into warmed glasses. Top with a pinch of finely grated lemon zest if desired and serve at once.
—Diana Sturgis

TIRAMISU

In Italy, this dessert—which literally means "pick me up," probably because it is so tempting—is always made with fresh mascarpone cheese, a light, nonsalty cream cheese. We have devised a simple substitute—a mixture of ricotta and cream cheese—that approximates the richness of the original.

6 to 8 Servings

1 pound fresh mascarpone or 8 ounces each of whole-milk ricotta and fresh cream cheese
¼ cup granulated sugar
2 tablespoons rum
24 biscotti all' uovo* or champagne biscuits
1 cup freshly brewed espresso, cooled
4 egg yolks
¼ cup superfine sugar
¼ cup plus 2 tablespoons Marsala
2 tablespoons unsweetened cocoa powder
Strawberries, for garnish
*Available at Italian and specialty food stores

1. In a food processor, blend the mascarpone (or the ricotta and cream cheese), the granulated sugar and the rum until smooth.

2. On a serving plate, arrange 6 biscuits, flat-side up, side by side. Moisten lightly with ⅓ cup of the espresso. Spread one-third of the cheese mixture over the biscuits. Repeat 2 more times, finishing with the cheese.

3. Halve the 6 remaining biscuits crosswise and make a fence around the layered cheese.

4. Whisk the yolks and the superfine sugar together in the top of a double boiler until pale yellow and fluffy.

5. Place over hot but not boiling water. Beat, adding the Marsala 1 tablespoon at a time, until the mixture is hot and thickened to the consistency of a light, fluffy batter. Immediately remove the zabaglione from the heat and beat for 3 minutes longer.

6. Pour the zabaglione over the top layer of the dessert. Sprinkle the cocoa over the top. Decorate with strawberries.

—Margaret and G. Franco Romagnoli

TIRAMISU WITH RUM AND CHOCOLATE

Tart whipped cream replaces the traditional but hard-to-find tangy mascarpone cheese. This recipe can be prepared the night before.

8 to 10 Servings

4 eggs
1 cup granulated sugar
½ cup all-purpose flour
2 tablespoons cornstarch
¼ cup freeze-dried coffee granules
¼ cup white or amber rum
4½ ounces bittersweet chocolate, chopped
1½ cups heavy cream, chilled
⅓ cup confectioners' sugar
3½ tablespoons fresh lemon juice

1. Preheat the oven to 350°. Butter a 13-by-9-by-2-inch pan and line the bottom and sides with parchment paper. Butter and flour the paper.

2. In a large bowl set over simmering water, beat the eggs at high speed with ½ cup of the granulated sugar until warm, about 5 minutes. Remove from the heat and beat until the mixture has tripled in volume, about 3 minutes.

3. Sift the flour with the cornstarch. Resift half the flour over the eggs and fold in. Repeat with the remaining flour, folding, only until no streaks remain.

4. Spread the batter evenly in the prepared pan and bake for 15 to 20 minutes, until the top is golden and the edges have pulled away from the pan. Unmold the cake onto a towel-covered rack and peel off the paper. Let cool.

5. Meanwhile, in a small saucepan, bring the remaining granulated sugar and 1 cup plus 2 tablespoons of water to a boil over high heat, stirring to dissolve the sugar. Remove from the heat and stir in the coffee. Let cool; add the rum.

6. Invert the cake onto a tray and pierce with a fork at 1-inch intervals. Drizzle the coffee syrup evenly over the surface.

7. In a double boiler, melt the chocolate with 3 tablespoons of water, stirring until smooth. Spread half the chocolate over the cake and refrigerate until it is set, about 20 minutes.

8. In a medium bowl, beat the cream, confectioners' sugar and lemon juice at high speed until stiff.

9. Cut the cake into 24 squares. Line a 2-quart glass bowl with cake squares, chocolate-side in. Spoon one-third of the whipped cream into the center and fill the bowl with the remaining cake. Cover with the rest of the whipped cream and smooth the top.

10. Reheat the remaining chocolate over low heat and stir in 1 or 2 teaspoons of hot water, if necessary, for a pouring consistency; drizzle over the top and refrigerate for at least 2 hours.

—Diana Sturgis

MASCARPONE CREAM DESSERT

This dessert improves when made one or two days ahead and all the flavors have time to blend in the refrigerator. You can vary the recipe by adding a little melted chocolate instead of coffee and by decorating it with grated chocolate or, in summer, raspberries. Because the filling is very soft and creamy, this may require a spoon for serving.

🍸 A small glass of Tuscany's dessert wine speciality, Vin Santo, such as Badia a Coltibuono or Brolio would add an authentic flourish to the dessert course.

12 *Servings*

6 *large egg yolks*
1 *cup sugar*
1¼ *cups dry Marsala*
2 *tablespoons instant coffee, dissolved in 1 teaspoon of hot water*
3 *cups mascarpone cheese (1½ pounds)*
12 *ounces ladyfingers (see Note, next page)*

¼ *cup (about 2 ounces) chocolate-covered coffee beans, for garnish*

1. In a large saucepan, bring 3 inches of water to a boil over moderate heat.

2. In a medium stainless steel bowl, whisk the egg yolks with the sugar until light in color, about 2 minutes. Whisk in 1 cup of the Marsala. Set the bowl over, but not touching, the boiling water. Whisking constantly, cook until the egg mixture becomes creamy and foamy and doubles in volume, about 4 minutes. (The mixture should reach a temperature of 160°.)

3. Remove the bowl from the heat. Stir in the dissolved coffee and the mascarpone cheese; mix gently but thoroughly until blended. Set aside.

4. Line the bottom of a 10-inch springform pan with a circle of parchment or waxed paper. Lightly brush both sides of the ladyfingers with the remaining ¼ cup Marsala. Arrange the ladyfingers, smooth-side up, in a daisy petal pattern on the bottom of the springform pan, being careful not to leave any empty spaces.

5. Cut the remaining ladyfingers in half crosswise and stand them, cut-sides down and smooth-sides in, all around the insides of the springform to completely line it. Pour in the cooled mascarpone cream. Cover with plastic wrap and chill until set, at least 8 hours but preferably for one to two days.

MASCARPONE

Mascarpone is a very soft, fresh cow's milk cheese. Similar to French crème fraîche and English Devonshire clotted cream, it is rich, creamy and buttery in flavor—not surprisingly, since it is 60 percent butterfat. In fact, some people think of it as more a cream than a cheese. Originally produced in the wintertime in Lombardy and Tuscany only, it is now made all over Italy, where it is often sold in small muslin bags. In the United States you are more likely to see it in plastic tubs. Mascarpone is frequently flavored with liqueur and used to make pastry fillings or served for dessert with sugar and fruit.

6. To serve, trim the tops of the ladyfingers so that they are flush with the mascarpone cream mixture. Invert onto a serving platter; remove the sides and bottom of the springform pan and the parchment paper. Decorate with the coffee beans and serve.

NOTE: Ladyfingers vary in size, so be sure to buy enough to completely line the bottom and sides of the pan.

—*Lorenza de'Medici*

MOLDED RICOTTA AND MASCARPONE WITH STRAWBERRIES

This dessert is particularly pretty when molded in a heart-shaped form, such as a *coeur à la crème* mold.

6 Servings

1 *envelope unflavored gelatin*
⅓ *cup plus 3 tablespoons orange liqueur*
½ *pound ricotta, preferably fresh*
½ *pound mascarpone*
½ *cup confectioners' sugar, sifted*
1 *teaspoon vanilla extract*
1 *tablespoon plus 1 teaspoon fresh lemon juice*
Pinch of salt
½ *cup heavy cream*
1 *pint strawberries, sliced*
¼ *cup raspberry jam*
Whole strawberries and fresh mint leaves, for garnish

1. In a small saucepan, combine the gelatin with ⅓ cup of the orange liqueur and let stand until softened, about 5 minutes. Set the saucepan over low heat and stir until the gelatin dissolves, 2 to 3 minutes. Set aside to cool slightly.

2. In a large bowl, beat the ricotta and mascarpone with an electric mixer. Beat in the confectioners' sugar, vanilla, 1 teaspoon of the lemon juice and the salt; then beat in the cooled gelatin mixture.

3. In another bowl, beat the cream until stiff peaks form. Fold the whipped cream into the cheese mixture and pour into a 4-cup mold or bowl lined with plastic wrap. Smooth the top and refrigerate until chilled and set, about 3 hours.

4. In a blender or food processor, combine ½ cup of the sliced strawberries with the raspberry jam. Puree until smooth. Strain the sauce to remove the seeds and stir in the remaining 1 tablespoon lemon juice and 3 tablespoons orange liqueur. Add the remaining sliced berries.

5. Unmold the cheese dessert onto a serving plate and surround it with the strawberry sauce. Decorate with whole strawberries and mint leaves.

—*Nancy Verde Barr*

Strawberry Sherbet with Cherry Caramel Sauce (page 218) and Mascarpone Cream Dessert (page 223).

Top left, Walnut Torte
from Aosta (*page 235*). Top right,
Piedmontese Molded Coffee Custard
(*page 229*). Near right, Florentine
Chocolate-Hazelnut Dome (*page 232*).
Far right, Crumb Cake from Treviso
(*page 237*).

Molded Ricotta and Mascarpone with Strawberries (page 224).

SICILIAN RICOTTA CHEESECAKE

Typically Sicilian, this ricotta cake is similar in style to an American cheesecake, but much lighter. Italian ricotta is much firmer and less watery than the typical American ricotta. If you live near a store that sells freshly made ricotta in perforated containers, use it for the creamiest results. Do take care to gently stir the ingredients together: Beating the batter will incorporate air, which will cause the cake to rise too much during baking and sink dismally as it cools.

10 to 12 Servings

2 pounds fresh whole-milk ricotta, or two 15-ounce containers
⅔ cup sugar
⅓ cup all-purpose flour
6 eggs
¼ teaspoon cinnamon
2 teaspoons finely grated orange zest
2 teaspoons vanilla extract
Pinch of salt

1. Preheat the oven to 300°. Butter and flour a 9-inch springform pan; tap out the excess flour.

2. In a large bowl, stir the ricotta with a rubber spatula until it is as smooth as possible. In another bowl, mix the sugar and flour; stir into the ricotta until blended. Add the eggs, one at a time, mixing gently but thoroughly after each addition. Gently stir in the cinnamon, orange zest, vanilla and salt.

3. Pour the mixture into the prepared pan. Tap the pan once on a work surface to release any air bubbles. Bake the cake in the middle of the oven for about 1 hour and 10 minutes, or until lightly golden and almost firm in the center. A cake tester inserted 1 inch from the center should emerge clean.

4. Transfer the cake to a rack in a draft-free place; it will sink slightly as it cools. When completely cool, cover with plastic wrap and refrigerate until serving time. Remove the sides of the pan. Leave the cake on the pan base and transfer to a platter for serving.
—*Nick Malgieri*

PIEDMONTESE MOLDED COFFEE CUSTARD

One of the most typical and traditional Piedmontese desserts, this *bonet al caffè* is from Tonino and Claudia Verro's charming restaurant and inn, Contea, at Neive, near Alba, in the beautiful Langhe hills. This delicate and creamy custard is a fine ending to a light meal. During baking, a crust forms on the top, so there is a firm layer on the bottom when the dessert is un-molded. This is best made a day ahead and refrigerated overnight.

8 Servings

½ cup plus ⅓ cup sugar
1 teaspoon fresh lemon juice
½ cup finely ground espresso coffee
1½ cups milk
1 cup heavy cream
7 large eggs
2 tablespoons white rum

1. In a small saucepan, combine the ½ cup sugar with the lemon juice. Stir well with a metal spoon. Cook over low heat undisturbed, until the sugar begins to smoke lightly, about 2 minutes. Then cook, stirring occasionally, until the sugar melts and caramelizes evenly, about 5 minutes. When the caramel is deep amber, carefully add 2 tablespoons of hot water and let the caramel return to a boil. Immediately pour the caramel into a 1½-quart glass loaf pan and tip the pan in all directions to coat it evenly. Pour out any excess caramel and let the lined mold cool.

2. Preheat the oven to 300°. In a small saucepan, bring ¾ cup of water to a boil over high heat. Remove from the heat and stir in the espresso. Cover and let steep for 5 minutes. Pour the coffee through a fine strainer into a measuring cup, then line the strainer with a sheet of paper towel or a coffee filter and strain again. Measure out ½ cup of the coffee.

3. In a medium saucepan, combine the milk, cream and the remaining ⅓ cup sugar. Bring to a boil over moderate heat, stirring occasionally.

4. In a large bowl, whisk the eggs to break them up, then whisk in the rum and the reserved ½ cup coffee. Gradually whisk in the boiled cream mixture and pour into the caramelized mold.

5. Set the mold in a baking pan and add enough warm water to reach 1 inch up the sides of the mold. Bake for about 1 hour, until well browned on top and a thin knife or cake tester inserted in the center comes out clean; the custard will firm up as it cools. (The water bath should never come to a simmer, so check occasionally during baking and add cold water if necessary.)

6. Let cool to room temperature for 30 minutes, then cover with plastic wrap and refrigerate for at least 8 hours or overnight.

7. To unmold, insert the tip of a paring knife between the custard and the loaf pan and, scraping against the mold, loosen it at the top. Invert a platter onto the pan, then invert the custard onto the platter. The pan should lift off easily; if not, gently shake it from side to side to loosen the custard. If not serving immediately, loosely cover the custard with plastic wrap and refrigerate. To serve, cut into 1-inch slices with a sharp knife.
—*Nick Malgieri*

CANNOLI SICILIANI

The dough for these chocolatey cannoli is quite soft and should be kept as cool as possible during shaping and rolling.

Makes About 20
Cannoli

2 cups all-purpose flour
½ cup plus 3 tablespoons unsweetened cocoa powder
1½ cups granulated sugar
4 tablespoons unsalted butter, at room temperature
1 cup Marsala
4 cups vegetable oil, for frying
1 egg beaten with 1 teaspoon water
1 cup heavy cream
⅔ cup plus 1 tablespoon ricotta
⅔ cup raisins, chopped

3½ ounces unsalted shelled pistachios, toasted and finely chopped
3½ ounces semisweet chocolate, finely chopped
Confectioners' sugar, for dusting

1. In a large bowl, combine the flour, cocoa powder and 6 tablespoons plus 2 teaspoons of the granulated sugar. Add the butter and Marsala and stir with a wooden spoon until a soft dough forms. Cover and refrigerate for 15 minutes. (The recipe can be prepared to this point up to 1 day ahead.)

2. On a well-floured surface, sprinkle one-third of the dough with flour and roll out ¼ inch thick. Stamp out 3½-inch circles and set the scraps aside. Roll the circles into oval shapes; transfer to a cookie sheet and refrigerate until ready to mold. Repeat with the remaining dough; then repeat with all the scraps.

3. In a medium saucepan, heat the oil to 350°. Wrap the ovals around cannoli forms, sealing the edges with the beaten egg wash. Fry the cannoli shells in batches for 2 minutes. Transfer to a rack to cool slightly, then remove the cannoli forms. Wrap and fry the remaining cannoli shells in the same fashion.

4. In a medium bowl, beat the cream until stiff. In another bowl, blend the ricotta with the remaining granulated sugar. Stir in the raisins, pistachios and chocolate, then fold in the whipped cream. Cover and refrigerate until ready to use.

5. Using a piping bag or a small spoon, fill the cannoli shells with the ricotta cream mixture. Just before serving, dust with confectioners' sugar.
—Cindy Pawlcyn, Tra Vigne, St. Helena, California

TORTA CAPRESE

This rich cake derives its intense flavor from walnuts and chocolate.

8 to 10 Servings

1⅓ cups walnut pieces (about 5 ounces)
6 ounces semisweet chocolate, finely chopped
1½ sticks (6 ounces) unsalted butter, at room temperature
⅔ cup granulated sugar
8 eggs, separated
⅓ cup all-purpose flour
Confectioners' sugar, for dusting

1. Preheat the oven to 350°. Butter a 10-by-2-inch round cake pan and line the bottom with parchment or waxed paper.

2. Place the walnuts in a food processor and pulse at 1-second intervals until finely ground; be careful that they do not turn into a paste.

3. Place the chocolate in a small bowl set over very hot but not simmering water and stir occasionally until melted. Set aside to cool slightly.

4. In a large bowl, beat the butter with ⅓ cup of the granulated sugar until creamy and light. Beat in the cooled melted chocolate until blended. Then beat in the egg yolks, one at a time, scraping the bowl and beaters frequently between additions. Continue beating until the mixture is smooth and light. Stir in the walnuts and then the flour.

5. In another large bowl, beat the egg whites until they hold very soft peaks, then beat in the remaining ⅓ cup granulated sugar in a slow stream. Continue beating until the whites hold soft, glossy peaks. Stir one-fourth of the whites into the chocolate batter, then fold in the

CANNOLI FORMS

Cannoli are delicious Sicilian pastries: Tubes of sweet pastry dough are deep-fried until crisp, then stuffed with a mixture of sweetened ricotta flecked with chopped chocolate, nuts or dried fruits, or all three. To make cannoli you will need cannoli forms, which are 5-inch-long hollow tubes, usually made of tinned steel, around which the cannoli dough is wrapped before frying. Cannoli forms most often come in sets of four and are relatively inexpensive.

remainder with a large rubber spatula until no streaks of white remain.

6. Scrape the batter into the prepared pan and smooth the surface. Bake for about 40 minutes, until the center of the cake feels firm when pressed. Let cool in the pan for 10 minutes; the cake may shrink slightly. Scrape off the loose crust with a sharp knife. Invert the cake onto a rack and let cool completely. Peel off the parchment paper. Dust the cake with confectioners' sugar, transfer to a platter and serve at room temperature.

—Nick Malgieri

LA PIGNA'S CHOCOLATE-ALMOND TORTE

This rich, dense cake develops a fuller flavor if made a day ahead. It is marvelous topped with a scoop of rich vanilla ice cream.

8 Servings

2 cans (4½ ounces each, about 2 cups) whole blanched almonds
6½ ounces unsweetened chocolate
7 egg yolks
1 cup sugar
1 stick (4 ounces) plus 5 tablespoons unsalted butter, at room temperature
¼ cup confectioners' sugar, for dusting

1. Preheat the oven to 350°. Butter the bottom of an 8-inch springform pan and line with parchment or waxed paper. Lightly butter and flour the paper and the sides of the pan.

2. In a food processor or blender, grind the almonds and chocolate to a medium-fine consistency.

3. In a medium mixer bowl, beat the egg yolks and sugar until light and fluffy. Add the butter and beat until smooth.

4. Add the almond-chocolate mixture and beat until well blended, 2 to 3 minutes. The batter will be very dense; scrape it into the prepared pan.

5. Bake the cake in the lower third of the oven for 45 minutes, or until a skewer inserted in the center emerges clean.

6. Let the cake cool in the pan for 5 minutes. Remove from the pan and place on a serving plate. Let cool completely. Just before serving, sift confectioners' sugar over the top.

—La Pigna, Capri, Italy

FLORENTINE CHOCOLATE-HAZELNUT DOME

There are many theories about the origin of the *zuccotto*. Some say that the name derives from *zucco*, Italian for pumpkin, since the dessert is a half sphere. Others explain that it is meant to resemble the dome of the cathedral in Florence. This version is based on one made at the elegant Pasticceria Robiglio in Florence.

12 Servings

Sponge Cake:
4 eggs, separated
¾ cup granulated sugar
Pinch of salt
½ cup all-purpose flour
½ cup cornstarch

Filling and Garnish:
½ cup hazelnuts (about 2½ ounces)
10 ounces semisweet chocolate, finely chopped
2 cups heavy cream
¼ cup granulated sugar

3 tablespoons white or amber rum,
  plus more for brushing
2 teaspoons confectioners' sugar
1 teaspoon unsweetened cocoa powder

1. *Make the sponge cake:* Preheat the oven to 350°. Butter a 10-by-2-inch round cake pan and line the bottom with parchment paper.

2. In a large bowl, using an electric mixer, lightly beat the egg yolks. Beat in 6 tablespoons of the granulated sugar in a stream. Beat the mixture at high speed until it has tripled in volume and forms a thick ribbon when the beaters are lifted.

3. In a medium bowl, beat the egg whites with the salt until very soft peaks form. Beat in the remaining 6 tablespoons sugar in a stream and beat on high speed until firm peaks form. Using a spatula, fold the beaten whites into the egg yolk mixture. Stir the flour and cornstarch together and sift over the batter in 3 or 4 additions, folding gently with a rubber spatula until blended.

4. Pour the batter into the prepared pan and bake for about 30 minutes, until the sponge cake has risen well and is firm in the center. Leave the oven on. Loosen the cake and invert it on a rack. Turn the cake right-side up and let cool completely. (*The sponge cake can be made up to 5 days ahead and refrigerated, tightly wrapped in plastic.*)

5. *Make the filling:* Spread the hazelnuts on a baking sheet and toast in the oven for 15 to 20 minutes, or until the skins blister. Transfer the hazelnuts to a kitchen towel and let cool slightly, then rub them together to loosen the skins. Coarsely chop the nuts and place in a bowl. When the nuts have cooled completely, stir in 2 ounces of the chopped chocolate.

6. In a heavy medium saucepan, bring 1¼ cups of the cream to a boil over moderately high heat. Remove from the heat and add the remaining 8 ounces chopped chocolate. Let stand for 5 minutes, then whisk until smooth. Pour the mixture into a medium bowl and let cool to room temperature, then refrigerate until cold and set.

7. In a bowl, combine the remaining ¾ cup cream with the granulated sugar and beat until stiff. Cover and refrigerate.

8. Butter a 1½-quart glass bowl and line with plastic wrap, pressing the wrap smoothly against the inside of the bowl. Cut a ¼-inch horizontal slice from the top of the sponge cake and set aside, covered. Cut ten ¼-inch-wide vertical slices from the sponge cake. Use these slices to line the prepared bowl, fitting them tightly against each other, without overlapping, to completely line the bowl. Reserve the remaining sponge cake for another use.

9. Sprinkle the sponge cake in the mold with 2 tablespoons of the rum. Beat the chilled chocolate filling on medium speed until light. Spread the filling over the sponge cake in the bowl in an even ½-inch layer.

10. Remove the whipped cream from the refrigerator and re-whip until firm, then beat in the remaining 1 tablespoon rum. Fold in the chopped hazelnuts and chocolate and spoon the filling into the mold. Smooth the surface. Trim the sponge cake slices flush with the filling. Cover with the reserved cake layer and trim it to fit neatly inside the bowl. Cover with plastic wrap and freeze the *zuccotto* for 4 to 5 hours to set the fillings, then refrigerate until serving time.

11. To unmold, invert the bowl onto a platter and lift off the bowl. (It should lift off easily. If not, wipe the outside of the bowl with a cloth wrung out in very hot water, so that

233

DESSERTS

the butter between the bowl and the plastic wrap melts.) Peel off the plastic wrap. If the outside of the zuccotto is very dry, brush with a little more rum. Dust first with the confectioners' sugar and then with the cocoa. To serve, cut into wedges with a sharp knife.
—Nick Malgieri

CHOCOLATE-GLAZED ALMOND CAKE FROM PESCARA

The half-sphere shape of this *parrozzo* recalls *pane rozzo*, "rough bread," for which it is named. This refined version of the cake is from the Pasticceria Berardo at the end of the corso in Pescara, near the shore of the Adriatic.

8 Servings

1 *cup whole blanched almonds (about 5 ounces)*
¾ *cup sugar*
5 *eggs at room temperature, separated*
½ *cup all-purpose flour*
6 *tablespoons unsalted butter, melted and cooled*
¼ *teaspoon almond extract*
Pinch of salt
4 *ounces bittersweet chocolate, finely chopped*
1 *teaspoon vegetable oil*

1. Preheat the oven to 350°. Butter and flour a 1½-quart ovenproof glass bowl; tap out the excess flour.
2. In a food processor, combine the almonds with 2 tablespoons of the sugar and pulse just until the nuts are very finely ground.
3. In a large bowl, beat the egg yolks with ¼ cup of the sugar until tripled in volume and the mixture holds a ribbon when the beaters are

lifted, about 5 minutes. On very low speed, gradually beat in the flour, melted butter and almond extract. Fold in the ground almonds.
4. In a medium bowl, beat the egg whites with the salt on high speed until very soft peaks form. Gradually beat in the remaining 6 tablespoons sugar until soft peaks form. Fold one-fourth of the beaten whites into the batter until incorporated, then fold in the remaining whites.
5. Pour the batter into the prepared bowl and bake in the middle of the oven for 50 to 55 minutes, until the cake has risen and is firm to the touch. Let cool on a rack for 15 minutes, then invert the bowl on the rack to release the cake. Let cool completely.
6. Place the chocolate in a small bowl set over a pan of hot, but not simmering, water and stir until melted, then stir in the oil. Set aside to cool slightly.
7. Brush any crumbs off the cake and spread the chocolate evenly over the dome. Refrigerate briefly to set the chocolate. Serve at room temperature, cut into wedges.
—Nick Malgieri

234

WALNUT TORTE FROM AOSTA

This wonderful walnut pastry is from Aosta, capital city of the Valle d'Aosta, in northwestern Italy. The region is famous for its butter and walnuts. This version, also known as *torta di noci d'Aosta*, is inspired by the walnut torte at the Pasticceria Boch in Aosta, one of the most elegant pastry shops in northern Italy.

8 to 10 Servings

1¼ cups granulated sugar
½ teaspoon fresh lemon juice
¾ cup light honey
2½ sticks (10 ounces) unsalted butter,
    at room temperature
Pinch of salt
2 cups coarsely chopped walnuts
    (about 8 ounces)
3 egg yolks
2 cups all-purpose flour
Confectioners' sugar, for dusting

1. In a heavy medium saucepan, combine ½ cup of the granulated sugar with the lemon juice; stir well to mix. Cook over moderate heat, stirring occasionally, until the sugar turns pale amber, 12 to 15 minutes. Stir in the honey and 1 stick of the butter and bring to a boil over moderately high heat. Cook until thick bubbles form, 2 to 3 minutes. Stir in the salt and walnuts and set aside to cool.

2. Preheat the oven to 350°. Butter a 9-inch springform pan. In a large bowl, beat the remaining 1½ sticks butter at high speed until smooth, then gradually beat in the remaining ¾ cup granulated sugar. Continue beating until the mixture is light and fluffy. Beat in the egg yolks, one at a time, beating until fully incorporated. Using a rubber spatula, gradually mix in the flour until blended.

3. Place half of the dough in the bottom of the prepared pan. With floured fingertips or knuckles, press the dough evenly over the bottom and about 1 inch up the sides of the pan. Spread the cooled nut filling evenly over the dough. Flour the remaining dough and pat it into a 9-inch disk on a cardboard template or tart pan bottom; cover and refrigerate until well chilled.

4. Peel off the template and set the dough over the filling in the pan. Press it into place, then seal around the edges with the tines of a fork. Pierce the top in 10 or 12 places with the fork.

5. Bake the torte for 45 to 50 minutes, until lightly browned around the edge. Let cool briefly in the pan, then unmold onto a rack to cool. Dust very lightly with confectioners' sugar before serving.
—Nick Malgieri

235

FRIULIAN ALMOND TORTE

6 to 8 Servings

3 tablespoons fresh white bread crumbs
1½ cups rye bread crumbs, from 4 to 5 slices seedless rye bread, crusts trimmed
¼ cup rum
4 eggs
1¼ cups granulated sugar
1¼ cups ground (see Note), blanched almonds (about 5 ounces)
1 teaspoon grated lemon zest
⅛ teaspoon ground cloves
⅛ teaspoon cinnamon
1½ teaspoons confectioners' sugar

1. Preheat the oven to 350°. Fit a 9-inch circle of waxed paper into the bottom of a 9-inch cake pan. Butter the sides of the pan and the paper and sprinkle with the white bread crumbs.

2. Spread the rye bread crumbs on a plate and sprinkle with the rum. Separate 1 of the eggs.

3. In a medium mixer bowl, beat the 3 whole eggs and 1 yolk. Gradually add the granulated sugar, beating until the mixture turns light yellow and falls in ribbons from the beaters, about 5 minutes.

4. Add the almonds, rye bread crumbs, lemon zest, cloves and cinnamon. Beat until incorporated.

5. Whip the remaining egg white until it stands in stiff peaks. Gently fold the egg white into the batter. Scrape the batter into the prepared cake pan and smooth the surface.

6. Bake in the center of the oven for 30 minutes or until the center is no longer wet when tested with a toothpick. Slide a knife around the edges of the cake pan and turn the cake onto a rack. Peel off the waxed paper. Let cool, then turn right-side up onto a serving dish. Sprinkle the torte with the confectioners' sugar before serving.

NOTE: If you cannot find ground almonds, grate blanched whole almonds with a rotary grater. A food processor will not produce the powdery texture that ensures a light cake.

—*Tom Maresca and Diane Darrow*

FILBERT TORTE

14 to 16 Servings

12 eggs, separated
2 cups granulated sugar
¼ cup all-purpose flour
1 teaspoon grated lemon zest
2 tablespoons fresh lemon juice
1½ teaspoons vanilla extract
½ teaspoon salt
¼ teaspoon cinnamon
1 pound filberts (hazelnuts), finely ground
Confectioners' sugar, for dusting

1. Preheat the oven to 325°. Lightly butter the sides and bottom of a 10-inch tube pan, preferably with a removable bottom. Cut a piece of waxed paper to fit the bottom; place the paper in the pan and butter the paper.

2. In a large bowl, beat the egg yolks with an electric mixer. Gradually beat in the granulated sugar; continue beating until light and lemon-colored. Beat in the flour, lemon zest, lemon juice, vanilla, salt, cinnamon and ground nuts. The mixture will be very stiff.

3. In another large bowl, beat the egg whites until stiff but not dry. Fold about 2 cups of the beaten whites into the nut mixture to lighten the batter. Gently fold the remaining egg whites into the nut mixture until no streaks of white remain.

4. Pour the batter into the tube pan; gently smooth the top with a rubber spatula. Bake in the middle of the oven for about 1¼ hours, or until the edges of the cake pull away from the pan and the center springs back when lightly touched.

5. Cool the torte in the pan on a wire rack for 10 minutes. Run a narrow spatula or knife around the tube and outside edge of the pan to loosen the torte. Invert the torte onto a wire rack, peel off the waxed paper and let cool completely. Just before serving dust the top of the torte with confectioners' sugar.
—Helen Millman

CRUMB CAKE FROM TREVISO

There are many documented versions of the *fregolotta*; some are actually sponge cakes made with ground nuts. This very simple one is sort of a giant crumb cookie that's cut into wedges and served with coffee or tea.

8 Servings

1 *cup unblanched almonds (about 5 ounces)*
2½ *cups all-purpose flour*
1 *cup sugar*
¼ *teaspoon salt*
2 *teaspoons vanilla extract*
2 *sticks (8 ounces) unsalted butter, melted and cooled*

1. Preheat the oven to 350°. Butter a 10-inch tart pan with a removable bottom or a 9-inch pie pan.

2. Place the almonds in a food processor and pulse repeatedly until they are coarsely ground; the pieces should be no larger than ⅛ inch.

3. In a medium bowl, combine the flour, sugar and salt. Stir in the ground almonds.

4. Stir the vanilla into the melted butter and add to the dry ingredients. Stir with a rubber spatula until evenly incorporated. Rub the mixture between the palms of your hands to make crumbs no larger than ¼ inch.

5. Scatter three-fourths of the crumbs in the prepared pan and press very lightly with your fingertips to compress. Scatter the remaining crumbs on top but do not press them down. Bake the *fregolotta* in the middle of the oven for about 25 minutes, until light golden and cooked through. Transfer to a rack to cool.

6. If a tart pan was used, remove the sides and slide the crumb cake off the pan base onto a platter before cutting into wedges. If a pie pan was used, serve directly from the pan.
—Nick Malgieri

ITALIAN DESSERT WINES

Italians are fond of serving dry cakes and cookies that are destined to be served with (and often dipped in) a dessert wine. Here are a number of options worth sampling:

• Asti Spumante: From the Piedmont; a sparkling wine made from the Muscat grape.

• Moscato d'Asti: The still version of Asti Spumante.

• Malvasia di Lipari: Made from the Malvasia grape; produced on several small islands off the coast of Sicily.

• Marsala Vergine: A fortified wine from Sicily.

• Picolit: A relatively rare dessert wine from Friuli-Venezia Giulia; made from the Picolit grape.

• Vin Santo: The classic biscotti-dipping wine; made all over Italy, but the best comes from Tuscany.

DESSERTS

PANETTONE

The origins of panettone (a sweet, fruit-studded, yeast-risen bread) are not clear, but the most romantic explanation involves the love of a rich 15th-century nobleman, Ughetto della Tela, for a baker's daughter, Adalgisa. It was during the month of December, and Ughetto, knowing that his family would never accept a poor man's daughter into their family, gave Adalgisa's father, Toni, the financial support to purchase the very best flour, eggs and butter in order to make the traditional Yule cake. Ughetto also provided Toni with fat sultana raisins and lemon to make candied peel, ingredients not included in the traditional version of the Christmas cake. Toni's bread—pan di Toni, or panettone—was so popular that the baker soon became a wealthy man, and his daughter became an acceptable wife for the nobleman.

SAND TART

This delicious, delicate cake has a pleasantly grainy texture that results from the combination of cornmeal and potato starch. It's related to a rich shortcake, but the baking powder and the beaten egg whites keep it light, and the flavor is subtle. Have a slice with a glass of dessert wine for a serene conclusion to your meal.

6 to 8 Servings

2 sticks (8 ounces) plus 2 tablespoons unsalted butter, at room temperature
1 cup fine white cornmeal
1 cup potato starch
1 tablespoon baking powder
½ teaspoon salt
1 cup plus 2 tablespoons granulated sugar
2 eggs, separated
1 tablespoon anisette liqueur
½ teaspoon vanilla extract
2 tablespoons confectioners' sugar

1. Preheat the oven to 350°. Butter a 10-inch cake pan with 2 tablespoons of the butter.

2. In a medium bowl, sift together the cornmeal, potato starch, baking powder and salt.

3. In a separate medium bowl, cream the granulated sugar and the remaining 2 sticks butter with an electric hand mixer until light and fluffy, 2 to 3 minutes. Beat in the egg yolks, anisette and vanilla. Gradually beat in the cornmeal mixture to make a dense batter.

4. In another medium bowl, beat the egg whites until they stand in soft peaks. Fold the beaten egg whites into the batter in 2 batches. Transfer the batter to the buttered cake pan.

5. Bake the cake for 35 minutes, or until a toothpick inserted in the center comes out clean. Remove from the oven and let cool completely.

6. Sprinkle the top with the confectioners' sugar. Because this is such a delicate cake, it's best to serve it directly from the pan. Cut with a sharp knife and remove the pieces carefully with a cake server.
—Tom Maresca and Diane Darrow

VALTELLINESE CHRISTMAS BREAD

Called *biscïola*, this *panettone valtellinese* is a cross between a bread and a cake chock-full of fruit and nuts. Fresh chestnuts are not always easy to find, but use them here if you can. Score their flat side with a knife, boil them for 15 minutes and then peel them and proceed. Canned peeled whole chestnuts are easier to use and to find. The best quality are those from France. You can also use dried chestnuts (soak and boil until soft before using) or jarred chestnuts in syrup (drain first).

🍷 *Biscïola*'s moderate sweetness invites occasional sips of a nice dessert wine between bites. We suggest two very different wines from opposite ends of the country. I Vignaioli di Santo Stefano (Piedmont) Moscato d'Asti has a whisper of sparkle to highlight its fresh grapey taste. Capo Salina (Hauner/Sicily) Malvasia di Lipari, of golden honey color, is rich with scents of apricots and citrus. If you've had plenty of wine with dinner, you might opt for the former. On the other hand, just a little of the latter goes a long way.

Makes an 8-Inch
Cake

½ *cup raisins*
5 *dried figs, ends trimmed, coarsely chopped*
¼ *cup grappa or other brandy*
¼ *cup unsweetened apple juice*
¾ *cup rye flour*
1¾ *cups all-purpose flour*
1 *teaspoon baking soda*
2 *tablespoons coarsely ground walnuts plus ½ cup walnut pieces*
2 *tablespoons coarsely ground hazelnuts plus ½ cup whole hazelnuts*
¼ *cup sugar*
4 *tablespoons unsalted butter, cut into pieces, at room temperature*
1 *egg*
¼ *cup honey*
10 *canned chestnuts, drained and coarsely crumbled*

1. In a medium bowl, soak the raisins and figs in the grappa and apple juice for at least 2 hours or overnight.

2. Preheat the oven to 350°. In a large bowl, sift together the rye and all-purpose flours with the baking soda. Stir in the ground nuts and sugar. Work in the butter with your fingers until the mixture is the consistency of small peas. Stir in the egg and honey and knead until the texture is uniform, about 2 minutes.

3. Using a slotted spoon, drain the raisins and figs and add them to the dough. Gently work in the dried fruit along with the whole hazelnuts, walnut pieces and crumbled chestnuts, until evenly distributed and the dough forms a ball.

4. Dust a pizza stone or cookie sheet with rye flour. Shake off any excess. Place the dough on top and flatten it to form an 8-inch round about 1¼ inches thick. Smooth the edges with moistened fingers. Bake for 45 to 50 minutes, or until lightly golden and a cake tester inserted in the center comes out clean. Remove from the baking sheet and let cool completely on a rack. Serve the bread sliced in thin wedges. (*Wrapped well, the bread will keep refrigerated for up to 1 week and frozen for up to 2 months.*)
—Constance and Rosario Del Nero

PEACH AND RAISIN RISOTTO

A mildly sweet dessert, this is an interesting risotto.
🍷 Sweet Vin Santo

4 *to 6 Servings*

2 *packages (10 ounces each) frozen peaches in syrup, thawed*
4 *tablespoons unsalted butter*
½ *cup currants*
1 *cup arborio rice*
2 *tablespoons dark rum*
2 *tablespoons granulated sugar*
½ *cup heavy cream*
Brown sugar

DESSERTS

1. Drain the peaches, reserving the syrup. Cut the peaches into ½-inch pieces.

2. In a medium saucepan, combine the syrup with enough water to measure 4 cups. Bring to a simmer and maintain at a simmer over moderately low heat.

3. In a large nonreactive saucepan or flameproof casserole, melt 2 tablespoons of the butter over moderate heat. Add the currants and cook for 2 minutes. Add the rice and stir for 1 to 2 minutes, until well coated with the butter and slightly translucent. Add the rum and cook until it evaporates.

4. Add ½ cup of the simmering syrup and cook, stirring constantly, until the rice has absorbed most of the liquid. Adjust the heat, if necessary, to maintain a simmer. Gradually adding syrup, ½ cup at a time, cook, stirring constantly, until the rice is almost tender but still slightly crunchy in the center, 20 to 25 minutes.

5. Add the granulated sugar, the reserved peaches and the heavy cream. Continue to cook, stirring and adding syrup as necessary, ¼ cup at a time, until the rice is tender but still firm and is bound with a creamy sauce, 3 to 6 minutes longer.

6. Stir in the remaining 2 tablespoons butter and serve immediately. Pass a bowl of brown sugar separately.
—F&W

FRUIT-FILLED GNOCCHI WITH NUT SAUCE

These gnocchi can be served as a dessert, particularly if the rest of the meal does not contain either potatoes or pasta. But they are also eaten as a first course in the area around Trieste. Prunes are usually used, but you can substitute apricots if you prefer them.
❢ Light white, such as Antinori Galestro

6 to 8 Servings

1 *pound baking potatoes*
1 *stick (4 ounces) plus 2 tablespoons unsalted butter*
24 *pitted prunes or dried apricots*
1 *egg*
¾ *teaspoon salt*
1½ *cups all-purpose flour*
¼ *cup sugar*
¾ *cup chopped walnuts*

1. In a medium saucepan of boiling salted water, cook the potatoes until tender, 25 to 35 minutes; drain. While still hot, peel the potatoes and pass them through a potato ricer or a food mill into a large bowl. Beat in 2 tablespoons of the butter and set the potatoes aside to cool.

2. If you are using apricots, soak them in a small bowl of boiling water until the water is cooled and the fruit is softened, about 30 minutes. Drain and dry on paper towels. Cut the prunes or apricots in half.

3. With a wooden spoon, beat the egg and ½ teaspoon of the salt into the potatoes. Gradually stir in as much of the flour as possible. When the mixture becomes too stiff to stir, turn out onto a lightly floured surface and knead in the remaining flour.

4. Shape the dough into a ball. Divide the ball into quarters. Shape each quarter into a cylinder about 1 inch in diameter and cut each into 12 pieces. Flatten each piece of dough slightly and press a piece of fruit into each. Sprinkle the fruit with ¼ teaspoon of sugar and pinch the dough up and around the fruit to enclose it. Roll the dough in your palms to form an egg shape. As they are formed, put the gnocchi on a baking sheet lined with waxed paper.

5. In a small saucepan, melt the remaining 1 stick butter over low heat. Add the walnuts and the remaining ¼ teaspoon salt and cook for 2 minutes. Keep warm over very low heat.

6. In a large pot of boiling salted water, cook the gnocchi in 2 batches, adding them a few at a time to prevent sticking. After the gnocchi rise to the surface, cook for 2 minutes longer.

7. With a slotted spoon or skimmer remove the gnocchi and transfer to a heated serving platter. Drizzle the nut sauce over the gnocchi, toss lightly.
—*Michele Scicolone*

VANILLA-WALNUT COOKIES

These crisp, thin cookies are delightful eaten with milk, and they make a fine accompaniment to vanilla ice cream. Their Italian name *brutte e buone* translates as "ugly and good." The large amount of vanilla extract is not excessive.

*Makes About 2
Dozen 3-Inch
Cookies*

1 cup sifted all-purpose flour
½ cup sugar
½ cup choped walnuts
1 stick (4 ounces) unsalted butter
½ teaspoon salt
2 tablespoons vanilla extract
3 eggs

1. Preheat the oven to 350°. Lightly grease two large cookie sheets.

2. In a medium bowl, stir together the flour, sugar and walnuts until mixed.

3. In a medium mixer bowl, beat the butter until soft. Add the salt and vanilla and beat until mixed. Beat in the eggs.

4. On low speed, beat in half of the flour mixture until just blended. Add the remaining flour mixture and beat again briefly until smooth. (At this point, the dough may be refrigerated, covered, for several hours.)

5. To shape each cookie, drop a rounded tablespoon of dough onto the prepared baking sheet. With the back of a spoon, spread the dough out to make a thin circle about 3 inches in diameter. Continue until you have filled both sheets with 9 cookies each. Cover and refrigerate the remaining dough. Bake the cookies 18 to 20 minutes, until they are browned at the edges and a

lightly golden color in the middle. Remove with a spatula to a rack to cool.

6. Form and bake the remaining cookies.

—Frank Caldwell

CORNMEAL CRESCENT BISCOTTI

These cookies, *crumiri*, come from Piedmont where cornmeal is often eaten in the form of polenta. These biscotti are very delicate and particularly well suited to pairing with light sparkling wines. Unlike other, denser biscotti, they require only a quick dip in the wine as opposed to a heavy dunking.

Makes About 4
Dozen Cookies

1¾ cups all-purpose flour
¾ cup fine yellow cornmeal
1 teaspoon salt
2 sticks (8 ounces) unsalted butter, at
    room temperature
¾ cup sugar
1 egg
1 teaspoon vanilla extract

1. Preheat the oven to 375°. Butter and flour 2 large cookie sheets.

2. On a piece of waxed paper, combine the flour, cornmeal and salt. In a large bowl, beat the butter and sugar with a hand-held electric mixer until light and fluffy. Beat in the egg and vanilla. Stir in the dry ingredients with a wooden spoon until well blended. Cover and refrigerate the dough until firm enough to handle, at least 1 hour.

3. Scoop up 1 heaping tablespoon of the dough and roll into a log about 2 inches long. Bend to form a crescent shape. Repeat with the remaining dough. As they are shaped, place the biscotti about 2 inches apart on the prepared cookie sheets. With your hands or the back of a wooden spoon, lightly flatten the biscotti.

4. Bake for 15 to 20 minutes, or until golden brown. Transfer to racks to cool.

—Michele Scicolone

TOASTED SESAME SEED BISCOTTI

Biscotti regina reign in Sicily, where sesame seeds were introduced by the Arabs who ruled there for hundreds of years. Unhulled sesame seeds, available in health food stores, will give the cookies an authentic flavor.

Makes About 2
Dozen Cookies

1 cup unhulled sesame seeds (about ¼
    pound)
2 cups all-purpose flour
⅔ cup sugar
1 teaspoon baking powder
½ teaspoon salt
½ cup vegetable shortening
2 eggs
1 teaspoon vanilla extract
1 teaspoon grated lemon zest

1. Preheat the oven to 350°. Spread the sesame seeds on a baking sheet or in a roasting pan and toast, shaking the pan occasionally, until golden brown, about 15 minutes. Set aside to cool.

2. Lightly grease a cookie sheet. In a bowl, combine the flour, sugar, baking powder and salt. Cut in the shortening until the mixture resembles coarse meal.

3. In a small bowl, beat together the eggs, vanilla and lemon zest. Pour into the dry ingredients and stir until thoroughly incorporated.

4. Shape the dough into 2-by-¾-inch logs. Roll the logs in the sesame seeds, patting the seeds into the dough. With your hands or the back of a spoon, lightly flatten the biscotti and place 1 inch apart on the prepared cookie sheet. Bake for 30 to 35 minutes, or until golden brown. Transfer to wire racks to cool.

—*Michele Scicolone*

CHOCOLATE-WALNUT BISCOTTI

Biscotti di cioccolata are sometimes called *mostaccioli* because of their mustache shape.

*Makes About 4
Dozen Cookies*

2 cups walnut halves (about 8 ounces)
3 ounces unsweetened chocolate
*5 tablespoons plus 1 teaspoon unsalted
    butter*
2 cups all-purpose flour
2 teaspoons baking powder
3 eggs
1 cup sugar
1 teaspoon grated orange zest

1. Preheat the oven to 350°. Place the walnuts on a cookie sheet and toast until golden brown, about 10 minutes. Let cool and then chop coarsely.

2. In a double boiler over simmering water, melt together the chocolate and butter. Remove from the heat and stir until smooth. Let cool for 10 minutes.

3. Sift together the flour and baking powder. In a large bowl, beat the eggs lightly. Gradually beat in the sugar. Add the orange zest. Stir in the cooled chocolate until blended. Stir in the flour and baking powder until incorporated. Fold in the chopped walnuts. Divide the dough in half, wrap in plastic wrap and refrigerate at least 1 hour or overnight.

4. Butter a large cookie sheet and preheat the oven to 350°. Shape each half of the dough into a 14-by-2½-inch log. Place about 4 inches apart on the prepared pan. Smooth the tops and sides with a rubber spatula. Bake for 40 to 45 minutes, or until the logs are firm when pressed in the center. Remove the baking sheet from the oven. Do not turn off the oven.

5. Slide the logs onto a cutting board. With a large knife, cut each log diagonally into ½-inch slices. Stand the slices upright on edge on the prepared cookie sheet. Return to the oven and bake for 15 minutes longer, or until crisp. Transfer to wire racks to cool completely.

—*Michele Scicolone*

BISCOTTI

Biscotti are Italian cookies. Literally translated, the word means "twice cooked," and many, but not all, biscotti are baked twice for extra crunch. They are generally made with less fat than most American cookies. Subtly flavored and not too sweet, biscotti seem to require slow savoring. One or two make a satisfying light dessert, especially when served with a glass of wine. To many Italians, the wine is essential and, in fact, it is traditional to dip biscotti into wine. The hard cookies absorb a little of the liquid, which enhances their flavor and softens them slightly. Usually a dessert wine is served (see "Italian Dessert Wines," p. 237), but biscotti also go well with dry wines.

—*Michele Scicolone*

DOUBLE-NUT BISCOTTI

Variations of *biscotti di noce* are made all over Italy. In Naples they are called *quaresimali*, meaning Lenten cookies, because they were traditionally made during that time. In Tuscany they are called *biscotti di Prato* for the town where the best are supposedly made. This recipe has a large yield, but the cookies keep very well for up to one month in a covered tin; in fact their flavor will even improve.

Makes 8 Dozen
Cookies

1½ cups blanched whole almonds
  (about 8 ounces)
½ cup hazelnuts (about 2 ounces)
4 cups all-purpose flour
2 teaspoons baking powder
1 teaspoon cinnamon
5 eggs
1 stick (4 ounces) unsalted butter,
  melted and cooled
2 cups sugar
1½ teaspoons finely grated lemon zest

1. Preheat the oven to 375°. Spread the almonds on a cookie sheet and toast, turning once, until golden brown all over, about 10 minutes. Transfer to a cutting board to let cool. In a food processor, finely grind ½ cup of the almonds.

2. Spread the hazelnuts on the cookie sheet and toast until the skins begin to split, about 10 minutes. Immediately transfer to a kitchen towel and rub to remove as much of the skin as possible. Add the hazelnuts to the remaining whole almonds on the board and chop coarsely.

3. Reduce the oven temperature to 350°. Butter 2 large cookie sheets. In a medium bowl, sift together the flour, baking powder and cinnamon. Stir in the ground almonds and the chopped almonds and hazelnuts.

4. In a large bowl, whisk the eggs until frothy. Stir in the butter, sugar and lemon zest until just combined. Stir in the flour and nut mixture until blended.

5. Shape the dough into four 12-by-2½-inch logs and place about 4 inches apart on the cookie sheets. Smooth the tops and sides with a rubber spatula. Bake for 25 minutes, or until the logs are firm when pressed in the center. Remove from the oven. Do not turn off the oven.

6. Slide the logs onto a cutting board and cut them diagonally with a large knife into ½-inch slices. Stand the slices upright on edge on the cookie sheets. Return to the oven and bake for 20 minutes longer, or until crisp and brown. Let cool on a wire rack.
—Michele Scicolone

Cannoli Siciliani (*page* 230).

Above, Hazelnut Biscotti with
Black Pepper (page 249). At right,
Sand Tart (page 238).

Raisins in Grappa (page 214).

CHRISTMAS CANTUCCINI

Cantuccini di Prato, a version of the popular biscotti, are a traditional Italian twice-baked cookie. To maintain the brilliant green color of the pistachios through the two stages of baking, it is important to begin with unroasted pistachios, which have a more intense flavor and color. If stored in an airtight container, these will keep for at least two weeks, and their sturdiness makes them great cookies to send by mail.

Makes About 3
Dozen Cookies

1¾ *cups all-purpose flour*
1 *cup plus 1 teaspoon sugar*
½ *teaspoon baking powder*
¼ *teaspoon salt*
½ *cup dried cranberries (about 2½*
   ounces)
4 *tablespoons cold unsalted butter, cut*
   into ½-inch pieces
1 *teaspoon vanilla extract*
1½ *cups shelled unroasted pistachios**
   (about 8 ounces)
2 *eggs, lightly beaten*
**Available at Indian and Middle*
   Eastern markets

1. Preheat the oven to 350°. Lightly butter a large heavy baking sheet.

2. In a food processor, combine the flour with 1 cup of the sugar, the baking powder and salt. Process for a few seconds to blend. Add the dried cranberries and process until coarsely chopped. Add the butter and vanilla. Pulse until the mixture resembles coarse meal.

3. Add the pistachios and eggs and pulse 10 times to blend. Scrape down the sides of the bowl and pulse 5 times, just until the dough is evenly moistened.

4. On a lightly floured work surface, divide the dough into 4 equal pieces. Roll each piece into an 8-inch log. Transfer the logs to the prepared baking sheet, leaving 2 inches between each. With your hands, flatten the logs to a width of 2 inches and sprinkle with the remaining 1 teaspoon of sugar. Bake for 25 minutes, or until golden brown. Using a metal spatula, transfer the logs to a rack to firm up slightly, 15 to 20 minutes.

5. Transfer the logs to a work surface. Using a sharp knife and a quick single motion, slice each log on the diagonal into ½-inch slices. Return the *cantuccini* to the baking sheet, cut-sides down, and bake just until the first hint of golden brown appears, about 7 minutes. Transfer to a rack and let cool completely.
—Peggy Cullen

HAZELNUT BISCOTTI WITH BLACK PEPPER

This is a version of the walnut-almond biscotti found on the menu at Trattoria Angeli.

Makes About 2
Dozen Cookies

1½ *cups hazelnuts (about 7 ounces)*
1¾ *cups unbleached all-purpose flour*
½ *teaspoon baking soda*
½ *teaspoon baking powder*
⅛ *teaspoon salt*
1½ *teaspoons freshly ground black*
   pepper
1 *stick (4 ounces) unsalted butter, at*
   room temperature
1 *cup sugar*
2 *eggs*

1 teaspoon finely grated lemon zest
1 teaspoon finely grated orange zest
1½ teaspoons vanilla extract
¼ teaspoon almond extract

1. Preheat the oven to 350°. Place the hazelnuts on a baking sheet and roast until lightly browned, about 12 minutes. Rub the warm nuts in a dish towel to remove most of the skins. Chop coarsely and set aside.

2. In a medium bowl, sift together the flour, baking soda, baking powder, salt and pepper.

3. In a large bowl, beat the butter and sugar with an electric mixer at medium speed until light and fluffy, about 3 minutes. Add the eggs, one at a time, beating well after each addition. Beat in the lemon and orange zests and the vanilla and almond extracts. Using a rubber spatula, fold in the hazelnuts and the sifted dry ingredients just until incorporated.

4. On a lightly floured work surface, shape the dough into two 12-inch logs, 3 inches wide and 1 inch thick. Place the logs on a large, heavy buttered baking sheet about 4 inches apart. Bake in the middle of the oven for 25 minutes or until the logs are lightly browned and feel firm when pressed in the center. Let cool on the baking sheet for about 10 minutes.

5. Carefully transfer the logs to a cutting board. Using a serrated knife, cut them crosswise into ¾-inch slices. Arrange the slices, cut-side down, on the cookie sheet and bake for 15 minutes until golden brown. Transfer to a rack and let cool completely. (*The biscotti can be stored for up to 2 weeks in an airtight tin.*)
—Evan Kleiman, Trattoria Angeli, Los Angeles

RICE FRITTERS

These substantial fritters are reminiscent of rice pudding, with a light, citrus fragrance. They are traditionally made for the feast of San Giuseppe on March 19.

*Makes 2½ to 3
Dozen Fritters*

4 cups milk
1 lemon or orange
1¼ cups arborio rice
2 tablespoons unsalted butter
2 tablespoons sugar, plus more
    for coating
Pinch of salt
6 eggs, separated
6 tablespoons unbleached
    all-purpose flour
4 cups vegetable oil, for frying
½ cup olive oil, for frying

1. In a medium saucepan, bring the milk to a boil over moderate heat. Meanwhile, using a vegetable peeler, remove the zest from the lemon or orange. Add the zest strips to the milk and stir in the rice, butter, the 2 tablespoons sugar and the salt.

2. Reduce the heat to low. Simmer, stirring occasionally with a wooden spoon, until the rice is completely cooked and the milk almost totally absorbed, about 20 minutes.

3. Scrape the rice into a bowl and let cool completely, about 2 hours. (*The recipe can be prepared to this point up to 1 day ahead. Cover and refrigerate the rice overnight. Let return to room temperature before proceeding.*)

4. Discard the citrus zest. Using a wooden spoon, blend the egg yolks into the rice mixture, one at a time. Stir in the flour until thoroughly incorporated.

5. In a large cast-iron skillet, heat the vegetable and olive oils over moderate heat to 375°. Meanwhile, in a large bowl, beat the egg whites until stiff but not dry. Gently fold the whites into the rice.

6. When the oil is hot, spoon tablespoons of the rice mixture into the oil and fry, turning, until well browned and cooked through, about 5 minutes. Using a slotted spoon, transfer the fritters to paper towels to drain. When all the fritters are cooked, roll them in sugar. Arrange on a platter and serve hot.
—*Giuliano Bugialli*

CHESTNUT FLOUR FRITTERS

These light, sweet fritters once were among the most common of all preparations made with chestnut flour. The batter is thin and is meant to be. It is best to eat these fritters as soon as they are made.

Makes About 18 Fritters

1 *cup chestnut flour,* * *sifted*
¾ *cup milk*
1 *tablespoon sugar, plus more for sprinkling*

Pinch of salt
1½ *tablespoons raisins*
4 *cups vegetable oil, for frying*
*Available at Italian markets

1. Place the chestnut flour in a medium bowl and make a well in the center. Gradually add the milk, stirring constantly with a wooden spoon to prevent lumps from forming. When all the milk has been added and the batter is smooth, stir in the 1 tablespoon sugar, the salt and raisins. Set aside.

2. In a large skillet, heat the oil over moderate heat until it reaches 375°. When the oil is hot, carefully spoon in the batter by tablespoons, leaving space between them to allow for spreading. Fry, turning, until evenly browned, about 2 minutes. Using a slotted spoon, transfer the fritters to a platter lined with paper towels to drain. Repeat with the remaining batter.

3. When all the fritters are done, remove the paper towels from the platter. Sprinkle the fritters with sugar and serve immediately.
—*Giuliano Bugialli*

251

THE BASICS 253

FOOD & WINE'S FRESH PASTA

Makes 1¼ to 1½ Pounds

About 2½ cups all-purpose or bread flour
3 whole eggs
1 egg yolk
2 teaspoons olive oil
Pinch of salt

1. Place 2½ cups of flour in a medium bowl. Make a well in the center and add the whole eggs, egg yolk, oil and salt. Using a fork or your fingers, blend the ingredients in the well.

2. Gradually work in the flour until the dough masses together and pulls away from the sides of the bowl. It should be soft, pliable and slightly sticky. If the dough is too stiff and dry, add up to 2 tablespoons of water, 1 teaspoon at a time; if too wet and sticky, add flour, 1 tablespoon at a time.

3. Turn the dough out onto a lightly floured surface and knead until smooth and elastic, 8 to 10 minutes.

4. Shape the dough into a ball, dust lightly with flour and cover with plastic wrap. Let rest for at least 30 minutes before rolling out.

FOOD PROCESSOR METHOD
In a small bowl, combine the whole eggs, egg yolk, oil, salt and 2 tablespoons of water. Place 2½ cups of flour in a food processor fitted with the metal blade. With the machine on, pour the egg mixture through the feed tube and process for 10 seconds. The mixture will resemble crumbly meal after 5 seconds and should form a ball after another 5 seconds. If the dough is still crumbly after 10 seconds, add another tablespoon or two of water as necessary. Once a ball has formed, transfer the dough to a work surface and knead it briefly until smooth and elastic. Shape the dough into a ball, cover with plastic wrap and let rest for at least 30 minutes before rolling out.
—John Robert Massie

EGG PASTA

This recipe makes enough for about 3 dozen tortelli. The pasta can also be used to make fettuccine, linguine, tagliarini or lasagna noodles.

Makes About 1½ Pounds

3 cups all-purpose flour
½ teaspoon salt
4 eggs

In a food processor, combine the flour and salt. Process briefly to mix. With the machine on, add the eggs one at a time to form a soft dough. If the dough isn't quite moist enough, add 1 to 2 teaspoons of cold water. Turn out onto a lightly floured surface and knead until smooth and elastic, about 3 minutes. Gather into a ball. Cover with plastic wrap and let rest for at least 30 minutes. (*The recipe can be made to this point up to 1 day ahead. Cover with plastic wrap and refrigerate; or freeze for up to 2 weeks.*)
—Carol Field

FRESH BUCKWHEAT PASTA

6 Servings

3 eggs, at room temperature
¼ teaspoon salt
1 cup buckwheat flour*
1 cup unbleached all-purpose flour
*Available at health food stores

1. In a small bowl, whisk together the eggs and salt. In the bowl of a food processor fitted with a metal blade, combine the buckwheat and all-purpose flours. Process briefly to blend. With the machine on, slowly pour in the eggs. Continue to process until a firm dough forms, about 10 seconds. Turn the dough out onto a work surface (it will be damp and crumbly) and knead until smooth. Wrap the dough airtight in plastic wrap and let stand at room temperature for 45 minutes.

2. Cut the dough into 4 equal pieces and flatten each with your palm. Adjust the rollers of a pasta machine to their widest setting and roll each piece of dough through the machine. Fold each strip of pasta dough over itself lengthwise and roll through the machine again. Reset the rollers to the next lowest setting, again fold the dough and run each piece through the machine twice. Adjust the machine to the next to the last setting and repeat the above procedure. The resulting pasta should be slightly thicker than typical fettuccine. Let the pasta dough rest at room temperature for 25 minutes.

3. Using the pasta machine's fettuccine cutter, cut the pasta into long strips and trim into 5- to 6-inch lengths. Toss the fettuccine with additional white flour to prevent it from sticking and spread out on a baking sheet. The pasta can be used at once or prepared several days ahead. When completely dry, wrap the dough in plastic wrap and store at room temperature.
—Michael McLaughlin

SPINACH PASTA

This makes enough for about 5 dozen 2-inch ravioli.

Makes 1¼ to 1½
Pounds

1 pound fresh spinach, washed and
    stemmed, or 1 package (10 ounces)
    frozen spinach
About 2½ cups all-purpose or
    bread flour
2 whole eggs
1 egg yolk
2 teaspoons olive oil
Pinch of salt

1. If using fresh spinach, steam for 2 to 3 minutes, or until wilted and tender but still bright green. If using frozen, cook as directed on the package. Drain and rinse under cold running water until cooled, to refresh and preserve the color; drain well. Squeeze the spinach by handfuls to remove as much water as possible. Puree in a food processor or food mill; scrape out onto a clean kitchen towel. Bundle the spinach puree in the towel and wring tightly to remove as much moisture as you can; there will be about ⅓ cup spinach puree.

2. Place 2½ cups flour in a medium bowl. Make a well in the center and add the spinach, whole eggs,

egg yolk, oil and salt. Using your fingers or a fork, mix together these ingredients in the well.

3. Gradually work in the flour until the dough masses together and pulls away from the sides of the bowl. It should be soft, pliable and slightly sticky. If the dough is too stiff and dry, add up to 2 tablespoons of water, 1 teaspoon at a time; if too wet and sticky, add flour, 1 tablespoon at a time.

4. Turn the dough out onto a lightly floured surface and knead until smooth and elastic, 8 to 10 minutes. This dough does not need a resting period and is best rolled out immediately, though it can be made the night before.
—*John Robert Massie*

TOMATO PASTA

This makes enough for about 5 dozen 2-inch ravioli.

*Makes 1¼ to 1½
Pounds*

*About 2½ cups all-purpose or
    bread flour*
5 tablespoons tomato paste
2 whole eggs
1 egg yolk
2 teaspoons olive oil
Pinch of salt

1. Place 2½ cups flour in a medium bowl. Make a well in the center and add the tomato paste, whole eggs, egg yolk, oil and salt. Using your fingers or a fork, mix together these ingredients in the well.

2. Gradually work in the flour until the dough masses together and pulls away from the sides of the bowl. It should be soft, pliable and slightly sticky. If the dough is too

stiff and dry, add up to 2 tablespoons of water, 1 teaspoon at a time; if too wet and sticky, add flour, 1 tablespoon at a time.

3. Turn the dough out onto a lightly floured surface and knead until smooth and elastic, 8 to 10 minutes. This dough does not need a resting period and is best rolled out immediately, though it can be made the night before.
—*John Robert Massie*

BASIC PIZZA DOUGH

This recipe makes 1¾ pounds of dough, enough for seven 7-inch flat pizzas or two 9-inch deep-dish pizzas. The ingredients can be easily doubled if you wish to make a bigger batch.

Makes 1¾ Pounds

1 envelope active dry yeast
1 tablespoon sugar
*1½ cups lukewarm water (105° to
    115°)*
*3¼ cups unbleached flour, preferably
    bread flour*
½ teaspoon salt
¼ cup olive oil, preferably extra-virgin

1. In a small bowl, combine the yeast and sugar. Add the water and

stir to mix. If the yeast is not active and bubbling within 5 minutes, discard it and repeat the procedure with a new envelope of yeast.

2. Measure 3 cups of flour by spooning into a one-cup measure and leveling off with a knife, and place in a large bowl. Stir in the salt, then form a well in the center of the flour.

3. Pour the yeast mixture into the well and add the oil. Stir in the flour, beginning in the center and working toward the sides of the bowl. When all the flour is incorporated and the dough is still soft but begins to mass together, turn out onto a lightly floured work surface.

4. Using a dough scraper to lift any fragments that cling to the work surface, knead the dough, adding just enough of the remaining ¼ cup flour until the dough is no longer sticky. (It is better that the dough be too soft than too stiff.) Continue to knead until the dough is smooth, shiny and elastic, 10 to 15 minutes.

5. Shape the dough into a ball and place it in a large, oiled bowl; turn the dough over to coat with the oil. Cover with plastic wrap, set in a warm draft-free place and let rise until doubled in bulk, 1 to 1½ hours. Punch the dough down and reshape into a ball. Cover and refrigerate until doubled in bulk, 20 minutes to 1 hour.

6. Punch the dough down. If making deep-dish pizza, divide the dough in half. If making flat pizza, divide the dough into 7 balls of equal weight (4 ounces) and use one for each flat pizza. To freeze, wrap each ball well in plastic; let the dough thaw before proceeding.
—Anne Disrude

QUICK SEMOLINA PIZZA DOUGH

This dough takes almost no time at all to assemble, and it can be made ahead of time. You can refrigerate or freeze it, but it must be at room temperature before you cook it. This crust employs baking powder rather than yeast, so there's no rising time.

To make sure your skillet is at the right temperature, do a test crust. Cut off a walnut-size piece of dough, roll it into a 1/16-inch-thick round and put it in the heated skillet. Bubbles should appear on the underside within the first 45 seconds; if they don't, increase the heat a little. If bubbles appear but then burn within the first three minutes, reduce the heat. The crust is cooked on only one side; it should be dark brown.

Makes 4 Pizza
Rounds, 7 Inches
Each

1 *cup semolina flour**
1 *teaspoon baking powder*
½ *teaspoon salt*
1 *tablespoon extra-virgin olive oil*
*Available at specialty food shops

1. In a food processor, combine the semolina flour, 1/3 cup hot water, the baking powder, salt and olive oil. Process until the dough masses together, about 45 seconds.

2. Cover with plastic wrap and let rest for at least 15 minutes or up to 2 hours. (*The recipe can be made up to this point 1 day ahead. Cover with plastic wrap and refrigerate. It can also be frozen. When you are ready to use the dough, roll it out, cover with plastic wrap and let it return to room temperature .*)
—Anne Disrude

CALZONE DOUGH

Makes Enough for
4 Calzone

1 *envelope active dry yeast*
1 *cup lukewarm water*
  (105° *to* 115°)
¼ *cup olive oil, preferably*
  extra-virgin
2½ *to* 3 *cups all-purpose flour*
1½ *teaspoons salt*

1. In a small bowl, sprinkle the yeast over the warm water; let stand until dissolved, about 5 minutes. Stir in the olive oil.

2. *Hand method:* In a large bowl, combine 2½ cups flour and the salt. Add the yeast mixture and stir until well blended. Turn out onto a lightly floured surface. Knead until smooth and elastic, 8 to 10 minutes, adding more flour if needed; the dough should remain slightly soft.

Food processor method: Combine the flour and salt in a food processor fitted with the metal blade. With the machine on, add the yeast mixture through the feed tube and process until the dough is smooth and cleans the sides of the bowl. Turn the dough out onto a lightly floured surface and knead briefly, adding more flour if needed.

Heavy-duty mixer method: In the large bowl of an electric mixer fitted with a dough hook, combine the flour and salt. With the mixer on low speed, gradually add the yeast mixture. Knead until the dough masses on the hook and becomes smooth and elastic, adding more flour as needed.

3. Place in a lightly oiled bowl; turn to coat. Cover with plastic wrap and let rise in a warm place until doubled in volume, about 1 hour.

4. Punch the dough down and divide into 4 equal pieces. (*If making the dough ahead of time, wrap the balls of dough tightly and store in the freezer for up to 1 month. Let the dough return the room temperature before proceeding.*)
—Michele Scicolone

ITALIAN PARSLEY PESTO

This pesto will keep covered in the refrigerator for up to one week.

Makes About
1 Cup

¼ *cup pine nuts or blanched*
  almonds
3 *medium garlic cloves*
2 *cups packed flat-leaf parsley leaves,*
  rinsed and dried
⅓ *cup extra-virgin olive oil*
3 *tablespoons freshly grated Parmesan*
  cheese
½ *teaspoon salt*
½ *teaspoon freshly ground pepper*

1. Preheat the oven to 325°. Place the nuts on a baking sheet and bake for 8 minutes, or until lightly toasted. Let cool.

2. In a food processor, mince the garlic. Add the parsley and nuts and process until minced. With the machine on, add the oil in a thin stream and process until well blended. Add the Parmesan and the salt and pepper and process to mix.
—*David Holben and Lori Finkelman Holben, The Riviera, Dallas*

OREGANO VINAIGRETTE

Makes About
⅔ Cup

1 small anchovy fillet, minced
2 medium garlic cloves, minced
1 teaspoon minced fresh oregano
 or ½ teaspoon dried
½ teaspoon Dijon mustard
2 tablespoons red wine vinegar
¼ teaspoon salt
¼ teaspoon freshly ground pepper
⅔ cup extra-virgin olive oil

In a small bowl, whisk together the anchovy, garlic, oregano, mustard, vinegar, salt and pepper. Whisk in the oil in a thin stream.
—*David Holben and Lori Finkelman Holben, The Riviera, Dallas*

SALSA TRICOLORE

This piquant sauce, flecked with brightly colored herbs and bits of roasted red pepper and hard-cooked egg, is a quick and delicious oil bath for grilled fish, chicken or meats. It's especially tasty on cold meats or vegetables or with boiled beef. My recipe is freely adapted from a sauce served by Lidia Bastianich at Felidia in New York City.

Makes About 2
Cups

1 medium red bell pepper
1 small red onion, minced
 (about ½ cup)
1 small celery rib, trimmed and
 minced (about ⅓ cup)
2 garlic cloves, minced
½ cup chopped flat-leaf parsley
3 to 4 tablespoons chopped
 fresh chives
2 tablespoons chopped fresh sage
 or ½ teaspoon dried
1 to 2 teaspoons chopped fresh
 tarragon (optional)
1 teaspoon salt
½ teaspoon freshly ground
 black pepper
3 tablespoons balsamic vinegar
2 tablespoons red wine vinegar
¾ cup fruity extra-virgin
 olive oil
1 hard-cooked egg, finely chopped

1. Roast the pepper under a broiler or directly over a gas flame, turning with tongs, until the skin is charred all over, about 10 minutes. Wrap in foil (or enclose in a paper bag) and let stand for 10 to 15 minutes. Peel off the skin, then remove the stem, seeds and ribs. Cut the

pepper into ¼-inch dice and place in a mixing bowl.

2. Add the onion, celery, garlic, parsley, chives, sage, tarragon, salt, black pepper, balsamic and red wine vinegars and the olive oil. Blend well. Stir in the hard-cooked egg. Taste and adjust the seasonings and vinegar-oil balance to your taste.
—Richard Sax

GREEN SAUCE

If you are making this sauce to go with Poached Chicken Breasts with Green Sauce (p. 79), use some of the poaching liquid in place of the chicken stock called for below.

Makes About 1½
Cups

1 cup (packed) flat-leaf parsley
½ cup fresh basil
1 medium garlic clove
1 tablespoon drained capers
3 cornichons (French gherkin
    pickles)
1 celery rib, cut up
½ cup extra-virgin olive oil
1 tablespoon red wine vinegar
1 to 2 tablespoons fresh
    lemon juice
2 to 4 tablespoons chicken stock or
    water (optional)
Salt and freshly ground pepper

In a food processor, combine the parsley, basil, garlic, capers, cornichons, celery, olive oil and vinegar. Chop but do not puree. Stir in the lemon juice to taste. If the sauce seems too thick, add a few tablespoons of stock. Season with salt and pepper to taste.
—Anna Teresa Callen

CHUNKY TOMATO SAUCE

Use this sauce on pizza or as a pasta sauce. If you use it on pizza, remember to use it sparingly because it's quite liquid.

Makes About 3
Cups

2 tablespoons olive oil
3 medium onions, thinly sliced
4 large garlic cloves, minced
½ cup canned tomato puree
1 can (16 ounces) Italian plum
    tomatoes with their juice, crushed
5 sprigs of parsley
12 fresh plum tomatoes (about 1½
    pounds)—peeled, seeded and
    coarsely chopped
½ teaspoon salt
¼ teaspoon freshly ground pepper
2 tablespoons minced fresh basil

1. In a medium saucepan over moderate heat, heat the olive oil until shimmering. Add the onions and garlic, cover and cook over low heat until softened and translucent, about 10 minutes.

2. Add the tomato puree, the crushed canned tomatoes with their juice and parsley. Simmer, uncovered, for 30 minutes.

3. Pass the sauce through a food mill of fine-mesh sieve to remove the seeds. Return to low heat and simmer until very thick (there will be about 2 cups).

4. Add the fresh tomatoes and cook for 2 minutes. Season with the salt, pepper and basil.
—Anne Disrude

MARINARA SAUCE

Many southern Italians refer to a quick tomato sauce as "marinara" because it could be made at a moment's notice by a fisherman's wife upon her husband's return. Served over breaded or fried foods or mixed into baked pasta dishes or spaghetti, it is the most common southern Italian tomato sauce. A simple marinara can be adjusted to suit a variety of pasta dishes by adding sautéed onions, other fresh herbs, such as oregano, parsley, marjoram or rosemary, or by adding hot peppers.

Makes About 3 Cups

¼ cup extra-virgin olive oil
2 small garlic cloves, minced or crushed and peeled (see Note)
2½ pounds plum tomatoes—peeled, seeded and finely chopped— or one 35-ounce and one 14-ounce can of Italian plum tomatoes, lightly drained and finely chopped
¼ teaspoon salt
½ teaspoon freshly ground pepper
2 tablespoons shredded fresh basil

1. In a medium nonreactive skillet, heat the oil over moderately low heat. Add the garlic and cook, stirring, until golden, about 4 minutes. Discard the garlic if desired.

2. Add the tomatoes, salt and pepper. Cook, stirring occasionally, until thickened, about 30 minutes. Soft bits of tomato will remain, and the sauce should be thick enough to hold its shape on a spoon. (*The sauce can be made ahead and kept covered in the refrigerator for up to 4 days or frozen for up to 3 months.*) Stir in the basil just before serving.

NOTE: Crushed, peeled garlic cloves can be discarded after browning for a very subtle flavor or left in and discarded at the end of cooking for a slightly more emphatic garlic taste. More often than not I use minced garlic and leave it in. This gives the sauce a strong garlic flavor.
—Nancy Verde Barr

TOMATO SAUCE

Makes About 4 Cups

⅓ cup olive oil
1 medium onion, chopped
2 garlic cloves, minced
1 tablespoon chopped fresh basil or 1 teaspoon dried
2 tablespoons chopped parsley
1½ teaspoons chopped fresh oregano or ½ teaspoon dried
2 pounds fresh plum tomatoes— rinsed, dried and cut into ½-inch dice—or 2 cans (35 ounces each) Italian peeled tomatoes, drained and chopped
1½ teaspoons sugar
1 teaspoon salt
Pinch of freshly ground pepper

1. In a large nonreactive saucepan, heat the olive oil over moderate heat. Add the onion and cook, stirring occasionally, until softened but not browned, about 5 minutes. Add the garlic, basil, parsley and oregano and stir to combine. Cook until fragrant, about 1 minute. Stir in the tomatoes, sugar, salt and pepper.

2. Cover the pot and simmer the sauce, stirring occasionally, for 30 minutes.
—Fred Ferretti

TOMATO SAUCE WITH GARLIC

This long-simmered sauce can be made up to 3 days ahead and stored, covered with plastic wrap, in the refrigerator or frozen for several months.

Makes About 3 Cups

1 can (28 ounces) Italian peeled
   tomatoes, with their juice
3 tablespoons olive oil
5 medium garlic cloves, crushed
   through a press
½ teaspoon salt
¼ teaspoon freshly ground pepper
¼ teaspoon sugar

1. Puree the tomatoes with their juice in a food processor or blender.
2. In a heavy medium nonreactive saucepan, heat the oil. Add the crushed garlic and sauté over moderate heat, stirring occasionally, until golden, 6 to 8 minutes.
3. Add the pureed tomatoes, salt, pepper and sugar; stir until blended. Reduce the heat to low, partially cover and simmer, stirring occasionally, until the sauce is thickened, 1 to 1½ hours.
—Da Celestino, Florence, Italy

CREAMY TOMATO SAUCE

*Makes About
1½ Cups*

1 can (35 ounces) Italian peeled
   tomatoes, drained
Bouquet garni: 5 sprigs of parsley, ½
   teaspoon thyme and 5 peppercorns
   tied in a double thickness of
   cheesecloth
¾ cup heavy cream
½ teaspoon salt
Freshly ground pepper

1. Place the tomatoes in a blender or food processor and puree until smooth. Strain the tomato puree through a coarse-mesh sieve to remove the seeds.
2. In a large skillet, bring the tomato puree with the bouquet garni to a boil over moderate heat. Boil, uncovered, for 5 minutes to reduce slightly. Stir in the cream and add the salt. Discard the bouquet garni. Season with additional salt and pepper to taste.
—John Robert Massie

TOMATO BUTTER SAUCE

*Makes About 3
Cups*

⅓ cup extra-virgin olive oil
1 small carrot, sliced into ¼-inch
   rounds
½ small red onion, cut into
   small dice
1 small leek, sliced into ¼-inch rounds
1 can (28 ounces) plum tomatoes
1 medium garlic clove, finely
   chopped
¾ cup chicken stock or canned low-
   sodium broth
½ cup dry white wine
⅛ teaspoon crushed red pepper
1 bay leaf
2 sticks (8 ounces) cold unsalted
   butter, cut into small pieces
1 cup minced flat-leaf parsley
¾ teaspoon salt
½ teaspoon freshly ground pepper

1. In a large nonreactive saucepan, heat the olive oil over moderately high heat until hot, about 2 minutes. Add the carrot, onion and leek and cook, stirring, until soft, about 5 minutes. Gently break up the tomatoes with your hands and add with their juice to the vegetables. Add the garlic and cook, stirring, until the mixture boils and is well blended, about 5 minutes. Add the chicken stock, wine, red pepper and bay leaf. Increase the heat to high and cook until the tomatoes have given off all their liquid and the sauce is thick, 20 to 25 minutes.

2. In a food processor, puree the sauce until smooth. (*The recipe can be prepared to this point up to 1 day ahead. Let the sauce cool completely, then cover and refrigerate.*)

3. To serve, reheat the sauce and gradually whisk in the cold butter. Add the minced parsley and season with the salt and pepper.
—*Steven Singer, Sfuzzi*

MEAT AND TOMATO SAUCE

*Makes About 3
Cups*

¼ cup olive oil
1 medium onion, chopped
2 garlic cloves, finely chopped
½ pound ground beef
1 can (28 ounces) Italian peeled
   tomatoes, chopped, with
   their liquid
1 tablespoon minced fresh basil or
   1 teaspoon dried
1 teaspoon salt
¼ teaspoon freshly ground pepper

1. Heat the oil in a medium saucepan. Add the onion and cook over moderate heat until softened but not browned, 3 to 5 minutes.

2. Add the garlic and the ground meat and cook, stirring frequently, until the meat begins to brown, about 5 minutes.

3. Add the canned tomatoes with their liquid, the basil, salt and pepper. Bring the sauce to a simmer and cook until thick, about 1 hour.
—*Michele Scicolone*

BECHAMEL SAUCE

*Makes About 4
Cups*

4 tablespoons unsalted butter
¼ cup all-purpose flour
4 cups milk
Pinch of nutmeg
¼ teaspoon salt

In a heavy medium saucepan, melt the butter over moderate heat. Whisk in the flour and cook, stirring, for 1 to 2 minutes, without browning. Slowly whisk in the milk. Bring to a boil, whisking until thick and smooth. Reduce the heat to low and add the nutmeg and salt. Simmer the sauce, whisking frequently, for 10 minutes. Pour into a bowl and place plastic wrap directly on top to prevent a skin from forming.
—*Palio, New York City*

BECHAMEL SAUCE WITH CHEESE

*Makes About 1½
Cups*

2 cups milk
Bouquet garni: 5 sprigs of parsley,
    ¼ teaspoon thyme and
    ½ bay leaf, tied in a double
    thickness of cheesecloth
2 tablespoons unsalted butter
3 tablespoons all-purpose flour
½ teaspoon salt
Pinch of freshly ground white
    pepper
Pinch of nutmeg
½ cup freshly grated Parmesan cheese

1. In a heavy medium saucepan, bring the milk with the bouquet garni to a boil.
2. Meanwhile, in another heavy medium saucepan, melt the butter over moderate heat. Add the flour and cook, stirring, for 1 to 2 minutes without browning to make a roux.
3. Whisking constantly, strain the boiling milk into the roux. Return to the boil and cook, whisking, until the sauce is thickened and smooth, 3 to 4 minutes. Season with the salt, pepper and nutmeg and stir in the cheese.
—*John Robert Massie*

VEGETABLE BROTH

*Makes About 6
Cups*

2 medium carrots, peeled and cut into
    2-inch pieces
2 medium onions, quartered
3 celery ribs, with tops, cut into
    2-inch pieces
2 peeled fresh or drained, canned
    Italian plum tomatoes
1 bay leaf
1 small bunch of parsley
½ teaspoon salt

In a large saucepan or stockpot, place the carrots, onions, celery, tomatoes, bay leaf, parsley and salt. Cover with 3 quarts of water and

bring to a boil over moderate heat. Reduce the heat to moderately low and simmer for 2 hours. Strain before using. (*The vegetable stock can be cooled and kept covered in the refrigerator for up to 3 days or frozen for up to 3 months.*)
—Nancy Verde Barr

CAPON BROTH

Capon makes a particularly luxurious broth. You can, of course, substitute a stewing hen or roasting chicken.

*Makes About 6
Quarts*

*3 carrots, peeled and quartered
3 medium celery ribs, coarsely
 chopped
2 medium onions, quartered
16 to 20 sprigs of flat-leaf
 parsley
1 tablespoon salt
1 small capon, about 5 pounds*

1. In a stockpot, bring 6½ quarts of cold water to a boil. Add the carrots, celery, onions, parsley and salt.

2. When the water returns to a boil, add the capon and cook, uncovered, over moderate heat for 2 hours, skimming the foam off the top occasionally.

3. Remove the capon and save for salad, sandwiches or any other use. Strain the broth and refrigerate it. When the fat congeals on top of the cold broth, carefully lift it off and discard.
—Carol Field

FISH STOCK

*Makes About 3
Cups*

*1 pound non-oily fish bones
Shells reserved from 1 pound
 shrimp
¼ cup chopped onion
½ cup chopped carrot
½ cup dry white wine
1 bunch of parsley stems
2 tablespoons peppercorns, preferably
 white
Pinch of thyme
2 bay leaves*

Rinse the fish bones under cold running water. In a medium saucepan, combine the fish bones, shrimp shells, onion and carrot. Add enough water to cover (about 3½ cups) and bring to a boil over high heat. Skim off any surface scum and reduce the heat to low. Add the white wine, parsley stems, peppercorns, thyme and bay leaves. Simmer uncovered for 25 minutes. Strain through a fine sieve lined with several layers of dampened cheesecloth.
—Jimmy Schmidt

Italians are passionate about their coffee. No other people feel so strongly about their coffee traditions, methods of preparation and ways of enjoying endless aromatic cups. But perhaps that's not so remarkable when you consider that coffee was first introduced to the West through Venice, which is also the birthplace of the European-style cafe (see "A Short History of Italian Coffee and Cafes," page 270). And remember, too, that Italians invented espresso—arguably the single greatest contribution to the world of coffee in modern times.

As any visitor to Italy soon realizes, Italians are never far from good coffee. You don't have to go to a *caffè* or a *ristorante* to get a perfectly prepared, steaming cup —you can get one at a train station, at a stop on the *autostrada*, even at a newsstand. Italians find it unthinkable that anyone would put up with watery brown brews, much less vending machine instant, when, with just a little more trouble, they could have a really aromatic, satisfying beverage.

If there's a secret to Italian coffee, it's taking the little extra time required to prepare it correctly. Of course that's all part of the Italian insistence on fresh ingredients and the appreciation of natural, forthright flavors in cooking.

THE COFFEE ITALIANS DRINK AT HOME

First, the coffee beans. Italy, with few exceptions, doesn't import the very highest quality coffees avail-

COFFEE, ITALIAN STYLE

A National Passion by Elin McCoy & John Frederick Walker

able on the international market. But the Italians know how to get the maximum pleasure out of the beans they do import. What makes Italian coffee taste so good in Italy is the emphasis on the careful blending of beans and an insistence on roasting for optimal flavor and freshness. The interest many Americans have in the different tastes found in coffees from various countries isn't shared by Italians, who know well that a good blend of beans from various sources is likely to be superior to all but a handful of single-source coffees.

It has been estimated that some 3,500 roasters supply the beans for Italian *caffès* and home kitchens, and each roaster has its own blend of beans to entice customers.

Then there's the question of the roast itself. Italians enjoy the deep, savory flavors that fully roasted coffee beans provide (especially for espresso). In Italy, coffee beans are typically given a gleaming, chocolate-brown roast, and the further south one goes in Italy, the darker the coffee is roasted. (In most cases the nearly blackened beans of so-called "Italian roasts" sometimes seen in American coffee outlets are actually far darker than would be found in Italy, even in the south.)

What you need to prepare the kind of rich, satisfying coffee Italians themselves drink at home is simple enough: Fresh, darkly roasted, good-quality coffee beans that are finely ground, good water and a drip pot. But it's the attention to detail that spells the difference. Let's go through these elements one by one.

Coffee: If you have a home coffee grinder—which is ideal—look for a good source of coffee beans. In addition to specialty stores, many grocery stores these days carry an excellent selection of high-quality coffees (including decaffeinated beans). As a factor, freshness outweighs a fancy name; the most prized coffees in the world won't taste good if they're stale. To approximate what Italians drink, choose a blend of dark-roast Latin American coffees. Remember that Italian taste leans toward darker but not necessarily the darkest available roast. Unfortunately, roasting nomenclature in this country is rather loose. A "Full-City" roast on the West Coast is often dark enough; on the East Coast, a "Continental," "Italian" or "Espresso" roast may be preferable.

Grinding: For maximum flavor, grind the beans yourself just before brewing. It's vital to match the grind to the method, which for Italian-style coffee requires a fine to extra-fine grind.

Water: Always use fresh, cold water to start. If you don't like the taste of what comes out of your tap, don't expect it to improve the taste of your coffee. Use a soft bottled water instead.

Proportions: Never guess amounts. Brew full-strength coffee using the proportion of 2 level tablespoons (or one "approved coffee measure") per 6 ounces of water. For coffee that will approximate espresso strength and be served in demitasse cups, use 4 level tablespoons per 6 ounces of water.

Method: You can use your familiar filter cone or electric drip machine, but Italians are wedded to old-fashioned drip pots variously called a *machinetta* or *Napoletana*. (In France it's called a *café filtre* pot.) There are numerous brands. We like the Ilsa Neapolitan Flip-Drip (about $35), which is stainless steel.

The design of these pots varies somewhat, but the idea is the same: The bottom pot holds the water, a two-part perforated basket holds the ground coffee and fits into the bottom pot, and the upper or serving pot (the one with the spout) fits upside-down on the basket. Place the bottom pot (filled with water) on a burner until the water boils (the pot will steam and hiss), then remove the whole thing from the burner and turn it over (use potholders). The serving pot will now be right-side up and the coffee will be brewed by the water from the bottom (now top) pot dripping through the coffee. Remove the empty water pot and the basket with the spent grounds before serving to prevent bitter, overly extracted coffee from continuing to drip into the serving pot. Give the coffee a stir before pouring.

This sort of flavorful home-style Italian *caffè* can be drunk on its own, perhaps with a little cream and/or sugar to taste or combined half-and-half with hot or steamed milk to make the favorite Italian breakfast coffee, *caffè latte*, traditionally served in a large cup. (The French call their version of *café au lait*.)

Italians also use another type of stovetop coffeemaker. A *Moka* pot uses steam to force hot water through the grounds, much the way the old vacuum method does.

It's important to keep all these metal pots clean to prevent a build-up of bitter tasting coffee oils, which can spoil the brew.

But good and flavorful as coffees made with these machines are, they shouldn't be confused with espresso. True espresso can't be made except in a special self-contained machine that utilizes pistons or hydraulic pumps to force steaming hot water through ground coffee.

ESPRESSO

Espresso is a form of coffee whose uniquely attractive taste is derived from its extremely rapid brewing method. The remarkable way in which a correctly prepared cup of espresso seems to capture the very essence of coffee flavor leads many experts (not all of them Italian) to deem it the peak of coffee drinking. At the least, the world of coffee would certainly be impoverished if there were no espresso.

The story of espresso begins at the turn of this century with an impatient Neapolitan asking a Milanese engineer if there wasn't a faster way to make coffee. As a result, the first espresso machine was patented by a Mr. Bezzera in 1903. Utilizing boiler tanks and steam pressure, these early ornate machines— bristling with valves and dials and often topped with small sculptures—could brew hundreds of cups per hour. Spigots on the sides supplied steaming hot water, which in turn was forced through very finely ground coffee to produce a delightfully fresh, aromatic cup in about 10 seconds. Technical improvements continued over the decades, culminating in Achille Gaggia's development in 1946 of a piston-operated machine. By the 1950s, electric pumps were introduced and today's state-of-the-art espresso machine is a sleek-looking, highly automated wonder—and small enough to fit on a kitchen countertop. (Expect to pay from $150 to $300 or more for a top-quality machine—Gaggia, Rotel, Rancilio, Krups, Bosch and the like. The more expensive models offer conveniences such as large-capacity water reservoirs and less recycling time between cups.)

Because darker, fully roasted shades of coffee are traditionally used to make espresso (although lighter shades can be used), the word "espresso" has become almost synonymous with "dark roast." But just because a coffee is made from "espresso roast" beans doesn't make the resulting brew a genuine espresso. The real thing, made from an espresso machine, consists of no more than 1¼ to 2 fluid ounces—derived from 6 to 8 grams (1 tablespoon) of ground coffee—that fills less than half a demitasse-sized cup, making those unfamiliar with the beverage feel they've been short-changed. If properly prepared, however, that single, concentrated mouthful will be topped with a thin layer of golden coffee foam (the *crema*) and be wonderfully aromatic, rich and syrupy in texture and intensely flavorful.

The espresso machines now available for home use vary in mechanical detail, making it difficult to offer step-by-step brewing advice. Apart from following the instructions that accompany the machine, however, pay special attention to the following:

1) Keep the machine clean. Residue build-up on the brewing surfaces will taint the flavor of the beverage.

2) For successful espresso, the grind must be powder-fine, with only a slight grittiness detectible when rubbed between the fingers.

3) The art of tamping the ground coffee (approximately one rounded tablespoonful) in the perforated metal filter to an even thickness takes practice. If done right, it should take about 10 seconds to pull a single shot of espresso. If packed too tightly, the coffee will ooze out drop by drop and taste burnt and bitter. If packed too loosely, coffee

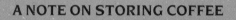

A NOTE ON STORING COFFEE

Air and moisture will stale coffee quickly. Ground coffee will become stale in a day if left exposed; roast coffee in bean form takes a week or more. Fortunately, it's possible to retard staling by keeping coffee in an airtight canister. Refrigeration—and even better, freezing—will slow the staling process considerably. But there is a drawback: Moisture in humid air will condense on cold beans or ground coffee if left out in a warm kitchen. If you don't get a fresh supply of beans at least weekly, freeze them in small airtight containers, removing them as needed for daily grinding (the beans don't have to be thawed) and promptly return unground beans to the freezer.

will gush out and taste watery. The art of packing grounds perfectly and the other attendant details of successful brewing (wiping the rim of the filter, observing the brew as it's dispensed, etc.) are best understood by having them demonstrated, which is why many specialty coffee shops actually offer clinics for purchasers of these machines. Once you master the technique, however, you'll have the satisfaction of watching true espresso gurgle out of your machine laced with the foamy *crema* that marks a successful cup.

ESPRESSO LEXICON

The world of espresso has its own special vocabulary. In an Italian *caffè*, an espresso will rarely exceed 2 ounces unless you order a *caffè lungo* or *caffè alto*, which are made with a little more water. When real espresso lovers want a larger cup, however, they ask for a *doppio*—a double shot (about 4 ounces) of full-strength espresso. If you ask for an *espresso ristretto*, you'll get a short pour of an ounce or less, accomplished by turning off the pump a few seconds sooner than usual. It is very concentrated—the essence of espresso—but as the Italians put it, *"poco ma buono"* (or, loosely, less is best).

U*n caffè corretto al rhum* or *alla grappa* is an espresso "corrected" with a dash of rum or grappa. As with all coffee drinks, sugar is optional, but no one adds milk or cream to plain espresso—except for *espresso macchiato*, which is "marked" with a trace of foamed milk, and *espresso con panna*, which is served with a dollop of whipped cream. An espresso served with a small curl of lemon peel on the side—a style popular in the United States—is called an *espresso Romano*.

FAVORITE ITALIAN COFFEE DRINKS

The invention of espresso inspired a series of coffee drinks, which the Italians were quick to perfect. Here are some of the most popular.

Cappuccino

Cappuccino is a widely popular coffee drink that gets its name from the cap of foam on top of the cup. Apparently it reminds Italians of the white-hooded, dark brown robe of Capuchin friars. The recipe varies from half espresso and half hot, frothy, steamed milk to one-third espresso, one-third hot steamed milk and one-third foamed milk, with sugar to taste. A sprinkle of cinnamon on top is an American variation.

Although a version of cappuccino can be made with strong, drip-brewed coffee and hot milk that has been frothed in a blender, it is really best made with an espresso machine. Virtually all such machines have a jet that allows you to bubble steam through milk, heating it and creating foam (*schiuma*). Fresh cold whole milk works best (although some experts swear by lukewarm milk). With a half-full pitcher of milk at the ready, open the steam valve for a second to clear any water from the line, then immerse the jet just under the surface of the milk and open the valve. The trick is to work fast and keep the jet in the milk—which means you have to raise the pitcher as the foam builds—and make sure not to scald the milk. It take practice, and Italian *barista*s are as proud of their artistry in steamed milk as they are with their skill in making espresso; some will swirl a *cuore* (heart) in your cappuccino with the foam.

Caffè Latte
Caffè latte can be made with strong coffee and heated milk, but it is particularly attractive when made with one or two shots of espresso and three times as much hot steamed milk. Unlike cappuccino, the foam is always omitted.

Latte Macchiato
Latte macchiato is basically a large mug of steamed milk with a shot of espresso poured down through the foamy top. It's even better served in a large glass so that as the dark espresso is dribbled down through the milk, it creates the layered look of a parfait.

Espresso con Ghiacco
Espresso con ghiacco is an iced version of *latte macchiato* using one or two shots of freshly made (or refrigerated) espresso and cold milk over ice. Espresso, sweetened to taste, can be poured over shaved ice. Or brewed and sweetened espresso can be frozen to a thick consistency to make a *granita di espresso*.

Then too, chocolate sauce, cocoa, cinnamon, raspberry and almond syrups, not to mention various liqueurs, are popularly used to contribute additional flavor to Italian coffee and coffee drinks.

A SHORT HISTORY OF ITALIAN COFFEE AND CAFES

It was the Arabs who first discovered the pleasures of coffee—after all, the coffee tree is indigenous to Ethiopia. The beverage spread throughout the Moslem world during the 15th century and travelers to Constantinople brought word of coffee to the West during the latter part of the 16th century. But it was the Venetians, who, because of their extensive trade with the Turkish Empire, first imported coffee beans to Europe in 1615.

Exotic and expensive, coffee was initially sold in apothecary shops as a medicine. It enjoyed immediate acceptance throughout Italy, and by the middle of the 17th century it was commonly sold by street vendors. The first coffee houses—*caffès*—appeared in Venice's Piazza San Marco by the end of the 17th century. At first tiny and windowless, later grand and airy, they embodied from the beginning that essential set of functions—part social club, part business address, part bulletin board—that accounts for the popularity of cafes to this day, not only in Italy, but throughout Europe and elsewhere. So closely linked are coffee and cafes in Italian culture that the word for both is the same: *caffè*. In fact, one-third of all coffee drunk by Italians is consumed outside the home.

One of the most famous early Venetian cafes, Caffè Florian, still survives in the Piazza San Marco. Opened in 1720 by Floriano Francesconi, a friend of the sculptor Canova, it became a fashionable meeting place and a source of news and gossip. Today, there are countless cafes in Italy, from famous ones like the Florian in Venice and the Greco in Rome to the touristy ones clustered in the Galleria and Piazza del Duomo in Milan to the rustic little coffee bars found in every village square. A typical cafe scene looks like a cross-section of Italian life, with pensioners discussing politics, children being indulged with sweets, students holding hands or reading books, businessmen laying plans, and travelers taking it all in.

Although an Italian cafe serves everything from an *aperitivo* to *gelati*, in all of them the ambiance is fueled principally by *caffè*, primarily espresso, either drunk standing up at the bar (at about 700 lira or 50 cents a cup) or lingered over (for a somewhat higher price) at a table. Italians drink coffee at all hours, but the choice is dictated by long-standing custom and time of day: *Caffè latte* in the morning, cappuccino after lunch (and perhaps after dinner) and espresso anytime.

271

272

273

275

CONTRIBUTORS

Jody Adams is executive chef at Michela's in Cambridge, Massachusetts.

Nancy Verde Barr is a food writer and cooking teacher. A number of the recipes that appear in *The Best of Food & Wine/The Italian Collection* are reprinted from her book *We Called It Macaroni* (© 1990 by Nancy Verde Barr) with the kind permission of the publishers, Alfred A. Knopf, Inc.

Lidia Bastianich is chef/owner of Felidia in New York City. She is also the author of *La Cucina di Lidia* (Doubleday).

Umberto Bombana is chef at Pazzia in Los Angeles.

Giuliano Bugialli is a cooking teacher (New York City and Florence, Italy) and the author of *The Fine Art of Italian Cooking* (2nd edition, Times Books/Random House), *Giuliano Bugialli's Classic Techniques of Italian Cooking* (Simon and Schuster), *Giuliano Bugialli's Foods of Italy* (Stewart, Tabori & Chang), *Bugialli on Pasta* (Simon and Schuster) and the upcoming *Giuliano Bugialli's Foods of Tuscany* (Stewart, Tabori & Chang).

Anna Teresa Callen is a food writer, cooking teacher (Anna Teresa Callen Italian Cooking School, New York City) and the author of *Menus for Pasta* and *The Wonderful World of Pizzas, Quiches and Savory Pies* (both from Crown).

Dolores Casella is a cooking teacher and chef/owner of Dolores Casella's Downtowner in Idaho Falls, Idaho. She is the author of *A World of Breads, A World of Baking, New Book of Breads* and *The Complete Vegetable Cookbook* (all from David White Publishing).

Mark Cox is chef at Tony's in Houston.

Peggy Cullen is a New York-based food writer, consultant and baker.

Diane Darrow is a food writer and co-author with her husband, Tom Maresca, of the upcoming *Seasonal Italian Cooking* (Grove Weidenfeld) and *La Tavola Italiana: A Regional Guide to the Classic Cuisines of Italy* (Morrow). A number of their recipes that appear in *The Best of Food & Wine/The Italian Collection* are from *La Tavola Italiana* (© 1988 by Diane Darrow and Tom Maresca) and are reprinted with the kind permission of the publishers, William Morrow and Company, Inc., New York.

Lorenza de'Medici is a food writer, cooking teacher (The Villa Table, Siena, Italy) and the author of a number of books, including *Italy the Beautiful Cookbook* (Collins), *The Renaissance of Italian Cooking* (Fawcett Columbine) and *The Heritage of Italian Cooking* (Random House). She is currently working on a book entitled *The Villa Table* scheduled for publication in 1992.

Constance and Rosario Del Nero are co-authors of *Risotto: A Taste of Milan* (Harper & Row). In addition, Constance is a cookbook illustrator and Rosario a cooking teacher. They are currently in Italy where Rosario is running a small restaurant in the Italian Alps and where they are both working on a book tentatively titled *Our Little Ristorante*.

Anne Disrude is a New York-based food stylist.

Bette Duke is a New York-based designer.

Fred Ferretti is the author of *Gourmet* magazine's monthly "A Gourmet at Large" column.

Carol Field is a food writer and the author of *Celebrating Italy* (William Morrow) and *The Italian Baker* (Harper & Row). She is currently working on another Italian cookbook to be published in 1993.

Jim Fobel is a cookbook author whose most recent books include *Jim Fobel's Diet Feasts* (Doubleday), *Jim Fobel's Old-Fashioned Baking Book* (Ballantine) and the upcoming *The Whole Chicken Cookbook* (Ballantine).

George Germon and **Johanne Killeen** are chefs and co-owners of Al Forno in Providence, Rhode Island, and the authors of *Cucina Simpatica* (HarperCollins).

Edward Giobbi is a painter-sculptor and the author of *Italian Family Cooking* (Random House), *Eat Right Eat Well—The Italian Way* (Knopf) and, most recently, *Pleasures of the Good Earth* (Knopf).

Vito Gnazzo is chef at Rex, Il Ristorante in Los Angeles.

Joyce Goldstein is a chef, restaurateur, food writer and the author of *The Mediterranean Kitchen* (William Morrow) and another, as yet untitled, cookbook due from Morrow in 1992.

David Holben and **Lori Finkelman Holben** are co-chefs at The Riviera in Dallas.

Marcia Kiesel is Associate Director of *Food & Wine's* test kitchen.

Evan Kleiman is a cooking teacher and chef/owner of Angeli Caffe, Trattoria Angeli and Angeli Mare restaurants in Los Angeles. She is also the co-author, with Viana La Place, of *Cucina Rustica* (William Morrow), *Pasta Fresca* (William Morrow) and *Cucina Fresca* (Harper & Row). She is currently working on two solo projects scheduled for publication in 1992: a book on Italian seafood dishes and one on Italian food and cooking for children.

Viana La Place is a food writer, cooking teacher and author of *Verdura, Vegetables Italian Style* (William Morrow). She is also co-author, with Evan Kleiman, of *Cucina Rustica* (William Morrow), *Pasta Fresca* (William Morrow) and *Cucina Fresca* (Harper & Row).

Nick Malgieri is a cooking teacher (the director of the baking program at Peter Kump's New York Cooking School) and the author of *Perfect Pastry* (Macmillan) and *Great Italian Desserts* (Little, Brown). He is currently working on a complete baking guide to be published in late 1993.

279

Tony Mantuano is chef/owner of Mangia and the soon-to-be-opened Tuttaposto, both in Kenosha, Wisconsin.

Tom Maresca is a food and wine writer and author of *The Right Wine* (Grove Weidenfeld) and *Mastering Wine* (Bantam), due out in its 2nd edition in 1993. He is also co-author with his wife, Diane Darrow, of the upcoming *Seasonal Italian Cooking* (Grove Weidenfeld) and *La Tavola Italiana: A Regional Guide to the Classic Cuisines of Italy* (Morrow). A number of their recipes that appear in *The Best of Food & Wine/The Italian Collection* are from *La Tavola Italiana* (© 1988 by Diane Darrow and Tom Maresca) and are reprinted with the kind permission of the publishers, William Morrow and Company, Inc., New York.

John Robert Massie is a New York-based food stylist.

Elin McCoy and **John Frederick Walker** are contributing editors of *Food & Wine* and the authors and publishers of *Coffee & Tea*, 3rd edition, a widely used reference in the coffee and tea trade.

Michael McLaughlin is a food writer and the author of *The Manhattan Chili Company Southwest American Cookbook* (Crown), *The Back of the Box Gourmet* (Simon and Schuster) and the co-author (with Sheila Lukins and Julee Rosso) of *The Silver Palate Cookbook* (Workman). Scheduled for publication in late 1992 are *Weekends in the New American Kitchen* and *Fifty-Two Meatloaves* (both from Simon and Schuster).

Bruce McMillan is chef at Anthony's in Houston.

Mark Militello is chef/owner of Mark's Place in North Miami, Florida.

Cindy Pawlcyn is chef/owner of Tra Vigne in St. Helena, California.

W. Peter Prestcott is Entertaining & Special Projects Editor of *Food & Wine*.

Carl Quagliata is chef at Giovanni's Ristorante in Beachwood, Ohio.

Margaret and **G. Franco Romagnoli** are food writers, TV chefs and the authors of *The New Romagnolis' Table*, *New Italian Cooking*, *Carnevale Italiano* and *The Romagnolis' Table* (all from Atlantic/Little, Brown).

Richard Sax is a food writer and cookbook author. He is currently working on a cookbook on old-fashioned desserts from all over the world, to be published in late 1992 by Simon and Schuster.

Jimmy Schmidt is chef/owner of The Rattlesnake Club and co-owner of Tres Vite, both in Detroit, and is currently working on two restaurants to open in late 1991 in the Detroit suburbs. He is also the author of *Cooking for All Seasons* (Macmillan).

Michele Scicolone is a food writer, cooking teacher (at The New School, New York City) and the author of *The Antipasto Table* (William Morrow), and an upcoming book on Italian desserts to be published in 1993.

Piero Selvaggio is owner of Valentino and Primi restaurants in Los Angeles.

Steven Singer is Corporate Executive Chef of the Sfuzzi restaurants. He is currently at work on a book entitled *Entertaining Sfuzzi Style* due out in mid-1992.

Diana Sturgis is *Food & Wine's* Test Kitchen Director.

We would also like to thank the following restaurants and individuals for their contributions to *Food & Wine* magazine and to this cookbook:

Allegro, Waltham, Massachusetts; **Amerigo's**, Bronx, New York; **Cibrèo**, Florence, Italy; **Sonny D'Angelo**, D'Angelo Brothers, Philadelphia; **Da Celestino**, Florence, Italy; **Donatello**, San Francisco; **Enoteca Pinochiorri**, Florence, Italy; **Hotel Palumbo**, Ravello, Italy; **La Capannina**, Capri, Italy; **La Pigna**, Capri, Italy; **La Riviera**, Metairie, Louisiana; **Helen Millman**; **Palio**, New York City; **Rosa Ristorante**, Baldwin Park, California; **Sambuco**, Porto Garibaldi, Italy; **San Domenico**, New York City; **San Pietro**, Positano, Italy; **Spiaggia**, Chicago; **Tony Vallone**, Anthony's and Tony's, Houston, Texas.

PHOTO CREDITS

Cover: Jerry Simpson.
Page 17: Mark Thomas. **Pages 18-19:** Steven Mark Needham. **Page 20:** Mark Thomas. **Page 37:** Mark Thomas. **Pages 38-40:** Jerry Simpson. **Pages 73-75:** Mark Thomas. **Page 76:** Steven Mark Needham. **Page 93:** David Bishop. **Pages 94-95:** Mark Thomas. **Page 96:** David Bishop. **Page 113:** Mark Thomas. **Pages 114-115:** Mark Thomas. **Page 115:** Thom de Santo. **Page 116:** Jerry Simpson. **Page 149:** Elizabeth Watt. **Pages 150-151:** Jerry Simpson. **Page 151:** Aaron Rezny. **Page 152:** Elizabeth Watt. **Page 169:** Dennis Galante. **Pages 170-171:** Jerry Simpson. **Page 172:** Steven Mark Needham. **Page 205:** Jerry Simpson. **Page 206:** Jerry Simpson. **Pages 206-207:** Mark Thomas. **Page 208:** David Bishop. **Page 225:** Mark Thomas. **Pages 226-227:** Maria Robledo. **Page 228:** Jerry Simpson. **Page 245:** Jerry Simpson. **Pages 246-248:** Mark Thomas.